Managing in a Strategic Business Cont...

David Farnham is professor emeritus of employment relations at the University of Portsmouth. He also is a visiting professor at the Universities of Greenwich and East London and visiting senior research fellow at the University of Glamorgan. He is chief examiner of the People Management and Development standard of the CIPD and co-director of the Personnel Policies Study Group of the European Group of Public Administration, Brussels. He has been visiting fellow at the Catholic University Leuven and works professionally with colleagues globally. He is a Chartered Fellow of the CIPD.

The CIPD would like to thank the following members of the CIPD Publishing Editorial Board for their help and advice:

- Pauline Dibben, Middlesex University Business School
- Edwina Hollings, Staffordshire University Business School
- Caroline Hook, Huddersfield University Business School
- Vincenza Priola, Wolverhampton Business School
- John Sinclair, Napier University Business School

The Chartered Institute of Personnel and Development is the leading publisher of books and reports for personnel and training professionals, students and all those concerned with the effective management and development of people at work. For details of all our titles, please contact the publishing department:

tel: 020 8612 6204

e-mail: publish@cipd.co.uk

The catalogue of all CIPD titles can be viewed on the CIPD website:

www.cipd.co.uk/bookstore

Managing in a Strategic Business Context

David Farnham

Chartered Institute of Personnel and Development

Published by the Chartered Institute of Personnel and Development
151 The Broadway, London, SW19 1JQ

First published 2005
Reprinted 2006, 2008

Typeset by Curran Publishing Services, Norwich, Norfolk
Printed in Great Britain by Cromwell Press, Trowbridge, Wiltshire

British Library Cataloguing in Publication Data
A catalogue of this publication is available from the British Library

ISBN 0-85292-998-6
ISBN-13 978-0-85292-998-8

Chartered Institute of Personnel and Development
151 The Broadway, London, SW19 1JQ
Tel: 020 8612 6200
Email: cipd@cipd.co.uk   Website: www.cipd.co.uk
Incorporated by Royal Charter.   Registered Charity No. 1079797

Contents

List of tables

Abbreviations and Websites

ACAS — Advisory Conciliation and Arbitration Service www.acas.org.uk

ACPO — Association of Chief Police Officers

AHAs — area health authorities

AI — artificial intelligence

BCG — Boston Consultancy Group

BCS — British Crime Survey

BMA — British Medical Association

CAP — Common Agricultural Policy

CBI — Confederation of British Industry www.cbi.org.uk

CC — Competition Commission www.competition-commission.org.uk

CEEP — European Centre of Enterprises with Public Participation

CIPD — Chartered Institute of Personnel and Development www.cipd.co.uk

CoR — Committee of the Regions

Coreper — Permanent Representatives Committee

DHAs — district health authorities

DNA — deoxyribonucleic acid

DTI — Department of Trade and Industry www.dti.gov.uk

ECB — European Central Bank

ECHR — European Convention on Human Rights

ECJ — European Court of Justice

ECSC — European Coal and Steel Community

EEC — European Economic Community

EESC — European Economic and Social Committee

EIB — European Investment Bank

EMU — European and Monetary Union

EPP-ED — European Peoples Party-European Democrats group

ESF — European Social Fund

ETUC — European Trades Union Confederation www.etuc.org

EU — European Union www.europa.eu.int

Euratom — European Atomic Energy Community

FE — further education

GATT — General Agreement on Tariffs and Trade

GDP — gross domestic product

GNP — gross national product

GPs — general practitioners

HASAWA — Health and Safety at Work Act

HE — higher education

HGP — human genome project www.genome.gov

HIV/AIDS — Human Immunodeficiency Virus/Acquired Immune Deficiency Syndrome

HR — human resources

HRM — human resources management

HSC — Health and Safety Commission

HSE — Health and Safety Executive

IBM — International Business Machines

IBRD	International Bank for Reconstruction and Development	OEEC	Organisation for European Economic Co-operation
ICSID	International Centre for Settlement of Investment Disputes	OFT	Office of Fair Trading www.oft.org.uk
ICTs	information and communication technologies	ONA	organisational network analysis
		P&D	personnel and development
IDA	International Development Association	PC	personnel computer
		PCTs	primary care trusts
IFC	International Finance Corporation	PDS	Professional Development Scheme
IMF	International Monetary Fund www.imf.org		
		PES	Party of European Socialists
IT	information technology	PESTLE	political, economic, strategic, technological, legal, environmental contexts
IVF	in vitro fertilisation		
KIFs	knowledge intensive firms		
KPIs	key performance indicators	PFIs	Private Financial Initiatives
LEAs	local education authorities	PLC	public limited company
LSE	London Stock Exchange www.londonstockexchange.com	PSA	Public Sector Agreement
		QUANGOs	quasi-autonomous government organisations
MDGs	Millennium Development Goals		
MEA	Millennium Ecosystem Assessment	R&D	research and development
		RHAs	regional health authorities
MEPs	Members of the European Parliament	RRA	Race Relations Act
MHSW	Management of Health and Safety (Regulations)	RTD	research and technological development
		SERPs	State Earnings Related Pension
MIGA	Multilateral Investment Guarantee Agency	SWOT	strengths, weaknesses, opportunities, threats
MNCs	multinational corporations		
MPs	Members of Parliament	TQM	total quality management
MPC	Monetary Policy Committee	TUC	Trades Union Congress www.tuc.org.uk
NHS	National Health Service	UK	United Kingdom
NATO	North Atlantic Treaty Organisation	UN	United Nations www.un.org
NFU	National Farmers Union	UNICE	Union of Industrial Employers' Confederations www.unice.org
NGOs	non-governmental organisations		
OECD	Organisation for Economic Co-operation and Development www.oecd.org	USA	United States (of America)
		WTO	World Trade Organisation www.wto.org

Foreword

Studying for qualifications that require you to demonstrate a good knowledge of the context in which organisations carry out their activities is difficult because of the wide range of different topic areas that need to be understood. Courses encompass subjects as diverse as technological developments, legal systems and demographic trends. What is more it is necessary to gain an understanding of how these various different developments interact with one another and the choices that organisations have in deciding how to respond. The fact that the business environment is dynamic, unpredictable and continually evolving makes the subject even harder to grasp fully. To succeed it is necessary to have access to a well-written, accessible, up to date and authoritative text that covers all the fields in sufficient depth and which helps you to develop your own views about the many issues and debates that you will encounter on your course. This book by David Farnham achieves all these objectives, being both introductory and comprehensive in its coverage of the field.

For students of the Chartered Institute of Personnel and Development's module entitled 'Managing in a Strategic Business Context' this book is essential reading. It has been written very closely around the CIPD's standards in this field, covering all in considerable depth. It starts with a guide to the standards, going on to introduce each of the nine major fields of study in separate chapters. An especially useful feature is the section that comes at the end of each chapter discussing the practical implications of the major contextual developments for organisations in general and for the human resources function in particular. Those preparing for CIPD national examinations in the subject will therefore find the book invaluable.

Why, a portion of CIPD candidates ask, is it necessary for prospective HR professionals to demonstrate such a wide range of knowledge about aspects of the business environment? Why, for example are we required to know about the legal system, EU initiatives, world economic institutions or technological developments that have little or nothing in themselves to do with the management of people? Why do we need to know about trends that have no great relevance for our organisations? These are good questions. To understand the answers you need to appreciate the purpose of the CIPD's membership requirements.

First, it is necessary that people entering and representing the HR profession have credibility with other managers and with members of other professional groups. Historically a major complaint of personnel professionals was that they were not listened to by managers in other disciplines, that they lacked authority and were not taken seriously when decisions were being taken. One of the reasons for this was an inability on the part of personnel specialists to contribute to discussions outside their particular range of professional expertise. They were listened to when giving advice about dismissals or performance-management, but not even asked when it came to wider strategic decision-making in the organisation. It is important that those now entering the profession do not suffer from this historic lack of credibility, that they are able to speak with authority about the major debates of our time and contribute effectively to thinking within organisations about long-term responses to environmental trends.

Second, it is important to remember that you are seeking membership of a profession whose members work across all the industrial sectors. You may work in the public sector now, but your

CIPD membership will assist you to move into other areas. In five years' time you may be working for an international company operating in a wholly different industrial sector (or vice versa). You thus need to gain a foundation of knowledge and understanding about developments in the business world that span well beyond your current daily concerns.

Third, as a member of the CIPD you should be able to make a very real contribution to wider debates that have relevance for the management of people in organisations. You need to know about long-term social and demographic trends because these effect your labour markets. You need to know how the legal system works because it produces and interprets law in ways that have direct relevance to the way people are managed. The same is true of European matters, technological developments and longer term economic and political trends. All these matters impact or have the potential to impact on your core HRM activities. Gaining this understanding enhances your professional standing, increases your credibility and thus helps give you sufficient influence to make a real proactive contribution to decision-making in your organisation.

Stephen Taylor
Manchester Metropolitan University Business School
CIPD Examiner, Managing in a Strategic Business Context

Preface

This book is written primarily for students studying the 'Managing in a Strategic Business Context' professional standard within the Leadership and Management Standards of the Chartered Institute of Personnel and Development's (CIPD) Professional Development Scheme (PDS). However, because of its subject matter, the book will also be of use to students on non-CIPD courses with units covering the business environment or business in context. Its chapters draw heavily upon the operational indicators, knowledge indicators and indicative content of the CIPD professional standard, which, because it is both strategic and contextual, is the benchmark for professional and postgraduate studies covering the business environment.

This book is distinguished from others in the field in a number of ways. First, it is a new, up-to-date text that has been written to enable CIPD students to meet the PDS standard, which is taught and examined at postgraduate or Master's level (M-level). The M-level standard requires postgraduate students to demonstrate:

- systematic understanding of knowledge and critical awareness of current problems and/or new insights
- comprehensive understanding of practice
- conceptual understanding enabling them to evaluate critically both current research and methodologies
- critical awareness of the role that contemporary personnel and development issues can play in the management of people and organisations
- comprehensive understanding of how and why personnel and development initiatives may be appropriate in different organisational settings.

Second, it has a strong managerial and interdisciplinary focus. Written from a managerial perspective, the book provides a framework within which readers can understand and interpret the strategic business context and its significance for those leading and managing complex organisations today. As a single-authored text, it presents an integrated and holistic approach to the subject matter through an interdisciplinary perspective. It draws upon a range of academic sources, thus enabling readers to review the strategic business context through a variety of conceptual frameworks.

Third, in line with the underpinning philosophy of the PDS, this standard aims to develop 'thinking performers' who are competent and knowledgeable in their field and are able to move beyond compliance to provide critiques of organisational strategies, policies and procedures. The competencies of thinking performers include ability to demonstrate:

- understanding of organisational strategy and its contexts
- thinking that is not limited to their own organisational level
- capability to evaluate and advise on the business implications of decisions
- knowledge of current research and current thinking to inform their views and proposals.

Fourth, students of the strategic business context are expected to develop a 'business partner' perspective of their roles. Business partners, whatever their managerial background, achieve value-adding contributions by working with others to plan, deliver and evaluate activity that enhances the capability of organisations to achieve their goals. The competencies of business partners include ability to:

- understand the managerial issues facing organisations in conditions of change
- act professionally and ethically
- keep informed about the implications of the internal and external changes affecting organisations
- carry out data-gathering and knowledge-sharing to produce added value for organisations.

Since the aim of this book is to help students meet this advanced level of understanding and analysis, and because it is written for an M-level audience, there is considerable emphasis within it on knowledge and understanding rather than on skills and competencies. 'Managing in a Strategic Business Context' is a conceptually demanding and intellectually stretching professional standard at postgraduate level, where students must show that they can:

- deal with complex issues systematically and creatively
- make sound judgements in the absence of complete data
- be original in tackling and solving problems
- plan and advise on how to implement tasks at a professional equivalent level
- propose or make convincing decisions in complex and unpredictable situations
- communicate their conclusions clearly to non-specialist audiences.

The text is presented rigorously, draws on a wide range of literature and provides keen insights into the complex contexts within which contemporary organisations operate. It is recommended that students use it as a source of knowledge and ideas and as a stimulus to wider reading. In this way, they can make their own judgements about the subject matter and commentary within it. To complement this book, students are very strongly advised to keep up-to-date with current strategic and contextual issues, by regularly reading the 'quality' press and accessing the websites of national and international organisations. Major newspapers include the *Financial Times, Guardian, Independent* and *Daily Telegraph* and Sunday papers such as the *Observer* and *Independent on Sunday*. They should also make use of *The Economist* and some of key websites listed at the beginning of the text.

Writing a book of this sort is a solitary task and I would like to acknowledge the contribution made in completing it by Dr Sylvia Horton, University of Portsmouth. Despite her own heavy professional commitments, she read the complete text very carefully, provided extremely helpful feedback to improve it, corrected it where necessary and enhanced its reader-friendliness. She also contributed to chapters 5 and 6, when the pressure of the publishing deadline was bearing heavily upon me. Without her energy, enthusiasm and collaboration, this book could not have been completed on time. Rob Thomas, University of Portsmouth, also read several chapters and provided additional, complementary comments to improve and develop the text. Responsibility for the final content, however, is mine alone. I would also like to thank Ruth Lake, Senior Commissioning Editor at CIPD, for commissioning this book and being patient and supportive to me, whilst it was being researched and written. Finally, I thank my family and special friends for just 'being there' and supporting me when I was planning, writing and working on the original manuscript.

David Farnham
University of Portsmouth
July 2005

Introducing the Strategic Business Context

'Managing in a Strategic Business Context' is a new professional standard within the Leadership and Management Standards of the Chartered Institute of Personnel and Development's (CIPD) Professional Development Scheme (PDS). It replaces the 'Managing in a Business Context' module within Core Management of the former Professional Qualification Scheme. This professional standard starts from the assumption that organisations and those responsible for managing them are increasingly subject to environmental turbulence and uncertainty. The external contexts within which businesses, public services and voluntary organisations operate are no longer stable and predictable but increasingly volatile and subject to change. As a result, managers have to identify, devise and implement appropriate strategies to ensure organisational survival, plan to achieve their goals and objectives and respond to market and contextual uncertainties. Managers also have to take account of the normative values and ethical standards within which organisations and society operate. In this chapter, the underpinning purposes of this standard are explained and the content of the book outlined.

THE PROFESSIONAL STANDARD

The main purpose of this standard is to ensure that personnel and development (P&D) professionals are able effectively to identify, examine and analyse the major contexts within which organisations operate and to contribute to the formation of responses which take account of contextual diversity, continuous change and ethical ambiguities. Developments in the business environment directly relevant to P&D managers are particularly significant, since P&D specialists need to respond to them and advise senior managers about them. Developments in labour markets and in employment regulation are major examples. A further purpose is to provide P&D professionals with information and understanding about the business environment more generally so as to increase their credibility and influence at senior levels within their organisations.

This standard is partly concerned with contextual factors, such as regulation, that affect the performance infrastructure of organisations and require compliance on the part of leaders and managers. It also aims to provide students with knowledge and understanding of developments in the business environment which provide opportunities for organisations to compete more effectively and/or provide improved standards of service to customer groups. In this respect, the standard concerns the achievement of performance differentiation. The focus within the standard is largely on the United Kingdom but international comparisons are introduced where appropriate. Unlike some other standards, there is greater emphasis within this one on knowledge than on skills and competencies.

The professional standard is divided into nine clusters, although many issues cut across these and they draw on ideas or practices that are identified in just one of the nine. For teaching and learning purposes the approximate percentage of time that is recommended should be devoted to each of these is:

- the competitive environment – 10 per cent
- the technological context – 10 per cent
- globalisation – 10 per cent

- demographic trends – 10 per cent
- social trends – 10 per cent
- government policy – 10 per cent
- regulation – 15 per cent
- developing strategy – 15 per cent
- social responsibility and business ethics – 10 per cent.

The competitive environment

This standard aims to ensure that CIPD graduates are familiar with the major features of a market economy and how organisations gain and subsequently maintain competitive advantage within it. The ways that organisations successfully respond to changes in markets for goods, services and labour are significant here, as is the role played by financial markets and institutions in the operation of market economies. The ways in which public and voluntary sector organisations interact with markets, which increasingly play an active role in their operation, also form part of this standard. Developments in labour markets and their significance for organisations are particularly important.

The technological context

CIPD graduates should have a broad grasp of the major technological developments affecting organisations. Information technology, telecommunications and the development of Internet-based activities are the most significant general areas of technology with which graduates should be familiar, but other areas are important too, especially where they impact either directly or indirectly on particular industries or organisations. Basic familiarity with developments in the fields of transportation, biotechnology, medicine, energy and robotics is also necessary. Understanding of the actual and potential impact of new technology on employment markets is especially important for P&D professionals. The desirability of many technological advances is contested and is often the subject of ethical critiques. These debates also form a part of this standard.

Globalisation

Another controversial development in the business context, from both a theoretical and a practical perspective, is internationalisation or globalisation. CIPD graduates are expected to have a good grasp of trends in this field and of the major debates surrounding them. The impact of globalisation on employment markets and practices is particularly significant, as illustrated by widespread hiring of overseas nationals to fill skilled jobs in the United Kingdom and the outsourcing of some organisational functions to other countries. On the institutional side, the major developments of significance are related to the European Union (EU), with their implications for UK employers. These form a significant part of this standard. Graduates are also required to have some basic understanding of the role played by other major international institutions whose decisions impact on UK organisations.

Demographic trends

The evolution, planned and unplanned, of the size and nature of the working population is a key area which P&D professionals need to understand and be in a position to advise their organisations about. While the focus in this standard is on the United Kingdom, broad familiarity with European and wider global population trends is also necessary. Future projections are significant, especially in so far as they have potential implications for supply of labour, the age profile of the workforce, retirement and pensions issues, and markets for goods and services. Government responses to demographic trends and their impact on organisations are of major concern, as are wider public policy debates about population issues.

Social trends

The principal aim of this standard is to ensure that CIPD graduates can identify the social trends that have implications for organisations in general and for employment markets in particular. CIPD graduates should be familiar with changing gender roles, new family structures, increased geographic mobility, decline in trade union membership, political affiliation and political participation, growth of consumerism and developments in the position of ethnic minorities. Attitudes towards work, marriage and family, religion and morality, and government are also important. The evolution of social structure in terms of income distribution, social class and social mobility also have significance for organisations and their labour markets, as well as being trends that are influenced by employing organisations. Finally, this standard focuses on the major social problems of our age and, in particular, on the role that is played by organisations in contributing to them and ameliorating them.

Government policy

Many areas of government activity impact directly and indirectly on organisations and on the activities of P&D professionals in particular. This standard aims to equip CIPD graduates with an understanding of the major debates about UK government policy, its aims and effectiveness. Familiarity with rival opposition platforms is also important, as is ability to develop original critiques based on experience and evidence. Economic and employment policy have the clearest direct impact on P&D activities but any policy area which has a long term effect on labour markets or on organisational activities is significant. CIPD graduates should be familiar with major developments in education policy, social policy and trade policy as well as government's long term economic strategy. Developments at EU level are also important, as is a broad understanding of alternative approaches pursued around the globe. Finally, CIPD graduates need to be able to advise organisations on how the direction of government can be influenced through lobbying activities, participation in consultation exercises and via the activities of employers' associations.

Regulation

The practical outcome of policy debates is often regulation and sometimes deregulation. This standard focuses on the major ways in which the state and its agencies regulate organisational activity and the purpose of such regulation. Central to this are the major principles of employment regulation and the ways in which it is enforced, as these are matters about which P&D professionals are required to give advice and which drive much P&D policy. The detail of employment law is covered in other sets of standards, so these only require a broad overview. The major areas are discrimination law, dismissal law, the regulation of employment contracts, health and safety law and regulations aimed at helping people combine their work and family lives. Other areas of regulation have an impact on organisations generally and are thus matters about which CIPD graduates need to have some understanding. Competition and consumer laws are major examples but regulation of specific sectors often has a significant practical impact on individual organisations. Knowledge of current and future regulation and its practical significance should be combined, with ability to present thoughtful critiques backed up with persuasive evidence. The main contours of the legal system are also covered.

Developing strategy

This standard focuses less on the business context and more on the ways in which organisations can develop responses to developments in their environments which are strategic in character. The operationalisation of business strategies are covered in other areas of the Leading and

Managing People standards, so the focus here is on the development of strategy and on effective strategic leadership. While organisational strategy in general terms is covered, emphasis as elsewhere in this standard is placed on P&D strategy, the role of P&D professionals in forming strategy and on long-term, considered responses to developments in the P&D environment. This standard requires students to engage with theories about strategy and the major different views of strategy formation that are found in the literature. They also focus on the many constraints on the fulfilment or implementation of strategic objectives.

Business ethics and social responsibility

The final standard focuses on business ethics, corporate social responsibility, environmental sustainability and professionalism. To a great extent these cut across the other eight clusters of the standards and should inform student thinking on technology, globalisation, social trends and regulatory issues. However, aspects can be studied in isolation and students should be able to engage with major theories and debates in these fields. Ability to reflect on the approaches taken by particular organisations should also inform study of these standards. There is a specific focus on the notion of organisational stakeholders, on ethical dilemmas and on the conflicts arising between ethical courses of action and those suiting the interests of the organisation.

OUTLINE OF THE BOOK

This book consists of 10 chapters which tightly follow the operational indicators, knowledge indicators and indicative content of the professional standard. A special feature of the text is that at the end of each chapter the implications of that standard is considered for organisations and P&D professionals.

Chapter 1 provides the background to the book. It defines the professional standard, sets out its purposes and then explains the aims of the nine clusters within the Leadership and Management standards. It also summarises the subject content of the remaining nine chapters.

Chapter 2 examines the competitive environment. It focuses on the structure and workings of market economies, the basics of economic policy and determinants of supply and demand. It also explores sources of competitive advantage for organisations, including an examination of Porter's five-forces model. The chapter goes on to outline the roles of capital markets, major financial institutions and contemporary debates about public sector organisations and the voluntary sector in the economy. It also summarises the main trends in the labour market.

Chapter 3 is concerned with the technological context. It describes and analyses some recent developments in technology and examines their impacts on organisations and markets. It also considers how resistance to technological change manifests itself and goes on to discuss the evolution of a knowledge economy and the applications of evolving technologies to problems and issues in the contemporary world. The chapter concludes by examining how technological developments impact on people, organisations and society.

Chapter 4 discusses major contemporary debates about globalisation. It examines the origins, causes and consequences of globalisation for governments and organisations. Debates about globalisation are linked with economic, social and technological developments and the likely evolution of the EU, as well as the implications of EU membership for organisations. There is also an analysis of major international bodies, such as the Organisation for Economic Co-operation and Development, the International Monetary Fund and the World Bank, and their impact on the business environment.

Chapter 5 examines current and future demographic trends in the United Kingdom and draws on some international comparisons. It provides a population profile of the United Kingdom, examines some of the main changes in the population structure and gives reasons for recent patterns of population change. The chapter also considers the evolving structure of the labour market, the changing occupational structure and the concept of an ageing population. The implications of these and related changes for organisations are also examined and discussed.

Chapter 6 examines recent social trends and identifies some social problems both in the United Kingdom and internationally. The social trends cover family structure, the changing role of women in society and social stratification. The chapter also considers the 'new' politics, participation in politics and the changing Welfare State. It discusses recent changes in social values and the central importance of individualism, secularism and consumerism in modern Britain, as drivers of organisational and personal behaviour. The chapter concludes by outlining recent social problems such as asylum seekers, drugs and crime, and protecting the environment.

Chapter 7 explores UK government policy, covering the economy, education and wider social field. It provides critiques of current policies and compares the espoused policies of the three main political parties in these key areas. The chapter goes on to describe and analyse the evolution of EU policy in terms of economic, employment, regional, social, agricultural, sustainable development and technological innovation issues. It also explains how organisations try to influence policy at national and EU levels.

Chapter 8 is about regulation of economic and business activity. The social and historical contexts of legal regulation are examined, a classification of law provided and the sources of English law outlined and debated. The chapter summarises the elements of contract law, competition law, consumer law and employment law. The impact of regulation on organisations and particular sectors is also discussed and debates about the need for and desirability of regulation from an organisational perspective are explored.

Chapter 9 focuses on strategy, what it is and how it is developed. It examines debates about strategy, particularly the major distinctions made between rational, emergent and other approaches to strategy. The tools and techniques of environmental analysis are outlined and the basic distinction between strategy formulation and strategy implementation is described and analysed. The external and internal constraints on strategy are also considered and debates about effective strategic leadership are outlined and commented upon. This includes a discussion of the role of the P&D function in the strategy process.

Chapter 10 examines the relevance of business ethics and corporate social responsibility for organisations and managerial decision-making. Starting with debates about corporate ethics and approaches to corporate ethics, the chapter discusses ethics and professionalism, explores recent models of stakeholder theory and contrasts them with classical stockholder theory. Issues of accountability, corporate social responsibility and ethical responses in organisations are also examined, especially in relation to the accounting, buying, HR, marketing and strategic functions.

The Competitive Environment |

CHAPTER 2

CHAPTER OBJECTIVES

By the end of this chapter, readers should be able to:

- review the major current trends in an organisation's employment markets and take appropriate action in response to their short and long term implications
- analyse the competitive environment of organisations through the use of internal Strengths and Weaknesses and external Opportunities and Threats (SWOT) and Political, Economic, Social, Technological, Legal, Environmental (PESTLE) analyses
- advise on the potential contribution of the P&D function in situations of intensified competition.

In addition, readers should be able to understand, explain and critically evaluate:

- major developments in employment and the labour market, their causes and consequences for organisations
- the concept of competitive advantage and ways in which it is gained and retained in the contemporary business environment
- capital markets and the roles played by major financial institutions
- contemporary trends and debates about the role of public sector organisations and their operating environments.

INTRODUCTION

The central economic problem facing humankind is how to satisfy the infinite wants of an ever-growing population within the constraints of the finite resources available. With the economic demands of people virtually unlimited, and the supply of economic resources to satisfy those demands fixed in the short term, conscious economic choices have to be made to determine economic priorities. Economic goods and services are those human-produced commodities whose production requires the use of scarce resources to create, exchange and distribute them. They include finished consumption goods and services, capital goods and raw materials. Although there are a limited number of 'non-economic' goods, such as fresh air and sunshine, which are normally freely available according to 'need', they are increasingly the exception rather than the rule. More generally, economic goods are commodities for which people's demands exceed the availability of scarce resources to meet them. It is the task of any economy to solve the economic problems associated with this universal feature of resource scarcity.

This chapter outlines some of the key issues in the UK market economy arising out of problems of economic scarcity, competition and choice. It also examines sources of competitive advantage. For the purposes of analysis, it makes the traditional distinction between macro-economic activity (the economy as a whole) and micro-economic activity (the economics of markets, prices, supply and demand). In this overview of economic activity, the chapter provides the setting for the rest of the book and it touches on related issues, such as economic policy, corporate strategy and key labour market trends, which are examined in more detail in subsequent chapters.

THE STRUCTURE AND WORKINGS OF MARKET ECONOMIES

In modern economic systems the fundamental economic actors are households, firms and government agencies. These are all units of consumption of the goods and services produced in an economic system, whilst households also supply key resources, such as labour and finance, to aid the production process. Firms are also agents in transforming and converting the scarce resources available into the goods and services demanded for consumption and investment purposes. Investment is the flow of expenditure channelled into activities producing new resources not intended for immediate consumption such as machinery and plant. Through planned investment, production capacity becomes possible. Government's economic role is a complex one, as it provides services to taxpayers, collects taxes from households and firms, transfers income and manages the macro-economy.

The scarce resources used by firms and government in creating new economic goods and services for consumption and investment are 'the factors of production', usually defined as land, labour and capital. Land incorporates those natural resources such as oceans, forests, minerals and soil fertility used in production. Labour is the sum total of human resources skills, knowledge and competencies that are available, nationally and internationally. Capital is those human-made aids to production, such as machinery, advanced technology and communication systems, which raise economic productivity and real output per worker over time. Capital is also used to describe money (ie finance capital) as a commodity, available for investment. The total output of all the commodities produced by a country over a given period, normally a year, is its gross domestic product (GDP); where net property income is included the aggregate is called gross national product (GNP).

Issues of scarcity and choice mean that all economic systems have a number of common problems to resolve. These are:

- What goods and services are to be produced and in what quantities, including the balance between consumption and capital goods?
- How are these goods and services to be produced, given current resources, technology and productive capacity?
- Who is to get the goods and services produced, or how is GNP to be divided among a country's economic and non-economic participants?
- How efficient are the methods being used in the production and distribution processes?
- Are existing resources being fully utilised or are some unemployed or underemployed?
- In monetary economies, are prices stable or are they rising out of line with productivity? This is described as 'inflation'.
- Is the economy growing and increasing its capacity over time?

Three types of economic system have provided institutional frameworks for solving these economic problems. These are free market economies, planned (or command) economies, and market (or mixed) economies, where free market and mixed economies are capitalist ones.

Free market economies

In free market economies, economic decisions about allocation of resources, and production of goods and services, are made through money prices, generated by voluntary economic exchanges among producers, consumers, workers and owners of factors of production. Decision-making is largely decentralised, with mainly private ownership of the means of production and some limited forms of social ownership. The market mechanism (or the price system) allocates resources, adjusts production and consumption decisions, distributes incomes to those owning factors of production, and paves the way for economic growth. In this case:

- Individual economic units decide what, how, where and when to produce and consume.
- They do so with reference to money prices.
- Prices respond to the forces of demand and supply for individual goods or factors of production.
- The outcome is a balance of demand and supply, with co-ordination of the economic activities of individual units and agents achieved through the working of the price system.

Planned economies

Planned or command economies are where economic processes are determined not by market forces but by planning agencies which determine and implement society's economic goals. The nearest approximations to such systems were the countries of Eastern Europe and the former Soviet Union until the breakdown of communism in the late 1980s and early 1990s. They have been replaced by 'economies in transition', as these states shift towards private enterprise and market-based economic systems.

Market economies

Market economies, combining private enterprise with varying degrees of government intervention and regulation, dominate the world economy today. Resource allocation between alternative uses is determined largely by the actions of individual firms and corporations seeking profits and market share in the marketplace, with governments influencing overall economic performance, distribution of incomes and welfare policies. Hutton (1995) has identified four principal types of market economy (or capitalist systems): the US, Japanese, European social market and UK economies. There are some similarities between the European social market economy and Japanese market economy and between the US and UK market economies. But the greatest contrast is between the UK market economy and the European social market economy, which is examined below. Within each market economy there is:

- a dominant set of basic business principles underpinning it
- a prevailing business ideology
- a distinctive financial system and labour market
- an institutionalised welfare system
- a range of government policies.

The main differences between the UK market economy and the European social market economy are summarised below. These are generic, stylised differences but are largely indicative of the major features of each.

- *Basic principles.* In the United Kingdom, the dominant factor is (finance) capital and the tradition of 'public spirit' in business is low. There is high reliance on price-driven markets, supply relations are at arm's length and also price-driven, and the extent of privatisation is high. In the European social market economy, the dominant relationship is partnership between capital and labour and the degree of public spirit in business is high. There is medium reliance on price-driven markets, supply relations are bureaucratic and planned, and the extent of privatisation is medium.

- *Firms.* In the United Kingdom, the main goal of firms is profits, managerial structures are hierarchic and social overheads are medium. In the European social market economy, the main goal of firms is market share, managerial structures are consensual and social insurance overheads are high.
- *Financial systems.* In the United Kingdom, the financial system is marketised, the banking system is advanced, marketised and centralised, and the stock market is very important. Required returns on finance capital are expected to be high and short-term. In the European social market economy, the financial system is bureaucratic, the banking system is traditional, regulated and regional, and the stock market less important. Required returns on finance capital are expected to be medium.
- *Labour markets.* In the United Kingdom, job security in the labour market is low, labour mobility is medium and labour management is generally adversarial. Pay differentials are large, labour turnover is medium and the level of skills in the labour market is generally poor. Unions are organised on a general or occupational basis and their power is weak. In the European social market economy, job security in the labour market is high, labour mobility is medium and labour management is co-operative. Pay differentials are medium, labour turnover is medium and the level of skills in the labour market is high. Unions are organised on an industrial basis and their power is strong.
- *Welfare systems.* In the United Kingdom, the basic principle of the welfare system is a mixed one, where universal provision is medium (and falling), means-testing is medium (and rising) and private welfare is medium (and rising). Participation in higher education is strongly related to social class. In the European social market economy, the basic principle of the welfare system is a corporatist-social democratic one, where universal provision is high, means-testing is low and private welfare is low. Participation in higher education is weakly related to social class.
- *Government policies.* In the United Kingdom, the role of government is strong and centralised. Government supports open trade and industrial policy is non-interventionist. The top rate of income tax is low. In the European social market economy, the role of government is encompassing. Government supports quite open trade and industrial policy is interventionist. The top rate of income tax is high.

To summarise, the essential features of contemporary market economies are market exchange of goods and services, motivated by competition in the marketplace, the drive for profits and market share by firms and the search for market value by individual and corporate consumers. Competition is rarely 'perfect', however, and most market structures are 'imperfect', so that government's role is to regulate markets and make sure that 'fair play' between producers and consumers takes place. Government also provides essential public services, paid out of general taxation. A central feature of modern market economies is the institutional frameworks within which they operate (Basu 2000). There is, nevertheless, intensive competition for business between firms for customers and consumers in such systems. This leads to mergers and acquisitions between businesses so that they can gain competitive advantage through economies of scale. Also within market economies, as Kay (2003, p17) has concluded: 'Economic differences persist because output and living standards are the complex product of the intersection of the economic environment with associated social, political and cultural institutions.' The economic lives of individuals 'are the product of the systems in which they operate.'

Consider the arguments for and against the three types of economic system identified above.

THE MACRO-ECONOMY: ECONOMIC POLICY AND THE CHANGING ECONOMY

The UK's modern market economy has emerged out of the historical legacies of the nineteenth and twentieth centuries. These legacies continue to influence the country's economic activities today. During the late twentieth century, further developments took place, so that the United Kingdom is often described as undergoing deindustrialisation or as a 'post-industrial' economy.

Laissez-faire

Britain was the first country to industrialise, from the mid-eighteenth century onwards, and to experience a shift from a predominantly agrarian economy to an industrial one. Changes in the techniques and organisation of production resulted in increases in investment, productivity and output, enabling Britain to feed a rapidly growing population and penetrate expanding overseas markets. By the mid-nineteenth century, Britain had become a largely urban and industrial economy, a net importer of food, and the world's leading producer (and a major exporter) of manufactured goods and services. Her staple industries were coal, textiles, cotton, engineering, iron and steel and, by this time, the benefits of the 'Industrial Revolution' were beginning to 'trickle down' to the 'lower orders'. This prosperity was achieved in a free market, private enterprise laissez-faire economy, where the state's role was the limited one of providing national defence and a framework of law and order (Pollard 1969).

The late nineteenth century was an economic watershed for Britain. There was an economic depression, with rising unemployment, caused by increased competition in world markets from a newly unified Germany and the United States. Britain's policy of 'free trade' and no restrictions on imports and exports resulted in cheap agricultural products coming in from the 'New World', which led to a crisis in arable farming. This was followed by a brief period of rapid economic growth in the early twentieth century and renewed expansion in the staple trades in terms of output, exports and employment. But rising prices and downturns in the economy followed (Landes 1998). During the First World War (1914–1918), markets were lost, new international rivals emerged, and national capital was consumed. There was a decline in Britain's stock of capital and a significant decline in her holdings of overseas assets (Aldcroft 1993).

The inter-war years

The inter-war years (1919–1939) were generally a period of slump, depression and high unemployment although, because of falling prices, those in employment enjoyed rising living standards. Britain's staple industries, upon which the economy had traditionally relied, declined but new industries expanded such as chemicals, electrical goods and motor vehicles. Following the Wall Street crash in the US in 1929, free trade was abandoned and import controls were introduced internationally. This triggered a worldwide slump between 1931 and 1934. It was not until the late 1930s, with military rearmament, that the UK economy, as well as other European economies, experienced renewed growth and falling unemployment. The Second World War (1939–1945), however, led to further capital consumption and loss of international markets. During the war, production and 'manpower' were centrally directed, prices controlled by government and basic goods such as food and clothing rationed, according to need. In order to maximise output and promote efficient use of scarce national resources, the United Kingdom had shifted to a planned, closed, command economy.

The post-war settlement

The period from 1945 to the mid-1970s has been described as the 'post-war settlement' or the era of the 'social democratic consensus'. The UK economy was slowly freed from its wartime constraints, industry was rebuilt and the pre-war private enterprise system replaced by a mixed market economy operating in an international economy of fixed exchange rates. The post-war Labour government (1945–1951) nationalised the Bank of England, the coal, gas, electricity, telecommunications and railway industries and introduced the modern welfare state. This was a state in which government would ensure the basic social and economic necessities of its citizens by providing, through its tax revenues and other sources, a series of public goods and services. These included the National Health Service (NHS), provided 'free' at the point of use, tax-funded secondary, technical and university education, and other universal social services (Booth 1995).

For over 30 years, successive governments – both Conservative and Labour – intervened in the management of the economy through the use of fiscal and monetary policies based on the economic theories of John Maynard Keynes (1936) known as 'Keynesianism'. These aimed to maintain simultaneously full employment, price stability, balance of payments equilibrium and economic growth, through using a combination of fiscal, monetary and industrial policies to manage the level of aggregate demand. It was assumed that demand or the overall level of purchasing power stimulated economic activity. There were, however, both technical and practical problems in doing this. The outcome was a 'stop-go' cycle of economic expansion, near full employment and rising prices followed by economic contraction, rising unemployment and slower price rises. Further, by the mid-1970s, 'stagflation' had taken root, where unemployment and prices rose together. This coincided with a breakdown of the fixed exchange rate mechanism, determined at the Bretton Woods conference in the US in 1944, a quadrupling of oil prices and balance of payments crises in the United Kingdom. In 1976, the Labour government turned to the International Monetary Fund (IMF) for help. Government, in return for a loan to support sterling, adopted strict monetarist policies involving tight control over money supply and tight fiscal policy to contain aggregate demand. The net result was a slowdown in price rises but rising unemployment (Owen 1999).

Neo-liberalism

The succeeding Conservative administrations (1979–1990), under Margaret Thatcher, continued initially with a monetarist policy (monetarism) but also adopted what became known as supply-side economic policies (Oulton 1995). Monetarism, in contrast to Keynesianism, contends that controlling inflation is the most important policy goal for government. Demand management, it is argued, is self-defeating because public spending crowds out private spending. Hence growth of money supply should be geared to the expected growth rate of real output in the economy or GNP, while the exchange rate is allowed to float freely, thus protecting the balance of payments. This means that public spending must balance tax revenues and be kept under tight control to prevent inflation.

Supply-side economics links with monetarism, since it rests on the assumption that market supply must be created before demand, if non-inflationary growth is to be sustained. It is the level of supply which ultimately determines the level of employment not, as Keynes argued, the level of aggregate demand. Supply-side economics and monetarism, it is claimed, allow taxes to be cut, leave more income to be spent by households, provide incentives to work and generate real growth. Growth, in turn, provides additional jobs in sectors where there is genuine private demand by households and consumers for new products or services. This 'genuine' demand is distinguished from the 'artificial' demand generated by government spending, which is often seen as keeping uncompetitive and technologically backward industries and firms in business when they should be left to go into liquidation. These theories reflected a resurgence of classical economic orthodoxy, which emphasises individual responsibility in the marketplace and denies government a major role in providing relief to the weak in the economy. Called 'neo-liberalism', these policies were associated with the ideas of the 'New Right' in politics and posited that market competition is the best way of promoting economic growth and political freedoms. Under neo-liberalism, economic efficiency supersedes social equity as the guiding principle of public policy (Britton 1991).

During the Margaret Thatcher and John Major (1990–1997) administrations, control of inflation was the main policy goal and governments relied upon interest rates as their primary means of regulating demand. Exchange rate policy presented ambiguities, however, since rates were never permitted to float as freely as advocates of monetarism argued. There were testy debates about whether the United Kingdom should become a committed member of the European Exchange Rate Mechanism and whether she should sign up to European economic and monetary union (EMU). There were attempts to deregulate markets by removing constraints upon competition especially in the banking sector, thus allowing the free interplay of supply and demand in the marketplace (Beatson 1995). Governments transferred important public assets, such as gas, electricity, telecommunications, water and railways, back to the private sector, through privatisation, and required the remaining public services to open their activities to the private sector through compulsory competitive tendering. Unemployment rose and continued at high levels throughout the period. This was a time when the UK economy was being transformed as the manufacturing sector declined rapidly and the service sector grew to account for more 75 per cent of employment. For some observers, this was when a 'new' global capitalism emerged and political democracy was weakened (Hertz 2001) and where alternative economic policies were deemed to be both necessary and tenable (Ormerod 1998, Stiglitz 2002).

The economy under 'new' Labour

The Tony Blair administrations, first elected to office in 1997, claim to have adopted a 'third way' in economic policy. In their project to renew 'social democracy', 'New' Labour governments have argued that they have integrated the need for economic efficiency (associated with neo-liberal market freedoms) with that for social justice (associated with protecting the economically weak). The party says that it has also moved 'beyond an Old Left preoccupied by state control, high taxation and producer interests; and a New Right treating public investment, and often the very notion of "society" and collective endeavour, as evils to be undone' (Blair 1998, p1). According to Giddens (1998, p26), the third way transcends 'both social democracy and neoliberalism' and is presented as an alternative to both state socialism, associated with the post-war Labour party, and market-liberalism advocated by the Conservatives in the 1980s and 1990s. Others have argued, however, that 'Labour governments have adapted neo-liberal approaches through their support of a Third Way in politics' (Budge *et al* 2004, p681). Whatever the debates concerning the theoretical underpinning of the New Labour project, the economic record of these governments was remarkably successful during the years following 1997, when Gordon Brown was Chancellor of the Exchequer. Overall, it was a period of steady economic growth, low unemployment, low inflation and a stable currency. Income tax remained the same as under the Conservatives and interest rates were also low. Public spending began to rise in their second administration as expenditure on health and education rose to nearer the levels found in continental Europe.

(i) What are the major differences between monetarism and supply-side economics and Keynesianism?

(ii) Why did governments adopt monetarism and supply-side economics and abandon Keynesianism?

(iii) Has this economic policy been more successful in achieving its objectives?

Structure of the UK economy

The structure of the UK economy has changed significantly over the past 50–60 years. In 1950 manufacturing accounted for over a third of national gross domestic product (GDP); now it has declined to about a fifth. Manufacturing covers a wide range of goods including engineering, machinery and equipment, vehicles, textiles, foodstuffs, wood and metal, chemicals, pharmaceuticals, paper, plastics, rubber and electrical goods. There is some debate about the causes and consequences of the relative (but not absolute) decline of manufacturing output in the United Kingdom, since real output in manufacturing continues to rise slowly due to capital investment, rising productivity and improved production systems. One reason for the relative decline of manufacturing is that as households and individuals become richer, demand for manufactured goods declines and rising incomes are spent on services including leisure, financial products and health care. Deindustrialisation or the post-industrial economy, however, is not limited to the United Kingdom; it is common to all developed economies (Ferguson and Ferguson 1994).

The United Kingdom is facing keen competition from other OECD countries and is losing her share of world markets in manufactured goods to countries like Germany, France, Sweden and Spain. She lacks competitive edge in terms of both price and quality. It is in service industries where growth is now located. The UK's exports of services such as finance, insurance and information technology continue to expand, compared with other economies, with some three-quarters of her workforce employed in the service sector. In this sense, the United Kingdom is in transformation from an industrial to a post-industrial, information or knowledge-based economy (Griffiths and Wall 2004).

A main reason for the relative decline of UK manufacturing is competition from the newly industrialising economies of South-East Asia – the so-called 'Tiger Economies' of Malaysia, Thailand, Singapore, Korea and Taiwan, as well as the emergence of China as a major economic force. Malaysia, for example, aims to be fully industrialised by 2020. Because firms in these countries pay lower wages, have lower social security costs and invest heavily in new plant and machinery, they have a competitive advantage over manufacturers in developed countries. It is these socio-economic conditions and higher levels of productivity which encourage Western multinational companies to locate in the Far East, so as to raise profits and get higher returns on their capital investments. Yet while these countries export manufactured goods, they also import them and their share of exports into developed countries remains fairly low. Indeed, most trade of developed countries is with other developed countries. Only about a fifth of manufactured imports into the United Kingdom are from developing countries.

Some take a less sanguine view of deindustrialisation. They argue not only that it results in job losses, deskilling and rising unemployment but also that a strong manufacturing base is crucial for economic growth, technological innovation and export potential (Blackaby 1979). Whether deindustrialisation can be accounted for by import penetration, low investment, low productivity or uncompetitiveness is the subject of debate. During the 1970s and 1980s, Keynesians argued that the UK's problem was that she could not get economic growth without suffering import penetration, and what was needed was reflation and economic protectionism to prevent import penetration. Writers like Bacon and Eltis (1976), in contrast, attributed the decline of manufacturing to growth of the non-market sector. They argued that public sector spending was crowding out the private sector, which was unable to expand for lack of sufficient resources. Further, such spending is seen as 'taxing' the private sector, which has less money to spend in the marketplace. It is evident that this was the view that influenced the Thatcher government in the 1980s, but deindustrialisation continued none the less.

Another important 'industrial' sector of the economy is energy and water supply. The share of output provided by this sector to GDP has remained fairly constant over the past 50 years at around 5 per cent, although it went up to over 10 per cent during the mid-1980s. Energy and water supply cover capital-intensive industries such as oil, gas, water and coal. The importance of coal supply has declined significantly during this period, while that of oil has grown. Other sectors remaining fairly stable over the past 50 years are: construction, public administration and defence, the wholesale and retail trades, hotels and restaurants, and transport and communications.

The sectors demonstrating the most significant rises in their shares in GDP over the last 50 years, as indicated above, have been services. The share of financial and business services has increased from some 3 per cent to about 20 per cent, while that of education, health and social work has increased from about 3 per cent to 12 per cent. Clearly, the United Kingdom is now largely a 'service' economy, where manufacturing industry plays a less significant and strategic role than it did 50 years ago (Cairncross 1992). For some commentators, new 'rules' are required for 'building wealth' in the knowledge-based economy (Thurow 1999).

The largest relative decline to UK GDP has been agriculture, forestry and fishing. They accounted for about 5 per cent of GDP 50 years ago but now constitute only 2 per cent. Again, agricultural and related output has not fallen absolutely over this period, only relatively, and at a much slower rate than the rest of the economy. The differential decline of agriculture can be explained in terms of more intensive farming methods, greater competitiveness, and the impact of the Common Agricultural Policy (CAP) on the supply of agricultural products in the marketplace, resulting in overproduction (Jewell 1993).

THE MICRO-ECONOMY: DETERMINANTS OF SUPPLY AND DEMAND

A market is where the buying and selling of goods or services takes place, but it does not need to have a physical presence. Markets may be local, regional, national or international. Although most economists regard markets as primarily economic phenomena, they are social constructs that enable buying and selling to take place within certain rules and conventions. In Far Eastern cultures, for example, there is often no 'fixed' market price for a particular good (say a suit) or a service (say a haircut), since it is expected that the parties will bargain the price at which the commodity is actually bought and sold.

Markets consist of producers and consumers or sellers and buyers, who may be individuals, households, business corporations or government agencies. In modern advanced market economies, business corporations and government agencies dominate the supply side of markets, with households, business corporations, public agencies and individuals buying commodities. A free market is one in which the forces of supply and demand are allowed to operate without interference of third parties or institutions. In free markets, it is the pressure produced by the interplay of market forces, or market supply and demand, which induces adjustments in market prices and/or the quantities traded in the marketplace. Prices are normally measured in monetary values, with equilibrium being where the quantity that consumers are prepared to buy equals the quantity that producers are prepared to sell at that price. Prices act as signals which co-ordinate the economic actions of individual decision-making units and provide a mechanism whereby changes in supply and demand affect the allocative efficiency of resources in the economy as a whole (Heather 2004).

Market supply

The quantity of a commodity supplied by a producer is the amount the producer is prepared to sell at a particular price at a particular time. It is influenced by four main factors:

- market price of the commodity
- costs of the factors of production
- goals of the producer
- current state of technology.

It can be hypothesised that the higher the market price of a commodity the greater the quantity that the producer is willing to supply, because more profit is made in doing this. Conversely, the lower the market price of a commodity, the smaller the quantity that the producer is willing to supply. Similarly, the lower the costs of factors of production, the greater is the quantity the producer is willing to supply, while the higher the costs of the factors of production the smaller is the quantity that the producer is willing to supply. Quantity supplied also changes according to the producer's goals – whether it is aiming to maximise profits, maximise sales, enter a new market or maintain an existing market position. Technological developments affect quantity supplied, because they lower unit costs of production and ensure higher output at lower cost.

Market supply increases when there is a rise in the quantity supplied at each price. It decreases when there is a fall in the quantity supplied at each price. Factors causing an increase in market supply include: falls in the prices of other commodities, falls in the costs of factors of production, changes in the goals of producers, and technological improvements. What causes a decrease in market supply are rises in the costs of factors of production, and changes in the goals of producers.

Market demand

The quantity of a commodity demanded by a consumer is the amount the consumer wishes to buy at a particular price at a particular time. It is influenced by a number of factors. These include:

- market price of the commodity
- prices of other commodities
- size of consumer income
- consumer tastes
- social factors.

It can be hypothesised that the lower the price of the commodity the greater the quantity the consumer is willing to buy. Conversely, the higher the price, the smaller the quantity the consumer is willing to buy. Where commodities are substitutes for one another – butter and margarine for example – a fall in the price of one causes a fall in the quantity demanded of the other. Conversely, a rise in the price of one causes a rise in the quantity demanded of the other. Where commodities are complementary, such as pipes and tobacco, a fall in the price of one causes a rise in the quantity demanded of the other, while a rise in the price of one causes a fall in the quantity demanded of the other. Where commodities are unrelated, a change in the price of one does not directly affect the quantity demanded of the other.

Normally a rise in consumer income results in a rise in the quantity demanded of a commodity. Similarly, a fall in consumer income results in a fall in demand. This is usually the case with consumer goods. In other cases a rise in consumer demand results in a rise in the quantity demanded up to a certain level; then it falls away. Consumer demand for basic foods, for example, is not infinite. Quantity demanded may decline above a certain level of income, as consumers transfer income to more expensive foods. In other cases, quantity demanded rises to a certain level of income and then remains unaffected. Social factors such as sex, age, social class, educational attainment and occupation affect quantity demanded, while changes in consumer tastes have similar effects.

Market demand increases when there is a rise in quantity demanded at each price, and decreases when there is a fall in quantity demanded at each price. The factors causing an increase in market demand include: rises in the prices of substitutes, falls in the prices of complements, rises in consumer income, and changes in consumer taste. Decreases in market demand are caused by: falls in prices of substitutes, rises in prices of complements, falls in consumer income, and changes in taste.

Market structures and market regulation

In 'free' or 'perfect' markets (with many small producers selling homogeneous or identical products), prices are determined by the interplay of supply and demand, and market equilibrium is reached where, in aggregate, consumers and producers are satisfied with the current combination of price and quantity of units bought and sold per period of time. However, there are few 'perfect' or 'free' markets in the real world and competition among producers or suppliers of goods and services is a normal part of economic behaviour, although the intensity of competition varies (Office of Fair Trading 2001). These market structures, together with lack of full knowledge of markets by consumers, lead to market imperfections resulting in:

- *Monopolistic competition*. These markets have many producers selling differentiated products.
- *Oligopoly*. These markets have few producers selling differentiated products.
- *Monopoly*. These markets have single producers selling one product.

Under perfect competition, there are many producers in an industry or sector (such as fruit or vegetable markets), the typical firm is small in size and the products sold are homogeneous. There are no barriers to entry to the market and the degree of market concentration in the sector is very low.

Under monopolistic competition, there are many producers in an industry or sector (such as clothes retailing), the typical firm is small in size and the products sold are differentiated. There are few barriers of entry to the market and the degree of market concentration in the sector is low.

Under oligopoly, there are few producers in an industry or sector (such as car manufacturing), the typical firm is large in size and the products sold are either differentiated or homogeneous. There are many barriers of entry to these markets and the degree of market concentration is high.

Under monopoly, there is one producer in an industry or sector, with no close substitutes, such as water supply; the typical firm is large in size and only one product is sold. There are high barriers of entry to the market and the degree of market concentration in the sector is very high.

Since markets are based on demand, backed up by ability to pay, not on need, they can operate at below optimum use of available resources. For these reasons, governments find it necessary to inter-vene in markets for various economic, social and moral reasons. One form of intervention is regulation of markets. Since the 1960s, there have been many examples of market regulation, covering:

- employment protection
- equal opportunities
- health and safety at work
- controls on prices, wages and profits
- regulation of financial markets
- competition policy through control of monopolies and mergers.

Since the 1980s, new forms of regulation have been introduced, including industry-specific regu-latory bodies linked to the privatisation of gas, water, electricity, railways and telecommunications (Corry 2003). At the same time, however, extensive deregulation has occurred, allowing markets such as bus transport and financial services to expand (Veljanovski 1991).

> Identify and analyse the factors affecting property prices in the United Kingdom over the past 10 years.

SOURCES OF COMPETITIVE ADVANTAGE AND RESPONSES TO COMPETITION

In competitive market economies, firms are always looking for sources of competitive advantage, with several factors generating 'a long-term tendency for competitiveness to increase in the cap-italist market economy.' These include increases in the quantity of business information, improve-ments in the quality and comparability of business data, the development of the accounting pro-fession, the adoption of recognised standards of reporting, improvement in communications, and the progressive professionalisation of the management function. This universalisation of modern business and management practices, as well as the emergence of multinational corporations, are central to the expansion of the geographical domain of economic activity and of 'competition onto a world-wide scale' (Auerbach 1988, pp112–114).

One of the most influential scholars to get competitive strategy recognised as an accepted part of management practice is Porter (1998a). His book, *Competitive strategy: techniques for analysing industries and competitors* (originally published in 1980) provides a framework for understanding the forces of competition in industries, tools for capturing the heterogeneity of industries and com-panies, and the concept of competitive advantage. Drawing on rich data from many case studies, Porter offers 'a more sophisticated view of industry competition' and brings 'some structure to the question of how a firm could outperform its rivals' and how 'competitive costs could be thought of in terms of cost, differentiation and scope' (Porter 1998a, pxi).

According to Porter (1998a, pp3,4,34), the essence of competitive strategy is relating a company to its environment. For him, 'the state of competition in an industry depends on five basic competitive forces.' These are 'threat of entry', 'intensity of rivalry among existing competitors', 'pressure from substitute products', 'bargaining power of buyers' and 'bargaining power of suppliers.' The goal of competitive strategy for a business unit in an industry 'is to find a position in the industry where the company can best defend itself against these competitive forces or can influence them in its favor.' Competitive strategy, in essence, is the ability to take 'offensive or defensive action to create a defendable position in an industry, to cope successfully with the five competitive forces and thereby yield a superior return on investment for the firm.'

The basic elements of Porter's analysis can be examined in terms of the contexts within which competitive strategy is formulated, his 'five forces' that drive industry competition, generic competitive strategies and analysing the competitive environment.

The contexts of competitive strategy

For Porter, formulation of competitive strategy involves four key factors that determine the limits of what a company can successfully accomplish: two are internal to the organisation and two are external. Internally, there are, first, the organisation's strengths and weaknesses in terms of its profile of assets and skills relative to its competitors, including financial resources, technologies and brand identification. Second, there are the personal values and motivations of the key executives responsible for implementing the chosen strategy. These strengths and weaknesses combined with these values determine the 'internal' limits to the competitive strategy that an organisation can effectively adopt.

The external limits of an organisation's competitive strategy are determined by the industry in which it operates and the broader expectations of society. The third factor, industry opportunities and threats, defines the competitive environment with its attendant risks and potential rewards. The fourth factor, societal expectations, reflects the impact on the organisation of government policy, social concerns, public mores and similar issues. All four factors – organisational strengths and weaknesses, the personal values of key executives, industry opportunities and threats, and societal expectations – have to be considered before a business can develop a realistic and implementable set of goals and policies.

The appropriateness of a competitive strategy is determined by testing its proposed goals and policies for consistency in terms of 'internal consistency', 'environmental fit', 'resource fit' and 'communication and implementation'. Developing an optimal competitive strategy requires three sets of questions to be addressed. The first is 'what is the business doing now?' For example, what assumptions need to be made about the organisation's relative position, strengths and weaknesses, competitors and industry/sector trends so that the strategy makes sense. Second, 'what is happening in the environment?' This requires an industry analysis, competitor analysis, societal analysis, and an examination of the organisation's strengths and weaknesses relative to present and future competitors. The third question is 'what should the business be doing?' This involves testing underlying assumptions in the strategy, strategic alternatives and strategic choice.

The five forces model

Porter argues that the five competitive forces that he identified 'jointly determine the intensity of industry competition and profitability, and the strongest force or forces are governing and become crucial from the point of view of strategy formulation' (Porter 1998a, p6).

Threat of entry

There are several barriers to entry into an industry. A major one is economies of scale (ie unit costs of production decline as the volume of the product/service per period increases). This barrier can deter entry of new entrants by forcing them to either come in at a large scale and risk strong reaction from existing firms or come in at a small scale and accept a cost disadvantage. Another barrier is product differentiation. This is where established firms have brand identification and customer loyalties stemming from past advertising or being first in the industry. Differentiation creates a barrier to entry by forcing entrants to spend heavily to overcome existing customer loyalties. Another barrier to entry is 'switching costs'. These are created by the one-off cost facing buyers of switching from one supplier's product to another, such as costs of employee re-training or of new equipment. A barrier to entry can also be created by the new entrant's need to secure effective distribution of its product or service.

The potential entrant's expectations about the reaction of existing competitors to its presence also influence threat of entry. If existing competitors are expected to react forcibly to make the entrant's position in the industry a difficult one, then entry may be deterred. This is most likely where there are histories of vigorous retaliation to new entrants, established firms with high commitment to the industry (with illiquid assets) or slow industry growth rates limiting the ability to absorb a new firm without pressure on sales and financial performance of existing firms.

Intensity of rivalry amongst existing competitors

This is the central focus of Porter's model, since increased rivalry amongst existing competitors leads to increased competition and possible reduction in profits for firms within an industry. A number of factors operates here including the relative number and size of competitors in an industry, its growth rate, high fixed costs relative to value added, lack of differentiation of products or services, and high exit barriers.

The number and relative size of competitors in an industry are important factors, since under monopolistic competition, for example, rivalry is intense, although under oligopoly it tends to be less. The growth rate of an industry affects competition since with slow growth, competition is intense but where growth is rapid, competition is less intense. In industries with high fixed costs (or storage costs), there is strong pressure for all firms to fill productive capacity and this often leads to price cutting when excess capacity is present. Where there is lack of differentiation of product or service, pressures for intense price and service competition are likely to follow. When exit barriers are high, excess capacity does not leave the industry. Firms losing the competitive battle do not give up the struggle but remain in the sector and, as a result, profitability in the entire industry can be persistently low.

Pressure from substitute products

All firms in an industry are competing with industries producing substitute products. Substitutes limit the potential returns in an industry by placing a ceiling on the prices that firms can charge. Where there are few (or no) substitutes for a product or service, producers face little competition, whereas with substitutes, competition is stronger.

Bargaining power of buyers

Buyers compete within an industry by forcing down prices, bargaining for higher quality or more services and playing competitors against one another – all at the expense of industry profitability. The power of each of the industry's important buyer groups depends on a number of characteristics of its market situation. It also depends on the relative importance of the group's purchases from the industry, compared with its overall business. A buyer group is powerful where: the products it purchases from the industry represent a significant fraction of the buyer's costs or purchases, the products it purchases from the industry are standard or undifferentiated, it earns low profits, the industry's product is unimportant to the quality of the buyer's products or services, or the buyer has full information of the market.

Bargaining power of suppliers

Suppliers can exert bargaining power over participants in an industry by threatening to raise prices or reduce the quality of purchased goods and service. Powerful suppliers can squeeze profitability out of an industry unable to recover cost increases in its prices. A supplier group is powerful where: it is dominated by a few companies and is more concentrated than the industry to which it sells, it is not obliged to contend with other substitute products for sale to the industry, the industry is not an important customer of the supplier group, the supplier's product is an important input to the buyer's business, or the products of the supplier group are differentiated.

Generic competitive strategies

To cope with these five competitive forces, Porter (1998a) identifies three potentially successful generic strategic approaches to outperforming other firms in the industry: overall cost leadership, differentiation and focus. Porter (1998a, p41–42) concludes that these three generic strategies are alternative but viable approaches for dealing with competitive forces. But firms failing to develop their strategy in at least one of these directions are 'stuck in the middle' and are placed in an extremely vulnerable strategic situation. A firm of this sort 'lacks the market share, capital investment, and resolve to play the low-cost game, the industry wide differentiation necessary to obviate the need for a low-cost position, or the focus to create differentiation or a low-cost position in a more limited sphere.' Such firms are almost guaranteed low profitability and are likely to suffer from 'blurred corporate culture and a conflicting set of organizational arrangements and motivation system.'

Overall cost leadership

Low cost generic strategy provides the firm with above-average returns in its industry, despite the presence of strong competitive forces, which gives it distinct market advantages. Its cost position provides substantial entry barriers to others in terms of economies of scale or cost advantages, defends the firm against rivalry from competitors, places the firm in a favourable position regarding substitutes relative to its competitors in the industry, defends it against powerful buyers and defends it against powerful suppliers. 'Thus a low-cost position protects the firm against all five competitive forces because bargaining can only continue to erode profits until those of the next most efficient competitor are eliminated.' Also 'the less efficient competitors will suffer first in the face of competitive pressures' (Porter 1998a, p36).

Achieving a low overall cost position often requires a high relative market share or other market advantages. It may well require having a wide line of related products or services to spread costs and serving all major customer groups to build sales volume. Implementing a low cost strategy may require heavy capital investment, aggressive pricing and start-up losses to build market share. Once achieved, the low cost position provides high profit margins that can be reinvested in new facilities so as to maintain the cost leadership position, such as in the case of Tesco.

Differentiation

The differentiation strategy is 'one of differentiating the product or service offering of the firm, creating something that is perceived industry wide as being unique' (Porter 1998a, p37). Differentiation takes many forms: design or brand image, technology, customer service or other dimensions. Differentiation is a viable strategy for earning above average returns in an industry because it creates a defensible position for coping with the five competitive forces, although it does so in different ways from the cost leadership strategy. Customer loyalty and the need for competitors to overcome uniqueness provide entry barriers. Because of brand loyalty by customers and resulting lower sensitivity to price, differentiation provides insulation against competitive rivalry. It also increases profit margins which avoid the need for a low cost position. Also the firm that has differentiated itself to achieve customer loyalty is in a better position *vis-à-vis* substitutes than are its competitors. Finally, differentiation yields higher margins for dealing with supplier power and it mitigates buyer power.

Achieving differentiation may preclude gaining a high market share. It often requires a perception of exclusivity, which is incompatible with high market share. More commonly, it implies 'a trade-off with cost position if the activities required in creating it are intensely costly' (Porter 1998a, p38). This might include extensive research, product design, high-quality inputs or intensive customer support, such as in the cases of cars manufactured by BMW and Mercedes.

Focus

The focus generic strategy targets 'a particular buyer group, segment of the product line, or geographic market.' The low cost and differentiation strategies are directed at industry-wide objectives, whereas the focus strategy 'is built round serving a particular target well, and each functional policy is developed with this in mind.' The firm achieves either differentiation from better meeting the needs of the particular target or lower costs in serving this target or both, such as in the case of the newspaper the *Financial Times*. 'Even though the focus strategy does not achieve low cost or differentiation from the perspective of the market as a whole, it does achieve one or both of these positions *vis-à-vis* its narrow market target' (Porter 1998a, p38f).

(i) Explain Porter's five forces model and comment on its usefulness as a tool of competitive analysis.

(ii) How can this model be applied to your organisation?

Analysing the competitive environment

The external environment of organisations is complex, because it is concerned with everything outside an organisation affecting its prospects and activities. This includes the industry and markets in which it operates, the competitors with which it competes, the customers it aims to satisfy and the general political, economic, social, technological, legal and global environments over which it has little control. Analysing the environment is therefore a difficult and challenging task for strategists.

First, there is fundamental disagreement about the nature of the strategic management process (see Chapter 9). Prescriptive strategic theorists, for example, argue that uncertainties in the environment can be predicted. Emergent strategic theorists, on the other hand, argue that the environment is so turbulent and unstable that prediction serves little purpose. Second, because the environment is dynamic, strategies have to be developed against a backdrop of continual change. Third, since the environment contains so many external influences affecting the strategic direction of organisations, only selected ones can be explored.

PESTLE analysis provides a useful starting point for analysing the general environment of an organisation. PESTLE stands for the 'political', 'economic', 'social', 'technological', 'legal' and 'environmental' contexts impinging on an organisation (although some commentators have recently added a further 'E' in the acronym for 'ethical' issues that are of concern to organisations). PESTLE produces a checklist for examining the factors most likely to influence an organisation's market and business prospects. The political ones include public policies and legislation at local, national and European levels and the distributions of political power at each of these levels. The economic ones include market competition, energy and communication costs, consumer spending, government spending, interest rates, currency fluctuations, exchange rate policy, inflation and investment spending. The sorts of social issues affecting demand for an organisation's goods or services and its labour supply include education, health, demography, attitudes to work and leisure, and general social trends. Technological factors include the impact of computers and information technology on working life, rates of technological change and levels of research, and development spending in an organisation. The main environmental factors affecting an organisation cover pollution, resource conservation, the 'social costs' of given policies and other 'green' issues. Ethical factors are concerned with the impact of business decisions on organisational stakeholders.

A SWOT analysis is useful in bringing together the environmental analysis of an organisation, its resource/competence analysis and its strategic capacity for dealing with them. SWOT stands for internal strengths and weaknesses and external opportunities and threats. Strengths are internal, positive attributes of organisations, helping them to gain advantage in order to achieve their strategic objectives. Some organisations define their strengths by benchmarking them through comparing their own processes, products, service, or activities with those of 'best practice' organisations. Weaknesses are internal negative attributes of organisations that may result in them failing to achieve their strategic objectives. Weaknesses, too, can be identified and possibly remedied by benchmarking and following 'best practice'. Opportunities are external factors that substantially assist organisations in their efforts to achieve their strategic objectives. Threats are external factors that may result in organisations failing to achieve their strategic objectives.

(i) Undertake either a SWOT analysis or a PESTLE analysis of your organisation.

(ii) What are the advantages and disadvantages of SWOT or PESTLE analyses for your organisation?

MAJOR FEATURES OF THE FINANCIAL SYSTEM

One of the most important markets in market economies is the capital or financial market. This is the group of interrelated markets where money is bought and sold and finance capital is raised, lent and borrowed on varying terms for varying periods of time. It incorporates submarkets such as the credit market, stock market and foreign exchange market. There are strong forces causing conditions in one set of financial markets to affect the others, nationally and internationally. In the United Kingdom, the money markets comprise three main sets of financial institutions: the Bank of England, the London Stock Exchange and commercial banks and related institutions.

The Bank of England

The Bank of England is the central bank of the United Kingdom. The Bank was founded in 1694, nationalised in 1946 and gained operational independence in 1997. Standing at the centre of the UK's financial system, the Bank is committed to promoting and maintaining a stable and efficient monetary and financial framework as its contribution to a healthy economy. The Bank's roles and functions have evolved and changed over its 300-year history. Since its foundation, it has been the Government's banker and, since the late eighteenth century, it has been banker to the banking system more generally or the bankers' bank. As well as providing banking services to its customers, the Bank manages the UK's foreign exchange and gold reserves and government's stock register. The Bank is most visible to the general public through issuing banknotes and, more recently, its interest rate decisions. The Bank has had a monopoly on the issue of banknotes in England and Wales since the early twentieth century. It is only since 1997 that the Bank has had statutory responsibility for setting the UK's official interest rate.

Monetary policy

One of the Bank's core purposes is maintaining the integrity and value of the currency. It pursues this core purpose primarily through the conduct of monetary policy. This involves, above all, maintaining price stability, as defined by the inflation target set by government, as a precondition for achieving a wider economic goal of sustainable growth and employment. High inflation can be damaging to the functioning of the economy. Low inflation or price stability can help foster sustainable long-term economic growth. In 1997, the Chancellor of the Exchequer announced that government was giving the Bank operational responsibility for setting interest rates. The Bank of England Act 1998 gave the Bank that responsibility, which came into force in 1998.

The Bank's monetary policy objective is to deliver price stability, as defined by government's inflation target, and to support government's economic policy, including its objectives for growth and employment. The government's inflation target is confirmed in each Budget statement. The Bank's inflation forecast is published in the form of a probability distribution and is presented in what is now known as the 'fan chart'. The price stability objective is to normally to achieve an inflation target of, say, 2 per cent, as measured by the 12-month increase in the Consumer Prices Index, which is the retail prices index excluding mortgage interest payments.

The Bank aims to meet the government's inflation target by setting short-term interest rates through its Monetary Policy Committee (MPC). Monetary policy operates by influencing the cost of money. The Bank sets an interest rate for its own dealings with the market and that rate then affects the whole pattern of rates set by the commercial banks for their savers and borrowers. This, in turn, affects spending and output in the economy and eventually costs and prices. Broadly speaking, interest rates are set at a level to ensure demand in the economy is in line with the productive capacity of the economy. If interest rates are set too low, demand may exceed supply and lead to the emergence of inflationary pressures so that inflation is accelerating. If they are set too high, output is likely to be unnecessarily low and inflation is likely to decelerate.

The MPC takes interest rate decisions and implements them through its financial market operations by setting the interest rate at which the Bank lends to banks and other financial institutions. The Bank has close links with financial markets and institutions. This contact informs a great deal of its work, including collating and publishing monetary and banking statistics. The MPC meets monthly and takes decisions by majority vote, with the Governor having the casting vote if necessary. The Treasury has the right to be represented in a non-voting capacity and legislation provides that in extreme circumstances, and if the national interest demands it, government has power to give instructions to the Bank on interest rates for a limited period (www.bankofengland.co.uk).

A stable financial system

The Bank is also responsible for maintaining stability in the financial system, since a healthy financial system is vital to the proper functioning of the economy. The Bank analyses and promotes initiatives to strengthen the financial system and monitors financial developments to try to identify potential threats to financial stability. It also undertakes work for handling financial crises should they occur and it is the financial system's 'lender of last resort' in exceptional circumstances. In this work, the Bank co-operates closely with Her Majesty's Treasury and the Financial Services Authority, the regulator of banks and other financial institutions in the United Kingdom.

Much of the Bank's work involves liaison and co-operation with government, financial institutions and other central banks. Given London's position as a large international financial centre, the Bank's work addresses international as well as domestic developments. The Bank participates in many international forums involved in promoting the health of the world economy and global financial system.

The Bank also works to ensure that the UK financial system provides effective support to the rest of the UK economy and that the United Kingdom remains an attractive location for the conduct of international financial business. This involves working on issues such as firms' access to finance and, over recent years, introduction of the euro and the evolution of the euro financial markets and infrastructure.

The London Stock Exchange

The London Stock Exchange (LSE) is one of the world's oldest stock exchanges and its origins can be traced back more than 300 years. Starting life in the coffee houses of seventeenth century London, the Exchange quickly grew to become the City's most important financial institution. Today, the LSE is at the heart of global financial markets and is home to some of the best companies in the world. The LSE grows its business through business development initiatives, acquisitions, joint ventures and alliances where appropriate.

To implement this strategy, it has three objectives, first, to reinforce and extend its position as the premier source of equity market liquidity, benchmark prices and market data in the European time zone. Second, it seeks to operate a diversified business that capitalises on the emergence of an increasingly innovative environment, through leadership in technology and market services. Third, it aims to deliver superior value to its customers and shareholders (www.londonstockexchange.com).

The LSE has a number of 'core businesses'. First, in equity markets, it enables companies from around the world to raise the capital they need, by listing securities on its highly-efficient, transparent and well-regulated markets. Through its main market, the LSE gives companies access to one of the world's deepest and most liquid pools of investment capital. Once companies have been admitted to trading, it uses its staff expertise of the global financial markets to help them maximise the value of their listing in London.

Second, through its trading services, the LSE provides the trading platforms used by broking firms around the world to buy and sell securities. Its systems provide fast and efficient access to trading, allowing investors and institutions to tap quickly into equity, bond and derivative markets. Internationally recognised standards of regulation and market practice make its markets some of the most attractive and liquid in the world. Over 300 worldwide firms trade as members of the LSE.

Third, the stock market supplies high-quality, real-time prices, news and other information to the global financial community. Strong relationships with data vendors help ensure the markets receive the information they depend upon. It invests heavily in the best technology to create new applications for its data and works closely with its world-class partners to constantly upgrade its products and services.

Commercial banks and related institutions

Commercial banks and related financial institutions, such as savings banks, building societies, insurance companies and credit organisations, are financial intermediaries. All these institutions are now networked and interconnected, using the latest information technologies. This means that their commercial responses are speedy and efficient. The big five banks take in funds principally as deposits repayable on demand or at short notice, which they use to make advances by overdrafts and loans to their customers. They hold financial stocks and maintain a money transaction mechanism by accepting deposits on current account and operate a system of transferring funds between banks by cheques and credit transfers. Other important banking functions include providing credit to businesses, providing foreign exchange services for customers, financing foreign trade, operating in money markets and providing advisory services to customers. Banks have the central position in the financial system and financial markets. They control the money payments mechanism and form a major element in the money stock and play an important role as short-term lenders.

With deregulation of financial markets since the late 1970s, the lines of division between banks and other financial institutions are increasingly blurred and overlap. However, with the renewed dominance of these reformed institutions in the financial marketplace, Augar (2000) has described this period as 'the death of gentlemanly capitalism', while Soros (2000), in turn, has argued for further reforms as necessary to manage and stabilise the new 'global capitalism.'

> Identify as many different organisations which supply money and consider the effect that this has on government's ability to control money supply.

THE BUSINESS CONTEXT FOR PUBLIC SECTOR AND VOLUNTARY ORGANISATIONS

Individuals or groups create private organisations for market purposes (for-profit organisations) and are ultimately accountable to their owners or members. Other 'not-for-profit', private organisations range from charities, voluntary organisations, trade unions and friendly societies, to sports clubs and self-help groups. The criteria of success by which business organisations are judged are primarily market and economic ones (Horton and Farnham 1999). On the other hand, government creates public organisations primarily for political (ie non-market) purposes. These 'not-for-profit' organisations are ultimately accountable to political representatives and the law for achieving their objectives.

Scope of the public and voluntary sectors

The criteria for success by which the performance of public organisations is assessed are less easy to define and measure than for private organisations, since they include social and political measures as well as market ones. Public organisations are involved in a wide range of activities and encompass all those public bodies involved in making, implementing and applying public policy throughout the United Kingdom. There are separate governmental systems for Scotland, Northern Ireland and Wales, which have their own law-making bodies for certain devolved matters. All the countries of the United Kingdom have common defence, foreign affairs and economic policies but there are significant differences in domestic policies, policing and legal systems between Scotland, Northern Ireland, and England and Wales. The rest of this section relates only to the latter, unless otherwise indicated. The major administrative organisations in England and Wales include central government departments, departmental agencies, non-departmental agencies (sometimes called QUANGOs or quasi-autonomous government organisations), the NHS and local authorities.

In practice, when it comes to providing a dividing line between private and public organisations, the distinction is blurred. Tomkins' (1987) spectrum of organisational types illustrates the interdependence and interrelationships between private and public spheres. Ultimately, the relative configurations of private and public organisations reflect political and economic choices in society. Tomkins identifies the following:

- fully private
- private with part state ownership
- joint private and public ventures
- private regulated
- public infrastructure, operating privately
- contracted out
- public with managed competition
- public without competition.

Central and local government organisations provide public services, which are funded largely from tax revenues, although there is a trend for some charging to individual users to be introduced – a process known as 'co-payment'. However, public services are generally provided collectively for individual consumption as citizen rights, not according to ability to pay. The services include: national defence, law enforcement, fire protection, environmental health, health care, personal social services, education, roads, recreational facilities and consumer protection. Central government has overall responsibility for public services and deciding policy on what services are to be provided, funded and administered. But there is no rational explanation for the current distribution of responsibilities between central and local government, which has evolved in a pragmatic fashion (Horton and Farnham 1999).

Central government is responsible for a range of services and encompasses all those bodies for whose activities a minister of the Crown is directly or indirectly responsible to Parliament. It includes the armed services, government departments, departmental agencies and non-departmental agencies. There are some 20 major government departments including Defence, Education and Skills, Work and Pensions, the Treasury, and Trade and Industry but most central government services are delivered through departmental agencies such as the Prison Service and Passport Service. There are around 90 departmental agencies which employ about 73 per cent of the total civil service workforce. There are also several hundred non-departmental public agencies, which are headed and run by boards which come under the umbrella of a central department but are not directly accountable to a government minister.

The largest public organisation is the NHS, which was created by the National Health Service Act 1946. It is based on the principle that medical care and comprehensive health services should be readily available and supplied, largely free of charge, to anyone normally resident in the United Kingdom. Many reorganisations have taken place since 1974 and there are now hundreds of primary care and hospital trusts each run by boards with the legal status of public corporations. The general thrust of the changes has been to encourage greater economic efficiency and effectiveness by using 'pseudo' internal market mechanisms and private sector business management methods. These initiatives reflected similar changes in other parts of the public sector, with increasing emphasis being placed on market values rather than welfare values.

More than 400 local authorities provide the remaining public services in the United Kingdom. In England, for example, there are non-metropolitan counties, non-metropolitan districts, metropolitan districts, London Boroughs, unitary authorities and the City of London. There are different structures in Wales, Scotland and Northern Ireland. Local authorities consist of elected councillors, working in co-operation with professional officers. Their task is to ensure the efficient provision of the wide range of services, laid down by law, which are either mandatory or permissive. These services include consumer protection, fire services, roads and traffic, and personal services, such as education, libraries, social services and housing. Other local services are cemeteries, development control, environmental health, art galleries, museums and provision for physical recreation.

The provision of local public services was transformed during the 1980s and 1990s, as some were privatised (such as bus services and the compulsory sale of council houses) and others were deregulated and exposed to market competition (such as the compulsory competitive tendering of local authority building and maintenance work). The remaining services were subjected to internal market structures and requirements to operate as if they were commercial businesses (Painter and Isaac-Henry 1999).

Voluntary associations include professional bodies, trade unions, pressure groups, political parties, employers' associations, charitable trusts, the churches and other religious organisations. They tend to be relatively small bodies, normally employing fewer resources than private businesses and public organisations. Their goals are welfare- and community-oriented, with private assets. In some cases they are democratically controlled bodies, run by their members on collegiate and participatory lines. Some voluntary bodies have become much more important in recent years, as they increasingly provide services to the public, under contract to public organisations.

Public management reform

Public management reform, sometimes described as administrative reform, 'new public management' or modernisation of public services, has been an issue of intense interest, scrutiny and review for over two decades and has been central to the public sector agenda during this period (Horton and Farnham 1999). The reforms that have taken place, at central government, local government and government agency levels, have had a number of purposes. These have included making economies in public expenditure, improving the quality of public service provision, making government operations more efficient and increasing the chance that public policies will be effective (Flynn 2002). The impact of these reforms has resulted in changes in how public services have been organised, structured, managed and delivered, and how public officials have been employed within them.

Several generic studies have traced the origins of public management reform programmes, classified and analysed them (Kickert 1997, Pollitt 1993). Other studies have concentrated on specific areas such as financial management reforms, organisational change, and performance management and performance measurement in the public sector (Pollitt 1998, OECD 1995, Peters and Savoie 1998). Further specialist studies have analysed and reviewed how public officials are recruited, deployed, rewarded, appraised, trained, promoted, disciplined and made redundant within public services (Farnham et al 1996, Farnham and Horton 2000, Horton et al 2002).

In their detailed international comparative study, Pollitt and Bouckaert (2004) suggest that public management reform can be analysed in a number of ways. Taking public reform as an example of 'strategic decision-making', for example, they identify four approaches to it: 'maintain', 'modernize', 'marketize' or 'minimise' the administrative system.

Maintaining the administrative system results in tightening up traditional controls, restricting spending and freezing recruitment. It also involves running campaigns against waste and corruption and generally squeezing the public sector.

Modernising the administrative system brings in faster, more flexible ways of budgeting, managing, accounting and delivering services to users.

Marketising institutes as many market-type mechanisms as possible within the public administration system, so that public organisations are made to compete with one another to increase efficiency and user responsiveness, which 'represents a penetration of the administrative system by the culture and practices of the market sector' (Pollitt and Bouckaert 2004, p176).

Minimising the administrative system involves handing over as many tasks as possible to the market sector, through privatisation and contracting out, resulting in what some have called the 'hollowing out' of the state. Clearly since the 1980s, those responsible for driving public management reform in the United Kingdom have adopted all these approaches at various times.

Horton (2005) has analysed public management reform in the United Kingdom using five possible trajectories:

- *Privatisation and marketisation.* Here the fundamental problem to be addressed is the role and size of government and the need to shrink it. It is assumed that markets are better than state provision, as co-ordinating mechanisms and in providing choice. They are more flexible, responsive to public demand and innovative. An entrepreneurial culture is needed to stimulate economic activity and growth. By privatising state activities, consumers benefit from better services and more accountability.
- *Structural reorganisation and re-engineering.* This is based upon the perception that public organisations need to be 'right for the job'. Old bureaucratic multi-functional bureaucratic structures with long hierarchies and over-centralised communication and control systems are seen as inefficient and ineffective and need to be replaced by uni-functional agencies with flexible matrix structures. Co-ordination through rules, regulations and supply-based financial systems has to be replaced by contracts, specifying desired outputs and performance indicators which chief executives and managers are responsible for delivering.
- *Enhancing the three Es.* Here the problem is seen to be inefficient and wasteful use of public money. Emphasis is on economy, efficiency and effectiveness. Management reforms are an opportunity to introduce private sector management skills into public organisations to address failures to deliver on policy outcomes. There is a need to eliminate obvious waste, introduce tight financial controls and pinpoint responsibility at every level of public organisations (Farnham and Horton 1996).
- *In search of excellence.* This sees the reform problem as one of a bureaucratic culture and excessive emphasis on standardisation, uniformity, regularity and risk avoidance. Reform means replacing bureaucracy with a culture committed to change and continuous improvement which is responsive to public needs and expectations. Total quality management (TQM) is introduced from the private sector, with its emphasis on getting things right first time, avoiding mistakes and waste and developing 'learning organisations'.
- *Reinventing democracy and public service orientation.* This approach emphasises decentralisation and democratisation of the policy and management processes. Services are provided at the lowest level and are accountable to their community, through traditional channels of local authorities and functional boards and by democratising the process and involving the public through subsystems of governance. Neighbourhood forums, community groups and joined-up government are used to meet public needs.

The public sector has been transformed since 1979 using each of these trajectories. It continues to be the target of the Labour government's modernisation agenda (Cabinet Office 1999).

(i)   What do you understand by the term public management reform?
(ii) What are the key characteristics of public management reform?
(iii) What have been the major effects of adopting it in UK public services since 1979 for
   (a) users
   (b) taxpayers and
   (c) public sector workers?

LABOUR MARKET TRENDS

The labour market consists of the working population, which is all those men and women available for and capable of work. It includes those who are unemployed (ie those seeking work), as well as those in paid employment. Over the last generation unemployment has fluctuated widely not only because of industrial restructuring and frequent recessions but also because of the way governments have recorded the numbers. Official figures have ranged from 5.6 per cent of the working population in 1976, rising to 12.4 per cent in 1983 and then down to 6.9 per cent in 1990. Figures rose again to 10.1 per cent in 1992, falling slowly to 5.8 per cent in 1997 and 4.8 per cent in 2004. There are variations in the population likely to be unemployed, with the young, black, unskilled manual worker and the over-50s being the most vulnerable. While gender, race, disability, age and geography are all factors influencing unemployment, the highest rates of unemployment are among young males between 16 and 20.

The labour market can be analysed in a number of ways including gender, age, employment status, occupation, industry and working patterns. This section summarises some major trends in the UK labour market in the early 2000s. These themes are explored in more depth in Chapter 5.

The working population

The working population (or labour force) is the economically active population, which is traditionally drawn from the 16–64 age groups. However, this will change with the introduction of a law preventing discrimination in employment on the grounds of age in 2006. The economic activity rate is the percentage of the population in the labour force and consists of those in work and those looking for work. The working population rose from around 25 million in 1971 to 26 million in 1979, peaking at 28.9 million in 1990. For some years, it remained fairly stable around 28.5 million but by 2004 it had risen to 29.7 million.

Traditionally, men have constituted the larger part of the labour force, but women now form an ever-increasing proportion as their participation rate rises and men's falls. In 1971, women accounted for 38 per cent of the labour force. By 1997, this had risen to 45 per cent, when some 54 per cent of women of working age were economically active, compared with 72 per cent of men. By 2004, 56 per cent of women were economically active, compared with 71 per cent of men, and women made up 46 per cent of the working population and men 54 per cent (Labour Force Survey 2004).

Because of the ageing profile of the population in general, the working population profile is also ageing. In 1971, 20.4 per cent of the working population was between the ages of 16 and 24 but this had fallen to 15.3 per cent in 1997. Conversely, 20 per cent of the working population was between 45 and 54 in 1971, and this had risen to 22 per cent by 1997. By 2005, only 10 per cent of the working population was between 16 and 24 and 22.8 per cent were between 45 and 54 (www.statistics.gov.uk/statbase).

Reasons for changes in the distribution of the working population are complex. One cause is the decline of the manufacturing and extractive industries (as indicated above), which were largely all-male occupations, and the growth of service industries (both private and public) employing mainly women. In 1978 there were 13.4 million men and 9.4 million women in employment. In 1997, this had risen to 14.4 million men and 12 million women. By 2004, following further rises in the employed workforce there were 15.3 million men and 13 million women. Women entering the labour market account for some 90 per cent of the increase in the labour force since the late 1970s. Most of the jobs lost in declining industries have been by the male workforce.

Linked to this is the increase in part-time employment or working for reduced hours (see below). Some 44 per cent of women are in part-time employment in contrast to only 10 per cent of men, although the proportion of men has been steadily growing. Part-time employment enables women with family responsibilities to enter paid employment and combine their dual roles. Further, changes in family structures, the increase in one parent families and the desire of many women to pursue their own careers have led to more women entering and remaining in the labour market than in the past. Although women with children have lower participation rates than those without, they are taking shorter career breaks and re-entering the labour market in much larger numbers.

Another trend has been the increase in self-employment. In 2004, some 3.8 million men and women ran their own businesses and, although the number of new businesses failing remains high, at around 60 per cent, there are always new ones being created to maintain and inflate the numbers.

Employment by occupation

In the United Kingdom, there is a fairly even distribution of people in employment across occupational groups. In 2004, six occupational groups (managerial, professional, 'associate' professional and technical, administrative, skilled trades and 'elementary' occupations) each employed between 12 and 15 per cent of those in employment. The remaining three occupations (personal services, sales and plant/machine operatives) employed 8 per cent each. However, there were twice as many women than men in secretarial, personal service and sales occupations, whilst in skilled trades and among plant/machine operatives the reverse was true (Begum 2004).

Occupations with the youngest workforces (16–24 years) were sales and elementary occupations, with sales having the highest proportion (39 per cent) of this age group in employment. Occupations having the oldest workforces (45–65 years) were plant/machine operatives (41 per cent), managers (38 per cent) and professionals (38 per cent). Elementary and administrative occupations had the highest proportions of people over 65 years old in employment.

In terms of qualifications, people employed in professional occupations were, unsurprisingly, most likely to have a degree (or its equivalent) as their highest educational achievement (69 per cent). Women in this group (73 per cent) were better qualified than men (66 per cent) in terms of degree qualifications. The professional group was followed by associate professional and technical occupations (30 per cent with degrees), managers (29 per cent) and administrative occupations (12 per cent). The proportion of people with no qualifications was greatest in elementary occupations (26 per cent), with women in this group (29 per cent) more likely to have no qualifications compared with men (23 per cent).

Employment by industry

Two industry groups – public administration including education and health (28 per cent) and distribution including hotels and restaurants (20 per cent) – accounted for almost half the people in employment, with women more than twice as likely to work in public administration as men. Financial services (including banking and insurance) and manufacturing employed 16 per cent and 14 per cent of those in employment respectively. Other services such as transport and communications and construction each employed between 6 and 8 per cent of those in employment. Essential services (including energy and water) and agriculture (including fishing) employed less than 1 per cent each.

Industries with the youngest workforces were distribution, financial services and 'other services', where at least 40 per cent of those in employment were 16–34 years of age. Industries with the largest proportions of older workers were essential services and public administration (39 per cent each). Over 9 per cent of the workforce in agriculture were over 65.

Financial services had the highest proportion of people with degrees (34 per cent), followed by public administration (31 per cent). Manufacturing, other services and essential services employed far lower proportions of those with degrees (between 15 per cent and 22 per cent each). Those least likely to be educated to degree level were in transport and communications, agriculture, construction and distribution. Men and women with degrees were most likely to be employed in public administration and financial services (41 per cent each). Public administration had the highest proportion of women with degrees (27 per cent) and agriculture had the largest proportion with no qualifications (21 per cent).

Working patterns

Growth and widespread use of computing technology and the World Wide Web, and the shift from a manufacturing-based economy to a service-based one, have encouraged changes in the ways people work. The standard pattern of work, from nine to five, Monday to Friday, is less common than in the past. This shift towards non-standard work is fuelled by employer-pull for more employment flexibility and worker-push for a balanced approach between working time and the needs of families and individuals. Changes have been noted in part-time working, temporary work and shift work. Such changes in working patterns over time point to attempts by individuals and employers to develop a more productive approach to work. As McOrmond (2004, p24) concludes:

> Employers may be using non-standard working arrangements to create a labour force that is more flexible and thus suited to meet market demand, and employees may be attempting to create a more effective work–life balance.

Part-time working

The reasons why people work part-time have changed between 1993 and 2003. There was a slight increase in the proportion of people not wanting full-time jobs and those who could not find full-time jobs. The largest increase (18 per cent compared with 12 per cent) in those taking part-time work was among students. Men also made up a larger proportion of part-time workers but men working part-time voluntarily were more likely to do so because they could afford not to work full-time. Women working part-time were most likely to want to spend more time at home with their families. Doogan (2001) has shown that part-time work provides long-term employment options. Indeed a majority of women who were in full-time employment before taking maternity leave had switched to part-time work on their return. This has contributed to long-term employment among women, who are now employed part-time. There is also a trend for people past retirement age or made redundant from full-time jobs pre-retirement age to take part-time employment.

People aged 16 to 19 were the most likely group to be working part-time in the United Kingdom. Just over a half of men (51 per cent) and two-thirds of women (69 per cent) in this age group worked part-time. Women aged 25 to 29 were the least likely to be in part-time employment. However, in all age groups, women were more likely to have worked part-time in the period 1993–2003. As indicated above, the proportion of women in part-time employment remained stable (44 per cent) over this period, while that for men increased (from 7 per cent to 10 per cent) and the proportion of all those in employment increased marginally (from 24 per cent to 26 per cent).

The proportion of employees working part-time was greatest in distribution (40 per cent), with women (58 per cent) being more likely to work part-time than men (21 per cent). This was followed by other services (35 per cent), public administration (32 per cent) and agriculture (16 per cent).

Temporary working

Temporary employment ranges from seasonal, casual work in sectors such as agriculture to independent consultants taking on a series of contracts for a single employer. It is work of limited duration. In the United Kingdom, the proportion of people working in non-permanent jobs remained fairly constant over the period 1993–2003, when temporary employment was most common amongst those under 25, irrespective of gender (11 per cent). Prime-age people were least likely to do temporary work, although women were almost twice as likely (5.9 per cent) as men (3.5 per cent) to do so. Temporary employment peaked in 1997 (8 per cent) but decreased by 2003 to what it had been in 1993 (6 per cent). The reasons for working temporarily include not being able to find permanent work or not wanting permanent work.

Shift work

The proportion of people doing shift work (working non-standard hours) has not changed over the period 1993–2003 and was about 16 per cent of the employed workforce. It was men who predominantly worked shifts and this was related to the higher proportion of men employed in manufacturing, where shift work is more common. However, there is also a strong history of shift work in health-related occupations, personal services and emergency services where there is a need for 24 hour, seven day coverage. A high proportion of women is found in healthcare, although emergency services such as police, fire and prison services are populated largely by male employees.

Among men, the group showing the greatest increase in the proportion doing shift work was those aged 16–19, which rose from 10 per cent in 1993 to 18 per cent in 2003. Men aged 60–64 were the group least likely to work shifts. Among women, those aged 16–19 had the highest proportion doing shift work, rising from 12 per cent in 1993 to 20 per cent in 2003. These trends were probably linked to the growing need to finance their post-secondary education. For the population as a whole, the proportion doing shift work showed a slight increase from 13 per cent in 1993 to 15 per cent in 2003.

In 2003, shift work was most common in transport and communications, where about 27 per cent of workers did shifts. About 33 per cent of male workers in this sector worked shifts, compared with about 19 per cent of females. In public administration, some 19 per cent of workers were on shifts. Working shifts was least common in construction.

Working time

In terms of working time, managers were most likely to work more than 45 hours per week (19 per cent), with the greatest proportion being men (85 per cent). Long working hours were also common among skilled trades (17 per cent), plant/machine operatives (15 per cent) and professional occupations (12 per cent). For all other occupational groups, less than 10 per cent of those in employment worked more than 45 hours per week. Those least likely to work more than 45 hours were in administrative employment. But in nearly all occupations over half of those employed in them were likely to be working between 31 and up to 45 hours per week. The exceptions were personal services (43 per cent), sales (36 per cent) and elementary occupations (44 per cent).

Agriculture had the highest proportion of people working more than 45 hours per week. Of these, the largest group was self-employed (79 per cent) and the smallest group were employees (19 per cent). People were least likely to work more than 45 hours in public administration. However, in most industry groups, the majority of people worked between 31 hours and up to 45 hours per week.

> (i)   Critically examine the reasons given for increased employment flexibility.
> (ii) Identify and evaluate four different types of flexibility, enabling an organisation to meet both its organisational needs and those of its employees.

IMPLICATIONS FOR ORGANISATIONS AND P&D PROFESSIONALS

Managing scarcity is a major task facing managements in all organisations. In practice, there are never sufficient resources available for businesses, public services and voluntary bodies to satisfy their economic wants. To fulfil their economic and other goals, private and public organisations require skilled human resources, finance capital and access to intermediate goods and services, and raw materials in the operations process. Since these resources are limited in supply, organisations compete in factor of production and commodity markets for these resources. Within markets, it is prices that act as signals and indicators to firms and public enterprises in their continuous search for resource sufficiency, organisational effectiveness and improved economic performance.

Managements also have to decide what resources to use, in what quantities, how to use them and how to maximise efficiency in the operations process. In carrying out these activities, managements are continually faced with the problem of making choices amongst combinations of resources, work methods and which products or services to supply. These tasks continually face managements in every organisation and there are both financial and opportunity costs in taking these decisions.

This raises the question: to what extent are top managers reactors to market forces or controllers of them? In product markets, given the relative imperfections of most market structures in the modern world, businesses are generally price-makers rather than price-takers. Anecdotal and research evidence suggests that 'big business' is able, to varying degrees, to influence market prices and hence returns on finance capital and corporate profitability. With vast amounts of finance capital at stake, managers' ability to work market forces in their favour and facilitate product success and corporate viability is not without its benefits. Whether this benefits business clients of firms or their individual clients is more open to debate. As Galbraith (1967, p204f) has argued, 'the control or management of demand [by big business] is ... a vast rapidly growing industry itself.' In everyday language, this great machine and the varied talents it employs claims 'to be engaged in selling goods.' In less ambiguous language, 'it means that it is engaged in the management of those who buy goods.'

In money and financial markets, management influence is less apparent. Indeed some commentators argue that there is increasing divergence between the City of London's interests and those of the manufacturing and service sectors. Money markets are internationalised and demonstrate more propinquity to free markets than do other markets. With high-speed computer technology, and interdependent international money markets, there is great volatility in global money markets. The major actors in international equity and security markets are themselves corporate bodies, not individual investors. Increasingly, it is business firms that own other firms, with corporate ownership traversing national, international and continental boundaries. Those supporting this interpretation of corporate capitalism argue that real economic power has passed out of the hands of the managerial elite running companies to the relatively small group of entrepreneurial capitalists who work the money markets and concentrate financial ownership in their own hands.

Writers such as Marris (1964) have argued that 'managerial capitalism' better describes the power structure of modern market economies, which are dominated by large business corporations and where power and resources are located within a definable managerial class that is distinctly separate from the property-owning class, as well as being independent of its control. This managerial class, it is argued, pursues goals and aims that are independent of workers, shareholders and the state. Theories of managerial capitalism are closely linked with managerial theories of the firm. These analyses of contemporary capitalism are characterised by the dominance of large enterprises in the corporate sector, where ownership and decision-making is largely divided between shareholders and top managers respectively. Given imperfect capital markets and uncompetitive product markets, it has been argued that managers have scope to pursue business goals other than profit maximisation, such as corporate growth, market security and maximising sales.

Writing 40 years after Marris's study, Sampson (2004, pp311–312) has concluded that anyone looking at the chief executives and chairmen of the United Kingdom's largest 20 companies and at others in the top 100 'must be struck by the smallness of the pool from which they come' and the repeating interlocking of boardrooms. These names kept 'recurring in corporations, banks or insurance companies as if they were really one immense organisation with separate subsidiaries.' He explained this phenomenon by claiming that 'London has been able to provide a stable base and environment to attract multinational businesses, with all the back-up of sophisticated financial services and a fair legal system.'

In making difficult economic choices in conditions of scarcity and globalisation, top managements attempt to act rationally and decisively. Some do this by drawing upon sophisticated cost benefit analyses in both the private and public sectors. Cost benefit analyses differ from straight financial appraisals by considering all potential gains and losses in taking business decisions, irrespective of to whom they accrue. In essence, benefits are any gains in satisfaction and costs are losses in satisfaction, measured as opportunity costs. In practice, many costs are not capable of quantification in monetary terms, such as destruction of natural beauty, loss of wildlife or threats to the environment, while benefits are measured in monetary terms. For this reason, shadow prices are often used in cost benefit analyses. These impute into them valuation of an economic 'good' or economic 'bad', which has no market price. Shadow pricing represents the opportunity cost of consuming or producing a commodity that is not normally traded in the economy. Strictly conducted, cost benefit analyses value all inputs and outputs at shadow prices.

Understanding the nature of economic scarcity and the principles underpinning markets and price determination is an important skill for managerial decision-makers, including P&D professionals. Managers need to know the types of products, capital and labour markets in which their organisations operate. They need to be sensitive to the sorts of market changes likely to affect these markets. In this way, they are better able to anticipate the opportunities and threats facing their organisations in conditions of change and market instability. Top managers also try to anticipate the actions of their competitors, thus maintaining or improving the market positions of their organisations wherever possible. Managers also need to understand the way in which government intervenes in markets to protect consumers, provide workers' rights, maintain the environment or prevent price-fixing. In public services, in turn, the introduction of market testing and internal markets has brought significant changes in organisational culture, managerial values and human resources practices within them.

CONCLUSION

This chapter outlines some of the major features of the modern, competitive market economy. The changing scope of UK economic policy reveals that the so-called 'third way' of the post-Thatcher 'new' Labour government is claimed to transcend neo-liberalism and provide an alternative to state socialism, associated with the post-war Labour party, and market liberalism advocated by the Conservatives in the 1980s and 1990s. Others claim that New Labour has only adapted neo-liberalism to its own policy agenda. The evolving structure of the UK economy shows that it is shifting from one largely dependent upon manufacturing, old staple industries and large-scale industry to a post-industrial, service oriented and increasingly knowledge-based one.

The main determinants of market supply for a commodity are its price, costs of the factors of production, goals of the producer and current state of technology. The main determinants of market demand of a commodity are its price, prices of other commodities, size of consumer income, consumer tastes and social factors. However, there are few perfect or free markets in the real world and intensity of competition among producers or suppliers varies. These market structures, together with lack of full knowledge of markets by consumers, lead to market imperfections resulting in varying degrees of monopolistic competition, oligopoly and monopoly.

How organisations gain and maintain competitive advantage can be examined within Porter's five forces framework. This identifies the forces of competition in industries and provides tools for capturing the heterogeneity of industries. Its five elements are threat of entry, intensity of rivalry, pressure of substitutes, bargaining power of buyers and bargaining power of suppliers.

Financial markets and monetary bodies, such as the Bank of England and Stock Exchange, are central institutions in the UK market economy. Public and voluntary sector organisations interact with markets, which increasingly play an active role in their operation. Within public organisations, public management reform is a major driver of change. Finally, developments in labour markets include changes in the structure of the working population, increases in atypical employment, changes in the occupational and industrial distributions of employment and changes in working patterns such as part-time work, temporary work, shift work and working time.

USEFUL READING

AUGAR, P. (2000) *The death of gentlemanly capitalism: The rise and fall of London's investment banks.* Harmondsworth: Penguin.

BASU, K. (2000) *Prelude to political economy: A study of the social and political foundations of economics.* Oxford: Oxford University Press.

FLYNN, N. (2002) *Public sector management.* Harlow: FT/Prentice Hall.

GIDDENS, A. (1998) *The third way: The renewal of social democracy*. Cambridge: Polity Press.

GRIFFITHS, A. and WALL, S.(eds). (2004) *Applied economics*. Harlow: FT/Prentice Hall.

HEATHER, K. (2004) *Economics: Theory in action*. Harlow: FT/Prentice Hall.

HERTZ, N. (2001) *The silent takeover: Global capitalism and the death of democracy*. London: Heinemann.

HORTON, S. (2005) Trajectories, institutions and stakeholders in public management reform. In: D. FARNHAM, A. HONDEGHEM and S. HORTON, *Staff participation in public management reform: Some international comparisons*. London: Palgrave.

KAY, J. (2003) *The truth about markets: Their genius, their limits, their follies*. London: Allen Lane.

LANDES, D. (1998) *The wealth and poverty of nations*. London: Little Brown.

OFFICE OF FAIR TRADING. (2001) *The role of market definition in monopoly and dominance inquiries*. London: HMSO.

ORMEROD, P. (1998) *Butterfly economics: A new general theory of social and economic behaviour*. London: Faber and Faber.

OWEN, C. (1999) *From empire to Europe: The decline and revival of British industry since the second world war*. London: HarperCollins.

PORTER, M. (1998a) *Competitive strategy*. New York: Free Press.

SAMPSON, A. (2004) *Who runs this place? The anatomy of Britain in the 21st century*. London: Murray.

SOROS, G. (2000) *Reforming global capitalism*. New York: Little Brown.

STIGLITZ, J. (2001) *Globalisation and its discontents*. London: Penguin.

THUROW, L. (1999) *Building wealth: The new rules for individuals, companies, and nations in a knowledge-based economy*. New York: Harper Business.

The Technological Context

CHAPTER 3

CHAPTER OBJECTIVES

By the end of this chapter, readers should be able to:

- identify ways in which technological developments affect the P&D function and an organisation's employment markets
- contribute to the formation of organisational responses to technological change.

In addition, readers should be able to understand, explain and critically evaluate:

- technological developments and their potential impact on the business environment of organisations
- the evolution of a knowledge economy and its implications for organisations
- likely long term applications of evolving technologies
- debates about the desirability of technological developments in terms of their impact on people and the environment.

INTRODUCTION

Technology is the application of scientific knowledge to help humans produce goods and services more efficiently. It can also make work processes more effective and less human-intensive. There are many types of technology and it is advances in technology that have generally accompanied major waves of economic change, wealth creation and social transformation. Toffler (1970, 1981) has pointed out that in all societies the energy system, production system and distribution system are interrelated parts of a 'techno-sphere', which takes specific forms at each stage of socio-economic development. Fossil fuels provided the energy for industrial societies and new technology spawned, first, steam-driven and, later, electro-mechanically-driven machines. These were then brought together into interconnected systems to create factories, mass production and Fordist, bureaucratic organisational structures.

The new technologies of today, which are energising post-industrial societies, are rooted in information technology (IT), which in its strictest sense is the science of collecting, storing, processing and transmitting information (Forester 1987). IT is itself the result of a convergence of three separate technologies – electronics, computing and communications – and the invention of the silicon chip. Discoveries of the transistor (1947), the integrated circuit (1957), the planar process (1959) and the microprocessor (1971) converged to constitute a new scientific paradigm. IT or as it is sometimes called information and communication technologies (ICTs) are playing a central role in contemporary technological and economic change.

This chapter concentrates on ICTs. These are important because they have emerged as one of the key technological developments over the past 20 years. They take a variety of forms including the World Wide Web, intranets, inter-organisational networks, computer aided design, computer aided manufacture, automated production systems, automated teller machines, biotechnology, telecommunications, robotics and many other systems (Horton 2000).

These innovatory technologies are significant because ideas such as flexibility, teamwork, tele-working, networks, and distributed and virtual organisations all point to radical new ways of work-ing and organising work, based on new technological possibilities. In the era of the 'automation of automation', sometimes called 'cybernation' or 'the digital age', the totality of an organisation's automated operations are electronically integrated and linked together. In the past, technology transformed processes rather than produced goods or services. Today ICTs are not only trans-forming processes but also producing information as an output. Information has itself become a commodity. ICTs are pervasive, since they are not confined to the economic sphere but are also fundamentally changing the social, cultural and political spheres of society at an accelerating rate, through a fundamental technological revolution. This chapter examines some of the main ICT technological developments taking place in the digital age and outlines their impact on people, organisations and society.

DEVELOPMENTS IN TECHNOLOGY

Grübler (1998, p117) has summarised the technological changes that have taken place in the world since the onset of the industrial revolution in the eighteenth century. For him, technological change is driven by a series of 'technology clusters.' A technology cluster is 'a set of interrelated technolog-ical and organizational innovations whose pervasive adoption drives a particular period of economic growth, productivity increases, industrialization, trade, and associated structural changes.' These clusters do not follow sequentially, one after another in a rigid temporal sequence. 'Various clusters coexist in any given period, although the relative importance of each keeps shifting.' In his view, elements of an emerging cluster develop initially within specialised applications or specific market niches. Eventually, they emerge as a new dominant technology after an intensive period of experi-mentation and cumulative improvements. Further, as the dominant technology structure expands, many technological developments of its successor are developed through subsequent scientific discoveries, innovation and small-scale applications.

Grübler has argued that there is no simple 'cause–effect relationship' between technological, insti-tutional, organisational and global change. The appropriate model is 'one of co-evolutionary processes, rather than one of linear cause–effect relationship' Grübler (1998, p119). He has iden-tified a series of technological, economic and organisational changes distinguishing particular technology clusters. These are:

- New products and markets emerge.
- Transportation infrastructures widen existing markets.
- New process technologies, forms of organisation and systems of management make it possible to raise productivity.
- Macro-economic and social policies help in distributing productivity gains.
- Rising incomes create a powerful demand-induced stimulus for output growth.
- Energy, transportation and communication infrastructures facilitate changes and adjustments in agriculture, industry and consumer markets.

Grübler has identified four historical technological clusters and an emerging one, each of which has important implications for economic growth and development. He has classified the industrial and economic developments that have taken place since 1750 into five overlapping periods (Grübler 1998, p121):

(i)   1750–1820
(ii) 1800–1870
(iii) 1850–1940
(iv) 1920–2000
(v)   post-1980.

Some of their characteristics are as follows:

- *Agriculture*. Technology clusters in agriculture involved 'agricultural innovations' between 1750–1820 and 1800–1870, 'mercantilist agriculture' between 1850–1940, and 'industrialisation of agriculture' between1920–2000.
- *Industry*. Technology clusters in industry involved 'textiles' between 1750–1820, 'steam power' between 1800–1870, 'heavy engineering' between 1850–1940, 'mass production' between 1920–2000, and 'total quality' post-1980.
- *Services*. The technology cluster in services was specified as one of 'mass consumption' between 1920–2000.

These technology clusters are characterised by dominant 'organizational styles' and distinctive economic and social institutions. Between 1920–2000, for example, the dominant organisational style of the technological cluster was Fordism and Taylorism, multinational companies (MNCs) and vertical integration of businesses. Post-1980, the dominant organisational style was 'Just-in-Time' management, total quality control and horizontal integration between businesses. Between 1920–2000, economy and society were linked with the welfare state, Keynesian economic management and open societies. Post-1980, economy and society were linked with economic deregulation, environmental regulation and networks of actors. The core countries experiencing technology clusters associated with industrialisation of agriculture, mass production and mass consumption during 1920–2000 were the USA, Canada, Japan, Australia, New Zealand, the United Kingdom and west European countries.

Post-1980, the core countries experiencing a total quality cluster are members of the OECD. ICTs have been central to this period, where the products of new IT industries are information processing devices or information processing itself. As Castells (1996, p67) has argued: 'A networked deeply interdependent economy emerges that becomes increasingly able to apply its progress in technology, knowledge, and management to technology, knowledge and management themselves.' The rest of this section outlines some selected examples of how digital technology has been developed, used and applied in the information age.

Compare and contrast Toffler's and Grübler's analyses of technological change.

ICTs

The scientific and industrial predecessors of ICTs were rooted in the years before 1940, such as the invention of the telephone by Bell in 1876, the radio by Marconi in 1898 and the vacuum tube by Forest in 1906. However, it was during the Second World War, and its aftermath, that major technological breakthroughs in electronics took place. The transistor, invented in 1947, made possible the fast processing of electrical impulses in a binary mode of interruption and amplification. This enabled the coding of logic and communication between machines. These processing devices were semiconductors and were eventually developed into 'micro-chips', now made up of millions of transistors. The shift to silicon manufacture of semiconductors achieved by Texas Instruments in 1954 and the invention of the planar process in 1959 opened up possibilities of integrating miniaturised components with precision manufacturing (Hall and Preston 1988).

By the early twenty-first century, ICTs comprised a set of converging technologies in microelectronics, computers, computing software, telecommunications, broadcasting and optoelectronics. In addition, they included developments in biotechnology, because genetic engineering is focused on decoding, manipulating and the reprogramming of information codes of living matter (see below). Around this nucleus of ICTs, a constellation of major breakthroughs took place in the last two decades of the twentieth century in advanced materials, energy sources, medical applications, manufacturing techniques and transportation technology. This process of technological transformation expands exponentially because of its ability to create an interface between diverse technological fields through a common digital language in which information is generated, stored, retrieved, processed and transmitted. In these ways, the advanced world has become 'digitalised' (Negroponte 1995).

Microelectronics

The decisive step in microelectronics was the invention of the integrated circuit by Kilby and Noyce in 1957. It triggered a technological explosion as prices of semiconductors fell and production increased. Developments in new microelectronic technology accelerated in the 1960s, as manufacturing technology improved and computers, using faster and more powerful microelectronic devices, helped better chip design. The average price of an integrated circuit fell from US$50 in 1962 to US$1 in 1971. However, according to Castells (1996, p41), 'only in the 1970s did new information technologies diffuse widely, accelerating their synergistic development and converging into a new paradigm.'

A major breakthrough in the diffusion of microelectronics took place in 1971, when Intel invented the microprocessor (ie a computer on a chip). Information processing power could now be installed everywhere. The race was on for an ever-greater integration capacity of circuits on a single chip, with the technology of design and manufacturing constantly exceeding the limits of integration previously thought to be physically possible, without abandoning the use of silicon material. Even today, technical evaluations still predict 10 or more years of silicon-based integrated circuits, although research in alternative materials has been stepped up. Combined with developments in 'parallel processing' using multiple microprocessors, the power of microelectronics is relentlessly increasing computing capacity. Greater miniaturisation, further specialisation and the decreasing price of increasingly powerful chips has made it possible to put them in every machine in everyday life. These include dishwashers, microwave ovens, motorcars, electronic tracking systems and many others. Speed, cheapness and reliability have become the hallmarks of new microelectronic technology.

Computing

Computers were born in 1946, when researchers at the University of Pennsylvania, under US army sponsorship, produced the first general purpose machine – the Electronic Numerical Integrator and Calculator (ENIAC). According to Forester (1987), this first electronic computer weighed 30 tons, was built on metal modules 9 feet tall, and consisted of 70,000 resistors and 18,000 vacuum tubes. It occupied the area of a gymnasium and, when it was turned on, its electricity consumption was so high that Philadelphia's lighting dimmed.

In 1958, Sperry Rand produced a second-generation mainframe computer, followed immediately by International Business Machines (IBM) with its 7090 model. But in 1964, IBM with its 360/370 mainframe machine came to dominate the computer industry that was populated at this time by both 'new' and 'old' business machine companies. By the 1990s, most of these firms were ailing or had vanished from the market. In these 30 or so years, the computer industry had organised itself into a well-defined hierarchy of mainframes, minicomputers, terminals and some supercomputers. Microelectronics changed all that, inducing a 'revolution within a revolution.' The advent of the microprocessor in 1971, with its capacity to put a computer on a chip, turned the electronics industry upside down. By 1982, Apple Computers had ushered in the age of diffusion of computer power, with its microcomputer. IBM reacted by producing its own version of the 'personal computer' (PC) that soon became the generic name for all micro-computers. However, because IBM's PC was based on technology developed for IBM by other sources, it was vulnerable to cloning. This eventually doomed IBM's dominance in PCs but also spread the use of IBM clones around the world. It also diffused a common standard in microcomputing, in spite of the superiority of Apple machines.

A fundamental condition for diffusing microcomputers was fulfilled by the development of new software adapted to their operation. In the 1970s, two young Harvard dropouts, Bill Gates and Paul Allen, went on to found Microsoft, today's software giant. The creation of this business organisation translated dominance in operating software into dominance in software for the exponentially growing microcomputer market as a whole.

In the last 30 years, increasing chip power has resulted in a dramatic enhancement of microcomputing power, thus shrinking the function of large computers. Networked microprocessor-based systems, composed of smaller desktop machines (clients), served by more powerful, more dedicated machines (servers), have supplanted more specialised information processing computers, such as traditional mainframe machines and supercomputers. Since the mid-1980s, microcomputers cannot be perceived in isolation. They perform in networks, with increasing mobility based on portable computers. This extraordinary versatility, and the capacity to add memory and processing capacity by sharing computer power in an electronic network, decisively shifted the computer age in the 1990s. The shift was from one based on centralised data storage and processing to one based on networked, interactive computer power sharing. The whole technology had changed but so had its social and organisational interactions, with the cost of processing information falling dramatically. This networking capacity had become possible because of major developments in computer technologies and telecommunications in the 1970s. The changes had been driven by new microelectronic devices and enhanced computer capacity and were striking illustrations of synergistic relationships in the ICT revolution (Stalling 2004).

Telecommunications
Telecommunications, in turn, have been revolutionised by the combination of 'node' technologies (such as electronic switches and routers) and new linkages or transmission technologies. By the mid-1970s, progress in integrated circuit technologies made the digital switch possible. This increased speed, power and flexibility and also saved space, energy and labour. Major advances in optoelectronics such as fibre optics and laser transmission technology dramatically broadened the capacity of transmission lines, enabling the introduction of Integrated broadband networks. This optoelectronics-based transmission capacity, together with advanced switching and routing architectures, provided the basis for the so-called Information Superhighway.

Different forms of using the radio spectrum – such as traditional broadcasting, satellite broadcasting, microwaves and digital cellular telephony – as well as coaxial cable and fibre optics offer a diversity and versatility of transmission technologies. These are being applied to a range of uses, making possible ubiquitous communication between mobile users. Each development in a specific technology amplifies the effects of related ICTs. Thus mobile telephony, relying on computer power to route messages, also provides the basis for ubiquitous computing and real-time, interactive electronic communication.

Biotechnology

The revolution in biomedical sciences can be traced to the discovery of the basic structure of life – the 'double helix' of deoxyribonucleic acid (DNA) – by Watson, Crick and Wilkinson in 1953. DNA is a nucleic acid found in all living cells, which carries the organism's hereditary information. However, it was not until the early 1970s that gene splicing and related developments made possible the application of cumulative knowledge in this field. Gene cloning was discovered in 1973, the first mammalian gene discovered in 1975 and the first human gene cloned in 1977. What followed was a rush to start up commercial firms to exploit these developments. These were driven by the possibilities opened up by the potential ability to engineer human life. Agro-business followed, with the decision to develop genetically modified foods. Yet scientific difficulties, technical problems and legal, social and ethical obstacles slowed down the so-called biotechnological revolution during the 1980s.

In the late 1980s and 1990s, a new generation of scientist–entrepreneurs revitalised biotechnology, focusing on genetic engineering and gene therapy. A major international collaborative programme, co-ordinated by James Watson, brought together some of the most advanced microbiological research teams to map the 'human genome' or the thousands of genes making up the 'alphabet' of the human species. This project was completed, ahead of time, in 2003. The Human Genome Project (HGP) was a 13-year project co-ordinated by the US Department of Energy and the National Institutes of Health (www.genome.gov). During the early years of the HGP, the Wellcome Trust (UK) became a major partner, with additional contributions from Japan, France, Germany, China and others. Although the HGP is finished, analyses of the data will continue for many years. The project goals were to:

- identify all of the approximately 20,000–25,000 genes in human DNA
- determine the sequences of the 3 billion chemical base pairs that make up human DNA
- store this information in databases
- improve tools for data analysis
- transfer related technologies to the private sector
- address the ethical, legal, and social issues arising from the project.

This study, of course, has opened up possibilities of acting on such genes, and those identified in the future, thus enabling humankind to not only control some diseases but also identify biological dispositions and intervene in them, potentially altering genetic conditions. However, Lyon and Gorner (1995, p567) have warned of the potential dangers of genetic engineering:

> *Emotionally ... we are still apes, with all the behavioral baggage that the issue brings. Perhaps the ultimate form of gene therapy would be for our species to rise above its baser heritage and learn to apply its new knowledge wisely and benignly.*

Genetic engineering techniques now allow scientists to insert specific genes into a plant or animal without having to go through the trial and error process of selective breeding. Genetic engineering is therefore extremely rapid compared to selective breeding. With genetic engineering, zoological and botanical species can be crossed very easily. There is a variety of techniques used to modify plants and animals through genetic engineering. For example, there is a widely used herbicide that kills any plant that it touches. Genetically modified soybeans and other crop plants have been created that are not affected by this herbicide. By planting genetically modified seeds, farmers can control weeds by spraying this herbicide over their crops. The crop ignores the herbicide but weeds are eliminated. Genetically modified seeds like these reduce production costs and increase yields, so food becomes less expensive. Other scientists have inserted genes that produce a natural insecticide into corn plants to eliminate damage from 'corn borers' and a variety of anti-fungal genes can be inserted too (Ratledge and Kristiansen 2001).

With scientists, regulators and philosophers debating the humanistic implications of genetic engineering, some researchers and entrepreneurs have tried to gain legal and financial control of the human genome. In 1994 however, Merck provided substantial funding to Washington University to make such data public, so that there would be no private control of this knowledge, which might block development of products based on systematic understanding of the human genome. Since the 1990s, with more open markets, expanded educational opportunities and greater research capabilities globally, the biotechnological revolution has accelerated, thus triggering an ongoing debate about the blurred frontier between nature and human society.

Transportation

In the digital age, road transport, passenger transport (such as high speed trains), sea and air transport provide one of the institutional underpinnings supporting economic and social changes taking place locally, nationally, regionally and globally. For example, real benefits accrue from using chips and computers in transport systems. This began with variations in classical information networks such as improving traffic flows by controlling city traffic lights, helping airport flight handling, organising railway signalling and taking the pressure off the routine work of airline pilots and ships' officers.

The impetus to using computer technology in motor vehicles was to improve the efficiency of motor transport, through control of ignition and fuel timing and throttle and gear selection. Motor vehicles used for both domestic and commercial purposes are now provided with wider dashboard information such as digital speedometers, clocks and radios, electronic control of air conditioning, calculations of distances left on particular journeys and warnings about fuel consumption. Today, matters have gone even further, with chip technology being used for navigating journeys by satellite, road charging by transport authorities and monitoring traffic density and flows. In public transport, computer-driven driverless trains have been introduced at some airports and parts of cities. And in Germany, a computer-based system taking over the main line driver's function – observing signals, controlling speed and responding to radio instructions – was tested as early as the 1980s. That system, and others like it, had triple security procedures: two microcomputers working simultaneously checking each other's performance, with a third computer taking over if one of the others were to fail.

Dial-a-bus schemes have been tried, again in Germany, to give public transport the flexibility that people gain from using private taxis. These have offered door-to-door services for disadvantaged people. With no fixed schedules and booking by phone call or mail, drivers were in radio contact with the computer control centre. This selected the best bus to go to each call, billed the customer for the journey provided and produced operational statistics for management to use. In other more sophisticated cases, buses could be called from computer terminals at bus stops. These terminals gave customers tickets, stated the fares required, when the bus would arrive, how long the journey would be, where customers would need to change for other services and details of that journey. In sea transport too, advanced computers provide navigation technology, safety protection during sailing and computerised operational and information systems.

Modern airbuses using ICT systems can 'fly-by-wire', with computers programmed to override the instructions of pilots. Silicon chip technology is used for controlling engines, flaps and slats. Each of these microchips controlling these movements has back-up technology. Both 'front-line' and 'reserve' chips have to agree. If they do not, they inform the plane's captain who can take manual action to override them. If flight crews order the computers to do something against the 'rules', computers are able to reject the order and inform the captain of the aircraft why. However, where the crew wants deliberately to try the unorthodox, in an emergency for example, the chips do as requested when the order is repeated. This automation goes still further in military aviation. Fast low-flying aircraft carry computers responding to touch. With the lightest of touches by the pilot, they can act faster on split-second decisions than computers taking instructions from buttons or voice commands. Computer technology has even brought the 'pilotless' aircraft to reality in frightening fashion, with laser-guided loaded missiles speeding at low level across the landscape, fitting their flight to the contours of the land and direction of their target (Hester and Harrison 2004).

Energy supply

Although gas, electricity and oil remain the main sources of energy supply in the global economy, some limited use is being made of solar power and in other cases of wind power. Related developments include use of clean technologies and recovery, recycling and control systems for energy production. ICTs can be applied in a variety of ways in energy supply. At macro-level, using integrated computer technology to control the production of gas, electricity and oil supplies has resulted in greater efficiency, lower real costs and conservation of existing resources. At micro-level, computers used in office and factory environments have saved greatly on power and its usage. For many years, computers have been used to run heating, lighting, air conditioning, burglar alarms and fire alarms within organisations. They can be programmed for a year in advance, with details about the days and hours when buildings are in use and what temperatures are required. They then 'learn' from the data provided to fine-tune the programming to deal with seasonal irregularities and unseasonable changes in weather conditions. Although these systems were very costly till microchips became cheaper, they are now cost-effective not only for large enterprises but also for smaller organisations and household buildings, which can save unnecessary expenditure on heating bills.

Microelectronics is also a key to a new source of power: solar energy. The basic case for solar power is that the sun's energy is readily available, it does not pollute the atmosphere and it is relatively cheap to produce. Basically, the earth gets more energy from the sun in one hour than the world uses in a whole year. Indeed, on a bright summer day, the United Kingdom receives almost as much energy from the sun as does Africa. It is estimated that a solar array mounted on a south-facing roof in the United Kingdom produces around 700 kilowatt hours for every kilowatt of panels installed. The Department of Trade and Industry has estimated that solar panels installed on buildings have the potential to provide most of the electricity currently used in the United Kingdom.

The technology providing energy from the sun uses photovoltaics. This semi-conductor based technology, similar to the microchip, converts light energy directly into electric current that can be either used immediately or stored for use later. Anything requiring electricity can potentially be powered by solar energy. The great benefit of solar power is that it is very reliable and requires little maintenance. Photovoltaics do not release carbon dioxide, sulphur dioxide or nitrous oxide, unlike conventional electricity generating systems. Given these advantages why is solar power not more widely used? Some reasons are that vested interests (such as electricity suppliers) have not promoted it, it can be expensive to install and people able to provide it are in short supply (European Commission 2002).

Medicine

The applications and potential applications of digital technology to medicine are immense. Indeed, ICTs are increasingly taking centre stage in the provision of health care, in both hospitals and general practice in the United Kingdom and elsewhere. Only selective examples are provided here. With ICTs making a massive move into medical practice, both in selected areas of high-technology ('hi-tech') medicine and throughout the medical field generally, research in information technologies is taking place in areas such as medical imaging, tele co-operation, education and training. Medical images are produced in such number and richness of detail that they can only be analysed with the help of computers. Computers not only improve the quality of images but also help in reconstructing structures, detecting anomalies and measuring sources. In particular, computers help with appropriate visualisation to make the image contents understandable to clinicians. Three-dimensional images are used more and more. They have the inherent problem that it is extremely difficult to visualise images consisting of a 'cloud' of material in different shades of grey. Mechanisms are being found that highlight the relevant detail of images, whilst hiding other structures that are not relevant for a particular situation. The selection and composition of mathematical modelling depend on the medical goals of a particular analysis and can only be determined together with medical experts. With images needed to plan and control micro-invasive surgical procedures, it is necessary to design systems that support medical practitioners with appropriate visualisations throughout the whole process from image acquisition, diagnosis, treatment planning, surgery to final control (Berlage 1997).

As medical professionals become more specialised, diagnosis and treatment occur in co-operation between different specialists who may be geographically separated. They use computers to exchange their medical data, in particular images. However, data transfer alone is not sufficient. They must also be able to communicate about their patients, talk freely about medical data and refer to that data during their discussions. Merging these two communication channels (verbal and data communication) is a challenge that needs to be addressed before fully effective tele-consultations become the norm.

Another example of the application of ICTs to medicine is medical information systems. This field applies IT to healthcare and provides skills and tools enabling the sharing and use of information to deliver healthcare solutions and promote the health of people and patients generally. Medical information systems include use of computers in medical consultations (as outlined above), of e-mail and the World Wide Web and of more advanced technologies, such as texting reminders for patients and using remote, palm-held devices by healthcare professionals. In 2005, for example, the NHS announced plans to invest over £2.3 billion in ICTs over the next four years, making it the largest procurer of ICT software and hardware in the world. The policy aimed at introducing 'The Common Health Record' to enable the NHS improve 'the way it stores and uses information about [patient] health needs so that we can provide faster and more convenient care.' New computer systems were being designed to make it possible to 'combine patient information from different parts of the NHS, allowing the Health Service to set a new type of health record.' These records were geared towards giving healthcare professionals 'the right information at the right time, enable staff to make informed decisions more quickly and reduce time wasted waiting for information' (Hampshire and Isle of Wight Community 2005, p1).

Other applications of medical information systems include:

- architectures for electronic medical records and other health information systems for scheduling or research
- decision support systems

- messaging standards for exchange of information between healthcare information systems
- controlled medical vocabularies allowing standard, accurate information exchange
- using handheld or portable devices to assist providers with data entry or retrieval and in medical decision making
- expert systems enabling both medical practitioners and patients to access information on treatments and drug therapies.

'E-health' uses ICTs that provide interactions between medical information systems, public health and the private sector. E-health enables health services and information to be delivered and enhanced through the World Wide Web and related technologies. Such systems can provide 'long distance' health service delivery, which has become even more viable with broadband World Wide Web connections. Other requirements of this approach to medical care include the availability of expert advice and adequate time to assess requests of this type (Lenaghan 1998).

Clearly, medical knowledge is increasing at an accelerating pace and medical practitioners have to keep up to date with new knowledge during their whole professional lives. To ensure quality of diagnosis and treatment, special emphasis on continuous education is needed. Computer-based techniques help with this task, by providing training on the job and assisting in the analysis of images and teleconsultation.

Robotics

A robot is an automatic device that performs functions normally done by humans or by machines. The first industrial modern robots were 'Unimates' developed in the late 1950s and early 1960s. Since then, industrial robots have increased in their capability and performance through controller and language development, improved mechanisms, sensing and drive systems. In the early to mid-1980s, the robotic industry grew very fast, due primarily to large investments in it by the car manufacturing industry in the United States. This quick leap into the 'factory of the future' subsequently failed, however, when the integration and economic viability of these efforts at robotisation were demonstrated as being neither cost-effective nor able to deliver quality outputs. More recently, robotics have been linked with ICTs, resulting in more reliable, cost-competitive and effective systems of automation (Castells 1996).

Basically, a robot consists of three elements: a mechanical device, sensors and systems. The mechanical device, such as a wheeled platform, arm or other instrument, is capable of interacting with its environment. Sensors on or around the device are able to sense the environment and give useful feedback to it. Systems process the sensory input in the device's current situation and instruct it to perform actions in response to that situation.

Robotic automation has many applications. It enables organisations to improve safety and quality, reduce costs, increase productivity and achieve good returns on investments. Integrated robotic systems are used in a variety of industries including aerospace, agriculture, construction, consumer products, electronic and telecommunication products, fabricated metals, furniture, marine and shipping, and motorcar assembly. Robotic systems are used in a number of job activities including arc welding, spot welding, gas metal arc welding, gas tungsten welding, gluing, grinding, material handling, machine tending, packaging, plasma cutting, part loading and unloading, plasma spraying, rooter cutting and thermal spraying (Craig 2005).

In manufacturing, robotic development has focused on robotic arms that perform manufacturing processes. In the space industry, for example, robotics have been applied to making highly specialised 'planetary rovers'. Unlike in a highly automated manufacturing unit, a planetary rover operating on the dark side of the moon, without radio communications, might run into unexpected situations. At a minimum, a planetary rover needs some source of sensory input, some way of interpreting that input and a way of modifying its actions in response to a changing world. Furthermore, the need to sense and adapt to a partially unknown environment requires 'artificial intelligence' (AI) by the robotic device (Wise 2000).

From military technology and space exploration to the healthcare sector and commerce, the advantages of using modern robots (incorporating electronic control, sensory systems and micro-controller systems) are so widely accepted that they are now part of people's collective experience and everyday lives. Their uses relieve people from both danger and tedium:

- *Safety.* Robotics have been developed to handle nuclear and radioactive chemicals for many different uses, including nuclear weapons, power plants, environmental clean ups and processing certain drugs.
- *Unpleasantness.* Robots perform many tasks that are very tedious and unpleasant but necessary ones, such as welding, lifting and cleaning work.
- *Repetition and precision.* Assembly line work has been one of the mainstays of the robotics industry. Robots are used extensively in manufacturing and space exploration, where minimum maintenance requirements are emphasised.

In the field of medicine, there are many applications where the precision of robots is better than that of a skilled surgeon. Precision is obviously critical in neurosurgery but also in orthopaedics, for example, when drilling out bone for hip replacements. The higher level of accuracy of robots can lead to a lower number of implants needing revision after a few years. Minimal access surgery, often called keyhole surgery, requires the surgeon and other human operators to hold and manipulate a number of tools, as well as an endoscope for viewing the operation. The endoscope can be held and manipulated by a robot, able to move under the precise control of the surgeon. In all these surgical applications the robot is not replacing human operators but enhancing their abilities.

Medical robots are used during operations in hospitals. There are, for instance, 'passive tool holders', 'autonomous active robots', 'synergistic systems' and 'master–slave' systems. Master–slave robotic systems are those in which the 'master manipulator' (often a kind of joystick) is controlled by the surgeon, where the 'slave manipulator' performs the operation on the patient. A computer interface provides the connection between 'master' and 'slave', enabling the surgeon to perform an operation at a distance and, more importantly, in an ergonomically better fashion.

The slave manipulator consists of a mechanism that follows the motions of the master manipulator and performs the operation with the help of surgical tools, while the surgeon gets visual feedback on a screen from a small camera in the operative area. This permits the use of scaled motions so that large movements of the master result in accurate micro-motions, with small forces and without tremor, applied by the slave. In this way, soft tissues in the body can also be handled appropriately. Currently, master–slave systems are being clinically used mainly for minimally invasive 'closed' heart surgery (ie the robot performs the operation through small incisions in the body, as keyhole surgery). One manipulator arm normally carries a small camera, while two other manipulator arms carry interchangeable tools, such as scissors and grippers. However, one of the key problems is that the systems are large and very expensive. Furthermore, there is no sense of 'feel feedback' from the slave to the master (ie no so-called 'tactile feedback'). During the operation, the surgeon relies solely upon high-quality endoscopic vision for monitoring the process. New designs of microsurgical instruments enable new surgical procedures with better outcomes for patients. Safety demands are very important, because the systems need to work in a complex and changing environment, with no harm being done to patients (Angeles 2002).

The field of robotics, then, has created a large class of robots with the same basic physical and navigational competencies. At the same time, society has moved towards incorporating robots into everyday life, from entertainment to healthcare. Robotics is beginning to free people from hazardous situations, essentially allowing robots to be used as replacements for human beings. Robots initially were developed for dirty, dull and dangerous work. Now, largely due to the benefits of ICTs, robots are considered as 'personal assistants'. Increasingly, robots are requiring more AI, not less, thereby having an even more significant impact on our society in the future as technology expands to new horizons.

(i) Provide examples of how ICTs are applied and used within your own organisation.
(ii) Technological determinism argues that technology evolves according to its own internally derived logic and needs, independent of the social environment and social culture. It holds that to use technology effectively and secure its benefits for society, its development and application must not be inhibited by considerations other than those of its developers – engineers and technologists. What are the cases for and against this argument?

THE IMPACT OF TECHNOLOGY ON ORGANISATIONS

Technologies including ICTs impact on organisations in a variety of complex, interrelated and sometimes disputed ways. Again in this section, only selected examples are provided. The starting point is the economic restructuring of the 1980s which induced a number of reorganising strategies in both the private and public sectors in advanced market economies. Three main sets of explanations have been provided for these changes. First, writers such as Piore and Sabel (1984) have argued that the economic crisis of the 1970s resulted in the exhaustion of the mass production system and this constituted a further stage in the development of industrial capitalism. Second, for others, the diffusion of new organisational forms, some of which had been practised in certain countries and firms for many years, was a response to a crisis of profitability and capital accumulation in business organisations (Harrison 1994). Third, Coriat (1994) and others have claimed that the long-term evolution from Fordism (based on mass production and mass consumption) to post-Fordism (based on flexible specialisation and fragmented consumption) represented an historical transformation of relationships between production and productivity, on the one hand, and consumption and competition, on the other.

There were, however, some common features arising out of all these analyses.

- Whatever the causes and development of these organisational transformations, there was from the mid-1970s a major divide in the organisation of production and markets in the global economy.
- Organisational changes interacted with the diffusion of ICTs but these changes were largely independent and generally preceded the diffusion of ICTs within firms.
- The fundamental goal of these organisational changes was to deal with the uncertainty caused by the fast pace of change in the economic, institutional and technological environment of firms. This was done by enhancing flexibility in production, management and marketing.

- Many organisational changes were aimed at redefining employment practices, by introducing 'lean production' systems, with the objective of saving labour through automating jobs, eliminating certain tasks and de-layering management structures.

Thus one major impact of modern technologies on organisations has been the trend, articulated by Coriat (1994) and others, from mass production to flexible production or from Fordist to post-Fordist systems. The mass production model was based on productivity gains obtained by economies of scale. This involved assembly-line mechanised production of standardised products, sold in mass markets dominated by big businesses. These businesses were structured on the principles of vertical integration and institutionalised social and technical divisions of labour. They used rationalist, scientific management methods for organising work and their workforces. However, as demand for goods (and services) has become more unpredictable, technological change has made mass production systems too rigid and too costly for the 'new' economy, resulting in the need for flexible production methods. One form is flexible specialisation, where production (or operations) accommodates to continuous change, without attempting to control it. Another form is dynamic flexibility or high volume flexible production. High volume production systems combine high volume production (permitting economies of scale) and customised, reprogrammable production systems (providing 'economies of scope' or where a range of products reduces unit costs). New technologies including robotics, automation and integrated computer networks enable transformation of assembly lines, characteristic of large corporations, into easy programmable production units sensitive to variations in the market (product flexibility) and changes of technological inputs (process flexibility).

A second impact, as argued by Piore and Sabel (1984), has been a relative decline of the large vertically integrated firm as an organisational model. In order to survive in the increasingly competitive, open, marketplace, large organisations have had to respond to growing demand in the developing world. To do this, they have had to change their organisational structures. ICTs, such as computer networks, e-mail, teleworking and mobile telephony, have enabled large organisations to both centralise and decentralise their structures, reorganise spans of control and stretch their internal communication systems (Jackson and Van der Wielen 1998). The traditional corporate model of organisation, based on vertical integration, and hierarchic, functional management, with its staff and line structure of strict technical and social division of labour, has become increasingly untenable. The vertical disintegration of production is replaced by a network of firms externally, which substitutes for the vertical integration of departments within a corporate structure. This network allows for greater differention of the labour and capital components of production units.

Third, in facilitating new production and operations systems, technology has also impacted on organisations by facilitating new methods of management, some of them originating in Japan. This has given them productivity gains and competitive advantage. This new model of management – sometimes called 'Toyotism' (Wilkinson et al 1992) – has been widely imitated, partially or wholly, by corporations around the world leading to substantially improved performance within them, compared with firms using more traditional production and management systems. The elements of this management model include:

- *Just-in-Time management*. This is a system by which inventories are eliminated or reduced substantially through delivery of supplies to the production site at exactly the required time, with the characteristics specified for the production line.
- *Total quality control*. This aims at near-zero defects of products on the production line and best use of resources facilitating that.
- *Employee involvement*. This enables workers to become involved in the work process, by using teamwork, decentralised workplace initiatives, greater autonomy on the shop floor,

rewards for team performance and a flat management hierarchy with few status symbols in the daily life of the firm.

Fourth, knowledge creation becomes a very important function within the firm (see below). As Aoki (1988, p16) has commented, whilst US firms emphasise efficiency through specialisation and job demarcation, Japanese firms emphasise 'the capability of workers' groups to cope with local emergencies autonomously, which is developed through learning by doing and sharing knowledge on the shopfloor.'

A fifth impact of technology on organisations has been in the ways in which work is done in them. During the 1980s and 1990s, several factors accelerated change in work processes.

- Computer technology and its applications became increasingly cheaper, better and affordable.
- Global competition triggered a technology/management race between MNCs.
- Organisations evolved and adopted new shapes that were generally based on flexibility and networking.
- Managers and consultants understood the potential of new technology and how to use it.
- The massive diffusion of ICTs caused similar effects in factories, offices and service organisations. The role of direct work increased because IT empowered direct workers on the shop floor. What disappeared through integral automation were routine, repetitive tasks that could be pre-coded and programmed for execution by machines. IT enhanced work that required analysis, decision and reprogramming activities that only the human brain could achieve.

Increasingly, the work process is determined by the characteristics of the information production process. The results are:

- Value added is mainly generated by innovation of process and products.
- Innovation is itself dependent upon research potential and applied to specific purposes in given organisational contexts.
- Executive tasks are more efficient when they are able to adapt higher-level instructions to their specific application and when they generate feedback.
- Most production activities take place in organisations, where ability to generate flexible strategic decision making and capacity to achieve organisational integration between all elements of the production process are key features of the work process.
- Information technology becomes critical in the work process because:
  - It largely determines innovation capacity.
  - It makes possible correction of errors and generation of feedback effects at executive level.
  - It provides the infrastructure for flexibility and adaptability throughout the management of the production process.
  - It also provides the capacity to increase and centralise control and direction.

The tasks in the work process create a new division of labour within organisations. In production systems organised around IT, whether of goods or services, the following fundamental tasks can be distinguished:

- Strategic decision-making and planning are performed by senior managers.
- Innovation in products and process is performed by researchers.

- Managing relationships between decision, innovation, design and execution is performed by executive managers
- Execution of tasks under their own initiative is performed by operators.
- Execution of ancillary, preprogrammed tasks that have not been automated are performed by implementers.

A sixth impact of technology is on political organisations and the political system. ICTs are transforming, for example, the structures and delivery systems of government, with one-stop shops and e-government (Bellamy and Taylor 1998). Government has an e-government policy and all public organisations now have websites and are accessible through the World Wide Web and through e-mail by the general public. ICTs are not only radically changing the way that politicians interact with the public and vice versa but also have the potential to transform the system of representative democracy into one of direct democracy, by using interactive television, referendums via electronic voting and transmission of instant text messages from politicians to the electorate.

Describe and evaluate

(i) the impact of technology on your work organisation in the last 10 years
(ii) the impact of technology on your personal lifestyle in the last 10 years
(iii) the impact of technology on the culture of society in the last 10 years.

THE IMPACT OF TECHNOLOGY ON MARKETS

Perhaps the major impact of technology, especially ICTs, on markets has been to open up new markets (see also Chapter 4). To do this, finance capital required great mobility and firms needed dramatically enhanced communication capabilities, linking valuable market segments of each country into a global network through ICTs.

It was deregulation of markets in the 1980s and 1990s and ICTs in close interaction together that provided such conditions. The earliest, most direct beneficiaries were high technology firms and financial corporations. Indeed, the global integration of financial markets since the early 1980s, made possible by ICTs, had a dramatic impact on the growing disassociation of capital flows from national economies. Chesnais (1994) has measured the movement of international capital by calculating the percentage of cross-border operations in shares and other financial obligations over GDP in the 1980s and 1990s. In 1980, this percentage was not over 10 per cent in any major country. But by the early 1990s, it varied between 72.2 per cent of GDP in Japan and 109.3 per cent in the United States and 122.2 per cent in France.

ICTs have extended the global reach of businesses and have integrated certain markets, such as consumer durables and financial services. They have also maximised comparative advantages of location and finance capital. Certainly during the 1990s, there was some evidence suggesting that firms in electronics, telecommunications and financial services increased their profitability, restoring at that time the precondition for investment upon which market economies depend. Throughout the 1980s, there was massive technological investment in the communications and information technology infrastructures. This made possible the twin shifts towards the deregulation of markets and globalised capital markets. Further, around this core of new, dynamic, entrepreneurial firms, successive layers of industries, firms and workplaces were either integrated into the new market system or were phased out of it.

There are, however, limitations to globalised markets. There is not, nor is there likely to be in the foreseeable future, a fully integrated, open world market for goods, services, technology or labour. As long as nation states exist, or there are associations of nation states such as the EU, governments foster the interests of their citizens and firms within their jurisdictions. Furthermore, corporate ownership is not irrelevant to corporate behaviour. As Carnoy *et al* (1993) have shown US MNCs have followed the instructions of their governments, European MNCs have been the objects of systematic support by their own governments (as well as by the EU) and Japanese companies have been supported by their governments. In all these cases, the objectives have been to support nationally owned firms in terms of their technologies, products or services, markets and labour forces. Nor is market penetration always reciprocal. While the USA and to a lesser extent the European economies are relatively open markets, the economies in the eastern world, such as Japan and Korea, remain very protective.

However, the overall dominant trend is towards the increasing interpenetration of markets, particularly after the creation of the World Trade Organisation and steady progress towards European integration. Other indicators of market integration include the signing of the North American Free Trade Agreement, the intensification of economic exchanges within Asia and the gradual incorporation of Eastern Europe and the Russian Federation into the global economy. There is also a growing role played by trade and foreign investment in economic growth, while the almost total integration of capital markets makes all economies globally interdependent.

Greater integration of markets leads to more competition for resources and customers. Four main processes appear to be instrumental in determining the forms and outcomes of this competition in global markets.

- *Technological capacity.* This includes the science base in the production and management process, the strength of research and development (R&D), the human resources (HR) necessary for technological innovation, adequate utilisation of new technologies and their level of diffusion into networks of economic activity.
- *Access to a large, integrated affluent market.* This includes the North American trading zone and EU. The best competitive position is one enabling firms to operate unchallenged in these markets, whilst still having access to other markets with as few restrictions on them as possible. It is the dynamics of trade and foreign investment between countries and regions that affect the performance of individual firms.
- *The differential between production costs and market prices.* This involves the differential between production costs at the place of production and prices at the market of destination. The winning formula appears to be the addition of technological and managerial excellence and production costs lower than those of competitors.
- *The political capacity of national/supra-national institutions.* This involves the ability of political institutions to steer the growth strategies of their countries or areas under their jurisdiction. This includes creation of competitive advantage in the world market for firms serving the interests of populations in their territories by generating jobs and income. In this respect, government markets for defence, ICTs, and telecommunications and subsidies for R&D and training have been critical in positioning firms in global competition. Governments may also provide support for technological development and HR training (Reich 1991, Evans 1995).

From this analysis, it would seem that ICTs have created ever-larger markets in geographical and regional terms. There are now fewer really local product and consumer markets than previously because transportation technology enables goods and services to be supplied to larger markets, covering wide geographical areas. Also in creating new markets for technological hardware and software, ICTs have facilitated the elimination of space and time and effective real-time communication takes place between individuals via the World Wide Web, telephone, e-mail and video conferencing. The major case where ICTs have not generally created a global marketplace is the labour market but, as shown below, ICTs have provided ample employment opportunities for people locally. Product markets may be increasingly global but labour markets remain predominantly local. As a rule, capital is mobile geographically because digitalisation leads to the concentration and globalisation of capital but labour is immobile for social and cultural reasons.

In the information age, work is plentiful and demand for labour is high. There are more jobs and a higher proportion of people of working age are employed in all developed countries. These people have been absorbed into the labour market, without major disruptions. The diffusion of ICTs, though displacing some workers and eliminating some jobs, has not, on balance, resulted in mass unemployment. Work becomes disaggregated in its performance and fragmented in its organisation. Those who work are diverse in their experience and divided in their collective action. Workers lose their collective identity, with work becoming increasingly individualised in its conditions, interests and projects. Owners, producers, managers and managed become increasingly blurred through systems of networking, outsourcing, subcontracting and team working.

The dominant model of labour in the information-based economy is that of a core labour force and a disposable labour force. The core labour force consists of information-based managers and by those described by Reich (1991) as symbiotic analysts' or collaborating professionals. The disposable labour force can be automated, hired, fired, outsourced or off-shored, depending on market demand and labour costs. Traditional forms of work based on full-time employment, clear occupational boundaries and a career pattern over a lifetime are slowly being eroded and flexible modes of working are increasing. In general, firms are able to adopt a variety of strategies in managing labour such as:

- downsizing
- subcontracting
- employing temporary and flexible labour
- automating or relocating some tasks and functions
- tightening labour control through more stringent working arrangements.

Another feature of labour markets in knowledge-driven economies is their changing occupational structures. Although simplified, the following structural changes are emerging:

- continued decline in agricultural employment
- steady decline in manufacturing employment
- a rise in business service and social services, especially health and social care
- increasing diversification of service activities as sources of jobs
- a rapid rise in managerial, professional and technical jobs
- the emergence of a 'white-collar' working class made up of clerical and sales staff
- a continued substantial share of employment in the retail sector
- a simultaneous increase of the upper and lower levels of the occupational structure
- the relative upgrading of the occupational structure over time, with an increasing share of occupations needing higher skills and advanced education than the increase of lower level categories.

Because of labour immobility and differences in language and culture, there is not a unified global labour force. However, there is global interdependence in the information economy, characterised by segmentation across borders, not between countries. Global interdependence operates, first, through global employment in MNCs and their associated cross-border networks and, second, through the effects of global competition and the impact of flexible employment practices. In each case, ICTs are the means of linking different segments of the labour force across national boundaries.

There is also a dichotomy in the work process. On the one hand, work is unified through complex global networks. On the other hand, there is differentiation of work, segmentation of workers and disaggregation of labour on a global scale. Capitalist production relationships still persist but capital and labour exist in different spaces and times as, for example, the instant time of computerised networks (capital) and the clock time of everyday work (labour). It would appear that the life of global capital depends less on specific labour and more on generic labour, driven by the demands of networked businesses. Working life goes on, with its recruitment, promotions, training, negotiations, conflicts, dismissals and retirements. But the interests of capital are mobilised and insulated in flows of global capital, while labour loses its collective identity which dissolves into infinite variations of employment and work. In the digital age, capital is co-ordinated globally; labour is individualised locally.

To sum up, new technology is not only influencing how things are done and how work is organised but also what is done. Whole new industries have emerged and this is fuelling the service economy. These industries are cutting across the traditional manufacture of goods and services to the creation of knowledge and virtual worlds and experiences. But as Schiller (2000, p209) has concluded: 'We may be confident, however, that digital capitalism has strengthened, rather than banished, the age-old scourges of the market system: inequality and domination.'

In what ways are labour markets likely to be affected by technological developments in the next 10 years

(i) generally
(ii) within your own organisation?

RESISTANCE TO TECHNOLOGY

Life has always been organised around and in response to technology, since technology is central to human existence. But technology is not a neutral phenomenon and resistance to it is common among those most affected by its impact upon their lives. Sometimes this resistance appears to be rational to some interests, as for example, when the jobs of workers are threatened by technological change. Sometimes this resistance appears to be irrational to some interests when groups who oppose technologies, such as birth control for example, do so not on scientific grounds but on ethical, moral or religious ones. Resistance to technology may be either by individuals or by organised groups. Individual resistance to technology is direct and immediate, while collective resistance is indirect and planned. In either case, the objective of resistance is to prevent or obstruct the introduction or application of new technology to a particular process or system.

The Luddite machine breakers in early nineteenth century England provide a classical case study of resistance to technological change, although machine breaking has a long history in England that both predated and postdated the Luddite rebellion (Hobsbawn 1964). The Luddites, or machine breakers, were workers opposed to mechanisation of the woollen industry at that time, where hand-spinning was being replaced by mechanised spinning jennies and hand working for raising the nap of wool before shearing by 'gig mills'. The wool trade was crucial to the economy of eighteenth and nineteenth century England and the centres of the industry were the West of England and West Riding of Yorkshire. Lancashire was also involved in Luddite protests, as was Nottinghamshire which had its share of Luddites associated with the lace industry. The West of England trade used a 'putting out' or 'outworking' system of production, while the Yorkshire trade used a 'domestic system' where large numbers of master manufacturers undertook all the work processes in their own homes (Randall 1991).

Luddite campaigns against the new mechanisation varied. In Yorkshire, for example, the Luddites were violent, aiming their attacks at machinery as much as at their masters. They sought to halt certain technological developments rather than to gain advantage from them. It was not just a form of bargaining with the masters but war against the new machinery. In Nottinghamshire, in contrast, the Luddites focused their attacks on the machines that threatened quality of work and they singled out individual masters who rejected traditional approaches to working methods. Their ultimate aim was to secure economic advantage for themselves, through bargaining by riot. Following these and other physical attacks on the masters and their machinery, a number of trials took place, over 90 rioters were executed and the revolts were gradually suppressed (Hobsbawn and Rudé 1969).

Grint and Woolgar (1997, p37) have argued that the case of the Luddites can be used to present alternative explanations of why social resistance to technology occurs, where the boundary between the social and technical 'is part of the problem to be investigated.' In their analysis: 'The nature and characteristics of technical capacity, what the machine can and cannot do, what it is for, how it can be enrolled and controlled and so on are crucial matters for the sociologist.' The interpretations they have presented of Luddism are summarised below.

- *Rational technology, irrational Luddites*. This 'establishment' perspective viewed the Luddites as either anarchists or ignorant of the machine technology. In both cases, the Luddites were seen as irrational. There was no concern on the part of the establishment that the new machinery and its associated factory employment could be anything other than self-evidently beneficial for both masters and workers. For the establishment, the combination of *laissez-faire* and new technology would ensure the hegemony of British trade throughout the world.
- *Rational technology, irrational capitalism*. This traditional anti-establishment perspective of Luddism, epitomised by Marxist analyses, interpreted Luddism as not so much as against machinery as against the power behind the machinery. The real conflict was the struggle of the various classes, some working in factories, some in their homes, to maintain their standards of living. To the machine breakers, the technology presented threats to their employment, customary working methods and established social relations between masters and workers.
- *The machine as metaphor*. This symbolic perspective suggests that the machine was merely a metaphor for a cultural revolution that the Luddites recognised as being inherently destructive of all that they held dear. The pre-industrial 'moral' economy was about to be destroyed by *laissez-faire* capitalism. This interpretation of Luddite resistance to technical change implied that the technology was insignificant in itself, except as a trigger to the process of uncertain change.
- *The actor-network perspective*. This view of the new machinery sees the arrival of the new machinery as tantamount to introducing a new set of actors into existing networks of masters and workers. The arrival of the new machinery presented a potential disruption to a relatively stable balance of power between them. With the social organisation of work

well-established in the woollen trades, organised around established social networks, the introduction of new actors into the production system presented potentially new power relationships in working arrangements.

- *Machinery as a Trojan horse.* For entrepreneurs of the time, the new mechanised machinery, incorporated within factories, could be interpreted as a solution to the problems of labour recalcitrance facing them and a means of securing compliance of the working population to *laissez-faire* economics and a new form of society. For the authorities, mechanisation was a 'Trojan horse'. Indeed, if the new working class could be coerced or persuaded to accept the new technology, this would enable difficult questions about moral responsibility for unemployment and poverty to be pushed through on the coat-tails of the new machinery.

In the event, Luddite resistance to change, the mechanising of work and putting it into factories during the early nineteenth century only slowed the rate of change, it did not appear to prevent it. The new machinery was only one of a series of potential threats facing the Luddites at the time and its potential impact was largely unknown. Geographical, temporal and gender differences all played significant parts in the fragmented, differentiated and diffused responses to mechanisation. Government played a reactive role in suppressing the revolt of the machine breakers but the crucial part was played by entrepreneurial masters who were intent on forcing through technological change and, at the same time, breaking the resistance of the most strategically-placed groups of hand workers. By taking on these groups, the new breed of masters forced government into repressive and coercive action against them. The freedom of the new factory owners to shed the remnants of the old moral economy was gained, at least in part, by the Trojan horse of new technology. 'The Luddites failed not because they misrecognized the machine but because the alliance of the forces arrayed against them was too great for their interpretation to prevail' (Grint and Woolgar 1997, p64).

More generally, one of the main reasons why people resist technological and other change is that the proposed change may break the continuity of the working environment, creating a climate of uncertainty and ambiguity. In these conditions, it is not uncommon for old established structures to be redefined and modified. Some workers may try to maintain the status quo and resist such changes. According to Dawson (2003), resistance has been identified as resulting from one or more, or a combination, of one of the following:

- substantive change in jobs (changes in skill requirements)
- reduction in economic security or job displacement (threat to employment)
- psychological threat (whether perceived or actual)
- disruption of social arrangements (new working arrangements)
- lower status.

Eccles (1994), in turn, has identified 13 possible causes why workers resist change:

- failure to understand the problem
- the solution is disliked because an alternative is preferred
- a feeling that the proposed solution will not work
- the change has unacceptable personal costs
- rewards are not sufficient
- fear of being unable to cope with the new situation
- the change threatens to destroy existing social arrangements
- sources of influence and control will be eroded

- new values and practices are repellent
- willingness to change is low
- management motives are considered suspicious
- other interests are more highly valued than the new proposals
- change will reduce power and career opportunities.

From this evidence, and from a managerial perspective, it is important to reflect critically on the need and reasons for change, taking into account the concern of others in the change process. This approach is preferable to assuming that, as resistance is inevitable, the reasons why people resist change should be ignored. For change agents seeking to overcome resistance to technological and other change, a number of strategies has been identified. Typically, these centre on participation, communication and support at one end of the spectrum to negotiation, manipulation and coercion at the other end.

In a case study reported by Dawson (2003, p82), a company developed a strategy to meet changing market needs, only to experience unanticipated market conditions in the business environment threatening the viability of its operations. Heavy investment in technology to produce large quantities of standard loaves was met by an unforeseen shift in demand for different types of bread that was not simply determined by price. Demand for greater customer choice was further reinforced by the purchasing policies of powerful supermarkets. These were acting to limit the strategic options available to the bakery company. Dawson showed that employee innovations were instrumental in making the technology work. They were both creative and accommodating in finding new ways of doing things that were able to circumvent the limitations imposed by the design and implementation of the new technology. 'During the course of employee engagement in using the technology, elements of the technology previously viewed as hard technical or structural constraints gradually became open to change.' Operations that had been seen earlier as technologically determined became refined through a social process and a degree of flexibility in the ways in which people viewed technology and in which the new technology was developed and designed. This case illustrated 'the temporal process of company transition and the complex interplay between politics, context and substance in the social shaping and use of technology.'

(i) Prepare a brief for your senior management team explaining the factors preventing the faster growth of e-business globally.
(ii) How do you think that these barriers might be overcome?

KNOWLEDGE IN ORGANISATIONAL AND ECONOMIC LIFE

As indicated above, knowledge is now recognised as an important resource and product of the information age. It is increasingly accepted that both explicit and implicit knowledge are a major resource that contributes to the competency of regions, countries and organisations. The central issues are how can such knowledge be discovered, applied and managed. Initially, ideas and theories linked IT and the potential of computers with storing, interpreting, creating and communicating knowledge but now it has moved beyond that by capturing knowledge, and applying it, through social and behavioural strategies.

Knowledge plays a major role in creating competitive advantage for organisations and for countries in a global economy, where R&D centres are heavily concentrated in certain areas, companies and institutions. However, communication of knowledge in global networks, such as through research networks, the World Wide Web and electronic diffusion, is at the same time both the condition to keep up with the rapid advancement of knowledge and the obstacle to its proprietary control.

Information and knowledge have always been critical components of economic growth and the evolution of technology has largely determined the productive capacity of societies and their standards of living. Yet the emergence of the current technological paradigm organised around powerful ICTs makes it possible for information itself to become the product of the production process. For both countries and organisations, knowledge in the information age is the key to increased productivity and profitability, which in turn drives the search for new knowledge.

Nelson (1994) has argued that agendas for economic growth should be built around the relationships between technical change, firm capabilities and national institutions. He did not view firms and nations as the actual agents of economic growth. In his analysis, they do not seek technology for its own sake or productivity enhancement for bettering humankind but they behave in given historical contexts, within the rules of an economic system that ultimately rewards or penalises their conduct. Firms are not motivated by productivity but by profitability. Productivity and technology may be important means for achieving this but they are not the only ones. Political institutions, which are shaped by broader sets of values and interests, are oriented economically towards maximising the competitiveness of their economies. By this analysis, it is profitability and competitiveness that are the determinants of productivity growth and technological innovation. This approach seems to be overlooking the search for knowledge for knowledge sake and the potential for applying knowledge to welfare objectives or to prevent death or disasters.

At organisational level, knowledge management seeks to make the best use of the knowledge available to an organisation, thus creating 'new knowledge' in the process. Knowledge management is particularly associated with 'knowledge intensive firms' (KIFs). These are organisations within the knowledge economy that employ highly skilled individuals who create market value through the application of knowledge to novel, complex client demands. These firms may work on their own or in collaboration with other firms (Drucker 1993). An important characteristic of KIFs is that a high proportion of their employees are knowledge workers compared with the number of support staff who are not knowledge workers. They want to work on interesting projects which make good use of their high level knowledge and skills, involving the latest technology where possible. As Swart et al (2003, p69 and p72) have commented: 'Consequently, importance is attached to the creation and development of knowledge at the individual level', sometimes referred to as 'learning-by-doing.' Whilst it is important for KIFs to satisfy the needs of individual knowledge workers for interesting work (which develops their knowledge and skills), they must at the same time facilitate the transfer of knowledge between separate project teams. Further, as noted in the study by Swart et al, successful KIFs 'were better able to convert human capital into intellectual capital because they had people management practices and processes that supported and enhanced this conversion process.'

Knowledge management is concerned with the critical issues of organisational adaptation, survival and competence in the face of increasing and continuous environmental change. Essentially, knowledge management embodies organisational processes that seek a synergistic combination of the data and information processing capacities of ICTs with the creative and innovative capacity of human beings. Broadly, data are information that is structured but has not been interpreted; information is 'messages' between senders and receivers that can be saved on computers; and knowledge is information that has a use or purpose, to which intent has been attached.

One branch of knowledge management is rooted firmly in the use of technology. This sees knowledge management as an issue of information storage and retrieval. It derives from systems analysis and management theory and is linked to the development of so-called 'knowledge technologies.' This branch of knowledge management develops sophisticated data analysis and retrieval systems, with little thought given to how the information contained is developed or used. Its failure to provide any theoretical understanding of how organisations learn 'new things' and how they act on this information mean that this knowledge is incapable of managing knowledge creation.

A second branch of knowledge management is based on the belief that organisations are capable of learning and that there is a link between learning theory and management. At the same time, hierarchical models of organisational structure are replaced by more organic models that see effective organisations as capable of structural change in response to their environment. This branch of knowledge management gives priority to the way that people construct and use knowledge. It derives ideas from complex systems, often making use of organic metaphors to describe 'knowledge growth.' It is closely related to organisational learning, which recognises that learning and doing are more important to organisational success than are dissemination and imitation (Nonaka and Takeuchi 1995).

Few doubt that better knowledge management within firms leads to improved innovation and competitive advantage. Everyone agrees on the goal of better utilisation of internal and external knowledge but how to achieve this goal is hotly debated. Some identify with a 'technology-driven approach', using state-of-the-art storage systems; others emphasise the soft side of knowledge management and the need to create 'a learning culture approach' so that knowledge management takes care of itself. It is arguable, however, that effective utilisation of knowledge and learning requires both technology and culture to be synergised. Explicit information and data can be codified, written down and stored in a data base. Yet collecting basic data is not where competitive advantage is found. An organisation's real edge in the market is often located in complex, context-sensitive knowledge which is difficult if not impossible to codify in binary form. This knowledge is found in individuals, communities of interest and their inter-connections and is usually referred to as tacit knowledge An organisation's data are found in its computer system; its intelligence is found in its biological and social systems.

Krebs (2005) has argued that the 'fast' economy requires flexible adaptive structures that self-organise internally in response to changes externally. He has proposed that organisational network analysis (ONA) is a software supported methodology that reveals the real workings of organisations. The rigour of systems analysis shows behaviour inside and between organisations.

> ONA exhibits both how knowledge is shared in emergent communities of practice, and how it is utilized in key business processes. In short, it uncovers the hidden dynamics that support learning and adaptation in the modern organization.
>
> (Krebs 2005)

For Krebs, ONA is basically an object-oriented model of an organisation with 'objects such as people, teams, and technologies interlinked sending messages to each other and invoking their respective methods to accomplish the goals of the firm' (www.orgnet.com/IMRIM.html). In his view, network models of how organisations get things done, drawing upon relevant ICTs, are as necessary in the new economy as organisational charts were in the industrial era.

(i) What do you understand by knowledge?
(ii) How can it be managed in organisations?

61

IMPLICATIONS FOR ORGANISATIONS AND P&D PROFESSIONALS

Technology is continually developing in response to new needs, the latest discoveries and advancing applications of it in everyday life. The emergence of new technology means, first, that businesses can remain competitive, find fresh markets, improve the quality of production and select appropriate technologies conducive to these ends. Second, governments encourage the development and dissemination of responsible innovatory technologies for further uses, as well as adopting them for their own activities, monitoring them and regulating them where necessary. But, third, there is also the need of humans to have some control over their working lives and private lives. While technology saves lives, empowers and enables humans to increasingly control the natural world, it also poses potential threats to civil and personal liberties. Technology can never be accepted unreservedly, without asking relevant questions about its human consequences and ethical implications. If the unplanned and unintended consequences of technological innovation become dominant, this creates new problems for society, organisations and individuals. The Doomsday scenario argues that humans will apply technology to destructive and amoral ends. The positive scenario is that humans have reason, choice and the opportunity to take moral and just decisions about the use and application of technology. The future is always uncertain and unpredictable but those with power to make decisions about technological innovation and its applications need to be discriminating and informed about which technologies are adopted and those that are not. This is the contrast between technological determinism, on the one hand, and political choice on the other. The ethics of new technologies and how they are used are particularly relevant to P&D professionals.

As indicated above, one of the main implications of ICTs for organisations is the centrality of knowledge creation and knowledge management within them. For Nonaka (1991) the knowledge-creating firm is based on organisational interaction between explicit (open) knowledge and tacit (unspoken) knowledge as the source of innovation. He has argued that knowledge accumulated in the firm comes out of experience and cannot be communicated by workers in formalised management procedures. Where innovation is critical to organisational success, organisational ability to increase sources of information from all forms of knowledge becomes the foundation stone for innovation. This requires the full participation of workers in the innovation process, so that they do not keep their tacit knowledge solely for their own benefit. It is here that online communication and computerised storage capacity are powerful tools in developing the complexity of organisational links between tacit and explicit knowledge. What makes KIFs different is the nature and quality of their skilled intellectual capital, their work processes that create market value through knowledge, and the deployment of knowledge that involves innovation, initiative and competence building (Swart *et al* 2003).

From the perspective of P&D professionals, two kinds of P&D practices seem to be important in managing knowledge workers. First, there are those associated with developing client management skills to gain business and ensure that the relationship is maintained. This has implications for selection and promotion criteria and for developing knowledge workers. Second, there are skills associated with collaborating and sharing information with partners in the network. As Swart *et al* (2003, p71) have put it: 'sharing the explicit knowledge is not likely to be the problem as much as communication skills that allow the transfer of tacit knowledge.' Such P&D practices would seem to be more effective when developed inductively, from the bottom up rather than from the top down.

Further, in knowledge-based work especially, there are potential tensions between the competing loyalties or identities of teams, organisations, professions and clients. Some problems can only be solved in interdisciplinary teams. Specialist professionals are needed who are open-minded to think about new computer-based approaches and applications to their work. Computer scientists, in turn, need to listen to the problems facing their professional colleagues. Psychologists may well have to look at human-to-human and human-to-computer interactions. Engineers and administrators may be necessary to make things work in practice. Very often, a single profession can no longer deal with all aspects of the complex problems associated with knowledge-based work. New systems have to be designed iteratively, with the users in mind, and they have to be addressed to real user problems. However, it is not possible to assess completely the value of a new development before it is taken into daily practice with users. Developers must be ready to change their systems radically until these meet user needs. Users, in turn, must be involved in these processes and a constructive dialogue between users and developers, involving a sequence of prototypical systems, is needed to satisfy user needs.

A second implication of ICTs is the changing occupational structure that is emerging in the information age. Two main types of employment structures seem to be present in the information, knowledge-based economy. One is the 'service economy model', epitomised by the United Kingdom, US and Canada. This is characterised by a rapid phasing out of manufacturing employment after 1970, as the pace of informatisation has accelerated. Having witnessed the elimination of almost all agricultural employment, this model emphasises a new employment structure where differentiation among service activities becomes the key element for analysing and structuring working arrangements. This model emphasises capital management services over producer services and keeps expanding the social service sector largely because of dramatic rises in healthcare jobs. There is to a lesser extent an increase in education employment. This model of the economy is also characterised by expansion of managerial work, including a considerable number of middle managers. This model arose following the neo-liberal, non-interventionist economic policies of the Thatcher and Reagan administrations in the 1980s, when in the midst of world turmoil, the manufacturing and trade bases of the UK and US economies were radically changed.

The other model, epitomised by the German and Japanese economies, is one that while reducing the share of manufacturing employment keeps it at a relatively high level. This allows for the restructuring of manufacturing activities drawing upon socio-technical systems. It reduces manufacturing jobs but reinforces manufacturing activity. Producer services are more important than financial services. Financial services remain important but the bulk of service growth is in services to companies and social services. In between these two models, France seems to be leaning towards a service economy but maintaining a strong manufacturing base.

A third implication is that in the new economy, teleworking becomes an increasingly important way of structuring work. In the 1980s, Toffler (1981) suggested that the information age would enable work to be relocated out of offices and factories, where the industrial revolution had put them, back into the home. Widespread interest in teleworking started in the 1970s, when interest began to be shown by organisations, workers, transportation planners, communities and the telecommunications industry. Developments in ICTs make it easier and enable more occupations to be performed from locations other than the employer base. Apart from homeworking, there are 'telecommuting cottages', other work centres and mobile work, when the 'office' can be in the car or suitcase, creating a results-orientated, trust-based mode of work.

Baruch and Nicholson (1997) have argued that four factors need to be considered before teleworking can become feasible and effective: the job, organisation, home-to-work interface and the individual. In terms of the job, the nature of the work and fit of technology for the specific work role need to be examined. For the organisation, how supportive the business culture is of homeworking arrangements, including willingness and ability of management to trust teleworkers, needs to be determined. In terms of the home–work interface, this covers a diverse range of factors from the quality of family relations to the kind of physical space and facilities available to the worker. For the individual, it needs to be determined to what extent there is a fit between teleworking and the individual's personal attitudes, values, norms and needs. Most of the early writing on teleworking focused on its innovative and positive influence. Recent views (Davenport and Pearlson 1998) are more balanced and raise questions about the idea of a 'best way' or suitability of teleworking to all types of work.

For individuals, the possible benefits of teleworking include less time spent on commuting, improved quality of working life and more time for family and non-working activities. The possible disadvantages of teleworking for individuals include fewer opportunities for group affiliation and detachment from social interaction, less influence over people and events at work, and fewer career development possibilities. For organisations, the possible advantages of teleworking include higher productivity and work performance, savings on space and overheads, and less absenteeism. The possible disadvantages of teleworking for organisations include less committed workers, difficulties in controlling and monitoring teleworkers' activities, and the need for alternative motivational mechanisms. The possible benefits of teleworking for national economies include less pollution, congestion and traffic accidents, support for local communities and more work opportunities for people. The possible disadvantages of teleworking for society include individuals becoming atomised and isolated from social institutions and the need to adapt the legal system (Jackson and Van der Wielen 1998).

In the digital age, P&D professionals are increasingly incorporating ICTs into their professional practices, through the use of computer technology, relevant software, e-mail, the World Wide Web, providing facilities for teleworking and other systems. One use of ICTs is, for example, in recruiting staff. The World Wide Web is now a common medium for advertising job vacancies, with the advantage of reaching a global audience for high level jobs – at least of potential recruits with access to this technology. Similarly, job applicants are using the World Wide Web to submit their curricula vitae (CVs), thus potentially speeding up the application process. References too can be requested and returned by e-mail. A key advantage of using such electronic applications is that CVs can be coded in terms of candidates' competencies and stored electronically so that they can be more easily searched, both for current job vacancies and for jobs in the future. Searches can be done on a global basis, provided the organisation has shared electronic databases for storing and retrieving applicant information (Batram 2000).

A second use of ICTs in P&D activity is in computer-based learning, especially involving jobs heavily dependent on technology. The shift towards self-managed learning offers the prospect of better focused and greater personal and professional development. Computer firms and publishers are expanding the range of materials available for this and are offering cheaper training and development facilities. Use of ICTs for supporting efficiency and effectiveness in both science-based pedagogy and instruction-based learning is an expanding field. Such computer-based training includes computer assisted learning, language laboratories and computer-based role plays. With increased access to electronic data, and a new generation of computers using AI to interact with learners, opportunities for this type of training are considerable. Further, in an era when knowledge management and 'intellectual capital' are increasingly important, these become the focus for reviewing organisational effectiveness. The structure, design and culture of organisations have to be built around managing knowledge. This suggests that cognition is more important than ever in working life. The implication is that possession and use of knowledge permeates all productive activity, at all levels in organisations, and developing human potential forms a greater part of ensuring organisational effectiveness than in the past. More people need to develop more knowledge than was the case previously and ICTs can play a key role in doing this.

A third use of ICTs in P&D activities are in databases for P&D information. Here ICTs are used in payroll systems, career development, succession planning, forecasting HR supply and demand, and monitoring productivity, efficiency and performance. In some cases, databases are developed matching staff competencies with the required competencies for specific jobs. The range of applications of computer technology to P&D issues go beyond these applications including monitoring equal opportunity policies, absence and labour turnover data, learning and development profiles, and staff appraisal. Indeed, when 360-degree appraisal is used, for example, audio and videotape equipment can record feedback responses and some organisations adopt online computerised data-gathering systems, as well as more informal systems where managers pass a diskette around a number of appraisees for their observations. Clearly, ICTs are impressively flexible in the applications to professional P&D activities.

A fourth use of ICTs in P&D activities is in creating direct communication channels between managers and employees within organisations, in both the private and public sectors. Such communication systems take various forms. These include staff surveys using e-mail distribution and response systems, organisational intranets providing briefings to staff, electronic information bulletins from managements to staff, and video-conferencing facilities for interactive communications between managers and staff. Managers using these processes claim that they deliver improved results and higher productivity and performance in their organisations. By developing and utilising the human capital of their organisations and enlisting its support for agreed organisational changes, they believe that the managing of change is made more effective (Farnham *et al* 2005, Preece 1995).

CONCLUSION

This chapter explains how advanced market economies have been undergoing a continuous technological revolution for some 20 years, based largely on ICTs. A networked, global economy has emerged that is using new technologies, incorporating computers, microelectronics and telecommunication systems. These are changing the ways in which goods and services are produced and distributed and how people work. These technologies are also changing how businesses, governments and people interact and communicate with one another.

The applications of ICTs are wide ranging. These include inter-organisational, intra-organisational and interpersonal communications, through intranets, the World Wide Web, e-mail and ICT networks. Other applications include biotechnology, transportation, energy supply, medicine, robotics and many other provisions. ICTs have enabled production systems to shift from mass production to flexible production. They have also enabled large organisations to centralise and decentralise their structures, reorganise spans of control and stretch their internal communication systems. Another impact has been changes in management methods in organisations, such as just-in-time management, total quality control and employee involvement.

Knowledge creation, knowledge transfer and knowledge management are also facilitated by ICTs. Where innovation is critical to organisational success, ability to increase information from all forms of knowledge becomes the basis for innovation. The ways in which work is done in organisations are also affected by ICTs. The jobs and tasks that disappear are routine, repetitive ones that can be precoded and programmed. The jobs and tasks that are created are those requiring analysis, decision and reprogramming that only the human brain can do.

The major impact of ICTs on markets has been to open up new markets for new products and new services in wider regional and geographical areas. In the digital age, demand for jobs and for work is high but the structure of the labour force changes. The dominant model of labour in the information-based economy is a core, secure labour force and a peripheral, insecure one. There is always resistance to technological change but resistance weakens following negotiation, manipulation or coercion. Finally, knowledge is an important resource and product of the information age. This knowledge is a major resource contributing to the competencies of countries, regions, organisations and people.

USEFUL READING

ANGELES, J. (2002) *Fundamentals of robotic mechanical systems*. New York: Springer.

BELLAMY, C. and TAYLOR, J. (1998) *Governing in the information age*. Buckingham: Open University Press.

BERLAGE, T. (1997) Information technology in medicine. *European Research Consortium for Informatics and Mathematics News*, No.29, April.

CASTELLS, M. (1996) *The rise of the network society*. Oxford: Blackwell.

CRAIG, J. (2005) *Introduction to robotics: Mechanics and control*. Upper Saddle River, N.J.: Pearson Education.

DAWSON, P. (2003) *Understanding organisational change: The contemporary experience of people at work*. London: Sage.

EUROPEAN COMMISSION. (2003) *Energy: Science and society – issues, options and technologies*. Luxembourg: Office for Official Publications of the European Commission.

FARNHAM, D., HONDEGHEM, A. and HORTON, S. (2005) *Staff participation and public management reform: Some international comparisons*. Basingstoke: Palgrave.

FORESTER, T. (1987) *High-tech society*. Oxford: Blackwell.

GRINT, K. and WOOLGAR S. (1997) *The machine at work: Technology, work and organisation*. Oxford: Polity Press.

GRÜBLER, A. (1998) *Technology and global change*. Cambridge: Cambridge University Press.

HALL, P. and PRESTON, P. (1988) *The carrier wave: New information technology and the geography of innovation*. London: Unwin Hyman.

HAMPSHIRE and ISLE OF WIGHT COMMUNITY. (2005) *NHS health records*. Hampshire and Isle of Wight Community.

HESTER, R. and HARRISON, R. (eds.). (2004) *Transportation and the environment*. Cambridge: Royal Society of Chemistry.

LENAGHAN, J. (1988) *Rethinking IT and health*. London: Institute for Public Policy Research.

LYON, J. and GORNER, P. (1995) *Altered fates: Gene therapy and the retooling of human life.* New York: Norton.

NEGROPONTE, N. (1995) *Being digital.* New York: Alfred A. Knopf.

PREECE, D. (1995) *Organisations and technological change: Strategy, objectives and involvement.* Routledge: London.

RATLEDGE, C. and KRISTIANSEN, B. (2001) *Basic biotechnology.* Cambridge: Cambridge University Press.

SCHILLER, D. *Digital Capitalism: Networking the global market system.* Cambridge, Mass.: MIT Press.

STALLING, W. (2004) *Data and computer communications.* Upper Saddle River, N.J.: Pearson Education.

SWART, J., KINNIE, N. and PURCELL, J. (2003) *People and performance in knowledge-intensive firms.* London: CIPD.

TOFFLER, A. (1970) *Future shock.* New York: Random House.

TOFFLER, A. (1981) *The Third wave.* New York: Bantam Books.

WISE, E. (2000) *Applied robotics.* Indianapolis: Sams Technical Publishing.

www.orgnet.com/IMRIM.html/krebs (2005)

Globalisation

CHAPTER OBJECTIVES

By the end of this chapter, readers should be able to:

■ assess the likely impact of trends towards globalisation on particular business sectors and organisations
■ advise on the role played by international institutions in shaping the business environment.

In addition, readers should be able to understand, explain and critically evaluate:

■ major contemporary debates about globalisation and its consequences
■ the current and likely future evolution of the European Union (EU)
■ the implications of EU membership for organisations.

INTRODUCTION

National economies in the developed world have become increasingly deregulated and opened up to international competition from other countries, including those of the developing world, in both their manufacturing and service sectors over the past three decades. As a result, global markets are playing an increasingly significant part in today's business relationships. Some UK businesses, for example, are competing not only with one another in the EU but also with their mainland European counterparts, which are sometimes parts of the same multinational corporations (MNCs), in both the EU and other international markets. Globalisation, which incorporates the internationalisation of economic activity as well as social, cultural and political dimensions, has implications for organisations in the private, public and voluntary sectors. It also impacts on those managing them, their workers and other corporate stakeholders, such as customers, suppliers and local communities. Globalisation impacts, in turn, on governments, state agencies and regional supra-national bodies such as the EU.

The essence of contemporary economic globalisation is its links with the international spread of production and new ICTs, which are promoted by the mobility of finance capital and changing patterns of international trade in what some have controversially called the 'borderless world' (Ohmae 1995). The key features of contemporary globalisation are expansion of cross-border trade, exponential growth of ICT systems, internationalisation of finance and production, and the downsizing of governments and the public sector (Cerny 1995). However, this increasingly international economic integration is complemented by mass communication systems and popular culture that promote individualism, consumerism and materialist cultures. It is a phenomenon described by the French as *mondialisation*, by Germans as *Globalisierung* and the Spanish as *globalización*. This chapter examines the phenomenon of contemporary globalisation, the responses of market economies to globalisation and the role of the European Union and major international organisations in the global economy.

THE CAUSES AND EXTENT OF GLOBALISATION

Globalisation is a complex and controversial phenomenon. Petrella (1996) has said that a new competitive era has emerged since the 1970s, especially in connection with the globalisation of economic processes. In his view, competition no longer describes a particular type of market configuration but 'has acquired the status of a universal credo, an ideology'. For industrialists, bankers and financiers, competitiveness has become the short-term primary goal of businesses, with profitability remaining their long-term *raison d'être*.

In the United Kingdom, for example, Hutton (1995, p13 and p170ff) has argued that the financial system, already biased to thinking only in the short term, has been further deregulated and this has intensified its greed for high, quick returns. In his view, 'the more market-based the financial system, the less effectively it mobilises resources for investment'. The reduced powers of trade unions and abolition of wages councils, in turn, have contributed to the deregulation of the UK labour market, thus making it more flexible. These changes have allowed employers to bid down wages and working conditions for the unskilled and poorly organised, with the impact particularly marked in the high-labour-content domestic services industries like hotels, catering and cleaning. For governments, too, national competitiveness is a major concern, because they want to attract and retain capital within their own territories 'in order to secure a maximum level of employment, access of local capital to global technology, and revenue needed to maintain a minimum of social peace' (Petrella 1996, p62ff).

The process of economic globalisation is associated with international trading between business corporations operating in relatively free, unregulated markets, uninhibited by tariff barriers and protectionist, national economic policies. Polanyi (1944, p69) has described the idea of the 'free market' as follows:

> *Nothing must be allowed to inhibit the formation of markets ... Neither must there be any interference with the adjustment of prices to changed market conditions – whether the prices are those of goods, labour, land, or money. Hence there must not only be markets for all elements of industry, but no measure or policy must be countenanced that would influence the action of these markets. Neither price, nor supply, nor demand must be fixed or regulated; only such policies and measures are in order which help to ensure the self-regulation of the market by creating conditions which make the market the only organizing power in the economic sphere.*

Seldon (1990, p1ff) has identified the free market with an 'imperfect capitalism', rather than an 'imperfect socialism'. For him, the market is a capitalist instrument that rewards the risks and penalties of individual ownership and judgement. It is 'not a socialist instrument subject to the irresponsible mercurial collective decisions of "public" men or women who control other people's resources, but are ultimately compelled, like the rest of fallible mankind, to put their personal interests first'.

One implication of the emergent global free market is that sovereign national states are set against one another in geo-political struggles for dwindling natural resources. What makes the 'new globalisation' different is that ICTs throw the economic and social division of labour into turmoil, as traditional Keynesian full-employment policies become unworkable and unsustainable within independent nation states .

Gray (1998, p6ff) has defined economic globalisation as the worldwide spread of industrial production 'promoted by unrestricted mobility of capital and unfettered freedom of trade', while Giddens (1990, p64) sees it as the displacement of local activities by networks of relationships whose reach is worldwide. He defines globalisation as the intensification of worldwide social relations 'which link distant realities in such a way that local happenings are shaped by events occurring many miles away and vice versa'. For Ruigrok and van Taulder (1995), globalisation encompasses a more complex set of features:

- globalisation of financial markets
- internationalisation of corporate strategies, in particular their commitment to competition as a source of wealth creation
- diffusion of technology and related research and development and knowledge on a world-wide basis
- transformation of consumption patterns into cultural products with worldwide consumer markets
- internationalisation of the regulatory capabilities of national societies into a global political economic system
- the diminished role of national governments in designing the rules for global governance.

The essence of the globalisation phenomenon, then, is that national economies become networked with other economies around the world, through international trading, ICTs – especially e-mail, electronic commerce and the World Wide Web – and a common consumerism. This consumerism is fuelled by sophisticated marketing techniques, a continual search for new products and services and large-scale MNCs claiming to be 'customer-centred', 'quality-focused' enterprises. Such companies are household names today such as Hewlett-Packard, Volkswagen-Audi, Sony, Nokia and News International.

Is globalisation a new phenomenon?

Some writers view globalisation as a new phenomenon; others see it as something that has been around, in one form or another, ever since the discovery of the 'new worlds' by European explorers in the sixteenth century. Those supporting the novelty of current global markets argue that the 'new' globalisation has rendered the nation state irrelevant and that it is powerless countries and homeless big business corporations that now inhabit the 'global economy' and 'global marketplace'. For Ohmae (1995, p20), 'in a borderless economy, the nation-focused maps we typically use to make sense of economic activity are woefully misleading'. In his view, people must 'face up at last to the awkward and uncomfortable truth: the old cartography no longer works. It has become no more than an illusion.' Others, such as Negroponte (1995, p1), have written:

> Like a mothball, which goes from solid to gas directly, I expect the nation-state to evaporate ... Without question, the role of the nation-state will change dramatically and there will be no more room for nationalism than there is for smallpox.

For 'new globalisers', global markets are the unique creations of late twentieth-century, early twenty-first century ascendant capitalism. Such markets are seen as orderly and stable institutions, operating under conditions of near perfect or perfect competition, where the nation state is perceived as an increasingly anachronistic and redundant entity (Mann 1997).

Those claiming that globalisation is not new argue that prior to 1914 the world already resembled a global market. Their view is that from about 1880–1914, money, goods and people flowed freely, and an international financial system based on the gold standard came into existence, which effectively limited the economic autonomy of national governments. Hirst and Thompson (1996, p6 and p31) have argued, for example, that present-day globalisation 'is a myth for a world without illusions', where it is held that Western social democracy and socialism of the Soviet block are finished. 'One can only call the political impact of "globalization" the pathology of overdiminished expectations.' In their view, international trade and capital flows were much more important relative to GDP before 1914 than they are today, among both the industrialising economies themselves and between these and their colonial territories. 'Thus the present period is by no means unprecedented.'

Whilst accepting that globalisation is an important contemporary phenomenon, Boyer and Drache (1996, p13) have argued that it is neither totally new nor completely overwhelming. According to their analysis, quantitative evidence demonstrates that globalisation is not novel when measured by national indicators such as share of exports as a percentage of GDP or share of foreign investment in total investment flows. In their estimation, the internationalisation of economic activity has not changed dramatically from the time when Great Britain was the leading global power; many features of the contemporary world were present then. They claim that the internationalisation of trade, production and finance has fluctuated widely over time, collapsing at the end of the 1930s and recovering only in the 1950s. Nevertheless, they see today's globalisation as quantitatively and qualitatively different from that of previous periods. 'State activity has been internationalized to an unprecedented degree in all industrialized countries.'

Even countries such as France, Japan and Sweden, which were not initially advocates of economic *laissez-faire*, have accepted the need to open up their national markets to international competition. Furthermore, with recurrent financial crises and a slowdown in economic growth, governments have not changed their basic policy frameworks. They continue to support the orthodoxy that external markets must be kept open, unlike state policy in the 1930s, when protectionism was in the ascendant. Boyer and Drache suggest, therefore, that it would 'be erroneous to conclude that capitalism has become global, since production methods, industrial relations, taxation and economic policy styles remain very specific to each national state'. They reject the contention that the nation state is *passé* or an accident of history.

Apologists for globalisation

Apologists of globalisation and the free market, such as the international financier and speculator George Soros (1995, p194), have argued that 'the collapse of the global marketplace would be a traumatic event with unimaginable consequences' and that reform of global capitalism is a necessary condition of continued prosperity and social peace (Soros 2000). Support for globalisation, and the transformation of social markets into free markets, is the overriding objective of transnational organisations such as the World Trade Organisation (WTO), International Monetary Fund (IMF), Organisation for Economic Co-operation and Development (OECD) and the World Bank. In advancing this project, they are following the lead of the United States, where progress today is seen as another step towards a universal civilisation – one based on a global free market. This model of a single worldwide civilisation, supported by the 'Washington consensus', Gray (1998, p105 and p108) has argued, expects 'democratic capitalism' to be accepted throughout a world in which a global free market becomes a final reality. He attributes this to the 'neo-conservative ascendancy' in the United States, where free markets are seen not only as a way of organising a market economy but also 'as a dictate of human freedom everywhere'.

Supporters of economic globalisation view it as being commercially and socially benevolent, adding to the total sum of human happiness, while its critics see it as potentially challenging, with several harmful effects. Thus, for the World Trade Organisation, the economic case for an open, international trading system, based on multilaterally agreed rules, rests largely on common sense, since economic protectionism leads to bloated inefficient companies, business closures and job losses.

Writers such as Fukuyama (1992), with his vision of the 'end of history', claim that the inevitability of 'democratic capitalism' constitutes 'the final form of human government' and its global reach is 'the triumph of the Western idea'. Those arguing for a global free market, then, see its growth as a period inaugurating a universal civilisation, replicating Western societies throughout the world.

Globalisation as modernisation

Another view of globalisation, articulated by Giddens (1985) and Robertson (1992), has challenged the capitalist interpretation of globalisation as too simplistic. Both have seen it as a multi-causal phenomenon and have put great emphasis on the importance of international relations in creating globalisation, which, in their view, has occurred independently of the internal dynamics of individual societies. For them, globalisation has its roots in the emergence of the culturally homogeneous nation state. Nation states, competing for resources, markets and territory, develop political, economic, military, administrative and diplomatic systems for exchanges with other states, which incorporate elements of both co-operation and conflict. As nation states multiply and the nation state becomes universal, so international relations have to accommodate to this development. The world comes to be conceptualised as a whole and new systems emerge to make it more unified. But this does not mean that it becomes more integrated or less conflictual, only more conscious of its oneness.

Giddens (1985) has explained the process as one in which the first European nation states successfully married industrial production to military action and succeeded in colonising tribal societies and destroying earlier empires. Their rational-bureaucratic systems enabled them to harness resources to industrial development and modernisation to manage relations with other states (Hardt and Negri 2000). The destabilisation of international relations caused by two World Wars in the twentieth century led subsequently to the blossoming of international organisations that offered more security and provided an environment within which new nations states emerged. Giddens (1990) has argued that globalisation has been driven by four, inter-related dimensions of 'modernism' or 'modernity'.

- *Capitalism*. The world that is emerging is a universal capitalist, market system.
- *Surveillance*. The nation state provides the institutional framework for internal surveillance and control. This is enhanced by the development of international information systems and the sharing of knowledge and data across national boundaries.
- *Military order*. War has been globalised and a system of alliances, centring on the hegemony of the United States, means that only local and peripheral conflicts occur but this depends on the stability of international alliances.
- *Industrialism*. Industrialisation has eroded western economic dominance but has resulted in commodification of services and information, with a globalised culture underpinning the whole process.

Diverse pathways to globalisation

For observers such as Held *et al* (1997, p257ff), globalisation is not a singular condition, 'a linear process or a final end-point of social change.' This means:

- Since different countries are developing along different pathways to the market economy, globalisation impacts on them differentially.
- Globalisation does not mean that world markets affect all aspects of economic life. Some economic activity, such as local, labour-intensive services or local public services, continues to be largely unaffected by world markets.

- Globalisation is not a homogenous phenomenon, since global markets, where capital and production systems move freely across national frontiers, depend on differences among localities, regions and nation states to operate effectively.
- Growth of global markets does not mean that US business culture is being copied throughout the world, since the spread of globalisation and ICTs does not result in convergence of national cultures. In fact, globalisation retains cultural differences among national economies.
- Globalisation does not lead irrevocably to the withering away of the nation state, which remains the decisive mediating structure that MNCs compete to control, whether in Europe, North America or Asia-Pacific.

Critics of globalisation

For critics of globalisation like Hirst and Thompson (1996, p10), in contrast, today's world economy shows many features bringing it closer to a disorderly global market, rather than an orderly one. According to them, the international system becomes socially disembedded as markets become truly global. 'Domestic policies, whether of private corporations or public regulators, now have routinely to take account of the predominantly international determinants of their sphere of operations.' Other critics, such as Gray (1998) argue that this is an Americocentric perspective, purveying a view of the world that is unrecognisable to most Europeans and Asians. By this view, indigenous varieties of capitalism emerging in Eastern Europe and the Far East cannot be contained within a single framework designed to reproduce the 'American dream' with its 'ideal type' of corporate, shareholder capitalism.

There is an 'anti-globalisation' movement, which is the umbrella term for a group of different protest causes, including environmentalism, third world debt, animal rights, child labour, anarchism, and anti-capitalism and opposition to MNCs. It also includes increasing numbers of cross-border social, cultural and technological links (Hertz 2001, Stiglitz 2002, Monbiot 2001). The targets of anti-globalisation protests have been meetings of the WTO, which promotes free trade between countries, IMF, which gives countries loans when their economies are in crisis, and the World Bank, which among other things gives longer term loans to countries for development. Other meetings of national leaders and businesses have also been hit, such as the Summit of the Americas in Quebec and the World Economic Forum in Davos. May Day, originally a pagan festival but now the day of workers and international socialism, is often a target for these protests. Protests have often resulted in violence. But most protesters are supporters of non-violent direct action and have used tactics such as 'guerrilla gardening' by giving pigeons food when authorities try to remove them.

Overview

To sum up, four main interpretations of contemporary economic globalisation have been outlined here: the 'Utopian' scenario, the 'sceptical' one, the 'modernist' one and globalisation as 'diversity'. Utopians argue that globalisation is associated with the establishment of a single global market, which benefits all interests concerned – suppliers, consumers, workers and societies. The aim is to establish a global free market – free from politics – where the manifold economic cultures and economic systems that the world has always contained will die out and become redundant. Most international agencies and many MNCs support this agenda, because they want to impose free markets on to societies throughout the world. The ultimate objective is to incorporate the world's diverse economies into a universal, global market, benefiting the corporate sector. It is MNCs overseeing the world economy that are the vehicles of this post-Keynesian orthodoxy. With the demise of Communist regimes in Eastern Europe and the former Soviet Union, Utopians believe that the advance of a singular, universal type of Western capitalism – the US free market model, in which government is a bystander – will eventually emerge triumphant throughout the world. As Ohmae (1995, p7 and p15ff) argues:

> with the ending of the Cold War, the long familiar pattern of alliances and oppositions among industrialized nations has fractured beyond repair. Less visibly, but arguably far more important, the modern nation-state itself – that artefact of the eighteenth and nine-teenth centuries – has begun to crumble ... For more than a decade, some of us have been talking about the progressive globalization of markets for consumer goods, like Levi jeans, Nike athletic shoes and Hermes scarves ... Today, however, the process of conver-gence goes faster and deeper. It reaches well beyond taste to much more fundamental dimensions of worldview, mind-set, and even thought-process.

Modernists interpret globalisation more pluralistically. They observe it as being driven by the forces of modernity itself. Noting the economic successes of 'first world' countries, developing countries seek to achieve the higher standards of living and quality of life of the western world. The end of colonialism and the emergence of newly independent states with their modernising elites mean that they welcome overseas investment and copy western ways of working, living and thinking. This results in a process of economic systemisation, an emerging global culture and global consciousness, and a global economy with a diverse cosmopolitan culture. For modernists, globalisation is a multi-faceted and uneven process but an inexorable one.

Those who see globalisation as representing diverse systems of economic production and exchange argue that it is a complex phenomenon, which takes different forms in different soci-eties. It is not a homogeneous phenomenon, following a sequential pathway to uniformity, but a heterogeneous one with diverse impacts on different countries.

Sceptics of globalisation, however, explore what is different about globalisation during a period of increased capital mobility, internationalisation of production and introduction of ICTs into business processes. They argue that if Keynes, Beveridge and Fordist employment relations structures were once the pillars of state policy, they no longer are (Hutton 1995, 2002). The emergence of a 'lean and mean' state, dedicated to providing lower levels of public services is symptomatic of the new economic order. For many countries grappling with new competitive pressures, home mar-kets remain where the best jobs are, where investment needs to occur and where indigenous firms make the difference. Petrella (1996) has argued that globalisation is partial and unstable and creates cleavages between social classes in advanced countries and between developed and developing countries. Sceptics also view markets as complex social institutions that are not self-organising and do not respond to universal laws of supply and demand. To be efficient, markets have to be embedded in national institutions, including money, labour and the environment.

Writers such as Cohen (1996), in turn, have addressed the way in which the nation state is being challenged and changed by new international trade agreements, such as the Canada–US Free Trade Agreement and the North American Free Trade Agreement. She concludes that free trade agreements adversely affect equality-seeking groups, by disenfranchising and excluding them from power. Such analyses lead Bienefeld (1996) and others to conclude that the nation state remains a necessary and feasible response to the pressures driven by increasing global disorder. In his view, the nation state is the only entity capable of restoring some congruence between the economic, social and political dimensions of modern life.

In Gray's analysis (1998, p194ff), the global economy that is emerging is a result of the worldwide spread of new technologies, not the spread of free markets. The outcome is 'not a universal free market but an anarchy of sovereign states, rival capitalisms and stateless zones'. He has argued that global free markets fracture societies and weaken states. Where there are weak governments, states have collapsed or ceased to be effective and market forces, over which governments have no control, have desolated societies. His prognosis is that only a framework of global regulation, involving currencies, capital movements, trade and environmental conservation, 'can enable the creativity of the world economy to be harnessed in the service of human needs'.

(i) What factors have led to globalisation?
(ii) Explain the following interpretations of globalisation:
    (a) globalisation as Americanisation,
    (b) globalisation as the restructuring of state power
    (c) globalisation as imperialism
    (d) globalisation as transformation

TYPES OF MARKET ECONOMY AND RESPONSES TO GLOBALISATION

Despite the claims of free market utopians, a universal model of contemporary market capitalism does not exist. It is precisely the combination of unfettered market competition, weakened social institutions (such as trade unions) and the torrent of technological innovation that produces the contemporary but diverse global economy. Specific responses by organisations, governments and societies to economic globalisation, therefore, vary by country, region, sector, location and time.

Hampden-Turner and Trompenaars (1995, pp6–10), for example, have examined seven cultures of capitalism, focusing on the United States, United Kingdom, Sweden, France, Japan, the Netherlands and Germany. They identify 'seven fundamental valuing processes' without which wealth-creating organisations could not exist, although each value has a tension within it. These are:

- *Making rules and discovering exceptions*: here the integrity of enterprises depends upon how well 'universalism' or rules of wide generality are reconciled with 'particularism' or special exceptions to rules.
- *Constructing and deconstructing*: here the mental and physical processes of 'analysing' and 'integrating' keep enterprises in a constant state of renewal or refinement.
- *Managing communities of individuals*: here the integrity of enterprises depends on how well the 'individualism' of employees, shareholders and customers is reconciled with the 'communitarianism' of the larger system.
- *Internalising the outside world*: here enterprises have to reconcile their 'inner-directions' and 'outer-directions' so that they can internalise the outer world to act decisively and competently.
- *Synchronising fast processes*: here the task is reconciling 'sequential time' with 'synchronised time' (ie how time is organised).
- *Choosing among achievers*: here the capacity to create wealth depends upon balancing 'achieved status' with 'ascribed status'.
- *Sponsoring equal opportunities*: here the integrity of enterprises depends on how to balance the need for 'equality' of inputs with 'hierarchy' in judging the merits of these inputs.

Tensions arise, Hampden-Turner and Trompenaars have argued, because any nation or organisation creating wealth must manage all seven valuing processes. Each culture in their study, however, starts in a different place, with the United States, for example, scoring highly on 'individualism' and Japan scoring highly on 'communitarianism'.

The typology outlined in Table 4.1 suggests that there are at least five types of market economy around the world. Each of these varies according to market regulation and accountability, the nature of the labour market and its underpinning value system. Using this typology (although there are others), Anglo-Saxon systems of market economy, such as those found in the English-speaking world in the United Kingdom, United States, Canada and Australasia, are typified by free markets, the centrality of contract law, dominance of shareholder interests, deregulated labour markets and an individualistic value system. In contrast, Central European economic systems are typified by social markets, public law, stakeholder interests, regulated labour markets and social cohesion.

In the Far East, two types of market system stand out – the Japanese and Chinese. In the Japanese system, businesses work within a framework of managed markets, market regulation is based on trust and market accountability is through networks of firms working together. Japanese businesses favour internal labour markets and a collectivist value system. In the Chinese case, including Hong Kong, Taiwan and other parts of the world with Chinese businesses, markets are largely interpersonal and, as in Japan, are based on trust, with market accountability being centred on family networks. Labour markets are parochial, since employers often rely on the recruitment and employment of ethnic Chinese workers, in a system incorporating strongly paternalist values. In the emergent economy of the Russian Federation, markets are anarchic, are regulated by naked power, and market accountability is to managers and workers. Russia has largely local labour markets and a 'mutual aid' value system based on extended families.

Table 4.1 Types of market economy

System	Market	Regulation	Accountability	Labour market	Value system
Anglo-Saxon	free	contract	shareholder	deregulated	individualist
Central-European	social	public law	stakeholders	regulated	social cohesion
Russian	anarchic	power	managers-workers	local	mutual-aid
Japanese	managed	trust	networks of firms	internal	collectivist
Chinese	interpersonal	trust	families	parochial	paternalist

In Anglo-Saxon market economies like that of the United Kingdom, for example, global forces impact on companies, national government, local government, customers, workers and other organisational and societal stakeholders in a variety of ways. Many private businesses, including MNCs, have to respond to increasing competition in their markets for goods and services and supplies of capital, labour and other resources by changes in their policies, structures and management systems. In order to gain 'competitive edge' and some control over indeterminate market forces, companies in the corporate sector adopt and develop a variety of business strategies to manage change, competition and uncertainty under globalisation. The principal responses of many private-sector businesses to globalisation include therefore:

- addressing competitive pressures in the marketplace
- seeking to retain and expand their market share of products or services, domestically and internationally
- searching for new markets, products and methods of providing them
- investing in information and communication technologies
- taking over and merging with other businesses
- investing and relocating operations overseas in trans-national groupings
- responding to pressures on productivity, quality and performance
- improving profits and profitability.

In terms of P&D policies and strategies, leading-edge companies in these circumstances are likely to seek greater commitment and motivation of their workforces. This is in the expectation that committed and motivated staff contribute to improved performance and higher productivity within their businesses and that 'people make a difference'. A number of linkages is claimed to exist between supportive corporate and societal contexts, specific HR practices and improved company performance and improved worker outcomes in 'high performance work systems.' A key assumption is that 'performance is a function of employee ability, motivation and 'opportunity'. In other words, it is argued that people perform well when they have the necessary knowledge and skills to do so and have the motivation to do so because they are incentivised for doing it. It is also necessary that the work environment provides the necessary support and avenues for expressing this performance (Boxall and Purcell 2003, p20). Pfeffer (1998) has identified seven components of high commitment HR practices:

- employment security
- selective hiring and sophisticated selection
- extensive training
- learning and development
- employee involvement and voice
- high compensation based on performance
- harmonisation of conditions at work.

In some respects, the impact of globalisation on governments at both national and local levels in Anglo-Saxon market economies is one of its most distinctive features. The main responses to globalisation by governments in such cases include:

- weakening the redistributive dimensions of the welfare state, since market solutions to resolving economic and social welfare problems become the preferred approach to making resource decisions
- emphasising the importance of flexible labour, product and capital markets
- regulating the economy is no longer a managerial one but a steering one
- recognising and accepting the central role of the private sector in creating wealth
- managing expectations arising from a 'low taxation' culture, where personal and corporate taxpayers have expectations of tax reductions, or at least a low tax regime
- dealing with a more limited concept of citizenship, where the boundaries of the public domain becoming narrower and more circumscribed
- accepting that financing public goods becomes harder to achieve and that government has to draw on the private sector as a major source of 'public investment'
- delivering a more limited range of 'public services' replaces a birth-to-death welfare state regime.

Some of the ways that those managing public services respond to globalisation, in turn, include:

- emphasising 'good' management and the effective managing of their limited resources
- addressing governmental demands for more efficiency, greater effectiveness and better value for money
- splitting public services into 'purchaser' and 'provider' units through the creation of internal markets or quasi-markets
- redrawing the boundaries between the public and private sectors, through subcontracting, market testing and creation of public agencies
- using private-sector benchmarks to guide best management practices
- responding more directly to client needs.

Some of the consequences of globalisation for the people employed in private businesses and public services include:

- less job security
- widening pay differentials
- more job flexibility
- changing job structures
- higher unemployment in flexible labour markets.

It is also argued that globalisation provides greater consumer choice and benefits to customers or consumers in the marketplace. It is asserted the 'consumer' once again becomes 'king' and that one of the main drivers of corporate and public service performance is 'customer satisfaction.' Consumer sovereignty replaces producer sovereignty as increasingly competitive markets propel the economic system to satisfy the economic wants of consumers. However, there are possible dangers in consumer sovereignty. First, consumers may be ill informed or persuaded by advertisers to make bad choices. Second, consumer preferences may be frustrated by monopoly or imperfect competition. Third, consumers can be considered the best judges of their needs and preferences, and making rational choices, only if they can learn by trial and error what to avoid and how to choose better. This is difficult to do in practice in complex consumer markets where consumer choice can often be too wide and confusing. Consumers may also make decisions which have high social costs resulting in the consumption of illness-inducing products that lead to health costs, absenteeism from work and high dependency.

(i) Drawing on Table 4.1 above, discuss and review the major differences between these types of market economy.
(ii) What are the major effects, both positive and negative, of the growth of MNCs locating in the United Kingdom for:
  (a) the UK economy
  (b) government
  (c) people?

THE EUROPEAN UNION

The EU is a unique political system, combining elements of supra-nationalism and inter-governmentalism. Its origins lie in the aftermath of the Second World War, when there was a need for rapid reconstruction and the reintegration of Germany into the community of western

European states. Anxious to assist Europe in becoming a strong buffer against the threat of Communist expansion from the Soviet bloc, the United States provided Marshall Aid and encouraged international co-operation within Europe. Proposals for a united states of Europe with a federal structure met with little support from post-war states. But six countries – Belgium, Luxembourg, France, the Netherlands, Italy and West Germany – agreed to co-operate in restructuring their coal and steel communities, when signing the Treaty of Paris 1951. Six years later, they signed the Treaty of Rome 1957, which created the European Economic Community (EEC) and the European Atomic Energy Community (Euratom). The EEC committed its members to creating a 'common market', by removing internal tariff barriers and adopting common external tariffs.

The benefits of economic co-operation led other countries to seek entry. The United Kingdom joined after years of procrastination (George 1998) as did Denmark and Ireland in 1973, Greece in 1981, followed by Portugal and Spain in 1986. The EU was further enlarged in 1995, when Austria, Finland and Sweden became members. In 2004, the biggest enlargement took place with 10 new countries joining: Cyprus, the Czech Republic, Estonia, Hungary, Latvia, Lithuania, Malta, Poland, Slovakia and Slovenia, making a total of 25 member states with a population of over 400 million (Nugent 2004).

The founding fathers of the EU always had a vision of a politically united Europe, but saw economic integration as the best means of achieving that. There was always ambivalence about political union amongst political leaders, because power was – and is – based on the nation state, not Europe. Their strategies have been essentially pragmatic and founded upon national interest. Between 1956 and 1986, there was some progress, but integration was impeded by the need to get unanimous agreement on every issue. The 1980s and 1990s saw greater political will for further integration, prompted partly by the reunification of Germany and the end of the Cold War. The Single European Act 1986, the Treaty of Maastricht 1992 and Treaty of Amsterdam 1997 transformed the EU, with its then-300 million citizens, and was a watershed in the development of this political experiment. The Treaty of Nice followed in 2001 and a new constitution was agreed in 2004, requiring ratification by all 25 states before it became European law. However, following rejection of the constitution in referendums in France and the Netherlands in summer 2005, the question of constitutional reform in the EU remained unresolved and had to be reassessed and reviewed by European politicians.

As the world moved into the twenty-first century, it was increasingly recognised that Europe collectively needed to face the challenges of globalisation. With revolutionary new technologies and the World Wide Web explosion transforming the world economy, these profound economic changes were bringing with them social disruption and culture change. Meeting in Lisbon in March 2000, the European Council of the EU adopted a comprehensive strategy for modernising the EU's economy and enabling it to compete on the world market with other major players such as the United States and the newly industrialised countries. The 'Lisbon strategy' included opening up all sectors of the economy to competition, encouraging innovation and business investment and modernising Europe's education systems to meet the needs of the information society (Kontrakou 2004).

Today's EU is the result of the hard work put in by men and women working for an integrated Europe. The EU is built on their concrete achievements. In no other region of the world have sovereign countries pooled their sovereignty to this extent and in so many areas of crucial importance to their citizens. The EU has created a single currency and a dynamic single market in which people, goods and capital move around freely. It strives to ensure, through social progress and fair competition, that as many people as possible enjoy the benefits of this single market (Dinan 2004).

The ground rules of the EU are set out in a series of treaties. These have forged strong legal ties amongst EU member states, with EU laws directly affecting EU citizens and giving them specific rights:

- Treaty of Paris which set up the European Coal and Steel Community (ECSC) in 1951
- Treaties of Rome which set up the European Economic Community (EEC) and the European Atomic Energy Community (Euratom) in 1957
- Single European Act 1986
- Treaty on European Union (Maastricht) 1992
- Treaty of Amsterdam 1997
- Treaty of Nice 2001.

> A visiting manager from the United States has asked you to explain what the European single market is. What would you say?

A number of fundamental principles underpin the EU. One is 'social peace', arising out of the two wars that ravaged the continent of Europe during the first half of the twentieth century. Politicians who had resisted totalitarianism during the Second World War were determined to put an end to international hatred and rivalry in Europe and build a lasting peace between former enemies. There was the desire for a new order in Western Europe, based on the interests that its peoples and nations shared and it was founded upon treaties guaranteeing the rule of law and equality amongst all countries. It was the start of more than half a century of peaceful co-operation between member states of the European Communities. With the Treaty of Maastricht 1992, Community institutions were strengthened, given broader responsibilities and the EU was born (Warleigh 2004).

The second principle is 'security and safety', especially as twenty-first century Europe has to deal with issues of safety and security beyond its own borders in North Africa, the Balkans, the Caucasus and the Middle East. One of Europe's challenges is to make the EU an area of freedom, security and justice where everyone has equal access to justice and is equally protected by the law. By the 1990s, European integration had reached a point where the EU began to go beyond its economic goals to acknowledge common problems of security and defence and to move slowly towards greater integration in those areas. The Treaty of Maastricht established two new pillars, foreign and security policy and justice and home affairs, but these remain areas of interstate co-operation. The war in Iraq exposed divisions within the EU, with each member state taking independent decisions on its position. More co-operation is being achieved on cross-border policing and there are attempts to get a common policy on immigration.

The third principle is 'economic and social solidarity'. The EU has been built to achieve political goals but its dynamism and success spring from its economic foundations: the 'single market' formed by all member states and the single currency (the Euro) used by 12 of them at the present time. The new entrants will adopt the Euro at the end of the transitional period. With EU countries accounting for an ever-smaller percentage of the world's population, they have to pull together if they are to ensure economic growth and be able to compete on the world stage with other major economies. No individual EU country is strong enough to go it alone in world trade. To achieve economies of scale and find new customers, European businesses have to operate in a bigger market than just their home country. But Europe-wide free competition has to be counterbalanced by Europe-wide solidarity, expressed in practical help for ordinary people and communities in terms of assistance from the EU budget, 'structural funds' managed by the European Commission, the Common Agricultural Policy and the European Investment Bank to improve Europe's transport infrastructure and boost trans-European trade.

The fourth principle is 'Working more closely together to promote the European model of society', which reflects the increasingly complex nature of Europe's post-industrial societies. Standards of living have risen steadily but there are still gaps between rich and poor and they will widen as post-Communist countries join the EU. That is why EU member states work more closely together on tackling social problems. The EU is based on the 'European social model', which is integrationist and collectivist in its underpinning philosophy. In periods of transition, continental member states in the EU traditionally give support to workers, who pay the price of economic reconstruction, with high welfare benefits and support with retraining. Social rights are rooted in many of the constitutions of the member states, which have sought to develop and protect these rights. The EU Charter of Fundamental Rights, which was proclaimed in Nice in December 2000, sets out all the rights recognised today by EU member states and their citizens. The United Kingdom has always been the reluctant partner in accepting this model and is currently, along with Spain, seeking to change it (Warleigh 2004).

The EU also wants to promote human values and social progress. Europeans see globalisation and technological change revolutionising the world and they want people everywhere to be in control – not victims – of this process of change. People's needs cannot be met simply by market forces or by the unilateral action of one country. So the EU stands for a view of humanity and a model of society that the vast majority of its citizens support. Europeans value their rich heritage that includes a belief in human rights, social solidarity, free enterprise, a fair sharing of the fruits of economic growth, the right to a protected environment, respect for cultural, linguistic and religious diversity, and a harmonious yoking of tradition and progress. Europeans have a wealth of national and local cultures that distinguish them from one another, but they are united by their common heritage of values that distinguishes them from the rest of the world (Cowles and Dinan 2004).

The UK has been described as the 'awkward partner' in the EU? Why do you think this is so?

Institutions of the EU

Under the treaties which make up the constitution of the EU, member states delegate some of their national sovereignty to the Union's institutions. These institutions represent not only their national interests but also their collective interests. The treaties themselves constitute what is known as 'primary' legislation and this juridical base enables the institutions to formulate 'secondary' legislation which takes the form of directives, regulations and recommendations. European legislation takes precedence over national legislation in those areas to which it relates. These 'laws', along with EU policies in general, are the result of decisions taken by three main institutions. This 'institutional triangle' can only function if the three institutions work closely together and trust one another (Warleigh 2004).

- Council of the European Union or Council of Ministers (representing member states)
- European Parliament (representing citizens)
- European Commission (the civil service or permanent bureaucracy of the EU that upholds the collective European interest).

Council of the European Union

The Council of the European Union is the main decision-making institution of the EU. Formerly known as the 'Council of Ministers', it is now called 'the Council'. Each EU country in turn presides over the Council for a six-month period. Every Council meeting is attended by a minister from each member state. Which ministers attend depends on the agenda. If foreign policy, it is the Foreign Affairs Minister from each country. If agriculture, it is the Minister for Agriculture. There are nine different Council 'configurations', covering all policy areas including industry, transport, the environment and so on.

Preparatory work for Council meetings is done by the Permanent Representatives Committee (Coreper), made up of the member states' ambassadors to the EU, assisted by officials from national ministries. Council's administrative work is handled by its General Secretariat, based in Brussels.

Council and European Parliament share legislative power, as well as responsibility for the budget. Council also concludes international agreements negotiated by the Commission. According to the treaties, Council has to take its decisions either unanimously, by a majority or by 'qualified majority' vote. On important questions such as amending the treaties, launching a new common policy or allowing a new country to join the Union, Council has to agree unanimously. In most other cases, qualified majority voting is used. In other words, a decision cannot be taken unless a specified minimum number of votes is cast in its favour.

The number of votes each EU country casts in Council roughly reflects the size of its population. Since 2004, the number of votes each country casts is as follows:

- Germany, France, Italy and United Kingdom   29
- Spain and Poland   27
- Netherlands   13
- Belgium, Czech Republic, Greece, Hungary and Portugal   12
- Austria and Sweden   10
- Denmark, Ireland, Lithuania, Slovakia and Finland   7
- Cyprus, Estonia, Latvia, Luxembourg and Slovenia   4
- Malta   3

Total   321

A minimum of 232 votes (72.3 per cent) is required to reach a qualified majority. In addition a majority of member states (in some cases two-thirds) must approve the decision and any member state can ask for confirmation that the votes cast in favour represent at least 62 per cent of the EU's total population (European Commission 2004a).

European Council

The European Council brings together the presidents and prime ministers of all EU countries plus the President of the European Commission. The President of the European Parliament also addresses every meeting of the European Council. It meets, in principle, four times a year, chaired by the President or Prime Minister of the country currently presiding over the European Council.

Given the importance of EU affairs in national political life, it is appropriate that national presidents and prime ministers have regular opportunities to meet and discuss major European issues. Following the Treaty of Maastricht, the European Council officially became the initiator of the major policies of the EU and was empowered to settle difficult issues on which ministers, meeting in the Council of the European Union, fail to agree. The European Council is thus the highest policy-making body of the EU and gives it strategic direction. Some member states would like it to become the government of Europe and want one of its members to represent the Union on the world stage.

The European Parliament

The European Parliament is the elected body representing EU citizens and takes part in the legislative process. Since 1979, Members of the European Parliament (MEPs) have been directly elected, by universal suffrage, every five years. Until the 2004 elections there were 626 MEPs. After enlargement of the EU (Nugent 2004), the number will increase to 732 in 2004–2007 and to 786 in 2007–2009, as shown in Table 4.2.

Table 4.2 Members of the European Parliament by member states

	1999–2004	2004–2007	2007–2009
Bulgaria	–	–	18
Belgium	25	24	24
Czech Republic	–	24	24
Denmark	16	14	14
Estonia	–	6	6
Germany	99	99	99
Greece	25	24	24
Spain	64	54	54
France	87	78	78
Ireland	15	13	13
Italy	87	78	78
Cyprus	–	6	6
Latvia	–	9	9
Lithuania	–	13	13
Luxembourg	6	6	6
Hungary	–	24	24
Malta	–	5	5
Netherlands	31	27	27
Austria	21	18	18
Poland	–	54	54
Portugal	25	24	24
Romania	–	–	36
Slovenia	–	7	7
Slovakia	–	14	14
Finland	16	14	14
Sweden	22	19	19
United Kingdom	87	78	78
TOTAL	626	732	786

Source: European Commission 2004a

Parliament normally holds plenary sessions in Strasbourg and additional sessions in Brussels. It has 17 committees that do preparatory work for its plenary sessions and a number of political groups that mostly meet in Brussels. The Secretariat-General is based in Luxembourg. Parliament and the Council share legislative power, by using three different procedures in addition to simple consultation. These are:

- *The co-operation procedure*: introduced by the Single European Act 1986. Here Parliament gives its opinion on draft directives and regulations proposed by the European Commission, which can amend its proposal to take account of Parliament's opinion.
- *The assent procedure*: also introduced in 1986. Here Parliament must give its assent to international agreements, negotiated by the Commission, to any proposed enlargement of the EU and to a number of other matters including changes in election rules.
- *The co-decision procedure*: introduced by the Treaty of Maastricht 1992, puts Parliament on an equal footing with the Council when legislating on important issues including free movement of workers, internal market, education, research, the environment, Trans-European Networks, health, culture and consumer protection. Parliament has the power to throw out proposed legislation in these fields if an absolute majority of MEPs vote against Council's 'common position'. However, the matter can be put before a conciliation committee. The Treaty of Amsterdam added another 23 and the Treaty of Nice a further seven to the number of fields in which the co-decision procedure applies.

Parliament and the Council also share responsibility for adopting the EU budget. The European Commission proposes a draft budget, which is then debated by Parliament and the Council. Parliament can reject the proposed budget and it has done so on several occasions. When this happens, the entire budget procedure has to be restarted. Parliament has made full use of its budgetary powers to influence EU policy-making.

Parliament is a driving force in European politics. It is the EU's primary debating chamber, a place where the political and national viewpoints of all the member states meet and mix. Parliament initiates many policy proposals. The Parliament is organised into groups which dominate debates. The largest of these are the European People's Party (Christian Democrats) and European Democrats (the EPP–ED group) and the Party of European Socialists (PES).

Parliament is the body that exercises democratic control over the Union. It has the power to dismiss the Commission by adopting a motion of censure but requires a two-thirds majority for this. It also has to approve the appointment of the President and the 25 commissioners that make up the Commission. It does not have the power to oppose individual members but only to support or reject the team proposed by the President. It checks that EU policies are being properly managed and implemented by examining, for example, the reports it receives from the Court of Auditors. The President of the European Council also reports to Parliament on the decisions taken by EU political leaders.

The European Commission

The Commission is another key institution, with one commissioner per country, appointed for a five-year period by agreement between member states, subject to approval by Parliament. The Commission acts with political independence. Its job is to uphold the interest of the EU as a whole, so it must not take instructions from any member state government. As 'Guardian of the Treaties', it ensures that the regulations and directives adopted by Council and Parliament are put into effect. If they are not, the Commission can take the offending party to the Court of Justice to oblige it to comply with EU law.

The Commission is also the only institution with the right to propose new EU legislation and it can take action at any stage to help bring about agreement both within Council and between Council and Parliament. As the EU's executive arm, the Commission carries out the decisions taken by Council. The Commission is largely responsible for managing the EU's common policies, such as research, development aid, regional policy and manages the budget for these policies. The Commission is answerable to Parliament and the entire Commission has to resign if Parliament passes a motion of censure against it (European Commission 2004a).

The Court of Justice

The Court of Justice of the European Communities, located in Luxembourg, is made up of one judge from each EU country, assisted by eight advocates-general. They are appointed by joint agreement of the governments of the member states. Each is appointed for a term of six years, after which they may be reappointed for one or two further periods of three years. The Court's job is to ensure that EU law is complied with and that the treaties are correctly interpreted and applied.

The Court of Justice is also the only institution that can, at the request of the national courts, give a ruling on the interpretation of the treaties and on the validity and interpretation of EU law. This system ensures that EU law is interpreted and applied in the same way throughout the Union. The Treaties explicitly allow the Court to check whether EU legislation respects the fundamental rights of EU citizens and to give rulings on questions of personal freedom and security.

The Court of Auditors

The Court of Auditors, set up in 1977, has one member from each EU country, appointed for a term of six years by agreement between member states, after consulting Parliament. The Court of Auditors checks that all EU revenue has been received and all its expenditures are incurred in a lawful and regular manner and that the EU budget has been managed soundly.

The European Economic and Social Committee

When taking decisions in policy areas covered by the treaties, the Council and Commission consult the European Economic and Social Committee (EESC). Its members represent the various interest groups that collectively make up 'organised civil society' and are appointed by Council for a four-year term. The EESC has to be consulted before decisions are taken in a great many fields such as employment, the European Social Fund and vocational training.

The Committee of the Regions

The Committee of the Regions (CoR), set up under the Treaty on European Union, consists of representatives of regional and local government, proposed by member states and appointed by Council for a four-year term. Under the Treaty, Council and Commission must consult the CoR on matters of relevance to the regions and the Committee may also adopt opinions on its own initiative.

The European Investment Bank

The European Investment Bank (EIB), based in Luxembourg, finances projects to help the EU's less developed regions and make small businesses more competitive.

The European Central Bank

The European Central Bank (ECB), based in Frankfurt, is responsible for managing the Euro and the EU's monetary policy (Eusepi and Schneider 2004).

You have been asked to brief a visiting manager from Canada about the processes through which European law is made and enforced.

(i) What will you say to her?
(ii) She is also interested to know how European law impacts on your organisation and how it affects organisational policy and practice.

MAJOR INTERNATIONAL ORGANISATIONS

There is a range of international institutions seeking to influence patterns of international trading, national economic policies and economic development. Most of them were created at the end of the Second World War. The functions and activities of four of them are outlined below. One critique made by some observers of these international institutions is that they are strongly free market in their economic approach and are encouraging neo-liberal economic policies, privatisation and tax-cutting initiatives, rather than Keynesian, interventionist policies.

Organisation for Economic Co-operation and Development (OECD)

OECD is made up of about 30 member countries sharing a commitment to democratic government and the market economy. It provides a setting for reflection and discussion based on policy research and analysis that helps governments shape policy that may lead to a formal agreement among member governments or be acted on in domestic or other international forums. With active relationships involving some 70 other countries, non-governmental organisations (NGOs) and civil society, OECD has a global reach. It grew out of the Organisation for European Economic Co-operation (OEEC), formed to administer US and Canadian aid under the Marshall Plan for the reconstruction of Europe at the end of the Second World War. After taking over from the OEEC in 1961, OECD's task has been to build strong economies in its member countries, improve efficiency, hone market systems, expand free trade and contribute to developments in industrialised and developing countries. In recent years, OECD has moved beyond a focus on its member countries to offer its analytical expertise and accumulated experience to developing and emerging market economies. Its member countries are shown in Table 4.3.

Table 4.3 OECD member countries

Australia	Hungary	Norway
Austria	Iceland	Poland
Belgium	Ireland	Portugal
Canada	Italy	Slovak Republic
Czech Republic	Japan	Spain
Denmark	Korea	Sweden
Finland	Luxembourg	Switzerland
France	Mexico	Turkey
Germany	Netherlands	United Kingdom
Greece	New Zealand	USA

Source: OECD 2004

The OECD is a group of like-minded countries. Essentially membership is limited only by a country's commitment to the market economy and pluralistic democracy. It is rich, in that its 30 members produce two-thirds of the world's goods and services, but it is by no means exclusive. The core of original European and North American members has expanded to include Japan, Australia, New Zealand, Finland, Mexico, Korea and four former communist states in Europe: the Czech Republic, Hungary, Poland and the Slovak Republic. Non-members are invited to subscribe to OECD agreements and treaties and the organisation is now working in some 70 non-member countries from Brazil, China and Russia to the least developed countries in Africa and elsewhere.

The organisation is also expanding its relationship with civil society. Initially focused on relations with business and labour, these have broadened to include a wide range of NGOs. OECD also increasingly invites public comment on various aspects of its work. As it opens itself to many new contacts around the world, OECD is broadening its scope, looking ahead to a post-industrial age in which it aims to weave OECD economies into a yet more prosperous and increasingly knowledge-based world economy.

OECD has around 2,300 staff in its Secretariat in Paris, who work directly or indirectly to support the activities of its 200 committees, working groups and expert groups. Some 40,000 senior officials from national administrations come to OECD committee meetings each year to request, review and contribute to work undertaken by the OECD secretariat. Even from home, they have access to OECD documents and can exchange information through the OECD online data network. Some 700 economists, lawyers, scientists and other professional staff, based mainly in a dozen substantive directorates, provide research and analysis. A Secretary-General directs the Secretariat, assisted by four Deputy Secretaries-General. The Secretary-General also chairs Council, which provides the crucial link between national delegations and the Secretariat. OECD works in two official languages: English and French. Staff members are citizens of OECD member countries but serve as international civil servants, with no national affiliation during their OECD posting (OECD 2005).

Member countries fund OECD. National contributions to the annual budget are based on a formula related to the size of each member's economy. The largest contributor is the United States, which provides 25 per cent of the budget, followed by Japan. With the approval of the Council, countries may also make separate contributions to particular programmes or projects.

The emergence of globalisation has seen the scope of OECD work move from examination of each policy area within each member country to analysis of how various policy areas interact with each other, between countries and beyond the OECD area. This is reflected in work on issues such as sustainable development, bringing together environmental, economic and social concerns across national frontiers for better understanding of the problems and the best way to tackle them together.

Best known for its publications and its statistics, its work covers economic and social issues from macroeconomics, to trade, education, development, and science and innovation. OECD also plays a prominent role in fostering good governance in the public service and in corporate activity. It helps governments ensure the responsiveness of key economic areas with sectoral monitoring. By deciphering emerging issues and identifying policies that work, it helps policy-makers adopt strategic orientations. It is well known for its individual country surveys and reviews.

OECD also produces internationally agreed instruments, decisions and recommendations to promote 'rules of the game' in areas where multilateral agreement is necessary for individual countries to make progress in a globalised economy. Sharing the benefits of growth is also crucial, as shown in activities such as emerging economies, sustainable development, territorial economy and aid. Dialogue, consensus, peer review and pressure are at the very heart of OECD work.

OECD has been called a think tank, a monitoring agency, a 'rich man's club' and a 'non-academic' university. It has elements of all of these but none of them captures the essence of OECD. It gathers together its 30 member countries in a unique forum to discuss, develop and refine economic and social policies. They compare experiences, seek answers to common problems and work to co-ordinate domestic and international policies to help members and non-members deal with an increasingly globalised world. Their exchanges may lead to agreements to act in a formal way by, for example, establishing legally binding agreements to crack down on bribery or by drawing up codes for free flow of capital and services. However, OECD is also known for its 'soft law' or non-binding instruments on difficult issues such as its guidelines for multinational enterprises. Beyond agreements, discussions within OECD make for better-informed work within member countries' own governments across the broad spectrum of public policy and help clarify the impact of national policies on the international community (www.oecd.org).

International Monetary Fund (IMF)

IMF is a specialised agency of the United Nations (UN) system, set up by treaty in 1945 to help promote the health of the world economy. With headquarters in Washington DC in the United States, it is governed by its almost global membership of 184 countries. Since IMF was established, its purposes have remained unchanged but its operations, which involve surveillance, financial assistance and technical assistance, have developed to meet the changing needs of its member countries in an evolving world economy.

IMF is the central institution of the international monetary system ie the system of international payments and exchange rates among national currencies that enables business to take place between countries. IMF's purposes have become more important, partly because of the expansion of its membership. The number of IMF member countries has more than quadrupled from the 45 states involved in its establishment in 1945, reflecting in particular the attainment of political independence by many developing countries and more recently the collapse of the Soviet bloc (Peet 2003).

Expansion of IMF membership, together with changes in the world economy, has required IMF to adapt in a variety of ways to continue serving its purposes effectively. Its purposes are to:

- Promote international monetary co-operation through a permanent institution which provides machinery for consultation and collaboration on international monetary problems.
- Facilitate the expansion and balanced growth of international trade and contribute to the promotion and maintenance of high levels of employment and real income and development of the productive resources of all members as primary objectives of economic policy.
- Promote exchange stability, maintain orderly exchange arrangements among members and avoid competitive exchange depreciation.
- Assist in the establishment of a multilateral system of payments in respect of current transactions between members and in the elimination of foreign exchange restrictions which hamper the growth of world trade.
- Give confidence to members by making the general resources of the Fund temporarily available to them under adequate safeguards, thus providing them with the opportunity to correct maladjustments in their balance of payments, without resorting to measures destructive of national or international prosperity.

- Shorten the duration and lessen the degree of disequilibrium in the international balances of payments of members.

IMF aims to prevent crises in the system by encouraging countries to adopt sound economic policies. As its name suggests, it is a fund that can be tapped by members needing temporary financing to address balance of payments problems. IMF works for global prosperity by promoting the balanced expansion of world trade through:

- balanced expansion of world trade
- stability of exchange rates
- avoidance of competitive devaluations
- orderly correction of balance of payments problems.

To serve these purposes, IMF:

- monitors economic and financial developments and policies in member countries and at global level
- gives policy advice to its members based on its more than 50 years' experience
- lends to member countries with balance of payments problems, not only to provide temporary financing but also to support adjustment and reform policies aimed at correcting the underlying problems
- provides governments and central banks of its member countries with technical assistance and training in its areas of expertise.

IMF helps member countries, in turn, by:

- reviewing and monitoring national and global economic and financial developments and advising members on their economic policies
- lending them hard currencies to support adjustment and reform policies designed to correct balance of payments problems and promote sustainable growth
- offering a wide range of technical assistance, as well as training for government and central bank officials, in its areas of expertise (www.imf.org).

As the only international agency whose mandated activities involve active dialogue with virtually every country on economic policies, IMF is the principal forum for discussing not only national economic policies in a global context but also issues important to the stability of the international monetary and financial system. These include countries' choice of exchange rate arrangements, avoidance of destabilising international capital flows and design of internationally recognised standards and codes for policies and institutions.

By working to strengthen the international financial system and accelerate progress toward reducing poverty, as well as promoting sound economic policies amongst all its member countries, IMF claims that it is helping make globalisation work for the benefit of all.

IMF was conceived in July 1944 at a UN conference held at Bretton Woods, New Hampshire (United States), when representatives of 45 governments agreed on a framework for economic co-operation designed to avoid a repetition of the disastrous economic policies that had contributed to the Great Depression of the 1930s. During that decade, as economic activity in the major industrial countries weakened, countries attempted to defend their economies by increasing restrictions on imports. But this worsened the downward spiral in world trade, output and employment. To conserve dwindling reserves of gold and foreign exchange, some countries curtailed their citizens' freedom to buy abroad, some devalued their currencies and some introduced complicated restrictions on citizens' freedom to hold foreign exchange. These fixes, however, also proved self-defeating and no country was able to maintain its competitive edge for long. Such policies devastated the international economy and world trade declined sharply, as did employment and living standards in many countries.

As the Second World War ended, leading allied countries considered various plans to restore order to international monetary relations and at the Bretton Woods conference the IMF emerged. Country representatives drew up the charter of an international institution to oversee the international monetary system and promote the elimination of exchange restrictions relating to trade in goods and services and stability of exchange rates. IMF came into existence in December 1945, when the first 29 countries signed its Articles of Agreement (Peet 2003).

The statutory purposes of the IMF today are the same as when they were formulated in 1944. Since then, the world has experienced unprecedented growth in real incomes. And although the benefits of growth have not flowed equally to all, either within or among nations, most countries have seen increases in prosperity that contrast starkly with the interwar period. Part of the explanation lies in improvements in the conduct of economic policy, including policies that have encouraged the growth of international trade and helped smooth the economic cycle of boom and bust. IMF has contributed to these developments.

In the decades since the Second World War, apart from rising prosperity, the world economy and monetary system have undergone other major changes; changes that have increased the importance and relevance of the purposes served by IMF. But these have also required IMF to adapt and reform. Rapid advances in technology and communications have contributed to the increasing international integration of markets and closer linkages among national economies. As a result financial crises, when they erupt, now tend to spread more rapidly among countries.

In such an increasingly integrated and interdependent world, any country's prosperity depends more than ever on both the economic performance of other countries and on the existence of an open and stable global economic environment. Equally, economic and financial policies that individual countries follow affect how well or how poorly the world trade and payments system operates. Globalisation thus calls for greater international co-operation, which in turn has increased the responsibilities of international institutions that organise such co-operation including IMF.

As the development of the world economy since 1945 has brought new challenges, the work of IMF has evolved and the institution has adapted to be able to continue serving its purposes effectively. Especially since the early 1990s, enormous economic challenges have been associated with globalisation and increasing international integration of markets and economies. These have included the need to deal with turbulence in emerging financial markets, notably in Asia and Latin America, help a number of countries make the transition from central planning to market-oriented systems and enter the global market economy, and promote economic growth and poverty reduction in the poorest countries at risk of being left behind by globalisation.

IMF has responded partly by strengthening the framework of rules and institutions of the international monetary and financial system and by enhancing its own contribution to the prevention and resolution of financial crises. It has also given new emphasis to the goals of enhancing economic growth and reducing poverty in the world's poorest countries. Reform is continuing.

The World Bank

The World Bank was created at the same 1944 Bretton Woods Conference as the IMF. Its 'dream is a world free of poverty' and its mission statement is (www.worldbank.org):

> To fight poverty with passion and professionalism for lasting results.
>
> To help people help themselves and their environment by providing resources, knowledge, building capacity, and forging partnerships in the public and private sectors.
>
> To be an excellent institution able to attract, excite, and nurture diverse and committed staff with exceptional skills who know how to listen and learn.

The stated principles of the World Bank are to be client-centred, accountable for quality results, dedicated to integrity and cost-effectiveness, inspired and innovative, and to work in partnership with others. The organisation espouses values of:

> personal honesty, integrity, commitment; working together in teams, with openness and trust; empowering others and respecting differences; encouraging risk-taking and responsibility; enjoying our work and our families.

The World Bank consists of members in over 180 countries, has 8,000 staff and is located in Washington DC in the United States, with country offices around the world. It is a development bank providing loans, policy advice, technical assistance and knowledge sharing services to low and middle income countries so as to reduce poverty. The Bank is one of the UN's specialised agencies and its member countries are collectively responsible for how the institution is financed and how its money is spent. Along with the rest of the development community, the World Bank centres its efforts on reaching the Millennium Development Goals (MDGs), agreed by UN members in 2002, which aims at sustainable poverty reduction around the world (Peet 2003).

The Bank promotes growth to create jobs and encourages people to take advantage of these opportunities. It is the world's largest external source of funding for education and Human Immunodeficiency Virus/Acquired Immune Deficiency Syndrome (HIV/AIDS) programmes. Amongst its other activities, the Bank:

- leads anti-corruption efforts
- supports debt relief
- funds biodiversity projects
- builds partnerships with other organisations
- brings clean water, electricity and transport to the poor
- involves civil society in every aspect of its work
- helps countries emerging from conflicts
- responds to the needs of poor people around the world.

In its work, the World Bank aims to bridge the divide between rich and poor nations, by turning rich country resources into poor country growth. With some of the world's largest sources of development assistance at its disposal, the Bank supports efforts of developing countries to build schools and health centres, provide water and electricity, fight disease and protect the environment.

The Bank consists of five closely associated institutions, all owned by member countries, with each institution playing a distinctive part in its mission to fight poverty and improve living standards in the developing world. The component parts of the World Bank 'Group' and their basic financial approaches are:

- International Bank for Reconstruction and Development (IBRD), which provides loans and development assistance to middle-income countries and creditworthy poorer countries. The IRBD obtains most of its funds through the sale of bonds in international capital markets.
- International Development Association (IDA), which provides interest-free loans to the poorest countries, by contributions from its wealthier members.
- International Finance Corporation (IFC), which promotes growth in developing countries by providing support to the private sector. In collaboration with other investors, the IFC invests in commercial enterprises through loans and equity financing.
- Multilateral Investment Guarantee Agency (MIGA), which encourages foreign investment in developing countries by providing guarantees to foreign investors against losses caused by non-commercial risks. The MIGA also provides advisory services to help governments attract private investments.
- International Centre for Settlement of Investment Disputes (ICSID), which helps promote international investment through conciliation and arbitration of disputes between foreign investors and host countries.

The MDGs, agreed by 189 nations at the UN Millennium Summit, embody an unprecedented level of consensus on what is needed for sustainable poverty reduction and the World Bank has a crucial role to play in this effort. The goals set specific targets towards which the entire development community should work. The breadth of this challenge requires the Bank, and the wider international development community, to scale up the impact of their work to achieve the needed development results. Its goals are:

- eradicate extreme poverty and hunger
- achieve universal primary education
- promote gender equality and empower women
- reduce child mortality
- combat HIV/AIDS, malaria and other diseases
- ensure environmental sustainability
- develop a global partnership for development.

Building on the consensus of how to achieve sustainable poverty reduction, a new global partnership has been forged, with clear roles for the development community. Developed countries have the obligation to reduce barriers to trade, help developing countries address constraints preventing them from fully realising the benefits from trade and investment flows, and ease debt burdens. Developing countries, in turn, have to focus on good governance, sound policies and robust institutions. To match the commitment to progress on policy reforms in developing countries, industrialised countries also need to ensure that adequate aid resources are available. The World Bank, as a partner in this scaling up effort, has a unique role to play, by using its knowledge and financial resources to play a catalytic role in the development process. It is concentrating on twin pillars of its strategic framework: building the climate for investment, jobs and sustainable growth and investing in and empowering poor people to participate in development. These are critical elements in achieving sustainable poverty reduction and in helping clients meet the MDGs.

World Trade Organisation (WTO)

The WTO's overriding objective is to promote globalisation and help international trade flow smoothly, freely, fairly and predictably by:

- administering WTO trade agreements
- acting as a forum for trade negotiations
- settling trade disputes
- monitoring national trade policies
- assisting developing countries in trade policy issues, through technical assistance and training programmes
- co-operating with other international organisations.

The WTO has nearly 150 members, which account for over 97 per cent of world trade. Around 30 others are negotiating membership. Decisions are made by the entire membership, typically by consensus. A majority vote is also possible but it has never been used in the WTO and was extremely rare under its predecessor, the General Agreement on Tariffs and Trade (GATT). WTO agreements are ratified in all members' parliaments.

The WTO Secretariat, based in Geneva, has over 500 staff and is headed by a director general. It does not have branch offices outside Geneva. Since members themselves take decisions, the Secretariat does not have the decision-making role that other international bureaucracies have been given. The Secretariat's main duties are to supply technical support for the various councils and committees and the ministerial conferences, provide technical assistance for developing countries, analyse world trade patterns and explain WTO affairs to the public and media. The Secretariat also provides some forms of legal assistance in dispute settlement and advises governments wishing to become members of the WTO (Peet 2003).

WTO was established in1995 and is one of the newest international organisations. As successor to GATT, which was established after the Second World War, WTO, whilst still a young organisation, has built upon the multilateral trading system that was originally set up under GATT over 50 years ago. In dealing with the global rules of trade between nations and ensuring that trade flows as smoothly and freely as possible, WTO claims that consumers and producers know that they can enjoy secure supplies and greater choice of the finished products, components, raw materials and services that they use. Producers and exporters, in turn, know that foreign markets will remain open to them. The result is a more prosperous, peaceful and accountable economic world.

The core of the WTO is the multilateral trading system, made up of WTO agreements, negotiated and signed by a large majority of the world's trading nations. These agreements are the legal ground rules for international commerce. Essentially, they are contracts, guaranteeing member countries important trade rights. They also bind governments to keep their trade policies within agreed limits to everybody's benefit. The agreements were negotiated and signed by governments but their purpose is to help producers of goods and services, exporters and importers conduct their business, with the goal of improving the welfare of the peoples of member countries.

The system was developed through a series of trade negotiations, or rounds, held under GATT. The first rounds dealt mainly with tariff reductions but later negotiations included other areas such as anti-dumping and non-tariff measures. The Uruguay Round 1986–1994 led to the creation of WTO. However, negotiations did not end there. Some continued after the end of the Uruguay Round. The current set of agreements was the outcome of the 1986–1994 Uruguay Round negotiations, which included a major revision of the original GATT. GATT is now WTO's principal rulebook on trade in goods. The Uruguay Round also created new rules for dealing with trade in services, relevant aspects of intellectual property, dispute settlement and trade policy reviews. The complete set runs to about 60 agreements and separate commitments (called schedules) made by individual members in specific areas such as lower customs duty rates and opening up services. Through these agreements, WTO members operate a non-discriminatory trading system that spells out their rights and their obligations. Each country receives guarantees that its exports will be treated fairly and consistently in other countries' markets. Each promises to do the same for imports into its own market. The system also gives developing countries some flexibility in implementing their commitments.

Any disputes over trade are channelled into WTO's dispute settlement process, where the focus is on interpreting agreements and commitments and how to ensure that the trade policies of countries conform with them. In this way, the risk of disputes spilling over into political or military conflict is reduced. By lowering trade barriers, it is argued, the WTO's system also breaks down other barriers between peoples and nations.

Over three-quarters of WTO members are developing or least developed countries. All WTO agreements contain special provision for them. These include longer time periods to implement agreements and commitments, measures to increase their trading opportunities, provisions requiring all WTO members to safeguard their trade interests and support to help them build the infrastructure for WTO work, handle disputes and implement technical standards. The 2001 Ministerial Conference in Doha set out tasks, including negotiations, for a wide range of issues concerning developing countries. Some people call the new negotiations the Doha Development Round. Before that, in 1997, a high-level meeting on trade initiatives and technical assistance for least developed countries resulted in an 'integrated framework' involving six intergovernmental agencies, to help least developed countries increase their ability to trade and some additional preferential market access agreements.

A WTO committee on trade and development, assisted by a subcommittee on least developed countries, looks at developing countries' special needs. Its responsibility includes implementation of the agreements, technical co-operation and increased participation of developing countries in the global trading system. The WTO organises around 100 technical co-operation missions to developing countries annually and holds on average three trade policy courses each year in Geneva for government officials. Regional seminars are held regularly in all regions of the world, with special emphasis on African countries. Training courses are also organised in Geneva for officials from countries in transition from centrally planned to market economies. The WTO has set up reference centres in over 100 trade ministries and regional organisations in capitals of developing and least developed countries. These provide computers and World Wide Web access to enable ministry officials to keep abreast of events in the WTO in Geneva, through online access to the WTO's immense database of official documents and other material.

(i) Outline the functions of the WTO, IMF and OECD.

(ii) What evidence is there to support the view that major international organisations are furthering the Americanisation of the global economy?

IMPLICATIONS FOR ORGANISATIONS AND P&D PROFESSIONALS

Global markets have become an increasingly significant part of the business context over the past two decades. Globalisation is not an uncontested phenomenon, however. It is a problematic one, which is difficult to objectify, define and categorise with precision. Some commentators emphasise its benevolent consequences for organisations and societies; others highlight its dysfunctional aspects. For some, globalisation is a neutral phenomenon rooted in the pragmatic behaviour of those engaged in mutually beneficial business exchanges in the marketplace. Others see it as an ideological construct, associated with the search for hegemony in the international economy by the developed world – led by the United States and some international organisations such as OECD, IMF, the World Bank and WTO. Not all economic life is affected by world markets, however, since local, geographically discrete markets persist. Nor does it mean the inevitable convergence of national cultures and the withering away of sovereign states, since globalisation affects different types of market economy in different ways. But, whatever its impact on specific organisations, managers in both the private and public sectors cannot escape the logic and organisational consequences of economic globalisation. These include increasingly powerful MNCs, growth in international market exchanges and migrations of people in developing countries seeking new lifestyles in the developed world.

In the private sector, globalisation encourages companies to search continuously for new products and new markets to remain competitive. Faced with increased uncertainties and change in the marketplace, the corporate sector invests heavily in information and communication technologies. Further, in seeking more 'added value' for their shareholders and investors, companies engage in takeovers, mergers and joint ventures and look for investment opportunities overseas. There are continued pressures to raise productivity and performance, improve the quality of their products or services and increase profits. The public sector, in turn, becomes more like the private sector in the ways in which it is organised and managed, with demands by politicians and taxpayers for increased efficiency, more effectiveness and better value for money. The emphasis becomes one of 'good management' or 'best practice management' rather than adherence to standardised rules and procedures. The boundaries between the public and private sectors become blurred and are redrawn.

The implications of globalisation for governments are equally far-reaching. One is that the redistributive functions of the welfare state are challenged and weakened. In order to promote business opportunities, governments deregulate labour, product and financial markets and encourage labour market flexibility. A more limited notion of citizenship emerges, rooted in what Galbraith (1993) calls 'a culture of contentment'. In Anglo-Saxon states, demands for lower taxation and a strong individualist culture become entrenched. Such forces, in turn, affect the ways in which public organisations are structured and managed.

Decisions taken within EU institutions also affect business and managerial policies. Managers have to be aware of EU regulations and directives affecting their operations, especially in employing and managing people and managing competition. Some try to identify the funds and resources available to their organisations and the procedures for applying for financial support, such as the farming community. MEPs are an important source of information, as are European Commission offices in member states within the EU. As the political power of the EU increases, the need for organisations to develop strategies in response to this power in areas such as P&D, consumer protection and environmental protection, and to establish links with relevant European bodies that can benefit them, are increasingly necessary. Other strategies for organisations include being represented on relevant committees, contacting employer groups in Europe and creating links with key European decision makers. Education and training programmes to update understanding of European issues are also provided by companies for their managers and other staff.

The external forces of global markets, EU institutions and other international bodies are complex and all organisations, private, public and voluntary, have to deal with the business consequences arising from each of them for themselves. These forces induce uncertainty and turbulence for organisations and for the managers leading them. Developing appropriate strategic, competitive and market responses to these forces are a necessary condition for organisational survival and growth in the contemporary world.

CONCLUSION

This chapter examines the origins, characteristics and consequences of the socio-economic phenomenon of globalisation. Globalisation, which has accelerated since the breakup of the Soviet Union in 1991, has a number of features. These include increased integration of individual economies, a rise in world trade, an impact by MNCs on ordinary people and movement of large sums of money in and out of national economies.

Those supporting globalisation claim that increasing world trade makes everyone better off, that global phenomena like the World Wide Web help those who are poor and that international links encourage countries to respect human rights. Opponents, on the other hand, claim that globalisation leads to exploitation of the world's poor, its workers and the environment, and it makes it easier for rich companies to act with less accountability and national cultures become overpowered by 'Americanisation'. Globalisation thus promotes the dominant values of 'big business' and the corporate sector. In this respect, several of the largest US brands (eg McDonald's and Starbucks) have faced particular opposition.

Responses to globalisation include expansion of the EU and other regional economic groupings around the world. The EU with its 25 member states, and its population of some 400 million, is the largest of these. It has created a single currency and a dynamic single market in which people, services, goods and capital are allowed to move freely. The EU strives to ensure, through social progress and fair competition, that as many people as possible enjoy the benefits of its single market.

Finally, some major institutional players in the contemporary global economy, most of which were created at the end of the Second World War, have played important parts in shaping the business environment in recent years. However, they have been criticised for being too free market in their economics and for encouraging neo-liberal economic policies, privatisation and tax-cutting initiatives, rather than Keynesian, interventionist policies, around the global economy.

USEFUL READING

CERNY, P. (1995) Globalisation and the changing logic of collective action. *International Organisation*, No 49, pp595–625.

COWLES, M. and DINAN, D. (eds). (2004) *Developments in the European Union*. Basingstoke: Palgrave.

DINAN, D. (2004) *Europe recast: A history of the European Union*. Basingstoke: Palgrave.

EUROPEAN COMMISSION. (2004a) *Key facts and figures about the European Union*. Luxembourg: Office of Official Publications of the European Commission.

EUSEPI, G. and SCHNEIDER, F. (2004) *Changing institutions in the European Union: A public choice Perspective*. Cheltenham: Elgar.

FUKUYAMA, F. (1992) *The end of history and the last man*. London: Hamish Hamilton.

GEORGE, S. (1998) *An awkward partner: Britain in the European Community*. Oxford: Oxford University Press.

GRAY, J. (1995) *False dawn: The delusions of global capitalism*. London: Routledge.

HAMPDEN-TURNER, C. and TROMPENAARS, F. (1995) *The seven cultures of capitalism*. New York: Piatkus.

HARDT, M. and NEGRI, A. (2000) *Empire*. Cambridge, Mass.: Harvard University Press.

HELD, D., GOLDBLATT, D. and PARRATON, J. (1997) *Global transformations*. Cambridge: Polity Press. 1997.

HERTZ, N. (2001) *The silent takeover: Global capitalism and the death of democracy*. London: Heinemann.

HUTTON, W. (1995) *The state we're in*. London: Cape.

HUTTON, W. (2001) *The world we're in*. London: Little Brown.

KONTRAKOU, V. (ed.). (2004) *Contemporary issues and debates in EU policy*. Manchester: Manchester University Press.

MANN, M. (1997) Has globalisation ended the rise and rise of the nation state? *Review of International Political Economy*. No 4, pp 472–496.

MONBIOT, G. (2001) *The captive state: The corporate takeover of Britain*. London: Pan Books.

NUGENT, N. (ed.). (2004) *European Union enlargement*. Basingstoke: Palgrave.

OECD (2005) *This is the OECD*. Paris: OECD.

OHMAE, K. (1995) *The end of the nation-state*. London: HarperCollins.

PEET, R. (2003) *Unholy trinity: The IMF, World Bank, and WTO*. London: Zed.

SOROS, G. (1995) *Soros on Soros*. NY: Wiley.

SOROS, G. (2000) *Reforming global capitalism*. New York: Little Brown.

STIGLITZ, J. (2001) *Globalisation and its discontents*. London: Penguin.

WARLEIGH, A. (2004) *European Union: The basics*. London: Routledge.

Demographic Trends

INTRODUCTION

Demography is the statistical study of populations and is concerned with the size, distribution and composition of the population of a country, region, area, or on a world-wide basis. Data are obtained through census returns, records of births, deaths, marriages, divorce, immigration, emigration and labour force analyses. Demography charts changes and trends in population and seeks explanations and causes of these changes. The demographic structure of a country clearly has implications for its economy. The size and age structure of the population, for example, affect the actual and potential availability of labour and demand for goods and services. They also affect public policy issues, such as healthcare, education, pension provision and social services. Governments at national and local levels need projections of population on which to base their policy decisions.

The size of a population is a dynamic social variable, as it changes over time. Its composition and distribution also change as people are born, die, move from one area to another, enter or leave the country. Because of the difficulty of keeping track of these changes, the size of a population at any one point in time is only an approximation. Demographic data are usually historic and based on samples, extrapolated to provide whole population statistics. It is estimated that the margin of error is plus or minus 4 per cent. The accuracy of such data requires careful definition of persons, places and time. For most analytical purposes, it is sufficient to know how many people are in a particular place at a given time. But it is also necessary to know about changes in population over time and their causes. This chapter indicates the main demographic trends within the United Kingdom in the early twenty-first century and considers their implications for markets, organisations and government. It does not provide depth of statistical detail, and is selective in its subject matter, since its aim is to indicate general trends and tendencies in demographic structures rather than provide sophisticated analyses.

THE POPULATION PROFILE OF THE UNITED KINGDOM

There are now more people living in the United Kingdom than ever before. In 2002, the population was just below 60 million at 59.2 million. This is 3.3 million more than in 1971. The populations of England, Wales and Northern Ireland all grew between 1971 and 2002, while the population of Scotland remained fairly stable. Population projections suggest that the UK population will reach 62.4 million by 2021, with longer-term projections indicating that the population will peak at almost 64 million around 2040 and will then start to fall. Around 19,000 more boys than girls are born each year but there are more females overall in the total population than men. In 2002, there were 30.3 million females compared with 28.9 million males – or 1.4 million more females than males. In addition to sex, the composition of a population can be analysed by age, ethnicity, region, household, occupation, education, and religious affiliation. The main features of these are summarised below (Office for National Statistics 2003a).

Age

The age structure of the population reflects past trends in births, deaths and migration and the number of people in any age group depends on how many people are born in a particular period and how long they survive. It is also affected by the numbers and ages of migrants moving into and out of the country. Between 1971 and 2002, the age structure of the population changed. The number of children aged under 16 fell by 18 per cent, while there was a 27 per cent increase in the number of people aged 65 and over. In other words, the United Kingdom has an ageing population. Between 1971 and 2001, the proportion of males aged 65 and over rose from some 11 per cent of the population to about 14 per cent, whilst that for women rose from some 16 per cent to about 18 per cent. For the years 1971–2001, there was an increase of 30 per cent of men aged 65 and over and 13 per cent of women. There have also been substantial changes in the age composition of the older population. Since 1981, there has been a declining proportion of both men and women aged 65 to 74 and a growth in the proportion of those aged 85 and over. This group of over 85s represented 1.1 per cent of men and 2.7 per cent of women in the population in 2001 (Arber and Ginn 2004).

The age structure of the population varies across different ethnic groups. In general, minority ethnic groups have a younger age structure than the White group. In 2001, 19 per cent of the White group were under 16, compared to 50 per cent of minority ethnic groups. The White group had the oldest age structure of all, with one-in-four people aged 65 and over. Among non-White groups, Black Caribbean's had the largest proportion of people aged 65 and over (11 per cent), reflecting the first large-scale migration of non-White groups into Britain in the 1950s. Bangladeshi, other Black and Pakistani groups had young age structures, with 38 per cent of Bangladeshi and other black groups and 35 per cent of the Pakistani groups being under 16. These patterns were influenced by past immigration to the United Kingdom. Much recent growth in the UK's minority ethnic population has been through children born in the United Kingdom. Progressive ageing of the non-White population is expected in the future but this will depend on fertility levels, mortality rates and future net migration.

How is practice in pension provision affected by an ageing population? Justify your response.

Ethnicity

Table 5.1 shows the UK population by ethnic group in 2001. The largest group was the White group, which made up 92.1 per cent of the population. Ethnic minorities accounted for the remaining 7.9

Table 5.1 UK population by ethnic group 2001

Group	Numbers	Per cent of total population	Per cent of non-white population
White	54,153,898	92.1	–
Mixed	677,117	1.2	14.6
Indian	1,053,411	1.8	22.7
Pakistani	747,285	1.3	16.1
Bangladeshi	283,063	0.5	6.1
Other Asian	247,664	0.4	5.3
All Asian	2,331,423	4.0	50.3
Black, Caribbean	565,876	1.0	12.2
Black, African	485,277	0.8	12.2
Black, Other	97,585	0.2	2.1
All Black	1,148,738	2.0	24.8
Chinese	247,403	0.4	5.3
Other ethnic groups	230,615	0.4	5.0
All minority ethnic population	4,635,296	7.9	100.0

per cent of the population. The largest minority was the All Asian group (4.0 per cent of the total population), followed by the All Black group (2.0 per cent). The Indian, Pakistani and mixed groups were the next largest subgroups (1.8 per cent, 1.3 per cent and 1.2 per cent respectively), followed by the Black Caribbean, Black African and Bangladeshi groups (1.0 per cent, 0.8 per cent and 0.5 per cent respectively).

> Access the last census data for your local area and identify and analyse its age and ethnic distributions.

Region

Regional populations are affected by people relocating within the United Kingdom, as well as births, deaths and international migration flows. During the twentieth century, there was a movement of people from the coal, shipbuilding and steel industry areas in the north of England, Scotland and Wales to the south of England and the Midlands, where many light industries and service industries were based. In 2002, Wales gained 14,000 people from migration within the United Kingdom and Scotland gained over 4,000 people, whilst England experienced a net loss of more than 18,000 people. Within the regions of England, the greatest net loss due to internal migration in 2002 was in London, where nearly 108,000 people moved to other parts of the United Kingdom. Over a third of people leaving London for elsewhere in the United Kingdom moved to the South East region and a quarter to the East of England. The South West experienced the highest net gain of 35,000 people, with 34 per cent moving from the South East and a further 17 per cent moving from London.

Non-White ethnic groups are more likely to live in England than other parts of the United Kingdom. In 2001, they made up 9 per cent of the population of England, compared to 2 per cent in Scotland and Wales and less than 1 per cent in Northern Ireland. They were also concentrated in the largest urban centres, with nearly half (45 per cent) living in the London Region where they constituted 29 per cent of that population. Seventy-eight per cent of Black Africans and 61 per cent of Black Caribbeans lived in London, along with 54 per cent of all Bangladeshis. This contrasts with less than 2 per cent of all non-White ethnic groups living in the North East and the South West of England respectively. Other areas of ethnic minority concentrations, particularly Pakistanis, were the West Midlands, Yorkshire, Humberside and the North West (Office for National Statistics 2003b).

Household

The types of household and families in which people live are becoming more diverse, reflecting changes in partnership formation and dissolution of relationships. People live in a variety of household types over their lifetime. They may leave their parental home, form partnerships, marry and have children. They may also experience separation and divorce, lone-parenthood and for-mation of new partnerships, leading to new households and second families. People are also spending more time living on their own either before forming relationships or after a relationship has ceased or broken down.

One of the most notable changes in household composition since 1971 has been the increase in the number of one person households. The proportion of one person households has increased from 18 per cent in 1971 to 29 per cent in 2003. The rate of change has not been uniform across all categories of those living alone. The largest increase has occurred among men under 65. The proportion of one person households comprising men under 65 was nearly 11 per cent in 2002 and more than three times the proportion in 1971. The proportion of households consisting of women aged 65 and over living alone was around 9 per cent in 2002. This proportion has remained fairly stable since the beginning of the 1970s. Over the same period, the proportion of households comprising of women under 65 living alone has increased by over 2 per cent. The increases, in part, reflect the decline in marriage and rise in separation and divorce, as well as the increase in the age at which people first married.

There have been considerable changes to family structures since the early 1970s. Children are living in an increasing variety of circumstances. Due to changes in cohabitation, marriage and divorce patterns, children may experience a range of different family structures during their lives. Parents separating can result in lone-parent families and new relationships can create step families.

The pattern of partnership formation has changed since the early 1970s but despite the decrease in the overall numbers of people marrying, it is still the most common form of partnership for men and women. Since 1971, the number of marriages in the United Kingdom has fallen from around 459,000 to just over 286,000 in 2001. The number of divorces increased from just under 80,000 in 1971, peaking at 180,000 in 1993. The number of divorces then fell by 13 per cent to 157,000 in 2001, when around half the population was married

Asian households are larger than any other ethnic group, with an average of 4.5 people per household in 2001, compared with the average White and Black Caribbean households of 2.3

people. Thirty-eight per cent of Black Caribbean households and 31 per cent of White households contained only one person. This contrasts with only 9 per cent of Bangladeshi households containing only one person. Seventy-four per cent of Bangladeshi households contained at least one child, compared with 28 per cent of White households. Asians are the least likely to be lone parent households at 10 per cent. Black Caribbean and Black African households are the highest at 48 per cent and 52 per cent respectively, with White households at 22 per cent. Households containing more than one family with dependent children are most likely to be headed by people from the Asian groups (Office for National Statistics 2004a).

A colleague has heard that government is expecting a growth of 5 million in the number of single households over the next 20 years. He is interested to hear your views about the reasons and consequences of this. What would you say and why?

Occupation

There are considerable differences in the socio-economic structure of men and women across the United Kingdom. In 2003, higher managers and professionals, small employers, the self-employed and the lower supervisory and technical class were all more likely to be male than female. Around 7 in 10 people in each of these categories were male. Women were more likely than men to be in the intermediate class, where more than 7 in 10 people were female. There were also variations in the proportions in each socio-economic classification across the regions. In 2003, the proportion of people working in managerial and professional occupations was highest in the South East and lowest in the North East.

Amongst ethnic minorities, Pakistanis and Chinese in employment are more likely to be self-employed than those in other ethnic groups with 22 per cent and 19 per cent respectively in 2002. Those most likely to be found in the professions are Indian, Chinese and non-British Whites, ranging between 17 and 20 per cent, which contrasts with only 11 per cent of Whites who are professional workers. Black Caribbeans, Bangladeshis and Pakistanis have the lowest proportions in professional occupations.

In 2002, two-thirds of Bangladeshis and half of Chinese men in employment were found in the distribution, hotel and restaurant industry, compared with 16 per cent of Whites. Pakistanis were most likely to work in the transport and communication industry. Bangladeshi and Chinese women were also concentrated in the distribution, hotel and restaurant industry, where 40 per cent of them were employed. Half of Black Caribbean women worked in public administration, education or the health sectors, which was the highest proportion for any ethnic group.

One in six Pakistani men were cab drivers or chauffeurs, compared to 1 in 100 White men. Two in five Bangladeshi men were either cooks or waiters, compared to 1 in 100 White men. The proportion of Indian men working as doctors (5 per cent) was almost 12 times higher than for White men. Among women, 1 in 10 Black African women were working as nurses, compared to 3 in 100 White women. Indian women were five times more likely to be working as machinists, packers, bottlers, canners and fillers than White British women (Office for National Statistics 2004b).

Education

For increasing numbers of people, experience of education is no longer confined to compulsory schooling from 5 to 16. Early learning and participation in pre-school education are seen as being important for building a foundation for future learning and most people continue in full-time education beyond school-leaving age. Many people return to education later in their lives and qualifications attained at school are increasingly supplemented by further education and training to equip them with the skills required by a modern labour market.

In 2002/2003 there were over 34,500 schools in the United Kingdom, with over 10 million pupils. State schools, not including special schools, were attended by over 9 million or 92 per cent of all pupils. Six per cent of pupils attended one of 2,400 non-maintained or 'private schools'. This proportion has remained unchanged since the mid-1990s, although there has been a rise in the number of pupils within them. One per cent of pupils attended one of 1,500 special schools in 2002/2003.

Following compulsory education up to the age of 16, young people can continue in full-time education, go into training or seek employment. However, not everyone working towards a qualification beyond the age of 16 will have worked their way continuously through the various levels of education. Whilst half of people of working age studying towards a qualification in the United Kingdom were aged between 16 and 24 in 2003, a fifth were aged 40 and over. In 2003, around a fifth of people of working age studying general certificate of education (GCE) advanced level or equivalent were over 25, as were nearly half of those studying for a degree or equivalent. There were nearly 5.4 million students in further education in 2001/2002, 58 per cent of whom were female. There were more than four times as many female further education students as in 1970/1971 but only around twice as many males. The majority of students in further education were part timers. Slightly more men than women studied full-time but far more women than men studied part-time.

There have also been substantial increases in the number of students in higher education over the last 30 years. There were six times as many women and two and a half as many men students in higher education in 2001/2002 than in 1970/1971. In 2001/2002, there were nearly 2.3 million students in higher education, 56 per cent of whom were female.

In 2001/2002, only 8 per cent of Black Caribbean men and 7 per cent of Pakistani and Bangladeshi men had degrees but 18 per cent of Indians and 20 per cent of Chinese had this qualification. Pakistanis and Bangladeshis were the most likely to be unqualified. Forty-eight per cent of Bangladeshi women and 40 per cent of men had no qualification and 40 per cent of Pakistani women and 28 per cent of men lacked any qualification (Department for Education and Skills 2003).

> How do you account for differences in the educational performance of different ethnic groups within the United Kingdom?

Religion

In the 2001 Census, 77 per cent of people in England and Wales, 67 per cent in Scotland and 86 per cent in Northern Ireland stated that they had a religion. Around 7 in 10 people in England and Wales said that they belonged to the Christian faith. These included 70 per cent of Black and 52 per cent of mixed ethnicity. After Christianity, the largest groups were Pakistani Muslims (658,000) and Indian Hindus (467,000) followed by Indian Sikhs (301,000), Bangladeshi Muslims (260,000) and White Jews (252,000). The Indian ethnic group are religiously diverse and include Hindus, Sikhs and Muslims while the Pakistani and Bangladeshi communities are more homogenous with

92 per cent of them Muslims. Fifteen per cent of people in England and Wales said they did not belong to any religion and nearly 8 per cent did not state their religion. It was notable that half of all Chinese people and 25 per cent of people from mixed ethnic backgrounds stated they had no religion but fewer than 1 in 200 Pakistanis and Bangladeshis agreed.

Can you infer from these statistics that the United Kingdom is not a secular society? Justify your conclusion.

POPULATION CHANGE

The rate of population change over time depends upon the net natural change – the difference between the numbers of births and deaths – and the net effect of people migrating to and from the country. Natural change is an important factor in population growth in the United Kingdom, although since the1980s net immigration has had an increased influence. Projections suggest that this trend will continue, with net immigration accounting for over half of population change by 2021.

In accounting for population changes, demographers identify the immediate causes as the relationship between births, deaths and migratory patterns. Changes in the total population of a country, therefore, consist of total births minus total deaths, while migratory changes consist of the number of immigrants minus total emigrants. Where both components cause a positive change or one causes a positive change, whilst the other remains stable, total population rises. Where both components cause a negative change or one causes a negative change and the other remains stable, then total population falls. Where natural change in both components remains the same or a change in one is offset by a change in the other, then total population tends to stabilise.

Births

There were 668,800 live births in the United Kingdom in 2002, 37 per cent fewer than in 1901. Fertility patterns influence the size of households and families and the age structure of the population. There was a downward trend in the fertility rate during the twentieth century, with 57 live births per 1,000 women aged 15–44 at the end of the century, compared with 115 live births per 1,000 women aged 15–44 at the start of the century.

The two World Wars had a major impact on births. There was a fall in number of births during the First World War, followed by a post-war 'baby boom', with births peaking at 1.1 million in 1920. The numbers of births then decreased and remained low during the inter-war years and the Second World War. A second baby boom followed the Second World War, with a further baby boom in the 1960s when women born in the baby boom after the Second World War reached childbearing age. In the mid-1970s, the number of births fell to similar levels as the number of deaths. There was a mini-boom in births in the 1980s and early 1990s before numbers began falling again. Projections suggest that the number of births will remain relatively constant over the next 40 years, ranging from 660,000 to 710,000 per year.

Fertility patterns also vary by age. In general, fertility rates for women aged 30 and over have increased since the 1980s, while those for women aged under 30 have declined. In 2002, the fertility rate for women aged 25 to 29 was still the highest but only slightly greater than the rate for the 30 to 34 age group which, since 1992, has exceeded that for those aged 20 to 24. Increased female participation in education and the labour market, and greater choice and effectiveness of contraception, have encouraged the trend towards later childbearing and smaller families (Office for National Statistics 2003c).

Throughout most of Western Europe, teenage birth rates have fallen rapidly since the 1970s. However, in the United Kingdom, rates have remained at 1980s level or above. In 2001, the United Kingdom had the highest rate of live births to teenage girls in the EU, with an average of 29 live births per 1,000 girls aged 15–19. This was nearly 44 per cent higher than Portugal, the country with the next highest rate. Sweden and Italy had the lowest rates at around seven live births per 1,000 girls aged 15–19 (United Nations 2004).

Deaths

The number of deaths has fluctuated around 600,000 people over the last century, with 608,000 registered deaths in 2002. It is projected that the number of deaths will increase as the number of people born in the baby boom after the Second World War begins to reach advanced ages. The number of deaths is expected to exceed the number of births from around 2029. Although the number of deaths each year remained relatively stable over the last century, death rates fell considerably. Rising standards of living and developments in medical science and technology help explain the decline in death rates. Between 1971 and 2002, the death rate for all males fell by 17 per cent, while the death rate for all females fell by 4 per cent. Infant mortality rates fell by 70 per cent during this period.

Large improvements in life expectancy at birth have been seen over the past century for both males and females. In 1901, males born in the United Kingdom could expect to live to around 45 years of age and females to around 49. By 2002, male life expectancy at birth had risen to almost 76 years and for females to just over 80 years. It was not, however, until the late twentieth century that life expectancy for adults showed any significant improvement and in recent years it has been the increase in life expectancy among older adults that has been particularly dramatic. For example, life expectancy for men aged 60 increased by 4.5 years between 1971 and 2001, compared with an increase of only 1.6 years between 1911 and 1971.

Over the past 30 years, circulatory diseases, including heart disease and strokes, have remained the most common cause of death among males and females of all ages but they have also shown by far the greatest decline. In 1972, death rates from circulatory diseases were 7,100 per million males and 4,400 per million females. By 2002, death rates had fallen by over half for both sexes to 3,200 per million males and 2,000 per million females, with cancer now accounting for about a quarter of all deaths in the United Kingdom (Chief Medical Officer 2003).

Migration

Migration flows influence the size, growth and location of the population. In the United Kingdom, the pattern of people entering and leaving the country changed over the twentieth century. There was a net loss due to international emigration during the first four decades of the century. However, since the 1950s there have been several waves of immigration. During the 1950s and 1960s, people came from the Caribbean. In the 1970s, people from the Indian subcontinent migrated to meet the labour market shortage for unskilled and semi-skilled workers. During the 1990s, people migrated to the United Kingdom from not only the old and new commonwealth countries but also mainland Europe, as the single market for labour encouraged cross border movement. During the 1950s and 1960s, there was emigration from the United Kingdom to Canada, Australia, New Zealand and other Commonwealth countries, which largely offset the inward flows of population. These patterns of emigration and immigration have changed since the

1980s. This is partly because of the EU and partly because of open markets in education and not least because of the increase in the number of refugees and asylum seekers.

In 2002, an estimated 153,000 more people arrived to live for at least a year in the United Kingdom than left to live elsewhere. The number of immigrants increased from 480,000 in 2001 to 513,000 in 2002. There were 359,000 emigrants in 2002, 51,000 more than in 2001. Net international immigration is projected to remain at a relatively high level in the near future.

In 2000, there were nearly 412,000 Irish nationals living in the United Kingdom, accounting for just under half of all EU nationals living here. Nationals from Italy and France each accounted for around 1 in 10. There were nearly 525,000 UK nationals living within the EU in 2002. Over 1 in 5 of these lived in Germany, with almost as many living in Spain. Nearly all other overseas nationals wishing to live permanently in the United Kingdom require Home Office acceptance for settlement. The number accepted for settlement increased by 7,600 to 116,000 between 2001 and 2002 (Eurostat 2003).

Asylum-related settlement grants rose sharply in 1999 and 2000. This was due to a change in the rules reducing the qualifying periods for people granted asylum and exceptional leave to remain, effectively increasing the number of people eligible for settlement. Of grants of settlement in 2002, 40 per cent were to Asian nationals and a further 34 per cent to African nationals. The fall in grants in 2001 was due mainly to a fall in acceptances of African nationals. They fell by 29 per cent from 2000 and then rose by 23 per cent in 2002. The number of people seeking asylum varies from year to year, although the total number of asylum applications, including dependants, to EU countries remained relatively steady between1999 and 2002. In 2002, the United Kingdom received 103,100 applications. This was 11,500 more than in 2001, a rise of 13 per cent. Belgium, Denmark, Germany, Italy, Spain and the Netherlands each recorded falls in applications between 2001 and 2002.

When the relative size of the countries' populations are taken into account, the United Kingdom ranked sixth in terms of asylum seekers in 2002, one place higher than in 2001. It had a rate of 1.7 asylum seekers per 1,000 of the population. Austria had the highest rate at 4.9 per 1,000 of the population, an increase of 32 per cent since 2001.The countries from which people arrive to claim asylum in the United Kingdom vary with world events. Iraqi asylum applications increased from nearly 6,700 in 2001 to over 14,500 in 2002. In 2002, large numbers of asylum seekers also came from Afghanistan, Somalia and Zimbabwe, which were areas with escalations in internal conflicts (Home Office 2003).

(i) Why have birth rates declined across much of western Europe since the 1970s?

(ii) Government forecasts estimate that the UK population will increase to 65 million (from about 59 million) by 2031, with most growth being concentrated in the South East. What factors are contributing to this increase and what are the main implications of this projection for:

(a) employing organisations

(b) government?

THE WORKING POPULATION

The working population, also known as the labour force or economically active population, consists of those people aged 16 and over who are employees, self-employed or participants in government training programmes plus the unemployed, looking for work. The labour force participation rate is the percentage of the population in a given group that is economically active. Most people spend a large part of their lives in the labour force, so their experience of the world of work has an important impact on their lives and attitudes. The proportion of time spent in the labour force, however, has been falling. Young people are remaining longer in education and older people, due to increases in longevity, are spending more years in retirement. A counter trend is that more women than ever are in paid employment and they tend to spend longer in work than in the past. Employment is increasingly in the service industries, whilst employment in manufacturing continues to fall (Gallie *et al* 1998).

People in employment

There are now more people in employment than at any other time in the post-war period and most working age households are 'work-rich'. These are households that include at least one person of working age and where all the people of working age are in employment. There were 11 million work-rich households in 2003, an increase of just over 800,000 more than in 1998. Work-rich households, as a proportion of all working age households, rose from 50 per cent in 1992 to 58 per cent in 2003. Around 16 per cent of working age households in 2003 was still workless. These were households where at least one person was of working age but no one was in employment. Although this proportion was virtually the same as in 1984, it rose during the early 1990s, peaking at 19 per cent in 1996, but has been decreasing gradually since then. Among lone parent households with dependent children, the proportion that was workless in 2003 was much higher at 43 per cent. This proportion had peaked in the early 1990s at 54 per cent.

The proportion of the working age population in employment remained fairly stable during the 1960s and 1970s. However, trends in the overall rate masked large differences for men and women, with the rate for men falling and the rate for women rising. While the economic cycle has affected the rates over all periods, there has been no sign of a long-run change in employment rates. The trend in employment rates for men has fluctuated between 78 per cent in 1984 and 79 per cent in 2003, with a peak of 82 per cent in 1990. This was followed by a low of 75 per cent in 1993. For women, employment rates have generally been rising from 59 per cent in 1984 to 70 per cent in 2003. As with men, the proportion of women in employment has followed the economic cycle. The difference in the employment rates between males and females was 19 per cent in 1984 but had fallen to 10 per cent in 2003.

Jobs density is an indicator of labour demand and is defined as the total number of filled jobs in an area divided by the resident population of working age. The overall UK figure in 2001 was just over 0.8 jobs per person of working age. Around 50 local authority areas had a jobs density of 1.0 or more. These had at least one job for every resident of working age. All except three of these authorities had rates below 1.4. The three authorities with densities more than 1.4 were all in Central London – City of London (60.1), Westminster (4.6) and Camden (2.1). East Renfrewshire had the lowest jobs density of 0.4 jobs per person of working age. This may be explained by high outward commuting to Glasgow. Large isolated rural areas, such as the highlands and islands of Scotland, tended to have relatively high jobs densities, as workers were less likely to travel outside the area.

Employment rates also vary by the qualifications people have obtained. For both sexes employment rates increase with level of qualifications. Ninety per cent of men and 85 per cent of women who had a degree or the equivalent were in employment in 2003. This compares with 57 per cent of men and 44 per cent of women who did not have any qualifications (Office for National Statistics 2004c).

Labour force participation rates

In 2003, there were 28.1 million people in employment in the United Kingdom, which was the highest number of people in work on record. Comparing the labour market in 2003 with that in 1988, the number of people in employment had risen by over 2 million, as more people were working full-time or part-time or were self-employed, while fewer people were unemployed. Twenty-six per cent of employees were working part-time in 2003, with 81 per cent of part-time workers being women. The number of part-time workers has increased by almost a third since 1988.

Labour force participation rates differ by sex and age. The male participation rate fell from 89 per cent in 1984 to 84 per cent in 2003. On the other hand, the female rate rose steadily from 67 per cent in 1984 to 73 per cent in 2003. The gap between economic activity rates for men and women has halved from 22 percentage points in 1984 to 11 percentage points in 2003. In that year, participation rates were highest for 25 to 34 and 35 to 49 year old men at around 92 per cent, while for women the rate was highest for 35 to 49 year olds at 78 per cent. Some people over state retirement age are also economically active, although the rates are low: 9 per cent for both men and women in 2003. Although economic activity rates for men have fallen over the last 10 years, while rates for women have risen, there have been different trends for men and women of different ages. The largest decrease in the economic activity rate between 1993 and 2003 was for 18 to 24 year old men, by five percentage points. The largest increase was for 50 to 59 year old women, by seven percentage points.

The labour force participation patterns of women without dependent children are similar, whether they are married, cohabiting or neither. However, the likelihood of women being economically active varies considerably according to whether or not they have dependent children. For both lone mothers and those with a partner, labour force participation rates are lowest when they have a child under 5. However, lone mothers with a pre-school child are less likely to be working than mothers with a partner. This differential decreases with age of the child, so that for mothers whose youngest child is aged 16 to 18, 72 per cent of lone mothers work, compared with 80 per cent of mothers with a partner. The lowest participation rate for women is amongst the Bangladeshi and Pakistani communities (Office for National Statistics 2004c).

Patterns of employment

Patterns of employment show how work is distributed. They vary by occupation, industry and the way in which work is done. There is also a growing sector of self-employment that accounted for just over 3.3 million people in 2003, representing 12 per cent of all people in employment. This subsection summarises the main developments in this area (Office for National Statistics 2004d).

Employment by occupation

The pattern of occupations followed by men and women is quite different. In 2003, 91 per cent of employees who worked in skilled trades were male. These occupations, together with work as process plant and machine operatives (84 per cent), were those where men accounted for a higher proportion of employees than women. Employees who were managers and senior officials were also more likely to be male than female (69 per cent compared with 31 per cent). This was also the case with professional occupations but to a lesser degree, with 58 per cent of professional employees being male and 42 per cent female. Occupations where employees were most likely to be female were personal services (83 per cent), administrative work (79 per cent) and sales and customer service (70 per cent).

Employment by industry

As outlined in Chapter 2, the UK economy experienced significant structural change in the post-war period, with a decline in the manufacturing sector and an increase in service indus-tries. In 1983, 29 per cent of male employee jobs were in manufacturing but by 2003 this had fallen to 20 per cent. The proportion of female employee jobs in the manufacturing sector also fell over the period, from 16 per cent to 7 per cent. The largest increase in both male and female jobs over the last 20 years has been in financial and business services, which accounted for about 1 in 5 of both male and female jobs in 2003. The total number of jobs done by women in 2003 was now virtually the same as the number done by men – 12.8 million compared with 13.0 million. In 1983, there were 2.5 million more male than female employee jobs.

Working patterns

There were 6.3 million people working part-time in 2003, of whom 5.1 million were women. However, only distinguishing between full-time and part-time work concealed a variety of working patterns. These included:

- flexible hours
- annualised hours
- four-and-a-half day weeks
- nine-day fortnights
- term-time working
- job sharing.

Government policy over recent years has stressed the importance of maintaining a healthy 'work–life' balance. One initiative cited as important is availability of flexible working. A fifth of employees working full-time and a quarter of those working part-time had some type of flexible working arrangement in 2003. Flexible working hours was the most common form of flexible working for full-time employees for both sexes. It was also the most common arrangement for men working part-time, whereas term-time working was the most common arrangement for women working part-time. In 2003, over half of all term-time workers were school teachers, post-compulsory education teachers or teaching assistants.

The most common length of working week for both male and female employees was between 31 and 45 hours. The next most common length for male employees was over 45 hours, whereas for female employees it was between 16 and 30 hours. Female employees were more likely to work shorter hours. Approximately 4 in 10 female employees worked up to 30 hours a week, compared with around 1 in 10 male employees. For women who were self-employed there were also different work patterns. A higher proportion of the self-employed than employed worked less than 16 hours. Similarly, a higher proportion of the self-employed worked longer hours with 43 per cent of self-employed males working over 45 hours, compared with 32 per cent of male employees. Although a higher proportion of self-employed females than employees also worked over 45 hours (17 per cent compared with 9 per cent), this was a smaller proportion than for males. Self-employed females were most likely to work from 16 up to 30 hours.

Self-employment

Self-employment was more common among men than women, where 16 per cent of men in employment were self-employed compared with 7 per cent of women. Men and women also varied considerably in type of self-employed work they undertook. Almost a third of self-employed men worked in the construction industry but very few women did. On the other hand, 23 per cent of self-employed women worked in 'other services'. These included, for example, community, social and personal services. A further 22 per cent were in public administration, education and health, where self-employed men were comparatively under-represented. The largest changes over the last 10 years in the type of self-employed work undertaken were the increase in the proportion of women in the banking, finance and insurance sector. This accounted for 14 per cent of self-employed women in 1993. There was a corresponding fall in the proportion working in distribution, hotels and restaurants.

In Britain in 2001/2002, people from Pakistani and Chinese groups were more likely to be self-employed than were those in other ethnic groups. Around one fifth of Pakistani (22 per cent) and Chinese (19 per cent) people in employment were self-employed, compared with around 1 in 10 White people and less than 1 in 10 black people.

Unemployment

People can be economically inactive for a number of reasons: some do not want a job, whilst others want a job but are either not available for or are not seeking work. In 2003, there were 7.7 million people of working age who were economically inactive. Approximately three quarters did not want a job, whilst just under a quarter wanted a job but had not sought work in the last four weeks. Looking after a family is a major factor in women's labour market participation and this was the reason given by about half the women who said they did not want a job. For men, long-term sickness or disability and being a student were the major reasons for not wanting a job.

The number of unemployed people is linked to the economic cycle, albeit with a time lag. In general, as the country experiences economic growth, so the number of jobs grows and unemployment falls, though any mismatches between the skill needs of the new jobs and the skills of those available for work may slow this process. Conversely, as the economy slows and goes into recession, so unemployment tends to rise. The latest peak in unemployment occurred in 1993, when it reached nearly 3 million according to official statistics. This recession had a much greater effect on unemployment among men than among women. In 2001, the number of unemployed people fell to its lowest level since 1990. More recently, unemployment increased slightly to 1.53 million people in early 2002 but then fell slightly again to 1.48 million by early 2003.

One measure of unemployment shown is based on Labour Force Survey estimates of the number of people without a job who are seeking work. It is based on internationally agreed definitions and is the official measure of unemployment. An alternative indicator of unemployment is the claimant count. This counts the number of people claiming unemployment-related benefits. Not all those looking and wanting work are officially registered hence the estimated figure for the early 1990s was 5 million unemployed.

In 2003, official unemployment was 5.0 per cent in England, 4.4 per cent in Wales, 5.6 per cent in Scotland and 5.3 per cent in Northern Ireland. London and the North East regions of England had the highest unemployment rates, at 7.0 per cent and 6.5 per cent respectively. The lowest unemployment rates were in the South East and South West, both at 3.8 per cent (Office for National Statistics 2004c).

A higher proportion of men than women are unemployed, as are a higher proportion of young people than older people. Unemployment rates peaked in 1993 and have since declined across almost all age groups, although there have been slight increases in some age groups in the early 2000s. The largest decline was for those aged 18 to 24, with a fall of nine percentage points for men and nearly five percentage points for women between early 1993 and early 2003. For those aged 16 to 17, unemployment rates have fluctuated over the past decade between around 20 and

24 per cent for young men and around 17 to 20 per cent for young women. The lowest unemployment rates in 2003 were among men and women over 50: 3.7 per cent for men and 2.3 per cent for women.

Age and sex also influence the length of time that people spend unemployed. Young unemployed people are less likely to have been so for a long period than older people and women are less likely than men to have been unemployed for a long period. In 2003, half of unemployed women aged between 16 and 29 had been out of work for less than three months and less than 1 in 10 had been unemployed for a year or more. However, around 1 in 10 unemployed men in their 30s had been unemployed for three or more years, rising to nearly 1 in 5 among those aged 50 to 64 (Office for National Statistics 2004c).

The dynamics of employment

In 2002, 1 in 10 employees of working age had been in their job for less than six months and about 1 in 3 had been with same employer for more than 10 years. At this time, twice as many employees left their job voluntarily (2.9 per cent) as involuntarily (1.4 per cent). Younger employees in particular were more likely to have left their jobs voluntarily than older employees. This could be because young people may undertake seasonal or temporary work while studying. Similarly young employees, new to the labour market often transfer voluntarily from job to job, until they feel their skills are being used and expectations realised. As people grow older, their financial responsibilities usually rise, so they may be less inclined to take the risks involved in changing jobs. The rate at which people voluntarily leave their job also varies by occupation. In 2002, the lowest rates were for professionals (1.4 per cent) and those in associate professional and technical sectors (1.9 per cent). The highest rates were in sales and customer service (4.0 per cent), followed by elementary occupations (3.6 per cent).

Overall, in 2001, 77 per cent of people working were very or fairly satisfied with their job. Women had slightly higher levels of job satisfaction than men (80 per cent compared with 74 per cent). Most people who wanted to move jobs were dissatisfied with aspects of their current job. In 2003, 6 per cent of male, and 5 per cent of female, full-time employees in the United Kingdom were looking for new jobs. For almost a third of men and over a quarter of women who were looking for a new job, unsatisfactory pay in their current job was the main reason. Around 15 per cent of both men and women were looking for a new job because their present job had come to an end, whilst around 7 per cent wanted shorter hours or their journey to work was unsatisfactory.

(i) What have been the most significant changes in patterns of employment over the last 25 years and what factors explain these patterns?

(ii) What are the main features of the labour market from which your organisation currently recruits its staff?

(iii) What are the current most important developments in your organisation's employment markets and what is their likely impact on it in the short term?

SOME INTERNATIONAL COMPARISONS

In 2003, the world's population exceeded 6.3 billion people. Nearly 61 per cent of the population lived in Asia, 13 per cent in Africa and 12 per cent in Europe. World population growth was at its highest between 1965 and 1970, when the annual growth rate was 2 per cent. Since 1970 the world population has been growing at a slower rate. The projected average population growth rate for 2000 to 2005 was 1.2 per cent. In 2002, Western Sahara had the lowest population density in the world with one person per square kilometre, while Singapore had the highest density with some 6,500 people per square kilometre. In contrast, there were 244 people per square mile in the United Kingdom. In 2001, almost half of the world's population lived in urban areas. However, there was wide variability between areas: 38 per cent of people in Asia and Africa lived in urban areas, compared with 78 per cent of those in North America.

In 2002, Africa had a high infant mortality rate at 89 infant deaths per 1,000 live births, while the rates in North America and Europe were less than nine and seven infant deaths per 1,000 live births respectively. The total fertility rate was also high in Africa, at 4.9 children per woman, whilst Europe had a rate of 1.4. There was also wide variability in life expectancy. Life expectancy at birth in Africa was 49 and expectancy for a 20 year old was 40 years, meaning that those children born in Africa who survive to their 20s can expect to live till they are around 60 years of age. The difference in Europe is much less pronounced at 74 years at birth and 55 years at age 20.

Within the EU, there are differences in mortality and fertility rates. In 2002, there were 5.9 infant deaths per 1,000 live births in Greece, whilst in Sweden the rate was 2.8. The total fertility rate was fairly low throughout Europe: Ireland had the highest rate with 2.0 children per woman, Italy, Spain and Greece had the lowest rates, with around 1.3 children per woman.

There are also differences in life expectancy. In Sweden, life expectancy at birth was 82.1 years for females and 77.7 for males in 2002, whereas in Ireland life expectancy at birth was 78.5 years for females and 73.0 for males. There was greater variability across 'candidate countries' of the EU countries (ie countries that were applying for membership of the EU at that time). In 2002, Turkey had 38.7 infant deaths per 1,000 live births, compared with 3.9 infant deaths per 1,000 live births in Slovenia. The total fertility rate was also lower in most candidate countries, compared with rates in EU countries. The lowest was in the Czech Republic, which had a total fertility rate of 1.2 children per woman. The highest total fertility rate occurred in Turkey, with 2.5 children per woman. Life expectancy ranged from 70.9 years for females and 66.2 for males in Turkey, to 81.0 years for females and 76.1 for males in Cyprus (United Nations 2004).

In March 2000 the Lisbon European Council agreed the aim of achieving an overall EU employment rate as close as possible to 70 per cent by 2010 and, for women, an employment rate of more than 60 per cent. In 2002, the overall employment rate in the EU was 64 per cent and the United Kingdom was one of only four out of the then 15 member states with employment rates above the 2010 overall target. Indeed, it had one of the highest employment rates across the EU, after Denmark, the Netherlands and Sweden. The range in employment rates across the EU differed greatly between men and women. For men, the Netherlands had the highest employment rate, at 83 per cent. This was 15 percentage points higher than that of Belgium, the country with the lowest rate. The range of employment rates for women was more than double that of men, from 73 per cent in Denmark and Sweden to 42 per cent in Italy. Although Finland had one of the lowest employment rates for males, it had the third highest rate for females. The United Kingdom had the third highest male rate and fifth highest female rate in the EU.

Men also work longer hours than women across the EU. In 2002, the EU average for men working full-time was 42 hours, compared with 38 hours for women. The United Kingdom has the fourth highest number of hours worked overall in the EU at 42 hours. This was one hour less than the countries with the highest. People working full-time in Italy worked 37 hours per week, the lowest in the EU.

Across the EU, unemployment rates in 2002 varied from 11 per cent in Spain to 3 per cent in Luxembourg and the Netherlands. Unemployment among men was highest in Finland and Germany (9 per cent each) and lowest in Luxembourg (2 per cent). For women the highest rate was in Spain (16 per cent) and the lowest was in the Netherlands (3 per cent) (Eurostat 2004).

(i)   Why do the patterns of employment vary so widely among member states of the EU?
(ii) Investigate and report on the pension systems in place across the EU.
(iii) Why is the UK state pension system one of the least generous?

IMPLICATIONS FOR ORGANISATIONS AND P&D PROFESSIONALS

Information and reliable data on the size and structure of the population are essential in understanding those aspects of society, such as household consumption and the labour market, which strongly impact on organisational decision-making and those responsible for managing organisations. The movement of people from inner cities, an ageing population, more one parent families, higher divorce rates, a falling birth rate and better educated people, all to varying degrees impinge on organisations and the work of P&D professionals. Thus the number of births and deaths, and number of people entering and leaving the country, and the population profile, are all factors likely to affect the size and distribution of the population, as well as demands in society for goods, services and public services. They also affect demand for labour, labour supply and how labour is employed.

As producers of goods and services, for example, organisations have to take account of a number of basic demographic factors in identifying their target markets and how to satisfy them. These include the distributional and structural features of the population such as age profiles, age projections, the sex ratio, ethnic composition, family and household size, geographical location, life expectancies and other related demographic factors. Profit-seeking businesses have to base their resourcing needs, corporate strategies and marketing plans on the expected consequences of demographic and similar factors acting on them. As population changes, these work through into the economy and create opportunities for developing new products and markets, as well as the decline of other markets, goods and services, which are substituted by novel brands.

An ageing population, for example, is likely to lead to increased demand for goods and services benefiting this social group. Older people, depending on their personal circumstances, demand appropriate leisure services, manageable housing stock and suitable healthcare products rather than luxury consumer goods, large houses and high-performing motor vehicles. Increased demand for financial services, such as private pension provision, is likely to be sought by the next generation of retirees. Lower birth rates and falling fertility, on the other hand, lead to decreased demand for baby products, children's clothes and toys.

More diverse households, additional one-person households, rising income households and dual income households, in contrast, create markets for new goods and services. A rise in one-person households, for instance, is likely to lead to demand for low-cost, smaller-scale housing, personal transportation and personal consumption goods. Rising income households and more dual income households, in turn, are likely to result in higher consumption spending on quality food, consumer durables and personal services, such as household cleaning, gardening services and suitable restaurants. People who are well-educated to degree level are likely to be more discerning and critical consumers, than those who are less educated, and therefore to demand superior goods and services for consumption.

Public services have to take account of the expected social and welfare demands of the population. On the one hand, older citizens will demand better healthcare, higher pensions and efficient public transport. A rise in family size or employment of women, on the other hand, leads to increased demand for more nursery provision, improved schools and good healthcare services for children. Any changes in the population profile leading to changes in the age structure, size of households and its social structure have potential knock-on effects for education, social services and healthcare especially. These social demands have to be met within the economic and financial constraints set by the country's political leaders.

As employers of people, both businesses and public services have to adapt their HR strategies in line with the changing demographic structure and shifts in population indicators. The composition and structure of the working population from which they draw their people resources are largely a function of demographic factors. P&D strategists and policy-makers need to respond effectively to pressing labour market factors, paying attention to the needs of their labour forces and their diverse interests. This means, amongst other things, taking account of the needs arising from increasing numbers of female employees (who may want flexible employment), ethnic minorities (with specific religious needs), the disabled (with special physical needs), parents (wanting maternity and paternity leave), quality of working life (better working conditions) and so on.

The age structure of the population is an important determinant of the availability of knowledge workers, HR competencies and labour skills demanded by employers in both the long and short terms. In a static economy, there is likely to be excess labour supply, whilst in a growing economy, with an imbalanced age structure, fewer young people and an ageing population, there is likely to be excess labour demand. In these circumstances, employers and organisations have to be imaginative and proactive in adopting suitable HR strategies, so as to deal with actual and potential labour shortages. These include recruiting effectively, using appropriate employment packages, retaining existing staff, using suitable motivational incentives, and utilising the maximum potential and personal contributions of all employees. It is also necessary to train and develop their workforces to be adaptable and flexible, thus enabling workers to meet the changing operational and challenging business demands made upon them. These managerial tasks clearly have cost implications for employers and need to be responded to effectively, if specific labour market shortages are to be met adequately.

As indicated above, because of family commitments and related reasons, such as dual income households, some women are only prepared to work flexibly on part-time employment contracts. This requires employers to provide appropriate flexible forms of employment and childcare facilities for workers with young children, especially for those women in lower-level routine jobs who cannot afford private childcare for their families. This is becoming less of a problem, however, as the state is now committed to providing pre-schooling for all three-year olds. Women want flexible hours to coincide with school starting and finishing times. Employers are increasingly conscious of the legal and moral needs to provide appropriate job opportunities and conditions of employment that do not discriminate against professional women or female managers, wanting progressive careers and career development. Women now expect equality of opportunity at work and managements need to provide the right conditions for this.

The problem for managements, however, goes beyond just providing fair and justified equal opportunities for women in employment. With more women in the labour force, and changing occupational and industrial structures, work–life balance is now an issue facing both men and women, especially those in professional and managerial jobs. Changes in economic behaviour have served to refocus attention on the relationship between employment and family life.

Work–life balance has increasingly become a major policy issue for national governments and at European level. The evidence suggests that work–life stress is most acutely experienced by men and women in professional and managerial occupations, even though their working conditions are better than those in routine and manual jobs. The longer reported hours of professional and managerial men and women are an important factor contributing to work–life stress. Developing a 'career' has become increasingly individualised, as organisations have been restructured and delayered, and stable career paths that once characterised formal bureaucracies have been increasingly eroded. Aspirations for promotion are associated with high levels of personal achievement and rising work–life stress. The relationship between working life and private life has become a 'problem' because of shifts in gender roles and changes in the economic behaviour of working women. There is also evidence that high commitment management policies are increasing workplace pressures on employees. In these circumstances, employers and senior managers need to be more sensitive to issues of work–life balance.

Perhaps one of the most pressing issues arising from underlying demographic changes, for organisations, individuals and the state, is pension reform. Life expectancy is increasing rapidly and will continue to do so in the future but combined with a forecast low birth rate this will produce a near doubling in the percentage of the population aged 65 by the middle of the century. The baby boom of the 1960s has delayed the effect of these underlying long-term trends but over the next 30 years there will be a very rapid increase in the dependency ratio. The dependency ratio is a measure of the portion of a population who are dependants in society (ie they are either too young or too old to work). The dependency ratio is calculated as the number of individuals aged 16 and below and above 65 divided by the number of individuals aged over 16 to under 65, expressed as a percentage of working population. A rising dependency ratio is a concern in countries like the United Kingdom, since both dependent groups rely on state expenditure on child welfare and education, on the one hand, and pensions and health and social care on the other. Although births look likely to stabilise or fall, the number of elderly is progressively increasing. With an ageing population, it becomes increasingly difficult for pension and social security systems to provide for a significantly older, non-working population without raising taxes and redistributing resources.

The implications of this for pensioner income will be more serious in the next quarter of a century than in 10 years' time. Over the long-term period many adjustments, for instance to savings rates and retirement ages, may occur, so a 'muddle-through' option appears to have been adopted. But it is highly likely that a muddle-through option will result in outcomes both less socially equitable and less economically efficient than could be achieved with a consciously planned response to the problems being faced.

The reason why the UK pensions system appeared to work well in the past was because it had one of the least generous state pension systems in the developed world and was complemented by a developed system of voluntary private funded pensions and means tested benefits. Nevertheless, this rosy picture hid multiple inadequacies relating to specific groups of people such as the low paid, women and people in flexible employment. But the system worked, with the percentage of GDP transferred to pensioners comparable to that in other countries. However, the state plans to provide decreasing support for many people in order to control expenditure in the face of an ageing population and the private system is not developing to offset the state's retreating role in the pension field.

Instead, it is in significant decline. With changes in the tax regime, a decline in the value of equity stocks and current demands on private pension funds, more and more firms are closing defined benefit schemes (ie those providing pensions based on final salaries, which are indexed-linked with prices) to new employees and replacing them with less generous defined contribution schemes. Overall, the present level of pension right accrual, private and state combined, is likely to leave many people with inadequate pensions in the future. There will be limits to solving the problem solely through increasing retirement ages. If state system plans are taken as given, a higher level of private saving is required.

This problem was addressed and analysed by the Pensions Commission (2004). It reported that, faced with the increasing proportion of the population aged over 65, society and individuals must choose between four options:

- pensioners will become poorer relative to the rest of society
- taxes/National Insurance contributions devoted to pensions must rise
- savings must rise
- average retirement ages must rise.

Some mix of higher taxes/National Insurance contributions, higher savings and later average retirement would be required. The Commission concluded that given present trends many people will face inadequate pensions in retirement, unless they have large non-pension assets or are intending to retire much later than current retirees.

According to the Commission's analysis, both the behavioural barriers to savings and the costs of provision have been made worse by the bewildering complexity of the UK pension system, both state and private. This complexity reflects the impact of multiple decisions made over the last several decades, each of which appeared to have made sense at the time but the cumulative effect of which has been to create confusion about pensions and mistrust in them. In its view, means-testing within the state system had both increased complexity and reduced, and in some cases reversed, incentives to save in pension systems which the tax system creates. The scope of this means-testing would grow over time, if current indexation approaches were continued indefinitely. Unless new government initiatives can make a major difference to behaviours, the Commission believed that it was unlikely that the present voluntary private system combined with the present state system would solve the problem of inadequate pension savings for the future.

For the Commission, one collective response to the demographic challenge should include a rise in the average age of retirement. Healthy ageing for many people makes this possible and an increase in employment rates among older people is now occurring. However, the increase needed to make later retirement a sufficient solution alone appears to have overlooked the significant inequalities in life expectancy and health across socio-economic groups which may limit the scope for across-the-board increases in retirement age. Increases in either taxes/National Insurance contributions and/or in private savings will also be needed to meet the demographic challenge. To achieve pension adequacy, the Commission concluded that there were three possible ways forward:

- a major revitalisation of the voluntary system
- significant changes to the state system
- an increased level of compulsory private pension saving beyond that already implicit within the UK system.

This is an ongoing debate that will not 'go away' and will be at the centre of public and private discourse over the next few years. The uncertain outcome of this policy debate has implications for the state, organisations, P&D professionals and individuals.

CONCLUSION

This chapter examines demographic trends in the United Kingdom and provides some international comparisons. The United Kingdom has an ageing population, including a growth in the proportion of those aged 85 and over. Generally, minority ethnic groups have a younger age structure than the White group. The most rapidly growing regions are the South West, South East and East of England, and London has the greatest net loss due to internal migration.

Major trends in households and families are the growth in one-person households and changes to family structures, with more one-parent families and a decline in marriages. Occupationally, men are more likely to be professionally employed, self-employed and supervisors, whereas women are employed in intermediate occupational groups. People are better educated today at all levels than in the past, with more women than men in further education, higher education and part-time education. Christianity is still the claimed largest religious affiliation but a growing proportion of people have no religious belief.

Population change depends upon the relationships between births, deaths and net migration, with net immigration having an increasing influence. Due to decreased fertility rates, births are projected to remain fairly constant over the next few years. Increased female participation in education and the labour market, and more effective contraception, have encouraged later childbearing and smaller family size. There have been large improvements in life expectancy at birth for both males and females. Rising living standards and developments in medical technology help explain the decline in death rates.

There are more people in employment than ever. The male participation rate has fallen and that for women has increased, while the pattern of occupations of men and women is quite different. The UK economy has shifted from a manufacturing base to a service-based one. About a fifth of the working population works part-time, of whom more than 80 per cent are women. Self-employment is more common among men than women and amongst ethnic minorities than Whites. Unemployment has declined in recent years, with a higher proportion of men than women unemployed and a higher proportion of young people than older people. Finally, international comparisons show wide variations in demographic growth, fertility and mortality rates, life expectancy and employment levels.

USEFUL READING

CHIEF MEDICAL OFFICER. (2003) *On the state of public health: Annual report of the Chief Medical Officer of the Department of Health.* London: The Stationery Office.

DEPARTMENT FOR EDUCATION AND SKILLS. (2003) *Education and training skills for the United Kingdom.* London: The Stationery Office.

EUROSTAT. (2003) *Migration statistics.* Luxembourg: Office of Official Publications of the European Communities.

EUROSTAT. (2004) *European social statistics*. Luxembourg: Office of Official Publications of the European Communities.

GALLIE, D., WHITE, M., CHENG, Y. and TOMLINSON, M. (1998) *Restructuring the employment relationship.* Oxford: Oxford University Press.

HOME OFFICE. (2003) *Asylum statistics: United Kingdom*. London: Home Office.

OFFICE FOR NATIONAL STATISTICS. (2001) *Census 2001*. London: The Stationery Office.

OFFICE FOR NATIONAL STATISTICS. (2003a) *Annual abstract of statistics.* London: The Stationery Office.

OFFICE FOR NATIONAL STATISTICS. (2003b) *Regional trends*. London: The Stationery Office.

OFFICE FOR NATIONAL STATISTICS. (2003c) *Birth statistics.* London: The Stationery Office.

OFFICE FOR NATIONAL STATISTICS. (2004a) *Population trends*. London: The Stationery Office.

OFFICE FOR NATIONAL STATISTICS. (2004b) *The state of the labour market*. London: The Stationery Office.

OFFICE FOR NATIONAL STATISTICS. (2004c) *Labour force survey*. London: The Stationery Office.

OFFICE FOR NATIONAL STATISTICS. (2004d) *Labour market trends*. London: The Stationery Office.

UNITED NATIONS. (2004) *United Nations demographic yearbook*. New York: United Nations.

Social Trends

INTRODUCTION

Social trends and social problems are reflected in the ways in which the major social institutions of society – such as family, social structure, politics and work – change and evolve over time. Social trends and social problems are underpinned by values that fashion people's behaviour, how they relate to others, how they interpret and understand their own experiences, and how they make sense of and perceive the world and themselves within it. Individuals acquire beliefs and values as a result of socialisation and through reflection. Their earliest experiences are within the family, which is the primary socialisation agency. It is here that children learn language, develop means of communication and have their first experiences of rules, rewards and punishments. They imitate the behaviour of their parents, siblings and peers. When children enter school, they learn how to play and relate to others in social settings. They also learn to read and write and are taught about history, geography and literature, so that they can locate themselves in the wider world around them and imbibe the cultural norms of society. They also learn the skills that they require in later life and in preparation for work. Socialisation continues throughout people's lives and secondary agencies, such as university, workplace, trade unions, professional associations, peer groups and increasingly the media, may challenge or reinforce earlier influences. People continue to be influenced by their personal experiences and observations of their environment, as the world changes around them.

Societies are continually evolving and changing. There is usually a cultural lag, however, since once acquired, attitudes and values are not easily replaced and institutional change is normally evolutionary and incremental. Most people are resistant to change because it threatens their security, understanding of the world and status within it. Change is accompanied by uncertainty, threats and risks, although it may also offer opportunities and benefits. Older people are often more resistant to change and new social trends than younger people, because they have invested so much in the past and are the least confident in their ability to cope with changing values, structures and institutions. Younger people generally find change and new social trends easier to cope with, because they lack the reference points of older generations and they often reject traditional values and behaviours to establish their own identities and independence. They also tend to learn more quickly and take on board new ideas and understand why society is changing. The United Kingdom, along with the rest of the industrial world, has experienced rapid and constantly accelerating social change in the last 50 years. This has affected all the major institutions of society, many of which have been transformed. This chapter explores some recent, selective social trends and social problems and considers how they impact on people, organisations and society.

FAMILY STRUCTURES

Family is a social group, within which there are many different structures including nuclear families, extended families, single-parent families, same-sex families and multicentric families. Although historically the family seems to be an enduring feature of society, it is in fact a constantly evolving and changing institution. Attitudes and perceptions of the family also vary. There are the idealised views of the family, which see it as a source of sustenance, nurturing, security and focus of loyalty for individuals. It is also seen as the cornerstone of society and the basis for stability, order, continuity and evolution of our culture. In contrast, some feminists see the family as an artificial institution, a social construction, which imposes collective goals on free personalities, particularly women, and interferes with the full development of the autonomous individual. In a similar vein, earlier philosophers such as Hobbes (1947 edition) and John Stuart Mill (1972 edition) saw it as an oppressive institution. For Hobbes, family relations were merely another exercise in power with male dominance over women and children, while Mill thought the family was a seedbed of despotism and the source of human misery. Berger and Carlsen (1993) go as far as to suggest that the family is the spawning ground for imperialism, racism, violence, homophobia and religious intolerance.

A recent definition of family is 'a kinship grouping of adults or adults and children, who may not necessarily have a common residence' (Abercrombie and Warde 2000, p265). In contrast, a definition widely accepted in the middle of the twentieth century was:

> A social group characterised by common residence, economic cooperation and reproduction. It includes adults of both sexes, at least two of whom maintain a socially approved sexual relationship, and one or more children, own or adopted, of the sexually co-habiting adults.

(Gittins 1993, p60)

Neither definition seems able to encompass the variety of social groups referred to as families in today's world. The nuclear family of a married couple with children, all living in the same household, and the extended family with a married couple living with children and grandparents and aunts or uncles still exist, especially amongst Asian communities. So too do kinship groups which live separately but are bound by birth and marriage. These families, although not having physical contact as frequently as in the past, do keep in constant or regular contact through telephone and ICTs such as e-mail. But, in addition, there are many one-parent families. Some 20 per cent of children live in one-parent families, headed mostly by women. There is also an increasing number of childless families and same sex families. The latter are now recognised in law and have recently acquired rights to adoption, whilst in vitro fertilisation (IVF), with sperm donors or surrogate mothers, makes it possible for them to have their own children. These families are likely to increase in the future.

The decline of traditional same-residence extended families can be attributed to greater social and geographical mobility, while relaxation of divorce laws has resulted in not only more one-parent families but also multicentric, extended families. One in two marriages ends in divorce and the percentage is rising. People continue to remarry, however, and have children with more than one partner. This suggests that marriage is still seen as an important social relationship. The reasons for marital breakdown are complex and multicausal but appear to be linked to unrealistic expectations about marriage, increased individualism, hedonism and the opportunities for developing new relationships, as both partners work and are more affluent than people in earlier generations. Also the importance of the family as an economic unit has declined, as more women are now employed and are economically independent of men. The family is becoming of increasingly emotional importance and the locus for love, affection and belonging. If those feelings change, then the reason for being in the relationship ceases and the search for those needs to be met elsewhere resumes (Smart and Shipman 2004).

During a lifetime, individuals may become a member of several families and households. This may include living in a family with natural or adoptive parents, involve a stepfamily, or be the result of divorce and remarriage by one or both original parents. During adulthood, people may marry or cohabit with a partner or several partners sequentially. This may be interspersed with periods of living alone. Women may have a child without a partner and live with the child or children, while the father may continue to support them or decline any responsibility. Many people live alone again, after divorce or death of a former partner. Social attitudes towards contraception, abortion, women working, cohabitation and divorce have changed among both sexes over the last 50 years. Thus traditional social constraints supporting 'conventional' family patterns have been removed or weakened (Whitmarsh 1995). However, there are still negative attitudes towards single-sex relationship marriages and parents and the law has only recently been changed to prohibit discrimination against gays and lesbians. The law is an important symbolic but blunt instrument and it will take time for such family situations to become generally acceptable.

One of the consequences of divorce, and the increase in the number of women choosing to have children without a permanent partner, is the fatherless family (Dennis and Erdos 1993) This is often seen as a social problem, partly because of the dependency of these families on the state and partly because they are seen as the cause of anti-social behaviour, particularly amongst youths, resulting in juvenile delinquency, truancy from school and low academic performance (Berger and Carlson 1993). Parenting problems that arise after divorce have been well researched and suggest that it is the social position of the fatherless family including income, occupation and education which is the important explanatory variable rather than the status itself (Silva and Smart 1999).

The state increasingly intervenes in family life, whether by providing income support, helping dysfunctional families and protecting vulnerable children. This is an area in which state intervention has increased in recent years. The government consultative green paper on families (Home Office 1998) implicitly saw the family with two parents as the most stable environment for children to grow up in. Therefore its policy was to help keep the family together. It advocated better services and support for parents including 'Sure Start', mediation services for couples contemplating divorce, better support services for families with serious problems and help for those experiencing family violence. It also promoted better financial support for families and helping them balance work and home by introducing more family-friendly employment rights. There was also a new deal for single parents and help with finding them employment. This was clearly intended to reduce the cost on the state and provide working 'models' for the children and assist women in becoming more independent. Most of these policies have been implemented in the last few years.

The Labour government's 'third way' approach to the family recognises that the family is the meeting point of many current social trends. These include increased equality between the sexes, more women in the labour force for longer periods of their lives, changes in sexual behaviour and a changing relationship between work and home (Giddens 1998).

What are some of the implications of single parent families for:
(i)   employers
(ii) government?

CHANGING ROLE OF WOMEN IN SOCIETY

One of the most significant social trends in the last 50 years has been the feminisation of the labour force. Although women have always worked, they have increased as a proportion of the working population from 29 per cent in 1901 to around 50 per cent in 2005. The expansion of women in employment can be attributed to changing labour market demands but particularly to the increased participation of women with children. In the past, it was marital status that was an indicator of women's economic activity but today it is responsibility for dependent children which is the most significant variable. Some 58 per cent of women with children aged under 5 are now economically active and this figure rises to 80 per cent of women with children aged 16 or above. Lone mothers have lower participation rates but these have risen since the Labour government came to power in 1997, partly because of availability of childcare which is still a determining factor whether a mother works full-time, part-time or not at all.

Working women

The pattern of women's employment has traditionally been different from men's and is characterised by both horizontal and vertical segregation. Women workers have been found in four main areas of employment: clerical and administrative work, the caring professions (teaching, nursing and social work), retailing and catering, cleaning and hairdressing. Their employment base has been widening in the last decade but horizontal segregation still persists. Women are still found mainly in the lower levels of organisations and men in higher positions. Even in organisations staffed predominantly by women, such as education and nursing, men hold most of the senior posts. The number of women in managerial jobs has been increasing, although they still only represent about 5 per cent of managing directors and chief executives. Black women are even more underrepresented at higher levels.

Women are far more likely to be in part-time work than men (see Chapters 2 and 5) and almost 10 per cent are in temporary posts. This means women tend to be in the least secure jobs and are particularly vulnerable to decisions by employers when reducing their workforces. Further, women tend to earn on average 25 per cent less than men. This is because they are in lower paid, lower status jobs and work less hours. This, in turn, has an effect on their career structures, career development, and pensions

There is a variety of explanations of women's unequal position in the labour market, which revolve around early socialisation into gender roles, personal and social expectations, the structure of the family and structure of employment. In addition, black women are discriminated against because of their colour and 'race'. Traditionally, the structure and organisation of work have been based on men as 'heads' of the family, working continuously throughout their lives. This continuous working day, week and work life takes no account of childbearing and childrearing and is difficult to reconcile with the dual role of women within society as parents and workers. Consequently, women temporarily withdraw from the labour market to raise children. This often results in downward occupational mobility, especially when they return to part-time work. Although the time taken out of work after childbirth is falling, and more women are returning full time, childbirth still interrupts their careers and limits their opportunities of gaining promotion, experience and rising to 'top jobs'.

The growing importance of women in the economy, the impact of the EU and pressure from the women's movement since the 1960s, have led governments to pursue a range of policies to get rid of unfair discrimination, assist women in their childcare roles and most recently mainstream gender equality throughout the public sector. Conservative governments in the 1980s and 1990s had no coherent strategy towards gender equality (Beveridge *et al* 2000), although in 1986 the then prime minister, Margaret Thatcher, established a Ministerial Group on Women's Issues. In general, however, government adopted a minimalist approach on equality by viewing equality for women as fundamentally an employment issue. There was no place on the equality agenda for wider issues such as childcare, social welfare, pensions or violence against women. Nevertheless, in the civil service, a Programmes for Action to further equality of opportunity was introduced in 1984 (Beveridge *et al* 2000) and other parts of the public sector followed.

Over 50 per cent of graduates are now women and they are entering the professions in large numbers, permeating the male bastions of the city, police, higher civil service and the law. Women are also the fastest growing number of self-employed, taking advantage of small business programmes and financial incentives. In the political sphere, women have been successful in gaining greater representation in both local and central government and in the many quangos which have been created since 1979 (Thomas and Wormald 1989). In 2004, there were 119 women MPs (18.1 per cent), 126 Members of the House of Lords (17.8 per cent) and six members of the cabinet (28.5 per cent), including the Minister for Women. The largest representation of women is in the Welsh Assembly (60 per cent), followed by the Scottish Parliament (39.5 per cent) and the European Parliament (24.4 per cent). These advances in women's position in the labour market and positions of power are the results of their demands for equal opportunities, willingness to take employers to tribunals and the European Court of Justice to establish their rights, and their recognition by employers as a valuable human capital resource.

On the other hand, there appears to be growing polarisation amongst women in the labour market. There are some women being increasingly integrated into higher management levels and the professions with well-paid jobs. On the other hand, there are those who are peripheral workers in low paid, part-time or temporary jobs, who fall in and out of the labour market. Women still far outnumber men amongst those living in poverty, as women are disproportionately represented in families living below the poverty line. These include pensioners and lone mothers who may or may not be in paid work. This increasing heterogeneity of women in the labour market is likely to increase over the next decade.

Gender equality policy

The Labour government elected in 1997 placed gender equality policy more centrally on the agenda and introduced a mainstreaming strategy (Women's Unit 1997). New gender equality machinery was installed and a Minister for Women was appointed and there was also an all-party Group on Gender equality in parliament made up of MPs and peers from the three major political parties. Under Labour governments, British gender equality policy has been streamlined, with a set of policy priorities covering childcare facilities, family-friendly working practices, bridging the pay gap, violence against women, legal and international obligations and increased participation of women in politics. Every new policy must be examined with reference to the implication for women.

Government policy and the advances of women notwithstanding, gender inequality still persists due to a number of structural, organisational, institutional and attitudinal barriers to gaining employment, better jobs and access to positions of power (Goode *et al* 1998, Callender 1996). Institutions, including the family, remain gendered. Equal opportunities legislation and the liberal equal opportunities policies of governments have proved blunt instruments in attacking organisational mobilisation of sexual bias (Blakemore and Drake 1996).

Gender occupational segregation is structurally determined by the growth of certain types of jobs, particularly part-time ones. Conversely, lack of part-time opportunities in managerial jobs and many professions and absence of family-friendly policies within organisations perpetuate vertical segregation. Further institutional barriers include access to qualifications, as women who take time out, work part-time or are lone parents are often denied the opportunities for training and work experience. Women still have a dual role as mothers and housewives, involving many hours of unpaid work. This leaves little time to pursue their careers. Although there is evidence that men now share domestic work, women still perform 75 per cent of it and have major responsibility for childcare. The introduction of paternity leave may shift that burden in the future, whilst introduction of nursery places for all children aged three and four is making it easier for women to enter or remain in the labour market.

However, government policies such as New Deal and Welfare to Work can be seen as pushing women into paid work to reduce the costs of social security. Further, as Goode *et al* (1998) point out, women's entry into previously male-dominated jobs does not necessarily herald a decline in segregation. Often these changes involve transformation of these occupations, leading to deskilling and/or downgrading of the pay, status and/or career opportunities associated with the occupation.

More significantly, contraction and restructuring of the welfare state have disproportionately affected women, partly because they constitute the bulk of public sector employees but also because they are the carers. Changes in social policies such as Community Care translate into care by families and by women. So, whilst there are far more opportunities for women to pursue careers and enlightened employers have taken positive action to promote this, women are still disadvantaged because of their generally weaker market position, unequal role within the family, lack of skills and experience and lack of financial or practical support to enable them to reconcile their domestic and employment roles. Further, there are the attitudinal barriers of employers but particularly of women themselves. Employer gender-stereotyping affects their willingness to recruit and promote women, whilst women's own attitudes affect their behaviour in the labour market. There is some evidence that these attitudes are changing, as more women are choosing not to have children or to restrict their families to one child. As women also delay having a family, they are well established in their careers and may have sufficient income to finance childcare.

Despite some 30 years of sex discrimination legislation, women in the United Kingdom remain underpaid in comparison with men and hugely underrepresented at senior management levels in business and public life. Why is this so and what can be done to address it?

SOCIAL STRATIFICATION

All modern societies are socially stratified and hierarchical, reflecting degrees of inequality among individuals, families, households and social groups in wealth, status and power. Those at the top of the hierarchy tend to have more of all three resources than those at the bottom. Social divisions within the United Kingdom reflect differing occupations, lifestyles, patterns of social behaviour and life opportunities. The major social divisions are traditionally seen as class, gender and ethnicity, although age, religion and regional cleavages are also important. This diversity, however, is overlaid and held together by systems of beliefs, language, law, national symbols and institutions. All societies consist of elements of heterogeneity and homogeneity. It is the integration of these elements that produces social stability, whilst at the same time enabling societies to change (Giddens 2001).

Defining social class

The term social class rather than social strata has traditionally been used by social scientists within the United Kingdom. Class is sometimes described as the British obsession and Britain is perceived as the most class-conscious society in the world. Even so, the concept of class has been disputed amongst social scientists. The Marxist view, for example, is a materialist economic one which emphasises that class is fundamental and determined by the relationship of people to the means of production.

- All those selling their labour constitute a 'working' class. In contrast, those owning the means of production constitute a ruling or 'capitalist' class described as the 'bourgeoisie'. Other classes, consisting of the self-employed, professionals and small businesses such as shopkeepers and artisans, are the 'petite bourgeoisie'.
- The relationship between the two major classes is inherently exploitative, as the capitalist extracts part of the value of the social production of the workers as profit and pays wages to the workers, which are less than the value of what they have produced.
- This exploitation causes class conflict, which is the engine of social change.
- Neo-Marxists have refined this by acknowledging a more complex class structure, consisting of lower, middle and upper classes. Each of these has differential economic rewards, affecting lifestyles and giving access to other resources such as property, wealth, social position and political power (Poulantzas 1975).

An alternative view, associated with Weber (1968, 1971), is that social position is a complex phenomenon with economic, social, political and cultural dimensions, linked to occupation, status and power.

- *Class situation*. Weber recognised three types of class situation: property classes, commercial classes and social classes. Property classes are determined by property differences and may be positively or negatively privileged. Commercial classes are determined by their ability to sell their skills or goods in the market. Social classes are wider groups including property and commercial classes, between which there is some mobility. These groups include the working class, intelligentsia, propertied classes, educated classes and small businesses. Weber identified a significant 'middle class' composed of the self-employed, public officials and those in liberal professions.
- *Group solidarity*. For Weber, classes can be identified in terms of their possessions and skills but it is status not class that is the root of group solidarity. Status refers to the way that society regards individuals or groups. It is conferred externally and reflects the positive or negative values attached to knowledge, skill, circumstances of birth, social position

or patterns of behaviour. It has its origins in the ability of groups to claim privileges denied to others. For Weber, conflicts between classes and status groups, and between status groups, cause social change.

■ *Power and party*. For Weber, power is the ability to influence decisions, either positively or negatively and to make things happen, reflecting one's own interest or collective interests. Parties are social groups established to influence or change the status quo. Their focus may be broad or narrow, national or local, but they try to influence particular communal outcomes and may or may not be related to class or status.

Debates about class today revolve around whether social class is any longer a meaningful concept that describes 'reality' and whether the meta-narratives of Marx and Weber can accommodate the complexity of modern classes that are increasingly fragmented. There is also debate about how to describe the new systems of social stratification that are emerging which seem to confuse the traditional divisions of working, middle and upper class. There are debates too about how to integrate the structuralist and behaviouralist elements of Marx and Weber into an analysis of class structures in modern societies (Giddens 1981). This debate identifies what Bradley (1996, p46) has described as a set of interrelationships arising out of the social organisation of production, distribution, exchange and consumption:

> *These include the allocation of tasks in the division of labour (occupation, employment hierarchies); control and ownership relationships within production; the unequal distribution of surplus (wealth, income, state benefits); relationships linked to the circulation of money (markets, shareholding and investment); patterns of consumption (lifestyle, living arrangements); and distinctive cultures that arise from all these (behavioural practices and community relations). Class is a much broader concept, then, than occupational structure, though the latter is often taken as a measure of it.*

Recent social changes have led some to the claim that the class system in the United Kingdom is coming to an end and that the United Kingdom is moving to a classless society. Observers point to a 'new' working class, more skilled, educated and affluent than the old working class, with similar lifestyles and consumption patterns to the middle classes. The 'new' working class is more likely to be homeowners, have holidays abroad, enjoy eating out and have a wide range of material possessions. In addition, increased social mobility within working class families, and the higher status attached to new occupations, are also seen as blurring boundaries between working and middle classes.

Another perspective is that class is a function of not only market position but also work situation. Market position is reflected in income, job security and opportunity for upward mobility, while work situation is reflected in the degree of autonomy, independence and control individuals have over work. The working class is distinguishable by not only the type of work they do and their market position but also their lack of control or autonomy over the work process (Lockwood 1958). Rather than 'embourgeoisification' of the working class, Lockwood and others (Wood 1989, Crompton 2000) point to the 'proletarianisation' of the middle classes. Changes in the work process affecting white-collar and lower professional groups (traditionally seen as middle class) are leading to loss of job autonomy, which is blurring the distinction between the classes, with negative effects. Further, the shift to flexible employment patterns is seen as reducing job security for manual, white-collar and professional workers. Thus the middle classes are being more exposed to risk and insecurity in employment, as job flexibility crosses the traditional manual/mental divisions of labour.

The changing social structure

The period between 1945 and the late 1970s was one of relative prosperity, full employment and a growing working population. New occupations and professions emerged, especially within the continuously expanding welfare state, and wages rose along with productivity. High levels of consumption led to a general rise in living standards and there was a high 'social wage' (ie 'free' public services and transfer payments by the state to individuals and households), resulting in some narrowing of the inequalities between social classes. There was also increased social mobility and distinctions and boundaries between classes became blurred, as general affluence resulted in converging consumption patterns and lifestyles across old class divisions.

A large working class of manual workers, a smaller middle class of white-collar workers, the professions, self-employed and a small upper class distinguished the old class structure. In 1951, about two-thirds of the working population and their families were in manual occupations and identified themselves as working class. Their shared economic or material position was the basis for a group identity, similarity of outlook and sense of common condition. This identity was expressed in terms of shared interests that provided a basis for political organisation and action (Abercrombie and Warde 2000). Between 1971 and 1981, the proportion of employed people in manual work fell from 62 to 56 per cent for men and from 43 to 36 per cent for women (Halsey 2000). By 2000, less than 30 per cent of the labour force had manual jobs and an increasing proportion of those were women and minority ethnic groups.

Explanations of these changes were to be found, first, in the decline of manufacturing and extractive industries where manual workers were employed, such as in mining, shipbuilding, iron and steel, docks, textiles and transport. Second, jobs have been lost to automation and new technology in industries such as printing and car assembly. Third, jobs have disappeared as corporations have transferred production to low labour-cost countries and UK plants have closed. This process of globalisation is creating a new international division of labour, so that the working class has not declined globally.

The social structure of the United Kingdom changed significantly in the second half of the twentieth century (Halsey 2000), with new patterns of social stratification emerging as it was transformed from an industrial to a post-industrial society. The major differences between industrial and post-industrial societies lie in their economic systems, types of commodities produced, the distribution of the labour force and the dominant technology. For Bell (1973), this involved:

- the change from a goods-producing to a service economy
- the emergence of new professions and technical classes
- the central role of knowledge as the key resource and source of innovation
- the dominance of new information-based technologies.

By the early twenty-first century, in contrast to the declining working class, the middle class had grown, as white-collar occupations had expanded, new professions had been created and technology had transformed working processes. The middle class has become numerically and socially the most significant social stratum and is predicted to grow between 10 and 14 per cent over the next decade. The middle class, however, is very heterogeneous and has been described by Dahrendorf (1982) as consisting of an 'upper' middle, 'middle' middle and 'lower' middle class. The upper middle class includes the higher professions, senior managers and those holding senior technical posts. The middle middle class consists of the lower professions, middle managers and technical grades, small business owners and farmers. The lower middle class are those in clerical and supervisory positions, shop workers and para-professional jobs.

The upper class remains the smallest class but that has also changed. It consists of interconnected families who own a disproportionate amount of property and wealth. In 2001, it was estimated that the top 1 per cent of people owned 23 per cent of marketable wealth and 33 per cent of marketable wealth less the value of dwellings (Summerfield and Babb 2004). The upper class also control and own large parts of industry, land and commerce, and hold top posts in major institutions of the state, commerce and the arts. In addition to the royal family and the traditional landowning aristocracy, it includes chief executives and directors of large national and MNCs, those at the top of the major financial institutions in the City including banks, finance houses and law firms, senior judges, military leaders and some top politicians and civil servants. This class is economically dominant, operates through national and international networks and is often referred to as 'the Establishment'.

Dahrendorf (1982) distinguishes between the 'old' and 'new' upper class. The latter are 'entryists' or *nouveaux riches* that have acquired property and wealth but generally lack the personal advantages deriving from birth and ascribed social status. Examples include Sir Richard Branson, Sir Paul McCartney, Sir Alan Sugar, Lord David Sainsbury and Dame Shirley Porter, all of whom appear in the list of the top 200 wealthiest people in the United Kingdom, along with the Queen and the Duke of Westminster. The *nouveaux riches* themselves are becoming increasingly heterogeneous, as the number of multi-millionaires continues to increase. In 2005, for example, the five richest people resident in the United Kingdom owned some £37.65 billion in assets between them and three of them were not born in the United Kingdom. These five individuals were (Beresford 2005):

- Lakshmi Mittal (an Asian), with investments in steel, had assets valued at £14.8 billion.
- Roman Abramovich (a Russian) with investments in oil, finance and football, had assets valued at £7.5 billion.
- The Duke of Westminster, with investments in property, had assets valued at £5.6 billion.
- Hans Rausing and family (Swedes), with investments in food packaging, had assets valued at £4.9 billion.
- Philip and Christina Green, with investments in retailing, had assets valued at £4.85 billion.

Only one of those five was a member of the old upper class (the Duke of Westminster). Clearly, the importance of inherited wealth is declining and the United Kingdom is fast becoming a plutocracy. This is seen in the growing power and control exercised by a trans-national capitalist elite, which is a crucial feature of the new globalisation. According to Sampson (2004, p354), the new elite is held together by a desire for personal enrichment, their acceptance of capitalism and the need for the profit motive, 'while the resistance to money values is much weaker'. Today the circles of Britain's power-centres look very different from the pattern 40 years ago.

> The palace, the universities and the diplomats have drifted towards the edge. Many institutions – including parliament, the cabinet, trades unions and industry – look smaller. The prime minister, the Treasury and defence loom larger at the centre. The bankers are more dominant, overlapping with corporations and pensions funds, while the nationalised industries have almost disappeared as separate entities. The media are more pervasive, seeping everywhere into the vacuum left by the shrinking of the old powers.

In spite of changes in social mobility, if class is an indicator of access to resources and therefore of life chances the United Kingdom remains a highly stratified society. In 2004, it was still the case that the distribution of income was more unequal than in most other European countries, with the gap between the highest and lowest incomes widening. The maldistribution of wealth was even greater with the bottom 50 per cent of the population owning only 5 per cent of marketable wealth, including dwellings, and only 3 per cent if dwellings are excluded. In 2002, 28 per cent of households had no savings. Greater absolute affluence has enabled convergence of life styles but is linked to the pervasiveness of popular culture and consumerism.

> A visiting manager from China is fascinated by the continued significance of social class in British society. He asks you to explain the main characteristics of the middle class and to explain why its numbers are rising, whilst those of other classes appear to be falling. What would you say?

THE NEW POLITICS AND PARTICIPATION IN POLITICS

Policy differences between the political parties were very large in post-war Britain in 1945. The Labour party, with its large majority in the House of Commons, began a series of reforms based on economic intervention and creation of the welfare state. The Conservatives subsequently realised that these reforms, especially the welfare state, were popular with voters and, if they were to win future elections, that they had to accept them. Between 1955 and 1964, the political positions of Labour and the Conservatives were very similar during the bipartisan heydays of the post-war settlement. Both major parties accepted the mixed economy, public ownership of large sectors of industry and the welfare state. After the general election of 1966, however, the Conservatives shifted to the right and the gap between the two main parties widened as Labour moved to the left. It was only in 1997 that 'New' Labour shifted decisively to the right, largely playing down economic intervention, whilst supporting welfare and education programmes. This meant that the whole of the political spectrum had moved to the right leaving the Liberal Democrats on the left, Labour as centre-right and the Conservatives still on the right but not significantly so. This social trend may be described as a 'new politics' which has a range of social implications.

Politics post-1997

The fundamental political aim of the Labour party since 1997 has been to win successive elections, after being out of office for 18 years between 1979 and 1997. This explains its financial and economic orthodoxies, that were designed to reassure the business sector, and its concern to manage the traditionally anti-Labour media and maintain good working relationships with media magnates such as Rupert Murdoch and the populist press. Labour had calculated that its traditional voters would continue to vote Labour and that affluent middle-class voters, especially in South East England, could be persuaded to vote for it on the grounds of general economic prosperity. Broadly, the party's electoral strategy was:

- creating a cross-class coalition of support in the country
- occupying the 'centre-ground' of British politics
- establishing a reputation for competence in government and in economic policy
- reorganising the party machine to make it more centralised and efficient
- managing the press.

By the early twentieth-first century, both Labour and the Conservatives had accepted the market as the major mechanism for distributing resources. Both agreed that bureaucracies and governments were at their best when organised as markets and when government limited its role to upholding markets. Indeed, one of the lasting innovations of the Thatcher years was reorganisation of state bureaucracies along market lines. In addition, the Thatcher governments had responded to the 'fiscal crisis', arising from open-ended social demands made on the public purse, by limiting public expenditure and encouraging a shift to private provision, such as in pension policy. Limiting government spending carried social costs in the 1980s and 1990s and had resulted in an increase in those living below the poverty line, mainly in conurbations. Labour, having been defeated in four general elections, remodelled itself to become electable. By taking on board many of the Conservative's neo-liberal ideas, Labour was renouncing the possibility of going back to the post-war settlement but offering to create a more just and fair society.

New Labour adopted a conservative approach to economic policy (see Chapter 7), which was confirmation of Labour's shift to the right in the political spectrum. 'New' Labour's 'new' political philosophy was based on the following principles:

- The free market is best at distributing resources, with government's role limited to regulating markets so that they function efficiently.
- Government should keep out of the economy as far as possible and its main role is providing financial stability and controlling inflation.
- High standards of public services should be established and, if necessary, markets and pseudo-market arrangements should be employed to deliver these services.
- Appropriate levels of taxation should support public spending.
- Government should protect the weak and vulnerable in society through state benefits but carefully targeted ones.
- Redistributing income should result from economic growth and equality of opportunity, not through redistributive taxation policies.
- The relationship between state and citizen should be renewed through constitutional reform.
- Economic relations between states should promote free international trade.
- Multilateralism should be supported in pursuing international security and justice.

By the early twentieth-first century, British politics had also changed because of the 'hollowing out of the state'. Central government had transferred powers upwards to the EU, outwards to the market though privatisation, and to an array of agencies and non-departmental public bodies through 'hiving off'. It had also created a devolved parliament in Scotland and an assembly in Wales. The role of the government now appeared to be one of steering a smaller ship of state rather than directing it. The aspect of this new hollowed out state that attracted most popular concern was the growing importance of the EU, which was seen as taking sovereignty away from the British government and transferring it to Brussels and the EU Council of Ministers.

The distinguishing features of UK politics by this time therefore were the impact of Europe and the radical policy changes of the 1980s and 1990s, which differentiated contemporary politics from those of the earlier post-war period. The goals and strategies of government had fundamentally altered. First, the issue of 'relative economic decline' was no longer on the political agenda, as it had been in the last quarter of the twentieth century. The United Kingdom had made adjustments to the global economy and discussion was dominated by questions of 'national sovereignty' versus 'Europe' and the reform and quality of public services. A new economic orthodoxy existed as Labour had accepted large parts of the Thatcherite legacy.

Second, New Labour had found its own distinctive set of policy initiatives. These incorporated modest grants of political devolution, a tempering of the market with a new stress on community, and pledges to improve the quality of life through improved public services. Labour governments since 1997 appeared to have adapted the neo-liberal legacy of the Conservatives to their own programmes through pursuing a 'third way' in UK politics (Budge *et al* 2004).

Participation in politics

Two other major trends in UK politics are discernible: electoral volatility and declines in electoral turnout. Electoral volatility reflects rapid changes in voting behaviour from one election to another; electoral turnout relates to the proportion of the electorate actually voting in elections.

Electoral volatility

As indicated earlier, modernisation and globalisation are creating an increasingly fluid and mobile society. Homogeneous social groups are being superseded by groups with socially mixed characteristics, for example manual workers now not only own their own houses but also are less likely to be members of trade unions or vote Labour in elections. There is, in short, a weakening of the relationship between social class and party preference. As fewer people are insulated from short-term economic and political processes, more are likely to either switch voting allegiances or abstain from voting in elections at all. Some of these effects are apparent from long-term decline in the level of support for the main political parties. It has been estimated that since 1970 the 'average share of the vote fell for both [main] parties, by 7 percentage points for the Conservatives, and by 10 per percentage points for Labour'. In both cases, 'their vote fluctuated more from one election to another in the later period' (Budge et al 2004, p388). The decline in the votes for the major parties was accompanied by substantial rises in votes for the Liberals and later Liberal Democrats, even though the Liberal vote itself fluctuated more from election to election in the period 1974–1997 than it did for the two major parties. There has also been a significant rise in support for nationalist parties in Scotland and Wales. This trend is indicative of 'partisan dealignment' in national politics or the weakening sense of identification that UK voters have with their preferred party and the rise of nationalist sentiments outside of England.

Each successive election since 1970 has recorded a slightly weaker attachment of electors to parties they had supported in the previous election. In 1964 and 1966, 44 per cent of the British public described themselves as 'very strong' party identifiers, with only 18 per cent saying that they were 'not very strong' party identifiers or identified with no party at all. By 1997 and 2001, only about 16 per cent declared themselves to be 'very strong' party identifiers, with about 44 per cent having a 'weak' identification or none (Norris 1997, Butler and Kavanagh 2001). Thus over three decades, the British electorate has moved from a position of committed partisanship to one of semi-detached voting preferences. Indeed, New Labour's election strategies in 1997, 2001 and 2005 appear to have been based on this trend towards partisan dealignment, by its attempts to attract such 'floating' voters to support it.

Electoral turnout

There has also been a steady decline in electoral turnout, which was slightly down in the 1980s but has been more dramatic since 1992. In 1950, turnout was almost 84 per cent of the electorate but by 2001 it had fallen to 59.4 per cent. A main purpose of elections is to make public policy conform to popular preferences. With low electoral turnouts, popular preferences may get distorted and even lost. Low turnout is a sign that many people do not value democratic processes and may be disinclined to defend them forcibly if they are threatened. In future, unless the main parties have major policy differences, and the election outcome has important consequences for the electorate, there is unlikely to be any increase in electoral turnout.

There are five possible explanations for low electoral turnouts.

- *Apathy*. This derives out of people's lack of knowledge, interest or involvement in politics.
- *Alienation*. This arises when people who are well informed about politics resent the failure

of politicians and parties to address their political interests, resulting in alienation to politics and political processes.

- *Indifference*. This happens when the main parties are seen to be so similar in their policies that the election result is unlikely to make any difference to way that the country is run.
- *Rational abstention*. This is where members of the electorate calculate that their vote will make no difference to the result, so they do not vote.
- *Non-registration*. Only registered voters can vote and in an increasingly geographically mobile society, the numbers not registered is likely to increase.

Based on recent trends, Curtice and Seyd (2003, p93) have claimed that 'there appears to be a crisis of political participation in Britain.' They have argued that this decline in electoral participation might seem particularly surprising given the expansion of educational attainment over the past few decades (see Chapter 5). 'Education is supposedly a "democratic good", meant to encourage adherence to democratic values, a sense of political competence and thus a greater propensity to vote.' In examining this 'puzzle of participation', they concluded that electoral turnout may have fallen 'but it has been accompanied by an increase in non-electoral participation' by the better educated. This means that the participation crisis has been confined to the ballot box but is not part of a wider decline in the willingness of citizens to engage with the political system. However, even among graduates, 'most forms of political activity are the preserve of a small minority, and are likely to remain so in the near future.' The implication is that most people, for most of the time, 'will still be relying on their elected representatives to make the right decisions for them.'

(i) Does a low electoral turnout in general elections matter?

(ii) How might electoral turnout be improved?

THE WELFARE STATE AND CHANGING SOCIAL VALUES

The British welfare state was established by the post-war Labour government between 1945 and 1951 (see Chapter 7). Broadly its aim was to meet the basic social and economic needs of its citizens by providing collectively, through its revenues raised from taxes and other sources, goods and services such as education, health, housing and social security to individual citizens and their families. Based on the Beveridge report (1942) which was initially resisted by the Conservatives, the welfare state became incorporated in the post-war political consensus and was subsequently supported by all political parties and the electorate for many years.

Reforming the welfare state

The first overt challenge to the welfare state came when the Conservative party came to power in 1979. Arguing that high public spending was at the root of the UK's economic difficulties at that time, and that levels of taxation needed to support the welfare state were unsustainable in the future, the Conservatives set about privatising public industries, reforming the remaining public sector and reducing public spending. They also sought to destroy the 'dependency culture', which they claimed the welfare state had reinforced, by reforming support systems. They favoured selectivity rather than universal services and targeting spending more effectively on those most in need. They also promoted more choice and a 'consumerist' attitude towards what were increasingly being called 'public services' rather than the welfare state. They also wanted to encourage greater use of privately-funded welfare services, emphasising personal responsibility in areas such as private healthcare and private pensions.

In many ways, New Labour governments have adapted rather than reversed the broad thrust of Conservative policies, although there have been attempts to improve the level of support for children, low income families and pensioners and to assist people getting into work. Social demands, however, continue to increase and make it difficult for governments to reduce public spending, which remains at around 40 per cent of GNP. As incomes rise, people want better education and improved healthcare services and an ageing population makes greater demands on health, social care and pensions.

There is general agreement that there have been significant changes in the welfare state over the past 20 years, although there is less agreement about whether it amounts to a new or modified form of 'welfarism' (Powell 1999). The major changes have included:

- tighter controls on public spending
- decline in social housing
- growth in private pensions
- increased involvement of private providers in welfare services
- increased private funding of welfare services
- more 'co-payments' for public services such as university 'top up' fees
- greater means-testing of benefits.

The question is have public attitudes to the welfare state changed over the past 25 years? In the early 1980s according to Bosanquet (1986), there was a collectivist attitude towards the welfare state, shared by two-thirds of the population and by people of differing ideological viewpoints. Today Sefton (2003, pp24–25) has concluded that there is, at one and the same time, resistance to attempts to reduce or redefine the welfare state, support for modernising it and a growing divide between these two positions, depending on which aspect of the welfare state is the focus of attention.

First, there has been public resistance to attempts by successive governments to restrict spending on public services. The evidence suggests that support for higher spending has been driven by general dissatisfaction with public services. 'Periods when support for higher spending increased have followed growing dissatisfaction with the National Health Service and state schools.' And debates about direct tax increases to finance higher spending have not dampened public enthusiasm for higher spending on public services.

Second, Sefton's research has shown that the public 'appear to be in sympathy with government's attempts to create a more "modern" welfare state.' Decline in support for spending on welfare benefits for the poor and redistribution, especially among Labour supporters, has occurred at the time when the Labour government was shifting its policy away from direct income redistribution towards a more preventative approach to tackle poverty. People have continued to favour higher spending on benefits to vulnerable groups and the retired 'but, like this government, they have become more selective about who should benefit from increased spending'.

Third, and surprisingly, increase in support for higher spending on public services has been concentrated among Conservative supporters, whereas hardening of attitudes towards benefit claimants has been concentrated among Labour supporters. But increased use of private health and education services does not appear to have undermined support for core public services. However, over this period, younger people have become less favourable towards increases in public spending and harder in their attitudes to the benefit system, relative to older generations. This has led Sefton (2003, p25) to conclude: 'In the process of modernising the welfare state, governments may be losing the support of those on whom the future of the welfare state depends.'

Changing social values

People's personal value systems reflect their enduring beliefs or philosophies that are held about what is 'good' or desirable. These, in turn, underpin a person's attitudes towards a range of issues such as religion, politics, social matters and morals (Alwin and Scott 1996). Two sets of value systems are especially relevant: 'left–right' values and 'libertarian–authoritarian' values.

Left and right values are often associated with economic issues such as the desirability of government intervention in the economy, income and wealth distribution, and relations between workers and managers. Left-wing values emphasise redistribution and the unequal relationship between workers and those employing them in the labour market. Right-wing values emphasise individualism, the value of competition and the impersonal allocation of resources in markets. This value dimension is closely related with political attitudes and opinion and support for left or right parties.

Libertarian and authoritarian values are concerned with authority. Libertarians stress the importance of individualism and freedom of personal action. Authoritarians stress conformity and obedience to authority. This value dimension is closely related to the ways in which people live their lives and their tolerance or intolerance of deviance from social norms.

These two sets of value system do not always go together. The four dimensions tend to be cross-cutting, which adds 'to the complexity of the ways in which they influence social and political attitudes in Britain and interact with the political party system' (Park and Surridge 2003). Three observations stand out:

- Traditionally, the notion of 'left' and 'right' has been closely connected with class, so that left-wing approaches have tended to favour working-class interests and right-wing ones the interests of the middle classes (Clark and Lipset 1996).
- Those who have been through higher education have tended to be more libertarian than authoritarian (Phelan *et al* 1995).
- There has been a tendency for people with left-wing values to support the Labour party and people with right-wing values to support the Conservative party (Sanders 1999).

The British Social Attitudes survey of 2003 examined the different values held by certain social groups and the ways in which they had changed over time. It was particularly interested in the impact that higher education had had on libertarian and authoritarian values, the extent to which social changes had affected the left/right values of different classes, and how the value of different party supporters had changed over the past two decades In terms of left-wing and right-wing groups, the evidence showed that there appeared to be a strong relationship between class and left–right values. Those in the working class and manual employment were especially likely to hold left-wing values and very unlikely to hold right-wing ones. Professional and managerial workers, in contrast, were more likely to have right-wing ones. There were also links between household income, house tenure, education and left–right values, with those in more advantageous socio-economic circumstances being more likely to have right-wing values than those who were less advantaged.

For authoritarian and libertarian groups, the evidence indicated that more highly educated people, especially graduates, were substantially more libertarian than those with lower levels of education. But if education remained the most important influence on these values, social class was important too. The most libertarian group was professional and managerial staff and the most authoritarian was manual supervisors and technicians. The relationship with household income followed a similar path, with those on very high incomes being the most likely to be libertarians and those on very low incomes most likely to be authoritarians.

The evidence also demonstrated that when a range of socio-economic characteristics were taken into account, people's left–right values were still the most important predictor of their being identified with the Conservatives or Labour. There were also marked differences in the libertarian–authoritarian values of party supporters. Conservatives were most likely to be authoritarians, Liberal Democrats were most likely to be libertarians and Labour supporters were towards the libertarian end of the spectrum.

The overall analysis was that there had been 'very small changes in left/right and libertarian/authoritarian values since 1986'. There was a small shift towards the middle of the scale of left-right values and a small shift away from the most authoritarian position of the libertarian-authoritarian scale. (Park and Surridge 2003, p143). The main conclusions of this study were:

- Education continued to relate closely to a person's libertarian–authoritarian values, as did income. However, age was no longer significant once other factors had been taken into account.
- If anything, the impact of social class on left–right values was stronger in 2003 than it had been in 1986, with routine manual workers significantly more left-wing than professional and managerial workers.
- In terms of party politics, decreasing proportions of people were identified with specific political parties, with slight shifts to the centre particularly among Conservative and Labour identifiers. There was some evidence of the value profiles of supporters of these two parties drawing closer together.
- Both left–right and libertarian–authoritarian values had important roles to play in party politics, especially among Conservative identifiers (at the authoritarian end of the spectrum) and Liberal Democrats (at the libertarian end).
- Those on lower incomes tended to have more left-wing and more authoritarian values than those on higher incomes.
- These values continued to play crucial roles in shaping the way in which people responded to the social world around them.

Explain why:

(i) people in working class and manual employment are more likely to hold left-wing values
(ii) people who have experienced higher education are more likely to hold libertarian values.

INDIVIDUALISM, CONSUMERISM AND SECULARISM

Globalisation, new technology and socio-demographic change are important contexts of the post-industrial economies of the contemporary western world. As shown in earlier chapters (especially Chapter 3), business leaders, politicians and individuals have no direct influence on these mega-trends and can only respond to them incrementally and reactively. However, there are other social forces at work within societies, and globally, which are affecting and changing individual behaviours and individual perceptions of the world. These forces are rooted in the renewal and reinforcement of individualist values, consumerism and secularism. They are resulting in increased social segmentation, social atomisation, commercialism and changing self-images.

Individualism is not a new concept of human behaviour and its origins lie in three movements: liberalism, the Reformation and the Enlightenment. Liberal theorists such as Locke (1947 edition) and Hobbes (1947 edition) saw individuals as beings endowed with natural, inalienable human rights by virtue of their humanity including rights to life, property and happiness. For Hobbes, individuals were selfish, acquisitive and aggressive by nature, whereas Locke saw them as moral, reasonable and capable of self-government. These ideas were translated into perceiving individuals as the best judges of their own welfare and that pursuit of individual interests is likely to result in maximum happiness within society. This utilitarian view underpins the argument today for neo-liberalism, free markets and business competition. It also underpins the contemporary human rights movement, liberal democracy and the basic tenets of market economics. These include property rights, the rights of individuals to produce and consume, enter into contracts, buy and sell, satisfy their wants in their own way and dispose of their property and labour as they themselves decide. Thus economic individualism underpins free enterprise, market economies and contemporary capitalism.

Individualism was also the child of the Reformation and religious Protestantism. Weber (1930) argued that the protestant ethic of hard work had a major impact on post-Reformation capitalism. Protestants, particularly the puritan sects, saw salvation being achieved through hard work and discipline in their daily lives. These led to capitalistic conduct based upon individualistic profit making and a moral responsibility towards using resources to increase wealth by effort, moderate consumption and saving for investment. The third strand of individualism can be traced to the Enlightenment with its rejection of superstition, religious faith, tradition and custom and using reason to explain the 'modern' world. Through reason and science, with its emphasis on empiricism and positivism, humankind could ultimately control nature in the interests of humanity. It was the Enlightenment that gave birth to modernism.

In the English-speaking world especially, individualism became the catchword for free enterprise, limited government, personal freedom and minimum state intervention in economic affairs, as opposed to socialism or collectivism (Lukes 2005). It reasserted itself in the 1980s with the political and economic reform movements discussed above and justified attacks on the 'big state', over-regulation and lack of personal choice.

Individualism today is also used to describe social 'atomism', where individuals pursue primarily individualistic, personal ends rather than collectivist, altruistic ones. Social atomism gives priority to individuals and their rights, which are seen as existing prior to any particular form of social life. This is neatly summarised by Macpherson (1962, p3) who has stated that 'possessive individualism' is based on 'a conception of the individual as essentially the proprietor of his [sic] own person or capacities, owing nothing to society for them.' The reassertion of individualist values has been reinforced by the decline of social democratic politics in western societies over the past 30 years and in changes within post-communist societies since the 1990s.

Individualism in economic and social affairs is further reinforced by mass 'consumerism' which is the driving imperative of contemporary capitalism. Continually rising levels of affluence and money incomes enable people to consume, with individual consumption of personal goods and services becoming the ultimate goal or 'good' for those in gainful employment and an expectation of those who are retired or unable to work. Sophisticated shopping malls, targeted marketing campaigns and readily available 'credit' are the agents of mass consumerism by individual consumers that take the forms of demands for niche products, luxury goods and customised services. Such patterns of economic consumption reinforce individualist values in western societies and they, in turn, reinforce personal consumption. The consumption culture spills over into the public sector, where users are increasingly seen as consumers, and satisfying their needs and expectations becomes the driving force of public managers and service providers.

The shift towards market individualism based on consumerism and personal choice based on personal freedom is, in turn, reinforced by another trend – secularism. There was a long-term trend in the decline of organised religion during the nineteenth and twentieth centuries. Religious attendance has continued to fall consistently across all western religions, as individuals have become their own arbiters of morality, choice and social action, in response to rising economic prosperity, wider accessibility to education and the 'consumer society'.

Some social scientists observing these changes in the dominant values and norms within society claim that there is a transformation of western cultures taking place which they call the movement from 'modernism' to 'postmodernism'. Postmodernism rejects the belief that reason and the scientific method can 'discover' the reality of the physical and social worlds. It rejects objectivism and claims there are no facts, only interpretations, and no objective truths only the constructs of individuals and groups. One person's reality is as real as any others and reason gives way to intuition, sentiment and imagination. Postmodern culture rejects the Protestant work ethic, order and discipline for nihilism, hedonism and experientialism (Smart 1993). Postmodernism is also associated with a new language which plays a key role in our understanding of postmodernist complexity and 'reality'. The words used are never neutral but value-laden, contingent and tied to periods of time, location, situations and conflicts. They are closely associated with particular modes of knowledge and understanding. This is clearly illustrated in this book, where the language of the strategic business context creates a picture of the world and a particular reality.

OTHER CONTEMPORARY SOCIAL TRENDS AND PROBLEMS

In this section, some remaining contemporary social trends and problems are outlined and briefly commented upon. They are important issues but selective ones. However, they do not demand the detailed analysis given to the earlier topics discussed in this chapter.

Asylum seekers and economic migrants

Asylum seekers are individuals requesting refuge into a foreign country due to fear of persecution in their countries of origin. The right to apply for asylum is a universal one but policies aimed at reviewing asylum cases have become very controversial in many EU states. EU governments, including that of the United Kingdom, stress the need to prevent 'bogus' asylum applications, whilst protecting the human rights of those with a genuine fear of persecution in their countries of origin. Because of high living standards and supportive welfare states, some economic migrants come to Europe not in fear of persecution but, as they cannot gain entry by other means, seek to do so by applying for asylum. Strict asylum policies have been created and many western countries have witnessed campaigns for migrants to be returned to their countries of origin and threats of deportation if they are unemployed or commit criminal offences. 'Moral panics' portraying migrants as criminals and dependent on the welfare state have prompted a tightening of immigration policies in many countries including the United Kingdom.

The countries from which people arrive to claim asylum in the United Kingdom vary with world events. Iraqi asylum applications increased from nearly 6,700 in 2001 to over 14,500 in 2002. Large numbers of asylum seekers in 2002 also came from Afghanistan, Somalia and Zimbabwe, areas that have seen escalations in conflict. Asylum-related settlement grants rose sharply in 1999 and 2000 due to a change in the rules reducing the qualifying periods for people granted asylum and exceptional leave to remain which effectively increased the number of people eligible for settlement. Of grants of settlement in 2002, 40 per cent were granted to Asian nationals and a further 34 per cent to African nationals. The fall in grants in 2001 was mainly due to a fall in acceptances of African nationals, which fell by 29 per cent from 2000 and then rose by 23 per cent in 2002.

Whilst these developments have taken place, there appears to have been an increase in anti-immigration sentiment in the United Kingdom since the mid-1990s. In 1995, about two-thirds of respondents to the British social attitudes survey wanted the number of immigrants reduced. By 2003, three-quarters of respondents held this view. According to McLaren and Johnson (2004), this was surprising because a dominant trend over the previous 20 years had been increasing liberalism on social issues. There was partial support for the view that the change was due to rising national pride. But there was also evidence that people were increasingly concerned about the perceived social consequences of immigration. Increased hostility was not particularly associated with people exposed to 'anti-immigration newspapers', the sentiment seemed 'to have affected everyone'. Indeed, change had been greatest among graduates and Labour supporters. A number of components seemed to have been at work: the increase in immigration, increase in government pronouncements about it plus increase in media coverage. For these researchers, it was a fertile area for further study. They especially identified the 'specific role played by the media and politicians in framing the immigration issues and shaping public opinion towards immigrants and immigration' (McLaren and Johnson 2004, p197).

Crime and drugs

Crime and drugs are both currently seen as social problems. But, as stated above, social problems are socially constructed and are therefore essentially political phenomena. Crime is what society determines is deviant behaviour and the degree of popular consensus or conflict about that behaviour. For example, murder, robbery, arson and physical assault are generally accepted as crimes, whilst public opinion is more divided about public disorder offences, use of drugs, anti-social behaviour, terrorism, political crimes and vagrancy. It is widely accepted that crime is rising and that governments should tackle the problem, although there is no consensus on how that should be done or on how to deal with offenders. Within the wider problem of rising crime, there is a perception that drug abuse is also rising and is itself linked to the rising crime rate.

What evidence is there to substantiate those assumptions? According to the British Crime Survey (BCS) crimes had been rising steadily since 1981 but peaked in 1995. Since then they have fallen by 39 per cent and by 30 per cent since 1997. The risk of becoming a victim has also fallen from 40 per cent in 1995 to 26 per cent in 2003/2004. Yet 65 per cent of respondents in the BCS thought crime had increased and one-third thought it had risen a lot. This may be due to the media tending to report incidents of crime in sensational ways, thus creating a 'moral panic'. It may also be because people mistrust official statistics, since most crimes are not reported. Only about a third of all crime is reported, 60 per cent is not recorded and 11 per cent is reported but not recorded. Also the BCS does not include 'victimless crime', such as drug abuse or corporate crimes.

There are different types of crime including crimes against the person, crimes against property, victimless crime and white-collar crime. Crimes against the person cover a wide range of actions from murder, to grievous bodily harm, to assault (physical and sexual). There is evidence that these crimes have been increasing, in particular the number of homicides, firearm offences and sexual assaults, although their numbers are still relatively low. Crimes against property account for the majority of crime (78 per cent) but these, according to the statistics, have been falling, with burglary halved since 1997. Nevertheless, there were more than 300,000 cases of shoplifting during

2003/2004 and more than 17,500 cases of theft by employees and over 1 million cases of theft and handling of stolen goods. Some 43 per cent of all crimes are committed in eight metropolitan police areas and 40 per cent of all robberies take place in the Metropolitan Police Area of Greater London. The detection rate is low and has been falling since 1980. It was only 23.5 per cent in 2003/2004.

Corporate and white-collar crimes are also rising but when such crimes as fraud, embezzlement and tax evasion are detected and convictions follow, punishments are less severe. Corporate crime is a fairly recent concept. It is usually committed by companies to increase profits, such as breaking health and safety laws or dumping waste to avoid paying for proper disposal. It has been estimated that in terms of harm caused to individuals and losses to the public in unpaid tax revenues, environmental costs and costs in health and welfare benefits, corporate crime is more serious than street crime and burglary. It amounted to around £16 billion in 2003/2004. It is often unclear who the victim is in corporate crime. It may be the consumer (faulty, dangerous goods), the employee (health and safety failures) or the public (tax evasion resulting in higher taxes).

White-collar crime is characterised by invisibility of victim and complexity. It often occurs when people with expert knowledge use it to steal and defraud. It is particularly difficult to catch the criminals and, when they are caught and convicted, sentences tend to be 'soft' or lenient. These crimes are not considered as serious as street crime or burglary, although recent developments in computer crimes committed by hackers are raising more concerns.

Drug offences are generally classified as victimless crimes. They have been increasing since the 1980s, when the issue of drugs came on to the political agenda. There were over 133,000 drug offences in 2003, an increase of 5 per cent over the previous year. Drugs are classified into three groups according to their harmfulness. Class A drugs include cocaine, crack, heroin, LSD, methadone and ecstasy. Class B drugs include amphetamines and Class C drugs include anabolic steroids and, since 2004, cannabis. Offences have been increasing in all three classes. More than 90 per cent of convictions have been for possession of drugs and, in 2003, before cannabis was reclassified, 70 per cent of all convictions were possession of cannabis. About 10 per cent of drug offenders were for dealing offences. Some 60 per cent of those found guilty of dealing received custodial sentences, while 20 per cent received a combination of community rehabilitation or community punishment orders. Most people convicted only of possession received cautions. Most offenders were young men (90 per cent were under 25), although those convicted of dealing or producing drugs were older, over the age of 25 (Mwenda and Kumari 2005).

Why do you think that white-collar crime, and in particular corporate crime, is not considered as serious as crimes against private property or the person?

Income inequality

Between 1979 and 1990, the income growth of the richest 20 per cent in society was over eight times that of the poorest 20 per cent. During this period, the rate of growth in income inequality in the United Kingdom was the fastest among western states for which data were available. By 2000, the poorest tenth in society received 3 per cent of the UK's total income, whereas the richest tenth received more than a quarter (Goodman and Shephard 2002). This inequitable distribution of income, in turn, has resulted in increasing inequality of wealth (ie ownership of assets) in the United Kingdom. Bromley (2003, p90) has argued, however, that income inequality was no more acceptable to people generally in the early twenty-first century than it had been in the early 1980s.

Whilst there was widespread aversion to income 'redistribution', there was little evidence suggesting that the principle of redistribution was less popular than previously. People's solution to the 'wages' gap tended to be 'a dramatic lowering of salaries for high earners (rather than a very large increase in salaries for lower income earners)'. This study claimed that there was little evidence supporting claims that 'Thatcherism' had encouraged people to be less questioning of large gaps between rich and poor. The generation coming to age during the 1980s were no less concerned about income inequality than some of the previous generations. In her analysis, the view that fewer politicians, rather than fewer people, questioned why incomes were distributed as they were 'might have been closer to the truth'.

The Institute for Fiscal Studies has investigated some of the possible explanations for changes in inequality seen over the last two decades and in particular why the trends are different over the economic cycles of the 1980s and 1990s. It found that wages growth played a part. Inequality tends to rise during periods of rapid wage growth, because the poorest households are the most likely to contain non-working individuals. The economic recovery in the 1980s was characterised by large increases in wages in each of the years from 1984 to 1988, matching the period when inequality increased rapidly. In contrast wage growth was very slow to return in the recovery of the early to mid-1990s, which was a time of stable or falling inequality.

Growth in self-employment income and in unemployment was also found to be associated with periods of increased inequality. It would appear that demographic factors such as the growth in one person households make a relatively unimportant contribution compared with labour market changes. However, the Institute found that changes in the tax and benefit systems have an impact in line with what economic theory suggests. The income tax cuts of the 1970s and late 1980s worked to increase income inequality, while direct tax rises in the early 1980s and 1990s, together with the increases in means-tested benefits in the late 1990s, produced the opposite effect. Recent increases in inequality appear to be driven by changes at the very top and possibly also at the very bottom of the income distribution.

Trade union membership

Since the late 1970s, union membership in the United Kingdom has dropped steadily over the intervening years from about 12.5 million members in 1980 to 7.7 million members in 2003. Also the number of unions fell from 389 in 1980 to 192 in 2003 and, whereas in 1980, the largest unions had represented 'blue collar' workers, by 2003 the largest unions were 'white-collar' organisations representing professional workers (Certification Officer 2004). At the same time, employers in about two-thirds of workplaces with less than 25 employees each recognised trade unions for collective bargaining purposes in 1980 but this had fallen to about a third of all workplaces by 2003. Indeed, by the early years of the twenty-first century, trade unions were largely a public sector phenomenon. These changes in the fortunes of trade unions can be accounted for by a number of factors including:

- the changing economy from an industrial structure to a post-industrial one
- a changing occupational structure from a predominantly manual to a non-manual one
- the shift from largely permanent employment to more flexible employment practices
- the introduction by managers of more individualised employment relationships between employers and employees
- a tight legislative framework for trade unions
- the difficulty for the unions in recruiting service sector workers, female employees and young workers into their organisations.

Trade unions were also marginalised by Conservative governments from 1979 to 1997 and large-ly excluded from the public policy-making process. The Labour government, recognising the need to enlist trade union support for its modernising agenda, reinstated the public sector unions by signing partnership agreements in the civil service and the NHS and encouraging other parts of the public sector and the private sector to do the same. Partnerships vary in the impact that they have had on trade union influence and power.

Work–life balance

Work–life balance has increasingly emerged as a major policy issues at European level and nation-ally (Council of Ministers 2001). It has been argued that increasing the amount of time spent at work is one way in which globalisation has affected family and working life. Employees in the United King-dom currently work the longest hours on average than any other country in Europe. They are also taking less vacation time than they did 20 years ago. Most significantly, the percentage of mothers working full-time has increased dramatically since the end of the Second World War. Taken together, these data suggest that today's couples and parents spend less time together and have less time to spend with their children than they did in the past (Hochschild 1997).

The research evidence suggests that work–life stress is most acutely felt by men and women in professional and managerial occupations. On average, men and women in routine and manual jobs express lower levels of work–life stress than do professional and managerial workers. Lower levels of work–life stress, however, are achieved at some economic cost. It is the longer reported hours of work of professional and managerial workers that contribute significantly to their report-ed levels of work–life stress. As Giddens (1990) and others have argued, contemporary societies are characterised by rising levels of 'individuation', as people in the absence of normative pre-scriptions and roles are faced with the necessity of working on their own 'biographies' to construct their 'reflexive selves.' With employment career patterns and stable career paths becoming increasingly eroded, and organisations being de-layered and downsized, work and employment have themselves become increasingly individualised. Individuals wanting to move up their occu-pational ladders have to further their 'promotability', by demonstrating their personal 'worth' to their superiors by exceptional effort and working consistently 'beyond contract'.

According to Crompton et al (2003, pp183–184), 'men are twice as likely to want to move up the job ladder as women, and professional and managerial employees are three times as likely to want to move up the job ladder as routine and manual workers.' In this study, promotional aspira-tions were associated with greater work–life stress, particularly among professional and manage-rial women and routine and manual men. In these writers' views, work–life balance had become a problem because of fundamental shifts in gender roles, attitudes and the economic behaviour of women. At the same time, however, UK governments have been embracing neo-liberal eco-nomic and labour market policies, promoting flexible employment and organisational and individ-ual competitiveness. 'High commitment' management strategies are also increasing workplace pressures on employees and increasing material inequalities among them (see above). These data have suggested that tensions have been greatest 'for two groups who have responded to these competitive changes and [have sought] advancement within increasingly individualised career structures ... aspirant managerial and professional women, and men in routine manual occupations' wanting to move up the job ladder.

Protecting the environment

All societies are now faced by concerns about the environment and environmental ecology and how best to cope with and contain environmental damage under the impacts of modern industry, technology and world population growth. The idea of the 'limits of growth' debate, popularised in the 1970s, was that economic growth and development was not compatible with the finite nature of the earth's resources (Hirsch 1976). Today sustainable development, in contrast, holds that growth should occur but should take place in ways that recycle resources rather than deplete them. In the case of the United Kingdom, the condition of the environment impacts on and is impacted by society locally, nationally and internationally. Phenomena such as industrial pollution and climate change have had, or are likely to have, profound implications for individuals, industry and the United Kingdom as a whole. For example, many activities produce pollutants, carbon dioxide emissions, resource depletion and result in global warming, which can harm the environment, as well as affecting human health and welfare.

Research shows that virtually all of the world's ecosystems have been significantly transformed through human actions, particularly in the last 50 years. Changes in ecosystems have been accelerating and today the fastest changes are taking place in developing countries. Ecosystems are particularly affected by large-scale fishing, freshwater use and intensive agriculture. They depend on fundamental environmental cycles such as the continuous circulation of water, carbon and other nutrients. Human activities around the world have modified these cycles, especially during the last 50 years, through increases in freshwater use, carbon dioxide emissions and fertiliser use. This, in turn, has affected the ability of ecosystems to provide benefits to humankind. Many animal and plant populations have declined in numbers, geographical spread or both. For example, a quarter of the world's mammal species is currently threatened by extinction. Human activity has caused between 50 and 1,000 times more extinctions in the last 100 years than would have happened due to natural processes. Increasingly, the same species are found at different locations on the planet and overall biodiversity is decreasing, because some rare species are lost and common ones spread to new areas. Overall, the range of genetic differences within species has declined, particularly for crops and livestock.

In March 2005, experts warned ecosystem changes were continuing to worsen, putting national and global development goals at risk. A landmark study, the *Millennium Ecosystem Assessment Synthesis Report* (United Nations 2005), revealed that approximately 60 per cent of 'ecosystem services' (ie the benefits people obtain from ecosystems) that support life on earth – such as fresh water, sea fisheries, air and water regulation, and regulation of regional climate, natural hazards and pests – were being degraded or used unsustainably. The Millennium Ecosystem Assessment (MEA) was an international programme designed to meet the needs of decision-makers and the public for scientific information concerning the consequences of ecosystem change for human well-being and options for responding to those changes. Scientists warned that the harmful consequences of this degradation could grow significantly worse in the next 50 years. The study said that any progress achieved in addressing the goals of poverty reduction, hunger eradication, and improved health and environmental protection in the world was unlikely to be sustained, if most of the ecosystem services on which humankind relies continued to be degraded. It specifically stated that the ongoing degradation of ecosystem services was a block to the Millennium Development Goals (MDGs) agreed to by world leaders at the UN in 2000 (see Chapter 4).

Although the evidence was incomplete, there was enough for the experts to warn that the ongoing degradation of 15 of the 24 ecosystem services examined was increasing the likelihood of potentially abrupt changes that will seriously affect human well-being. These included the emergence of new diseases, sudden changes in water quality, creation of 'dead zones' along coasts, collapse of fisheries and shifts in regional climate.

The MEA focused on ecosystem services, how changes in ecosystem services have affected human well-being, how ecosystem changes may affect people in future decades and response options. These responses might be adopted locally, nationally or globally to improve ecosystem management and thereby contribute to human well-being and poverty alleviation. The MEA was intended to be used (United Nations 2005):

- to identify priorities for action
- to be a benchmark for future assessments
- to be a framework and source of tools for assessment, planning and management
- to gain foresight concerning the consequences of decisions affecting ecosystems
- to identify response options to achieve human development and sustainability goals
- to help build individual and institutional capacity to undertake integrated ecosystem assessments and act on the findings
- to guide future research.

To what extent is economic growth compatible with the finite nature of the world's resources and the capability of the planet to carry population growth and absorb pollution?

IMPLICATIONS FOR ORGANISATIONS AND P&D PROFESSIONALS

British society has changed significantly over the past 50 years. The population is growing slowly, ageing and becoming more multicultural. Family structures are more diverse than in the past and single-person and single parent households are common features of contemporary Britain. The working population is highly feminised, as more women have entered the labour market and more women are becoming financially independent of men. Also new patterns of flexible employment reflect the transition from an industrial to a post-industrial, knowledge-based economy. These changes are reflected, in turn, in the system of social stratification, as household incomes generally rise, social mobility increases and differences between social classes and statuses simultaneously become both more blurred and more distinctive. All these factors and others outlined in this chapter have implications for organisations and P&D professionals.

Organisations in the private sector, for example, need to respond to the diverse needs of their customers in ever-increasingly segmented and competitive product markets. More social diversity, changing family structures, rising affluence and assertive individualism are putting pressures on businesses to diversify their product ranges, product choices and product development, so as to meet the rising expectations of demanding customers in the marketplace. What both household consumers and business customers generally want today are quality products, competitive prices, choice and service. Where there is international competition for customers, pressure on suppliers is even greater. In the private services sector too, potential customers expect niche services, variety and good customer service. Seeking and retaining their customer bases, in short, have become major objectives and imperatives for private businesses.

It is also apparent that the social changes outlined in this chapter are resulting in individual identities now being increasingly structured to a greater extent around personal lifestyle choices. Organisations and businesses have to respond to these changes and the challenges arising out of them. Such lifestyle choices are centred less on traditional class indicators such as employment and work status and more on how to dress, what to eat, how to care for one's body and where to relax.

Bourdieu (1986) has identified social class groups according to their levels of cultural and economic capital. As time passes, individuals are distinguishing themselves not according to economic or occupational factors but on the basis of cultural tastes and leisure pursuits. This has resulted in new businesses and new enterprises being created to satisfy customer-perceived needs. In an age of personalised consumption, individuals are helped by the proliferation of 'needs merchants' facilitating this process. These new business professionals are the growing number of people involved in presenting and representing goods and services, either actual or symbolic, in the globalised economy. They include advertisers, marketing people, fashion designers, style consultants, interior designers, personal trainers, therapists and webpage designers. All are involved in influencing cultural tastes and promoting lifestyle choices amongst an ever-widening community of consumers.

Building on this analysis, Savage *et al* (1992) have identified three distinctive lifestyles and consumption patterns within the middle class, on the basis of their cultural tastes and assets. These are, first, professionals in public service who are high in 'cultural capital' and low in 'economic capital'. They tend to pursue healthy, active lifestyles involving exercise, low alcohol consumption and participation in cultural and community activities. Second, there are managers and bureaucrats who have 'non-distinctive' patterns of consumption involving average or low levels of exercise, little engagement in cultural activities and a preference for traditional styles in home furnishings and fashion. The third group, the 'postmoderns', pursue lifestyles lacking any defining principles and may contain elements not traditionally enjoyed alongside each other, such as interests in classical music, extreme sports, drinking large quantities of alcohol or taking drugs.

Clearly, rapid expansion of the service economy and the entertainment and leisure industries reflect an increasing emphasis on consumption in modern society. The United Kingdom, like other contemporary western countries, has become a consumption society, geared to the acquisition and use of material goods. This provides a myriad of opportunities for organisations to satisfy a variety of customer wants in the 'consumer society' and its marketplace. In such a societal order, social class differences are partially overridden, with people from different social backgrounds watching similar television programmes and films or shopping in the 'same' high streets and shopping malls. But social class differences also become intensified through variations in income, lifestyles and 'tastes'.

The public sector too is having to adjust to rising expectations by taxpayers, as 'customers', 'clients' or 'consumers' of public services, who are better informed about their rights and what choices are available to them than in the past. With the marketisation of public services, schools, universities and hospitals, for example, are competing for pupils, students and patients. Public organisations are responding to this competition by marketing and promoting their services and trying to meet their targeted 'customers' needs'. Starting under the Conservatives in the 1980s and 1990s, governments argued that injecting a degree of competition into welfare services would provide the public with choice and ensure high quality services. Consumers would in effect 'vote with their feet' in choosing educational and healthcare services from specific providers. Institutions providing substandard services would be forced to improve their services or 'withdraw' from the market. Critics argued, on the other hand, that internal markets and quasi-markets would lead to lower quality services and a stratified system of service provision, rather than protecting the espoused value of 'equal services for all citizens', 'free at the point of use.'

Within the changing economy and social structure, there is a changing labour market to which organisations and P&D professionals are having to respond. On the supply side, more women are available and willing to work than in the past. This requires employers taking into account in their P&D policies issues such as working hours (to meet women's needs in their dual roles as workers and carers, as well as diversity of family life), gender equality and work–life balance. Women continue to experience inequalities in the labour market. Occupational gender segregation results in women being concentrated in different types of work than men. Many 'female jobs' are clustered in low-pay occupations and women are over-represented in part-time employment. The gender pay gap results in women on average, and throughout their life-times, earning less than men with the same qualifications. All these issues have recruitment, selection, reward, and learning and development implications for organisations.

On the demand side, the changing labour market needs of employers include the need for more knowledge workers, professional staff and other specialist workers in response to skills shortages and the changing economic and social structures impacting on organisations. Recruiting and employing overseas economic migrants, such as computer and IT analysts, research scientists, foreign language speakers and medical staff, have been one reaction to such labour market short-ages. Another initiative has been drawing from overseas sources to provide less skilled labour resources at the other end of the labour market, where certain types of labour are also in short supply. On the other hand, there is also the issue of an unquantifiable number of illegal often over-seas workers, employed in the 'informal', alternative economy, who do not pay taxes or national insurance, receive derisible rates of pay and whose health and safety at work is at risk.

It is also clear that transformations in the world of work are overlapping to produce new challenges to achieve some degree of work–life balance between working life and family life. Changes in house-hold structures have coincided with enormous changes in the economy and workplace. Organisa-tions are trying to become more efficient and streamlined, by cutting jobs and flattening hierarchies, whilst employees are working longer hours. One side effect of this is the growing gap between 'work-rich' households, with too much work to do, and 'work-poor' ones with not enough. Another side effect is the growing divide between dual-income households and one or no earner households. There is, however, no consensus on the precise criteria for developing an effective family-friendly, work–life balance policy. Harker (1996) has identified four objectives needing to be met. Such policies should:

- enable employees to meet home and work demands
- support gender equality and the sharing of family obligations
- not discriminate and be friendly to the needs of employees
- be underwritten by an 'invisible contract' between the needs of the employer and worker.

A number of 'family friendly' policies are being adopted by some employers to assist households to balance working life and non-working life commitments. These are far from universal but are increasing in importance. They include:

- *Flexitime*. This allows workers to choose their own working hours, within set limits, and shifts the workload around into a new pattern of attendance.
- *Job sharing*. This restructures the way in which is organised. Job-shares allow two peo-ple to share the responsibility and rewards of a single job and can also be arranged for two part-time workers.
- *Homeworking*. This allows employees to perform some or all of their responsibilities from home, with the help of a computer and modem. The phenomenon of 'wired workers' seems likely to grow in importance in the future.
- *Parental leave*. By law, working mothers and fathers in the United Kingdom are limited in the number of weeks of unpaid leave that they can claim from their employer. But in many other European countries, such as in Scandinavia, parental leave policies have been implemented to encourage fathers in particular to take off time to assist with childcare.

Flexible work policies, however, are not available in many workplaces and they are often only given to 'preferential' staff. The take-up rate for flexible policies by staff varies enormously. Also some commentators have argued that family-friendly policies alone do not integrate women fully into the labour market and ensure their economic independence. Nevertheless, family friendly policies have become more popular in some organisations, in part because they see them as attractive benefits to offer valued or potential employees.

CONCLUSION

This chapter examines some of the major social trends within the UK today. The family is a central institution in society, which satisfies basic human needs for emotional security, economic welfare and reproduction and helps socialise children and young people into the adult world. Its forms and structure change over time, however, in response to evolving economic structures, gender power relations and social norms. Today the family consists of a myriad of different types.

One of the major social changes over the past 50 years has been feminisation of the workforce, where women now make up 50 per cent of all workers. Nevertheless, despite recent attempts by government to initiate gender equality policies, horizontal and vertical segregation of jobs between women and men remain. There are also signs of increasing polarisation in female employment between high status well-paid jobs and low status poorly-paid ones.

The United Kingdom remains a socially stratified society, although there are different ways of defining social class. However, despite rising living standards and a changing occupational structure, concentrations of economic power, social status, political influence and large differentials in income and wealth distribution remain. Also a new politics has emerged, where the 'New' Labour Party has rejected traditional old Labour economic interventionism and redistributive policies and substituted them with sound public finances, support for market solutions and public service reforms. In national politics, there has been continuing partisan dealignment and weakening identification between voters and their preferred parties. There has also been a declining electoral turnout for many years.

The welfare state is changing too, with declining social housing provision, increasing involvement of private providers and greater means-testing of benefits. People's changing social values have resulted in decreasing proportions of them identifying with specific political parties and shifts to the political centre among both Conservative and Labour identifiers.

Individualism, consumerism and secularism are dominant forces in the contemporary world. They underpin personal preferences and individual choice, the market allocation of resources and a postmodern perspective of human life where there is no objective reality. Finally, a series of other social trends and problems has been identified and briefly examined: asylum seekers and economic migrants, crime and drugs, income inequality, trade union membership, work–life balance and protecting the environment.

USEFUL READING

ABERCROMBIE, N. and WARDE, A. (eds). (2000) *Contemporary British society.* Cambridge: Polity.

BEVERIDGE, F., NOTT, S. and STEPHEN, K. (2000) Mainstreaming and the engendering of policy making: a means to an end? *Journal of European Public Policy.* Vol.3, No. 3, pp385–405.

BUDGE, I., CREWE, I., MCKAY, D. and NEWTON, K. (2004) *The new British politics.* London: Pearson Education.

GIDDENS, A. (1981) *The class structure of advanced societies.* London: Hutchinson.

GIDDENS, A. (2001) *Sociology.* Cambridge: Polity Press.

GOODE, J., CALLENDER, C. and LISTER, R. (1998) *Purse or wallet? Gender inequalities and income distribution within families on benefits.* London: Policy Studies Institute.

GOODMAN, A. and SHEPHARD, A. (2002) *Inequality and living standards in Great Britain: Some facts.* London: Institute for Fiscal Studies.

HALSEY, A. (2000) A hundred years of social change. *Social Trends No. 30*, London: Office for National Statistics.

MWENDA, I. and KUMARI, K. (2005) *Drug offenders in England and Wales.* London: Home Office.

NORRIS, P. (1997) *Electoral change since 1945.* Oxford: Blackwell.

PARK, A., CURTICE, J., THOMSON, K., JARVIS, L. and BROMLEY, C. (eds). (2003) *British social attitudes: the 20th Report.* London: Sage.

POWELL, M. (ed). (1999) *New labour, new welfare state? The third way in British social policy.* Bristol: The Policy Press.

SAMPSON, A. (2004) *Who runs this place? The anatomy of Britain in the 21st century.* London: Murray.

WHITMARSH, A. (1995) *Social focus on women.* London: HMSO.

Government Policy

CHAPTER 7

> **CHAPTER OBJECTIVES**
>
> By the end of this chapter, readers should be able to:
>
> - advise organisations on the impact of current and future government policy
> - positively contribute to activities aimed at influencing the direction of government policy.
>
> In addition, readers should be able to understand, explain and critically evaluate:
>
> - the objectives of government and EU policy on the economy, trade, industry, education and in the wider social field
> - critiques of current government policy and rival opposition platforms
> - the current and likely future impact of government policy on organisations.

INTRODUCTION

Government policies are actions taken by the political executive to implement its decisions, such as on taxation, public spending, managing the economy, health and education that affect citizens, families and organisations as taxpayers, consumers and users of public services. Policy decisions, whether in economic, social, international or other affairs, derive out of party manifesto commitments, the governmental agenda, the resources at government's disposal and the circumstances at the time. When discussing government policy, it is customary to distinguish between the institutional context, style of policy-making and its substantive content. As with many aspects of UK politics, the most notable institutional characteristic of government policy is its highly centralised nature. This derives from the parliamentary system, with its dominant political executive, and the relative weakness of regional and local government. This contrasts with the federal systems of government in Germany and the United States, where power is shared between the federal or national government and *Länder* and states respectively. In each case, the *Länder* and states derive their powers from written constitutions and have their own legislative spheres of influence and tax raising powers. This chapter identifies and discusses some of government's major policy initiatives, and those of the main opposition parties, placing them in their historical perspectives. It also considers the evolution of EU economic and social policy and their impact on the United Kingdom.

INSTITUTIONS OF GOVERNMENT

The dominant institutions in public policy-making in the United Kingdom in terms of executive power are the Prime Minister's Office, Treasury, Cabinet Office and government departments. Although Parliament is the legislature and can veto or amend legislation, because of the nature of the party system and the electoral system which usually produces single party majorities, its major role is to support the government. The House of Lords is largely a legislative, reforming and debating chamber, although it can on occasion throw out government legislation but only for one year. The select committees of both houses of Parliament perform a useful scrutiny role, especially the Public Accounts Committee of the House of Commons. The EU is itself a major source of policy which is binding on the United Kingdom but many of the directives have to be incorporated into British law. The primary actors involved in taking policy decisions include the prime minister, chancellor of the exchequer, treasury officials, cabinet ministers, spending department officials, relevant pressure groups, local government and EU officials.

In terms of the style and substance of how policy is made, it depends on the area of policy. Areas of social policy are generally more open, although during the Thatcher administrations there was far less consultation and involvement of stakeholders than before 1979 and since 1997. The major feature of policy-making for much of the post-war period was 'tripartism' with government consulting the 'peak' associations of labour and business, namely the Trades Union Congress (TUC) and Confederation of British Industry (CBI). Constellations or networks of interest groups surrounded each major area of policy, including agriculture, education, health, defence and local government, and policy emerged from departments and was discussed in advisory and consultative committees. In areas such as foreign and defence policy, the process was relatively closed and secretive on the grounds of national security. Politicians and senior civil servants tended to initiate policy which was then presented and defended, sometimes modified and changed after consultation but was clearly top down. In some areas, it appeared to be characterised by 'crisis management', as governments pursued 'stop-go' economic policies. Because of the post-war political consensus, however, it was characterised in most areas by incremental change.

The election of the Conservatives in 1979 was followed by a period of transformational change in which the policy style was quite different. Policy emanated from politicians and their advisors and external think tanks. Senior civil servants were relied upon less as policy advisors and more as policy implementers. Tripartism was abandoned and the trade unions marginalised. Although the policy networks continued to be consulted, it was on a much reduced scale except in areas where government needed key stakeholder co-operation as in the case of the police. Governments were able to push through their radical policies without much resistance, because of large majorities in the House of Commons and the built-in Conservative majority in the House of Lords. During the Major administrations, when the Conservative party was more divided, there were more constraints on government but most policies were accepted.

When the Labour party came to office under Blair, they were committed to increasing democracy in the policy-making process and, in particular, pursuing a more open and consultative process. They created a people's forum of 5,000 randomly chosen citizens, who are consulted on all government proposals before they proceed to draft legislation. All government organisations are required to pursue a similar stakeholder involvement approach. The government also makes extensive use of green papers, consultative papers and the Internet to inform the public of its proposals and invites responses. There has been a return to a more pluralist approach to policy.

Between 1997 and mid-2005, Labour governments generally had an easy time in getting their policies accepted in Parliament. The prime minister was broadly supported by both the cabinet and Parliamentary Labour Party in his administration's policy initiatives and enjoyed an unusual degree of support regarding the fundamentals of government policy. Although there were some problematic policy areas such as foreign affairs, social security cuts, 'top up' fees in higher education, identity cards, immigration and asylum seekers, support for the government held up. One factor was acceptance of the primacy of economic policy and the almost universal perception that the main aim of economic policy under recent Labour administrations was control of inflation, as a means of maintaining economic growth and low unemployment.

After involvement in the Iraq War in 2003, the party became more divided and support for the prime minister fell among both labour supporters and the country at large. There were smaller majorities in the House of Commons and coalitions of Labour rebels in the Commons and cross-bench opposition in the House of Lords frustrated some policies, although they did not stop them. These included House of Lords reform, banning fox hunting and introducing legal powers of house arrest and restriction of civil liberties from getting on the statute book. In the period after the 2005 general election, however, the Labour government, with its reduced majority in the House of Commons, found it more difficult than previously to get its legislative initiatives relatively unchallenged through the House. In this Parliament, Parliamentary Labour Party 'rebels' had more potential power to keep the government in check, when it pursued policies that were unpopular with these MPs.

ECONOMIC POLICY

The basic distinction in economic policy is between macro-policy and micro-policy. Macro-economic policy is concerned with total or aggregate economic performance and includes monetary policy, covering interest rates, money supply, exchange rates, and inflation, and fiscal policy covering taxation and government spending and borrowing. Micro-economic policy is concerned with the performance and behaviour of individual units within the economy such as firms, trade unions, consumers and regional and local government. Clearly, the two areas are interrelated, since how firms, consumers and trade unions behave influences the macro-economy, overall level of demand for goods and services and the savings rate. Such micro-activities inform macro-economic management by government (Curwen 1997).

The post-war settlement

As outlined in Chapter 2, British economic policy has been dominated historically by free market and free trade principles. Indeed, Britain was a leader of free market economic thinking and principles during the nineteenth and early twentieth centuries. In contrast to France, Germany, Japan and Russia, industrialisation in Britain took place with little direct intervention by government. By the third quarter of the nineteenth century, the British economy was the largest in the world but it was private capital and free markets that had been the driving forces behind the construction of the institutional infrastructure and development of manufacturing and extractive industries. At the same time, Britain was a champion of international free trade. By the early 1930s, however, the system of world free trade was breaking down. This was one of the effects of the First World War, where the leading trading nations had fought themselves to economic and fiscal standstills. This led to major ideological and policy shifts in Britain involving abandonment of free trade and support for substantial government intervention in the economy and society.

The interventionist macro-economic reforms initiated by national governments in the 1930s, which included some nationalisation, public works to stimulate employment and low interest rates to encourage investment, were carried further by the Labour governments of 1945–1951 and were supported by both Conservative and Labour governments during the so-called 'post-war settlement', sometimes called the 'social democratic consensus', from 1945 until 1979. This consensus was underpinned by Keynesian economic policies, which gave a central place to government action in smoothing out the economic cycle. This consensus advocated government intervention in the economy to achieve economic stability, steady growth and full employment especially. The consensus was an implicit agreement amongst all political parties, up till 1979, that the fundamental economic and social policies of the reforming post-war Labour governments should remain unchallenged and unchanged (Deakin 1994).

Both Conservative and Labour governments during this period adopted Keynesian economic policies, 'free' health provision, increased social benefits and accepted state ownership of major public utilities. Keynesianism was its bedrock and aimed at avoiding unemployment by drawing upon relevant fiscal and monetary policies. This resulted in public spending being raised and taxes cut during recessions and public spending being cut and taxes raised when the economy overheated. There were also attempts at controlling prices and incomes through various monitoring bodies and at economic planning (Brittan 1964, Budd 1978).

Neo-liberalism

The end of the long post-war economic boom in the early 1970s revealed the limits of the bipartisan social democratic consensus and government intervention in the economy. Chronic balance of payments crises, abandonment of fixed exchange rates, a rapid rise in commodity prices, poor economic performance and low productivity in the United Kingdom were symptomatic of an under-performing economy. Under Conservative governments led by Margaret Thatcher and John Major between 1979 and 1997, support for and belief in free trade and free markets reasserted themselves thus replacing the social democratic consensus with a 'neo-liberal' one. Neo-liberalism incorporated ideas associated with the 'New Right' of the 1980s that market competition was the best means of guaranteeing economic growth and political freedoms. Substantive policies included privatising key public services, promoting free markets, supporting deregulation and introducing supply-side economic policies (Gamble 1994). The underlying assumption was that the economy was best left to 'run itself' with a minimum of government regulation. What regulation there was should be undertaken on financial grounds alone, thus favouring City interests, and should be aimed at reducing inflation. Public services were to be run on the 'market model', with incentives for efficient providers, penalties for inefficient ones and the welfare state being more selective in the ways it distributed social benefits.

Supply-side economics comprised a range of measures, aimed at unleashing market forces, raising productivity and encouraging greater market competitiveness (Grant 2002). These measures included:

- cutting back public spending to release more resources for the private sector
- lowering direct taxes to increase economic incentives
- weakening the bargaining power of trade unions
- challenging the political power of trade unions and their links with the Labour party
- encouraging flexibility of pay and working practices
- reducing entitlement to certain welfare benefits
- encouraging investment and enterprise
- promoting competition through deregulation and privatisation
- removing barriers to the free movement of finance capital.

'New' Labour

When the Labour party returned to power in 1997, under the label of 'New' Labour (in contrast with the 'New Right'), after 18 years in opposition, it retained much of the Thatcherite economic policy agenda including a commitment not to raise direct taxes and also to keep to the projected public expenditure targets for the first two years in office. There were two main strands to its economic policy. The first was a strategy for delivering both economic stability and economic growth through fiscal probity and a strong financial system. The second was to remove the barriers to economic growth by tackling supply side barriers including the lack of skills and employability of the labour force. Both of these strategies were in turn linked to improving public services as increased and sustainable economic growth would generate the revenues needed to increase expenditure on public services without raising income tax. One of the first actions of the new government was to give the Bank of England a measure of independence by handing the power to set interest rates to its Monetary Policy Committee, which would take decisions about interest rates out of political control (see Chapter 2). This alerted business to the new hands-off approach that the New Labour government intended to follow and raised its credibility, particularly with the financial sector.

The economic policy of New Labour that evolved comprised seven main elements, which drew upon neo-liberal antecedents and theories of 'endogenous growth'. This theory argues that long-term economic growth is generated by technological progress coming from investment and innovation. Within this context, the role of government is to stimulate investment and innovation by supporting basic research, promoting entrepreneurship and investing in public capital (Thomas 2001). These seven elements are outlined below.

- *Keeping inflation low.* Low inflation is government's prime economic policy objective. Previously, low unemployment and high growth were government's top priorities, with low inflation in a weak third position. With the internationalisation of finance capital, governments almost everywhere identify low inflation as the basis for economic prosperity and economic progress.
- *Fiscal responsibility.* During the 1960s and 1970s, UK governments believed that it was possible to 'spend their way out of trouble'. This meant stimulating the economy through raising public sector borrowing and increasing public spending to speed recovery. Today government is convinced that the only way to spend responsibly is to finance expenditure through taxation. Government borrowing is permitted but is not expected to rise to more than 3 per cent of GDP. During periods of sustained growth it is less than this. Such spending is designated as 'investment in public services,' with government borrowing being limited to support public investment spending.
- *Public spending of about 40 per cent of GDP.* In 2004/2005, total public spending in the United Kingdom was around £480 billion, which represented about 40 per cent of GDP or about £7,000 per year for every man, woman and child. This compared with about 30 per cent of GDP in Australia, Ireland and the United States, around 40 per cent in Greece and the Netherlands, and around 50 per cent in Denmark, Hungary and France (OECD 2004). Social security payments and other personal social services were the largest items of expenditure in the United Kingdom (31.1 per cent), followed by the National Health Service (15.6 per cent), education (12.9 per cent), defence and law and order (5.7 per cent each), and housing and the environment (4.8 per cent). The remaining expenditure was spent largely on debt interest, industry, agriculture and employment, and transport (HM Treasury 2004).
- *Low and preferably indirect taxation.* High direct taxation is assumed to be an economic 'bad'. Formerly, Labour governments supported high progressive income taxes and low indirect taxes. It is argued that high income taxes are disincentives to work and undermine economic efficiency. Indirect taxes, on the other hand, it is argued, provide consumers with the choice to save rather than to spend on low tax as opposed to high tax items. New Labour has broadly accepted this point of view.
- *The market rather than the state should provide goods and services.* Traditionally, Labour governments believed in public or common ownership of 'the commanding

heights of the economy' and Conservatives in privatisation. Today all political parties accept the advantages of privatisation, although Labour accepts the need for more regulation of companies previously in public ownership (see Chapter 8). However, it does not propose renationalising them.

- *Support for free trade.* Labour governments now support open international markets, with free and open competition at home and abroad, and only a minimal role for the state in protecting UK industry or firms.
- *Internationalisation of economic policy.* Economic policy in the United Kingdom is increasingly affected by external events, such as in the EU and international capital markets. EU regulatory, environmental and competition law now have precedence over national law and largely affect micro-policy. If the United Kingdom joins EMU (the Euro), then the European Central Bank will set all aspects of macro-economic policy, such as interest rates and exchange rate policy. Only fiscal policy will be left to central government, although even here it will be subject to the Stability and Growth Pact. In terms of international capital markets, with abolition of fixed exchange rates and removal of capital movement controls, there is pressure on government to have low levels of domestic inflation and of public debt. If markets sense that inflation or debt is out of control, investors will move out of what they perceive to be a vulnerable currency to a stronger one. In this case, to maintain the value of its currency, government will be forced to take drastic corrective actions such as cuts in public spending, raising interest rates or increasing taxation.

The commitment was to keep within the Conservative spending plans, not to raise direct taxes, to reduce public debt and only to increase public expenditure when prudent to do so (ie without borrowing so emphasising that this was 'New' Labour not 'Old' Labour). However, Annesley and Gamble suggest (2004, p148): 'early insistence on fiscal prudence and monetary credibility made the government appear far more orthodox than it was'. In fact, it did raise considerable extra revenue during its first administration from a one-off windfall tax on the profits of privatised utilities, which provided over £5 billion pounds to fund expenditure on the NHS, education and its new welfare-to-work programme. Pension funds tax credits were also abolished and this was estimated to raise another £5 billion. Tax relief for married couples and mortgage relief were also abolished in 1999 and later National Insurance for higher income groups was raised, effectively lifting the highest rate of income tax to 41 per cent. Early in their first administration, New Labour introduced comprehensive spending reviews and five-year unrolling expenditure plans based on projections of increases in GNP.

In order to increase public investment in public services without borrowing, New Labour used the Conservative invention of private financial initiatives (PFIs). These invited private investment in the construction of schools, hospitals and other public infrastructure. They were then leased back to public agencies for a specified period of 30 to 40 years. Although this involved higher government spending, it was spread over a longer period of time and did not appear on the public expenditure accounts. There are close similarities between the Conservative and New Labour approaches to economic policy but there are significant differences. There has been a major recasting of public expenditure and implicit in the government's comprehensive spending reviews was an element of Keynesian counter-cyclical thinking. New Labour's economic policy can best be described as 'eclectic' with a blend of monetarism, macro-economic pragmatism and Keynesian activism. Furthermore, their supply-side approach involved spending on training and removing the skills bottleneck, as well as introducing more regulation of the privatised public services to encourage both investment and also control over price increases which had a big impact on the rest of industry.

In summary, New Labour's economic policy has been effectively driven by the need to increase the size of the national economic cake, so that employment and standards of living would rise and so would tax revenues. Increased purchasing power would stimulate industry, which would also benefit from low inflation and low interest rates and a supply of money in line with GNP. The government's policies appeared to be successful as after two terms in office inflation rates were the lowest for 40 years and the lowest in the EU; growth was consistent at between 2 and 3 per cent per annum and the highest in the EU. Critics argue that New Labour is simply building on and continuing the neo-liberal policies of the Thatcher and Major years. Others argue, however, that New Labour's 'third way' is quite distinctive marrying the benefits of the market with the pursuit of social justice, greater equality and a fairer society.

(i) What are the differences of New Labour's economic policy and that of the Conservatives?
(ii) Identify and explain how recent government economic policies have affected your organisation.

SOCIAL POLICY

Social policy, broadly defined, is those policies that relate to personal welfare and the state's role in meeting people's welfare needs. It covers areas such as health care, income maintenance, housing and education, where government plays a major role in providing 'public services' and 'state benefits' to individuals and households, as opposed to these services being supplied by the market. In many modern economies, such as that of the United States, most state benefits are provided on a selective basis. The criteria normally used to determine eligibility include income, wealth, age and disability. In some countries, state benefits are provided universally, such as the NHS in the United Kingdom. All social groups are eligible for such benefits which means that the same benefit is provided to everyone on the basis of personal need. Elements of both systems are present in most western countries. In this section, the NHS, income maintenance and social housing are examined, with education policy being discussed in the following section (Blakemore 1998).

The welfare state

A 'welfare state' is where the state takes responsibility for providing at least minimum levels of economic and social security for its citizens. These include health care, social housing, sickness and unemployment benefits, education and pensions. The reforming Labour governments of 1945–1951 created the welfare state in the United Kingdom, although the Liberals had established a rudimentary unemployment insurance scheme and a low state pension in 1908. The modern welfare state was the product of the inter-war depression of the 1930s and the Second World War, which had shown how high levels of government spending could eliminate mass unemployment and address large-scale poverty. Its intellectual basis was rooted in Keynesian economics (Keynes 1936) and Beveridge's report on full employment and social welfare (Cutler et al 1986).

Beveridge argued that the new tools of economic management would enable mass unemployment to be eliminated and 'full employment in a free society' to become the norm, with government providing a system of social protection for those unable to work and provide it for themselves. Based on the principle of universalism, a comprehensive welfare state would ensure that everybody was secure – 'from the cradle to the grave' – from the five great 'evils' of 'want', 'ignorance', disease', 'squalor' and 'idleness'. These social benefits included health care and education 'free at the point of use', subsidised public housing and flat-rate social security benefits, including a state pension, irrespective of ability to pay for them. The new welfare system was in place by 1950.

The system appeared to work reasonably well until the late 1960s, although quite early on payments for medical prescriptions were introduced in the NHS. The main reasons for its success were, first, Keynesian full employment policies, which kept the cost of the welfare state down and tax revenues up. Second, benefits were set at relatively modest levels, with unemployment benefits and pensions being self-financing through National Insurance contributions. Health care services were relatively limited and the standards quite low and thus relatively inexpensive to provide. Limited supplies of public housing stock under local authority control ensured that the housing system worked reasonably effectively, although there were waiting lists for council accommodation and a points system determined allocation. Education was universal from 5 to 15, later 16, but further and higher education was limited to a small minority and therefore not a major drain on public expenditure. Third, there was a remarkable degree of consensus on the need for a welfare state (Timmins 2001), with all ages, social classes and regions believing 'welfare' was a good thing.

By the 1970s, welfare spending had grown, however, and become the largest item in the national budget. Right-wing commentators were arguing that unless public spending was reduced, the system would be unsustainable (Bacon and Eltis 1976). With the election to office of neo-liberal Conservative administrations during the 1980s and 1990s, ministers began rolling back the frontiers of the welfare state, although public support for welfare spending especially on health care and education remained high. Reforms saw the transfer of some services from the public to the private or voluntary sector or private businesses and voluntary organisations being enlisted to deliver public services under contract.

With the return to office of New Labour in 1997, 'modernisation' of what are now referred to as 'public services' rather than 'the welfare state' has continued unremittingly, with successive waves of public management reform. Some of these services are now selective, targeted and subject to 'co-payment'. This means that they are paid for mainly by taxes but involve 'top up' payments by users when they receive the service, such as dental charges and prescription charges. The government has also encouraged people to take responsibility for their own needs by stimulating private health insurance and pensions and permitting the building of private hospitals.

> What have been the objectives of public management reform or 'modernisation' of the welfare state?

The National Health Service

When the NHS was created in 1948, its administrative structure was a compromise between existing and new institutions. Its fundamental principle was that comprehensive health care should be provided to patients 'free at the point of use'. General practitioners (GPs) worked as independent contractors, hospitals were run by the central government and local authorities ran the remaining mental health and community health services. No further structural change was introduced until 1974, when the hospitals and local health services were united and Regional Health Authorities (RHAs) and area health authorities (AHAs) managed primary and secondary care. The rationale was to facilitate better management and control of the service from the centre.

In 1982, further restructuring took place but more significantly a new system of management was introduced. Multiprofessional boards were replaced with chief executives in hospitals and community authorities at the same time that government spending on health was reduced. During the 1980s, governments introduced compulsory competitive tendering, imposed new systems of funding and encouraged the managerialisation of the service to reduce the powers of the professionals and make the service more responsive to consumer needs.

The final change under the Conservatives was the most radical and saw the introduction of internal markets and the split between purchasers and providers. Under the NHS Community Care Act 1990, government created hospital and community trusts which were to be in competition with each other for patients and funding. GPs were encouraged to become fund holders and to compete for patients by offering them better services and buying those services from hospitals. In the internal market then, the 'purchasers' were District Health Authorities (DHAs), Family Health Service Authorities (non-funded GPs) and GP fund holders and the 'providers' were NHS Hospital and Community Trusts and GPs who would bid for business from the purchasers (North 2001).

Supporters of these reforms claimed that some improvements in performance took place, whilst critics argued that reform had resulted in large increases in the number of managers employed and that the quantity and quality of health care had not improved. During the 1990s, the rationing element in NHS provision (which had always been present) was made more explicit but some politicians and some members of the public believed the creation of the internal market to be a backdoor route to privatisation (Allsop 1995).

Reform did not cease with the Conservatives. After coming to power in 1997, the Labour government published a white paper *The New NHS: Modern, Dependable* (Ministry of Health 1997) identifying three themes for further reform: partially abolishing the internal market and replacing it with integrated care; mandating GPs to form primary care trusts (PCTs); and improving clinical care. In opposition, Labour had said that it would abolish the internal market but in office they were reluctant to do so. Instead, they tried to reduce the transaction costs of the internal market by streamlining the relationship between purchasers and providers. However, Labour's reforms went in the same direction as those of the Conservatives, with large PCTs setting up long-term service agreements with NHS trusts. The reforms were ambitious but incorporated within them were plans to increase spending on the NHS, so as to reach European average expenditure on health and retain the principle of 'free healthcare' at the point of use. As North (2001, p138) has commented: 'this is certainly a "rolling forward" rather than a "rolling back" of the state, but it is an engagement which is predicated on the citizen's involvement.'

Reform continues with the National Health Plan introduced in 2000. New regulatory bodies have been set up to monitor improvements. These were: the Commission of Health Improvement to improve health services, the Modernisation Agency to spread good practice, and the National Institute for Clinical Excellence to ensure cost effective drugs and medical practices. Increasingly tight targets have been set for all health trusts. The Department of Health sets these and rewards or punishes trusts depending on their performance. There certainly have been improvements in waiting times and patients have more choice and there have been significant changes in the contracts and roles of medical practitioners. However, there are clearly perverse effects and ever-closer links between the public and private health sectors.

Income maintenance

Following the Beveridge report and election to power of the reforming Labour governments of 1945–1951, a basic income maintenance system was established within the United Kingdom.

This comprised a flat-rate state pension, National Assistance payments for those past school leaving age not in receipt of unemployment benefit and a flat-rate family allowance paid to second and subsequent children. In each case, levels of these universalist benefits were relatively modest, certainly compared with similar systems in mainland Europe and the Nordic states.

With poverty among the elderly a continuous problem, in 1975, the Labour government introduced a State Earnings Related Pension (SERPS), with an earnings related element in it. In 1986, however, the Conservatives legislated to restrict the scope of SERPS because of its future costs. In 1990, it removed the connection between pensions and incomes and linked basic pension increases to price rises rather than to wage rises, so the relative value of the state pension has declined over time. By the early 2000s, politicians of both major political parties were committed to reducing the dependence of pensioners on the state pension by encouraging people to invest in private pensions. As an immediate response to the so-called 'pension crisis', however, the New Labour government introduced a means-tested Minimum Income Guarantee to supplement the basic state pension for those needing it because of 'pensioner poverty.'

Family poverty was originally addressed through National Assistance payments but in 1966 these were replaced by supplementary benefits. These means-tested payments were available to all in need, including pensioners and the unemployed. By the early 1970s, many families were in the 'poverty trap', where adults who took jobs found family income falling and this income being less than state benefits. Subsequent legislation in the 1970s and 1980s allowed benefit recipients to work without losing all their benefits. However, by the late 1990s, a general consensus had emerged that the disincentive effect of state benefits remained considerable for many families. In 1996, the unemployed were redefined as 'jobseekers' and unemployment benefit was designated as the 'jobseekers allowance', with unemployed individuals having to be available for work (Deakin 1994).

In 1998, the New Labour government stressed the need to help the poor and remove their dependency on state benefits. Subsequent Labour policy has emphasised the need to 'empower' the poor and remove benefit dependency. A series of New Deals have been introduced. The first was for the younger long-term unemployed and aimed to increase long-term employability among young people. Others were for the long-term unemployed, lone parents and disabled people to help them get into jobs and to 'improve their prospects of staying and progressing in employment' (Finn 2001, p77). Government also provided a minimum income guarantee for working families with children, with tax credits and income tax reductions. This 'New Deal', 'Welfare to Work strategy' or 'workfare' system, obliging parents to work rather than to depend on state benefits, was a sea change from the universalist welfare policies of the 1960s and 1970s.

The flat-rate element in the family allowance (now called child benefit) remains, although family allowances became taxable in 1968. The allowance was paid for all children in 1975, with one-parent families receiving a higher level of benefit. As a result of the changes outlined above, and a buoyant economy, expenditure on public income maintenance schemes levelled off during the late 1990s and early 2000s.

Social housing

It was the Labour government that provided a new system of housing subsidies through local authorities at the end of the Second World War. Most new housing at this time was to be provided by local councils and was called 'council housing', with the private sector being relegated to a secondary status. As housing was in short supply, waiting lists were created, where family size, income and job status were the determining criteria for allocating the public housing stock.

Generally, Labour governments supported local authority public sector housing and the Conservatives the private sector. But council house building decreased from the mid-1970s and the Conservatives applied a system of means tests from 1972, where rent rebates were given to needy tenants in both the public and private sectors (Lund 1996).

The Thatcher administrations from 1979 to 1990 were fundamentally opposed to council housing and a series of housing reforms took place:

- Tenants were given a 'right to buy' their council houses in 1980.
- Government provided further incentives for council house sales in the late 1980s.
- The Conservatives attempted to increase the role of private landlords in housing provision.
- The Housing Corporation was created to distribute government funding and housing corporations grew up to provide social housing.
- Many local authorities transferred their housing stock to housing corporations.
- Local authorities were limited to building mainly sheltered accommodation and prevented from using the funds accumulated from the sale of their housing stock.

As a consequence of these incremental but radical reforms, it was housing associations (supported by housing benefits) that largely provided for 'social housing' by the early 2000s. In the meantime, owner occupation accounted for over two-thirds of the total housing stock. Although housing shortages remain, politicians from all parties now believe that the private sector should have the dominant role in housing provision. New Labour policy has been to support an extension of owner occupation to the less advantaged through tax and interest-deferred mortgages, 'starter homes' and social housing for those ineligible for mortgages. As Durden (2001, p153) has concluded: 'UK housing policy has never had the pursuit of equity as a major objective.'

(i) Why is there continued high support for public provision of health care in the United Kingdom?

(ii) What are the implications of this for employing organisations?

(iii) Today about two-thirds of housing is owner occupied, whereas about 30 years ago most people rented their housing. To what extent has public policy produced this change in housing arrangements?

EDUCATION POLICY

In post-war Britain, developing an effective and socially just education policy was a major concern of the Labour party. From the 1940s until the 1970s, Labour education policy was aimed at facilitating social and occupational mobility in a meritocratic society. For Labour reformers, education was the means for promoting individual merit and promoting greater social equality. Educational opportunity would enable people with intelligence and personal application to become meritocrats and develop into 'tomorrow's leaders' (Young 1958). The Education Act 1944 provided the basis for the new meritocracy, followed by the extension of university and higher education opportunities in the 1960s and 1990s.

A generation-and-a-half after the 1944 Act, Kendall and Holloway (2001, p154) argued that education was central to the 'New Labour project'. It was seen as pivotal to 'reform in a number of key economic and social policy areas.' But by this time, underpinning New Labour policies were 'the beliefs that education enables individuals to obtain employment and stable income sources in a competitive global market.' For New Labour, education was 'crucial to overcoming the low-skill equilibrium of the British economy – low productivity and supply-side constraints to sustained growth.' Education had become, in short, less a vehicle for individual advancement and personal growth than one for satisfying national and employer needs in the flexible labour market.

Primary and secondary education

Under the reforming 1944 Act, central government assumed responsibility for universal free primary and compulsory secondary education up to the age of 15, raised to 16 in 1972. It was to be a national system, administered locally by local education authorities (LEAs). The task was a difficult one largely because in the United Kingdom, unlike in other countries such as the United States and France, the private rather than the public sector had traditionally provided elite education, especially at secondary level. The Conservatives have always been strongly supportive of private education and this has been the main distinguishing feature of their policy on education from that of the Labour party. The 1944 Act was the defining piece of legislation in that policy dichotomy, since the Labour government could have abolished private schools or incorporated them into that new settlement but it did neither. With rising household incomes and parental dissatisfaction with state secondary education in the intervening years, parents in the professional classes were increasingly able and willing to send their children to private schools during the 1990s and 2000s so as to optimise their children's chances of gaining entry to elite universities.

The 1944 Act established a tripartite, selective system of secondary schools: grammar schools for the academically able, secondary modern schools for the mass of the population and technical schools for boys with more practical skills. In 1964, the Labour government pledged to introduce only one form of school, the neighbourhood or community comprehensive, catering for all abilities. In 1965, LEAs were instructed to draw up plans for introducing comprehensive schools and, in 1974, Labour made the change mandatory. By 2003, there were over 3,000 comprehensive schools in the United Kingdom, but over 200 grammar schools, 100 modern schools and 200 'other' secondary schools remained (Summerfield and Babb 2004). This was because the earlier reforms had proved very controversial and many Conservative-controlled LEAs had refused to comply with the law. Indeed, in 1979, the Conservative government removed the directive and later actively encouraged authorities to maintain grammar schools.

The crucial issues in the secondary education debate in the 1980s and 1990s were parental choice and educational standards. Those on the political right, for example, argued, first, that comprehensive schools developed a culture of under-achievement in poorer communities. Second, they claimed a new generation of schoolteachers infused with egalitarian social principles was aggravating this culture of underachievement by emphasising development of children's personalities rather than essential skills for the job market. The Conservatives were also keen to encourage private education and, in 1980, introduced an assisted place scheme enabling children of parents with low incomes to obtain subsidised places in elite private schools. This scheme was abolished when Labour returned to power in 1997 (Fielding 2001).

During the 1980s, the thrust was to introduce new managerialism into the school sector. In 1986 and 1988, legislation devolved the management of schools to governing bodies, allowed schools to opt out of LEA control altogether and enabled central government to maintain them. These laws increased the power of head teachers who became managers. Boards of governors had elected parent governors, local business people and staff representatives. The schools had devolved budgets and responsibility for all staffing issues including appointments, promotions, training and development.

The Conservatives introduced a national curriculum and appointed the Office of Educational Standards to monitor standards of performance and produce league tables. Once again, it was thought that this would encourage competition between schools and raise their levels of performance and efficiency. These policies have not been abandoned but reinforced under Labour, with schools having to conform to central performance indicators and central financial directives. The national curriculum is being continually revised but still requires pupils to study English, mathematics, science and IT, along with up to seven foundation subjects. League tables on examination performance are widely published at both primary and secondary levels and classroom teachers are formally assessed and graded. The School Standards and Framework Act 1998 created up to 25 education action zones, consisting of two or three secondary schools together with feeder primary schools. Action forums of parents, representatives from business and LEAs were given the job of raising standards. However, selective schools remain, local government has not been given back its management function and performance indicators persist. So in most areas of education policy, Labour governments have followed Conservative policies. If anything, they have been tougher on failing schools than their predecessors were and they have given support to 'specialist' schools. Their latest initiative in the creation of new types of specialist colleges, which have close links with local businesses, is once again an example of partnership between the state and the market. (Kendall and Holloway 2001).

Further education

In post-war Britain further or post-compulsory education provided largely part-time education in further education (FE) colleges to people working in commerce, skilled trades (such as construction and engineering), as technicians, and as supervisors in industry and the public sector. The courses provided were on a day release, block or evening basis. From 1979 till 1997, however, following some critical reports regarding performance in the sector, successive Conservative governments changed the structure, governance and curriculum of the further education sector. Underpinning these changes was a set of political and ideological beliefs that FE colleges were inflexible, dominated by 'producer' interests and unresponsive to the needs of employers, local economies and communities. The approach of the Blair administrations has been characterised by a range of policy initiatives and legislation, culminating in the Learning and Skills Act 2000. These have indicated that while New Labour has a stronger commitment to the sector than its Conservative predecessors did, it has been 'profoundly influenced by the legacy of marketisation, privatisation and, crucially, the funding methodology' of earlier Conservative administrations (Kendall and Holloway 2001, p163).

Higher education

Higher education (HE) escaped major reforms until the 1990s. At the end of the Second World War, all HE was university education and it was free to those able to gain entry to university, with a system of means-tested maintenance grants for those needing them. With only some 5 per cent of 18 year olds going to university, the system was not a drain on the public purse. However, expansion of the universities in the 1960s was not accompanied by financial reform, so the system became more expensive to administer. Following further expansion of a more diverse system of HE from the late 1980s, a serious financial crisis occurred and government instituted tighter financial controls first through the University Funding Council and then through the Higher Education Funding Councils of England, Wales and Scotland.

After Labour had been elected to office in 1997, it continued to implement the Conservative policy of annual tuition fees of £1,000 for all HE students for the first time and abolished what remained of the student grant system. Students were offered loans in place of maintenance grants. Loans were to be repaid after graduation and when a certain income threshold had been reached. In 2001, government set a participation target of 50 per cent of 18–30 year olds in HE by 2010 and subsequently proposed a limited form of maintenance grant for those on very low incomes. More importantly, following legislation in 2004, universities were to be given the freedom to charge 'top up' fees of up to £3,000 per year in England and Wales, with effect from 2006, although the Scottish Parliament decided not to legislate top up fees. In general, however, by the mid-2000s, HE had become increasingly marketised and privatised, providing potential students with a range of choices in a mass emerging marketplace.

(i) What is the difference between 'education' and 'training'?

(ii) To what extent is current government education policy aimed at training a skilled workforce and educating informed citizens?

(iii) What are the implications of university 'top up' fees for potential students, universities and employers?

SOME COMPARISONS OF PARTY POLICIES AND REFORMS

In the post-Thatcher neo-liberal consensus, all three major political parties – Labour, Conservatives and Liberal Democrats – were generally agreed about the ends of public policy. What divided them was the means to achieve these ends. In general, the Labour party favoured sound public finances, investment in public services but partnership in their delivery. The Conservatives favoured a more market-based approach to policy and the Liberal Democrats favoured a more devolved community-led approach. Where the three major political parties broadly agreed was that the United Kingdom should have:

- an economy that is privately-owned where government's role is limited to ensuring fair competition and protecting consumers (see Chapter 8)
- an economic orthodoxy aimed at low inflation
- 'caps' on welfare and public service expenditure
- support for organised pressure groups
- support for the North Atlantic Treaty Organisation (NATO) and US leadership in the 'new world order'.

Table 7.1 provides some comparisons of the main public policies of the three major political parties. As indicated above, policy differences among the parties are now often ones of emphasis rather than of principle. However, the parties are still divided on fundamental issues such as Europe and political reform including devolution, individual rights and civil rights. Table 7.2 shows the party positions on selected public management and constitutional reforms. New Labour accepts that there is no going back to state socialism, so it has adapted neo-liberal approaches to policy through its support of a 'third way' in politics. In terms of public management reforms, the major dimension is improving the quality of public services, especially health care and education. This has resulted in Labour forcing a change in the political agenda and obliging the Conservatives to champion public services, with the Liberal Democrats shifting to the left of the other two parties on reform. But in essence in the area of public management reforms:

- Labour advocates joined-up government and increased consultation as a guide to policy.
- Conservatives advocate privatisation, hiving off, deregulation, decentralisation.
- The Liberal Democrats advocate subsidarity, decentralisation of administration to local bodies.

Table 7.1 Main policies of the political parties

Policy	Labour	Conservatives	Liberal Democrats
Economic	Supports balanced public finances, low inflation, no rises in direct tax	Supports balanced finances, low inflation, tax cuts where possible	Supports more Keynesianism, more progressive tax system but also balanced public finances
Social	Supports internal market in NHS, private finance initiative, tax credits for poor, new deal 'workfare' schemes for the unemployed	Supports public–private mixes in public services, targeted benefits, privatised pensions	Strongly supports public services including free care for the elderly and higher pensions
Education	Supports education as means of meeting labour market needs, central inspection and controls, specialist schools, top-up fees in HE	Supports more private education, more power for parents and vouchers to be used in public or private sector	Supports more expenditure on education through dedicated taxes and abolition of university fees
Environment	Supports genetically modified food (with qualifications), right to roam, international environmental treaties	Supports commercial agriculture, fox hunting, opposed to access, cautious about international treaties	Strongly supports environmental protection, public access
Transport	Supports improved public transport and new roads	Supports motorists and new roads, limited regulation of rail companies	Supports improved public transport, regulation of road building and motorists
Law and order	Supports a tough approach to crime, restriction of rights of asylum seekers, some extension of freedom of information	Supports a very strong approach to law and order, more prisons, war against drugs, against abuse of social benefit fraud	Strongly supports individual and civil rights, sceptical about war on drugs, against identity cards
Foreign affairs and defence	Supports EU, with strong support for NATO, USA leadership and free world trade	Opposes extension of EU powers, very committed to USA leadership and free world trade	Strongly supports EU, the single currency, qualified support for USA
The Constitution	Supports limited reforms such as devolution, House of Lords	Opposes further constitutional reforms or devolution and elected House of Lords	Supports proportional representation, strong regional governments

Table 7.2 Party positions on selected public management reforms

Issue	Labour	Conservatives	Liberal Democrats
National Health Service	Supports increased spending, bought-in private services, free at point of use	Supports market inputs, using private sector for some care, some selective means-tested charges	Supports increased spending from higher tax, greater autonomy for hospital and primary care trusts, free at point of use
Education	Supports increased quality and choice in schools, specialist schools, 50 per cent participation in HE, top-up fees in HE	Supports more choice in schools, Vouchers, access for poor children to private sector, More independence for schools, quality in HE	Supports increased spending through tax rises, greater local autonomy, against top fees
Transport	Supports investment in roads, private–public partnerships, part privatising London underground	Supports investment in roads, using private sector in rail transport	Supports reductions in road spending, increases in public transport, local authority control
Law and order	Supports more community policing, heavier sentences for serious offences, softer law on cannabis	Supports more police, tougher sentencing, no relaxation of drug laws, tougher custodial sentences	Supports devolved powers to run police authorities, more community policing, community participation in crime prevention

> Imagine that you have seen a TV programme in which business leaders appear to be arguing the case that the main political parties in the United Kingdom are increasingly converging in terms of their values and policy agendas. As far as business is concerned, they argue, it makes little difference today which party wins elections. What evidence is there supporting this point of view?

EVOLUTION OF EUROPEAN UNION ECONOMIC AND SOCIAL POLICY

The idea of a united Europe was once just a dream in the minds of philosophers and social visionaries. Victor Hugo, for example, imagined a peaceful 'United States of Europe' inspired by humanistic ideals. The dream was shattered by two world wars that ravaged the continent during the first half of the twentieth century. After the Second World War, new hope emerged. People who had resisted totalitarianism were determined to put an end to international hatred and rivalry in Europe and to build a lasting peace between former enemies. Between 1945 and 1950, a handful of statesmen including Konrad Adenauer, Winston Churchill, Alcide de Gasperi and Robert Schuman set about persuading their peoples to enter a new era in European politics. They wanted a new political order in western Europe, based on the interests of its peoples and founded upon treaties guaranteeing the rule of law and equality between countries (Cowles and Dinan 2004).

Economic policy

Robert Schuman (French Foreign Affairs Minister) took up an idea originally conceived by Jean Monnet and, in 1950, proposed setting up a European Coal and Steel Community (ECSC). In countries that had once fought each other, the production of coal and steel would be pooled under a shared authority. This bold move was a big success. It was the start of more than half a century of peaceful co-operation between member states of the European Communities (see Chapter 2). With the Treaty of Maastricht 1992, Community institutions were strengthened and given broader responsibilities and the 'European Union' was created. The EU worked hard to help unify Germany after the fall of the Berlin wall in 1989 and, after the Soviet Union collapsed in 1991, the countries of central and east Europe decided that their future lay within the family of democratic European states.

The EU has been built to achieve political goals but its dynamism and success spring from its economic foundations – the 'single market' formed by EU member states and the single currency (the Euro) currently used by 12 of them. EU countries account for an ever-smaller percentage of the world's population and they have decided that co-operating together is essential, if they are to ensure economic growth and compete on the world stage with other major economies. No individual EU country is strong enough to go it alone in world trade. To achieve economies of scale and find new customers, European businesses have to operate in a bigger 'domestic' market than just that of their home country. That is why the EU has worked hard to open up the single European market, by removing obstacles to trade and cutting away the red tape entangling economic affairs.

Europe-wide free competition is counterbalanced by Europe-wide solidarity in a continent-wide market of 380 million people. When European citizens become victims of floods and other natural disasters, they receive assistance from the EU budget. The 'structural funds' managed by the European Commission encourage and back up the efforts of EU national and regional authorities to close the gap between different levels of development in different parts of Europe. Both the EU budget and money raised by the European Investment Bank are used to improve Europe's transport infrastructure, extend the network of motorways and high-speed railways, provide better access to outlying regions and boost trans-European trade.

The Treaty of Rome 1957 set the European Economic Community the task of establishing a common market and, by progressively approximating the economic policies of member states, 'to promote throughout the Community a harmonious development of economic activities, a continuous and balanced expansion, an increase in stability, an accelerated raising of the standard of living and closer relations between the States belonging to it'. These goals have been largely achieved, thanks to the free movement of goods, people, services and capital and the EU policy of ensuring fair competition between businesses and protecting consumer interests. The single market was completed in 1993 and the Euro came into circulation in 2002.

However, to enable all sectors of the economy and all regions of Europe to benefit from these achievements, they had to be backed up by 'structural' policies financed and pursued with commitment and determination by the EU itself. Also Europe's political leaders realised that European solidarity needed action taken to strengthen 'economic and social cohesion'. In other words, the gap between richer and poorer regions had to be narrowed. In practice, this meant introducing regional and social policies. These policies have become more important with each successive enlargement of the EU (Kontrakou 2004).

Employment policy

Because around 10 per cent of the EU workforce was unemployed in the late 1990s, a new chapter on employment was inserted into the Treaty of Amsterdam 1997, making job creation a priority policy. At the European Council in Luxembourg in November 1997, leaders of the then 15 member states agreed a co-ordinated strategy for making individual national policies more effective. It provided a strategy for better vocational training, helping start up new businesses and improving 'social dialogue' or relations between employers and employees. It laid down guidelines for boosting employment. Progress on implementing these guidelines is regularly reviewed by member states and EU institutions, using a jointly agreed assessment procedure.

The 'Luxembourg strategy' was strengthened and given broader scope by the European Council in Lisbon in March 2000. It became the 'Lisbon strategy' and was directed towards a new and ambitious goal of making the EU, within a decade, the most competitive and dynamic knowledge-based economy in the world, capable of sustainable growth with more and better jobs and greater social cohesion. The long-term objectives of the Lisbon strategy related to competitiveness, more and better jobs and social inclusion.

A report by the High-Level Group on the Future of Social Policy in an enlarged EU identified, in 2004, three major challenges facing the EU's new social agenda: enlargement, population ageing and globalisation. In terms of employment policy, it made three recommendations (European Commission 2004b, pp54, 55, 61). These were to extend working life for the young, women and older workers, to implement lifelong learning, and to address economic restructuring. The Group believed that the EU could extend and improve working life 'by offering men and women a more flexible pattern of life, combining working periods, training periods and periods dedicated to children and the elderly.' This implied promoting mobility over the life cycle, through both working arrangements and social protection.

Regional policy

EU regional policy consists essentially of making payments from the EU budget to disadvantaged regions and sections of the population. The total amount allocated for 2000–2006 was €213 billion. The payments are used to boost development in backward regions, convert old industrial zones, help young people and the long-term unemployed find work, modernise farming and help less-favoured rural areas. The money is paid through specific funds – the European Regional Development Fund, the European Social Fund (ESF), the Financial Instrument for Fisheries Guidance and the European Agricultural Guidance and Guarantee Fund.

In addition to these 'structural' funds there is a 'Cohesion Fund'. This is used to finance transport infrastructure and environmental projects in EU countries where per capita GDP is less than 90 per cent of the EU average. The countries benefiting until recently have been Greece, Ireland, Portugal and Spain. Thanks to structural schemes, financed by the EU, member states have been better able to bring their economies into line with one another. Economic 'convergence' is also the result of action by EU governments to meet the requirements for economic and monetary union.

Social policy

The aim of EU social policy is to correct the most glaring inequalities in European society. The ESF was set up in 1961 to promote job creation and help workers move from one type of work and one geographical area to another. For 2003, the ESF was allocated €4.8 billion from the EU budget. Financial aid is not the only way in which the EU seeks to improve social conditions in Europe. Aid alone will not solve the problems caused by economic recession or by regional under development. Social progress in market economies springs, first and foremost, from economic growth and is nurtured by both national and EU policies.

Social progress in the EU is also supported by legislation guaranteeing all EU citizens a solid set of basic rights. Some rights are enshrined in the Treaties including, for example, the right of men and women to equal pay for equal work. Others are set out in directives about the protection of workers (such as health and safety at work) and essential safety standards.

In December 1991, the Maastricht European Council adopted a Community Charter of basic social rights, setting out the rights that all workers in the EU should enjoy:

- free movement
- fair pay
- improved working conditions
- social protection
- the right to form associations and undertake collective bargaining
- the right to vocational training
- equal treatment of women and men
- information, consultation and participation for workers
- health protection and safety at the workplace
- protection for children, the elderly and the disabled.

At Amsterdam in June 1997, this Charter became an integral part of the Treaty and is applicable to all member states.

The High-Level Group on the Future of Social Policy in an enlarged EU wanted to improve the contribution of social policy to growth, competitiveness and social cohesion. This could be done: 'by developing life long learning, modernising work organisations and reforming social protection'. The Group also wanted to foster social inclusion and invest in children and young people who 'will play a key role in the future of our societies' (European Commission 2004b, p61).

The Common Agricultural Policy

At the Berlin summit, when agreeing the 'Agenda 2000' arrangements, the European Council decided to reform the Common Agricultural Policy (CAP) to cut costs and keep European farming competitive. The aims of the CAP, as set out in the Treaty of Rome, have largely been achieved: a fair standard of living has been ensured for the farming community; markets have been stabilised; supplies reach consumers at reasonable prices; and structures have been modernised. Other principles that were adopted in the course of time have also worked well. Consumers enjoy security of supplies and the prices of agricultural products are kept stable and protected from fluctuations on the world market.

As farming methods have been modernised and agriculture in Europe has become increasingly competitive, more and more people have left the countryside and the farming community and the proportion of the EU workforce in agriculture has shrunk from 20 per cent to less than 5 per cent. Initially production grew far faster than consumption and the EU budget had to bear the heavy cost of disposing of surpluses. Steps had to be taken to reform this policy, which is why Agenda 2000 changed the aims and methods of the CAP. The main objective now is to encourage farmers to produce high-quality products, in quantities more in line with demand, and to move away from intensive farming methods that damage the environment. Aid to farmers is no longer related to the volume of goods they produce.

Reform is beginning to succeed and production has been curbed. The EU is one of the world's leading exporters and importers of agri-foodstuffs. Farmers are being encouraged to use sustainable farming practices that safeguard the environment and preserve the countryside. The new role of the farming community is to ensure a certain amount of economic activity in every rural area and maintain the diversity of Europe's landscapes.

In 2002, the Commission proposed further reforms that would enable Europe to influence the way in which the WTO draws up its rules. The Commission wants emphasis to be on food quality, the precautionary principle in agriculture and animal welfare. Similarly, the EU has begun reforming its fisheries policy. The aim is to reduce overcapacity in fishing fleets, preserve fish stocks and provide financial assistance to people who leave the fishing industry.

Policy on sustainable development

EU policies were originally focused on supporting the single market but they have gradually come to embrace many other aspects of daily life and address the challenges facing European society today. These are: environmental protection; public health; consumer rights; competition and safety in transport; education and access to culture.

In Johannesburg in August 2002, the United Nations held its 'World Summit on Sustainable Development'. To prepare for the summit, the European Council met in Barcelona in March and set a clear priority for the EU. This policy was to make its own sustainable development policy an example for the world to follow. The policy includes conserving and managing natural resources in a sustainable way, an international system for managing the environment, action to boost Europe's technological capacity and greater efforts to share that technology with the developing world. Some major challenges include how economic growth can be encouraged without damaging the environment, how water resources should be managed, how sustainable sources of energy can be accessed and how Africa can be saved from famine and disease. These issues can be tackled more effectively by concerted action at EU level rather than by individual European nations working alone.

Policy on technological innovation

As scientific and technological innovation has gathered pace, European research has diversified, bringing a wide variety of scientists and research workers together. The EU has had to find new ways of funding their work and new industrial applications for their discoveries. Joint research at EU level is designed to complement national research programmes and focuses on projects bringing together a number of laboratories in different EU countries. It supports fundamental research in fields such as controlled thermonuclear fusion through the Joint European Torus programme. It also encourages research and technological development (RTD) in key industries such as electronics and computers, which face stiff competition from outside Europe. It is expected that RTD will be stimulated in individual member states and the amount spent on it will rise to 3 per cent of national GDPs. The priorities include the life sciences (genetics and biotechnologies), treatment of serious illnesses, nanotechnologies, aeronautics and space research, sustainable energy systems, global environmental change and the ecosystem (Nugent 2004).

> Identify any three areas of EU policy that affect your organisation and explain how your organisation is responding and addressing these policies.

HOW ORGANISATIONS INFLUENCE POLICY

In modern society, formal participation in politics beyond voting in elections to influence government policy is normally channelled through secondary political groupings. When individuals or organisations become involved politically, they join and participate in organised groups reflecting their political interests and opinions. Organised political groups are of two kinds, political parties and pressure groups, and their memberships can overlap.

Nature and scope

Political parties seek to influence policy decisions directly by getting their leading members into formal positions of political authority in the House of Commons, devolved Scottish and Welsh Assemblies, local authorities and the European Parliament. Parties try to win political control to use political power. What distinguishes pressure groups from political parties is that they seek to influence policy decisions, not get their representatives into positions of formal political authority. Some pressure groups, such as Shelter, Age Concern or the Ramblers' Association, are politically independent; others have links with parties or even a single political party and help them fight elections, such as some trade unions and the TUC that generally support the Labour party. While it is relatively easy to distinguish between the Conservative party and the National Union of Teachers, for example, it is less easy to distinguish between minor parties and pressure groups. Sometimes pressure groups transform themselves into political parties such the Greens, whilst in other cases political parties seem to be little more than pressure groups such as Plaid Cymru.

Both political parties and pressure groups are concerned with power. The power of political parties depends on electoral success and support at the ballot box; the power of pressure groups depends on their membership base, resources, appeal and effectiveness. Since political parties need to have relatively wide appeal to win votes for their candidates, their political programmes tend to be broadly based. Pressure groups have much narrower political objectives, sometimes based on a single issue, such as the Society for the Protection of the Unborn Child and Abortion Law Reform Society. These lead to differences in organisation between political parties and pressure groups. Political parties contest elections, so they are organised nationally and locally. Pressure groups are much more varied and may be international, national or local.

Pressure groups have been defined as 'social aggregates with some level of cohesion and shared aims which attempt to influence the political decision-making process' (Ball and Millard 1986, p33). Pressure groups can be classified in a number of ways, including:

- *Interest groups.* These are national or central organisations, created because of their members' common socio-economic goals. Members of employers' organisations such as the Engineering Employers Federation, for example, combine to protect the common interests of federated engineering firms, which may be large or small, multi-plant or single-plant, and geographically concentrated or geographically spread companies. Managers representing them may be young or middle-aged, professionally qualified or not, and religious or agnostic. What brings these enterprises and corporate representatives together is their common commercial interest as organisations, not the organisational characteristics or personal aspirations of their managers. The Institute of Directors performs similar functions, as do other interest groups such as the British Medical Association (BMA), National Union of Students and trade unions.

- *Attitude groups.* These groups are based on the commonly held beliefs and values of their members. The motivating force behind joining the Royal Society for the Protection of Birds is not economic self-interest but concern for the protection and well-being of birds. Similarly, members of Age Concern share a compassion for, and commitment to, the elderly. Such groups contain men and women, professional people and non-professionals, atheists and religious people. Other examples of attitude groups are the Consumers' Association, Amnesty International and the Ramblers' Association. What draw their supporters together are the attitudes they share as individuals and their wish to organise collectively to protect the rights of the interests they represent.

- *Peak associations.* These are umbrella organisations that co-ordinate the activities of other pressure groups. Examples include the CBI and TUC. A European-wide association of private-sector employers is the Union of Industrial and Employers' Confederations of Europe. Other international peak associations include the Red Cross and International Labour Organisation.

- *Insider groups.* These have access to government officials and decision-making bodies and usually speak on behalf of legitimate mainstream interests in society, such as the National Farmers Union (NFU). These groups play by 'the rules of the game', and either have expertise which the government needs or whose co-operation is necessary if government policies are to be seen as legitimate and are to be implemented eg BMA, Association of Chief Police Officers (ACPO). These groups often have considerable influence on policy content.

- *Outsider groups.* These do not normally have access to key officials or decision-makers and are kept at arm's length by 'the establishment' because of who or what they represent. Examples include the Campaign for Nuclear Disarmament (CND) and animal liberation groups. Other outsider groups are of no threat or use to the government or the issues they are concerned about are not high on the government's agenda eg the darts group that achieved recognition of their activity as a sport rather than a game.

- *Crossbench groups.* These groups maintain party neutrality, knowing that they must deal with whatever party is in power.

- *Fire brigade groups.* These groups are formed to fight specific issues and dissolve when the issue is settled, such as the Anti-Poll Tax Federation during the Thatcher administration or the Anti-fuel tax protestors in 2000.

- *New social movements.* These are 'political' groups, such as Greenpeace, that have broader concerns than many interest and attitude groups but they are more loosely knit than political parties.

Activities, power and influence

In attempting to influence government decisions, pressure groups try to gain access to those taking decisions and to do this they lobby key individuals at different levels of power. They try to influence the prime minister, cabinet, ministers, government officials, local councillors or MEPs and European officials. They also seek to influence public opinion. The methods and levels each pressure group uses to communicate its opinions and demands vary widely, according to its power and circumstances. The most powerful pressure groups have almost instant access to the important parts of the political system, such as leading employers' and workers' organisations, but weak organisations have to improvise to make their views heard (Grant 2000).

In outline, the main internal features affecting pressure group power and influence include:

- membership size, type and density
- ability to recruit members
- membership unity
- internal structure
- financial resources
- quality of leadership
- possible sanctions.

The features of the external political environment most affecting the impact of pressure groups include:

- public opinion
- legitimacy of interest
- insider status
- degree of politicisation
- whether there are opposing groups
- institutionalised power within the social structure.

Some powerful groups have well-established relations with government, on a permanent or semi-permanent basis, sometimes channelled through advisory or standing committees, staffed by civil servants and pressure-group representatives. As indicated above, the NFU has close links with the Ministry of Agriculture and ministers. Relatively few pressure groups have the power to gain access to policy-making machinery but use representatives to pursue their objectives. If pressure groups cannot influence the main decision makers directly, they are forced to lobby MPs, members in the Lords, or MEPs. If pressure groups cannot influence Parliament, or if parliamentary supporters do not carry enough political weight, they are forced to operate outside Parliament. They may try to influence political parties, for example, by building up support for their policies within them. CND used this approach in its early days. For many years its main policy was unilateral nuclear disarmament and CND supporters tried to persuade both the Liberal party and Labour party to accept non-nuclear defence policies. They were unsuccessful with the Liberals but were eventually successful with the Labour party. However, Labour moved away from a policy of unilateral nuclear disarmament to a more complex multilateral position, thus requiring CND to adapt its political strategy in response.

Where it is not possible for pressure groups to influence national political parties, even outside Parliament, or if they are unsuccessful in doing so, they are forced to use the mass media and influence public opinion. The objective of campaigning at local level is to try to create shifts in public opinion in the hope that those in political power, and with influence, respond to these pressures. Tactics used include rallies, marches, petitions and media campaigns to get the message across. These can lead to media coverage, television documentaries and other in-depth analyses, thus putting pressure on government to modify its policy. Recent examples have been concern for the environment. Some pressure groups, such as Friends of the Earth and Greenpeace, have mounted strong grassroots campaigns to influence public opinion and government policies on lead-free petrol and organic farming. In 2000, there was a series of *ad hoc*, spontaneous nationwide fuel protests, organised by farmers, small businesses and some in the transport sector, against rises in indirect taxes on diesel and petrol fuels. In 2004/2005, the Countryside Alliance demonstrated against the legislation making fox hunting a criminal offence, as well as using the media and other avenues to influence the government.

Pressure groups vary widely in their power bases and in the ways in which they operate. Sometimes the more visible a pressure group the less its influence, and the more likely it is to operate at media and grassroots levels. The most powerful pressure groups rarely use such tactics. The most important determinant of pressure-group power is its position in the economic system and the potential sanctions that it has to back its demands. These may be positive, such as co-operating with the authorities, or negative, including withdrawal of financial resources or taking punitive actions against those in power. Large employer pressure groups, such as those representing banks, finance and insurance, are crucial to the economy and most governments listen to their views with some degree of deference. Unions had a great deal of power in the 1970s but were rarely consulted or listened to during the 1980s, 1990s and 2000s, since governments largely excluded them from the policy process. Examples of powerful pressure groups having close relations with the machinery of government include the ACPO, the Police Federations, Law Society, Bar Council and BMA. All these bodies have professional expertise that governments need to draw upon. Thus, in general, these and similar pressure groups have good working relations with government rather than antagonistic ones.

Financial resources and effective leadership of pressure groups are also important determinants of group power and influence, since they affect the types of campaigns and activities that pressure groups pursue. Size of membership is another factor, especially in interest groups as it determines their representativeness. The NFU, for example, represents most farmers hence government channels all its agricultural communications through that body. If there were several farmers' unions, each would be much weaker than the NFU is collectively. Public support is particularly important for attitude groups, since they have few sanctions to use against the public authorities. Powerful groups, with aims generally acceptable to the political system, such as the business community, find it easier to influence policy decisions than those whose views clash with dominant opinion such as fuel protest organisers.

Specify a named pressure group to which your organisation (or one known to you) belongs. Report and discuss:

(i) how the pressure group operates
(ii) what benefit the organisation gets from being a member of this pressure group.

IMPLICATIONS FOR ORGANISATIONS AND P&D PROFESSIONALS

The working of the macro-economy is complex. Even today it is not fully explained by the most advanced economic theory. Nevertheless, changes and developments in the international economy, national economy and public policy have significant impacts on businesses, public services and voluntary organisations. One of management's prime tasks is to plan for, or respond to, macro-economic changes that are driven by government policy and their likely impact on the organisations they manage.

Projected growth of the national economy, for example, is a starting point for any business forecasting. The direction and expected rate of growth in aggregate demand and national output indicate likely demand for an organisation's goods and services. They also have implications for what HR skills are required, current labour demand and future staffing needs. Too rapid a rate of national economic growth can result in skill and labour shortages for firms in the short term, with pressures on them to raise pay rates, since getting extra staff tends to lag behind rising sales. Where economic growth is sluggish, with national output falling, organisations find that they want less capacity. This makes it more difficult to maintain productivity and keep labour costs down. This, in turn, affects competitiveness and a company's ability to maintain its market position.

The components of national growth are important when examining their possible effects on product and labour market demand. Strong consumer spending is good for producers of consumer commodities, retail outlets and service-related industries selling direct to final consumers. Weak consumer spending, on the other hand, has the opposite effect. Investment spending trends are particularly important in industries producing capital goods for the domestic market. When interest rates fall, rises in investment expenditure can be expected but when interest rates rise, falls in investment spending are likely, although this depends also on the state of the economy and business expectations of future trends. Changes in government or public spending, in turn, affect not only provision of public services but also demand for human resources and the intermediate goods used within them. Cutbacks in public spending can result in lower demand for private-sector goods, services and resources and vice versa.

Capital-intensive industries tend to borrow more heavily than other sectors and so are considerably influenced by interest rates and their movements. The relative proportion of debt capital to equity capital in a company does not necessarily indicate the impact of high interest rates on it, since one company may have raised its debt at a low rate of interest, whilst another may have to cope with a much higher rate of interest. High interest rates help attract overseas money into the economy, which is needed to finance any balance of payments current account deficit but they also push up the exchange rate.

Those managing organisations, therefore, need to understand changes in the national economy and how these are likely to affect their organisation's business plans and operational activities in the short and medium terms. They also need to understand how the different fiscal policies of governments are likely to affect their sector in terms of tax liabilities, profitability, product markets, labour markets and the raising of finance capital.

Political parties in the United Kingdom provide the electorate with choices in local, regional, general and European elections. At every election, each political party publishes a manifesto outlining its policy proposals to voters and what it intends doing if it is elected to office. In national elections, given the plurality or 'first-past-the-post' voting system, the majority party usually has immense power in carrying out its election pledges. But once in office cabinet reshuffles and changes in political office holders often result in changes in economic, social or education policy. These can clearly affect an organisation's marketing, operations and financial strategies, as well as its business opportunities as a provider of goods or services in the market. Consequent changes in legislation affecting consumers, workers or competition demand relevant responses from senior managers and their organisations. Changes in economic or social policy, in turn, influence managerial decisions on resource requirements, resource use and resource allocation. They can also affect demand for welfare provision in the community.

The impact of EU decisions on management policies, planning and business practices is increasing. EU policies, implemented through directives and regulations, cover areas such as employment, competition, consumer protection and social policy. All these affect the ways in which organisational decisions and business policies are determined. These EU 'rules' have to be taken into account by corporate policy-makers. With the extension of the single European market, and more integration of the European economy, large companies have their own research departments and task forces to evaluate their corporate strategies, marketing plans and transnational investments.

Given the party system in the United Kingdom, its prevailing political culture and UK membership of the EU, those leading and managing organisations, in both the private and public sectors, need to be especially alert to the strategies available to them to influence national policies and EU institutions in the policy-making process. Few organisations are overtly party political but some, at different times, need to act politically to defend or extend their position as economic interest groups, so as protect their markets and business interests. Sometimes this is done on a one-off basis. At other times, it is done collectively through trade or business associations. Given the political contexts of public and European policy-making, managements need to establish effective working relations with the political authorities, if they wish to influence policy decisions. As indicated above, this can be done on a company-by-company basis or by membership of relevant employers' or trade associations and, at national level, through the CBI. Organisations can also be represented on permanent advisory or consultative committees of government departments or be invited to join ad hoc bodies of inquiry. Trade and business associations may also use full-time lobbyists or contact MPs to protect their members' commercial interests when these are being dealt with in Parliament. Increasingly, large organisations and pressure groups are opening offices in Brussels so they can keep close to the policy-making process of the EU.

In UK politics, because political power is concentrated at Westminster, most pressure groups tend to operate at that level. However, local authorities influence the local environment, exercise regulatory powers over planning controls and facilitate business development. In seeking to influence local authorities, managements need to lobby council members, contact council officers or operate through chambers of commerce.

CONCLUSION

This chapter analyses the nature and scope of government policy and how it is similar to and different from policies of opposition parties. It also takes account of the historical and EU contexts of policy. Traditionally, British economic policy has been dominated by free market and free trade principles. Only during the social democratic consensus, from 1945 until 1979, were UK governments strictly interventionist in the economy, relying primarily on Keynesian techniques of demand management. In recent years, neo-liberal policies under the Conservatives, and modified neo-liberal ones under New Labour, have dominated micro-economic and macro-economic management. The emphasis has been on keeping inflation low, fiscal responsibility, low direct taxation, support for free trade and using the market rather than the state to provide goods and services. New Labour is now the guardian of the new orthodoxy in economic policy.

Since 1945, social policy has been delivered by the welfare state. However, the old principle of policy provision – universalism – has increasingly given way to selectivity, targeting and co-payment by citizens. More recently, the values underpinning policy reform have shifted from those associated with managerial efficiency to those associated with the discipline of the market. In education policy, the main issues have centred around parental choice, educational standards and centrally imposed performance indicators and financial targets. FE and HE under New Labour inherited much of the Conservative legacies associated with marketisation and privatisation. HE has become massified and is linked with the ultimate co-payment requirement – university top-up fees.

While differences between Labour and the Conservatives remain in public policies, there are few fundamental divisions between the parties in most policy areas. New Labour, like the Conservatives, is committed to the state employing market-like solutions to a range of policies and reforms. The EU plays an increasingly important role in micro-economic policy and in some areas of social policy. It seeks to improve the contribution of EU policy to growth, competitiveness and social cohesion, extend working life and foster social inclusion. Finally, a diverse set of pressure groups tries to influence government policy by targeting top civil servants, ministers, the cabinet, political parties, the mass media, public opinion, local councils and the EU.

USEFUL READING

ALLSOP, J. (1995) *Health policy and the NHS*. Harlow: Longman.

BLAKEMORE, K. (1998) *Social policy: An introduction to social policy*. Milton Keynes: Open University Press.

BRITTAN, S. (1964) *The treasury under the Tories 1951-64*. Harmondsworth: Penguin.

BUDD, A. (1978) *The politics of economic planning*. Manchester: Fontana.

COWLES, M. and DINAN, D. (eds). (2004) *Developments in the European Union*. Basingstoke: Palgrave.

CURWEN, P. (ed). (1997) *Understanding the UK economy*. London: Macmillan.

DEAKIN, N. (1994) *The politics of welfare*. Hemel Hempsted: Harvester Wheatsheaf.

DINAN, D. (2004) *Europe recast: A history of the European Union*. Basingstoke: Palgrave.

EUROPEAN COMMISSION. (2004b) *Report of the high-level group on the future of social policy in an enlarged European Union*. Luxembourg: Official Publications of the European Communities.

FIELDING, M. (ed). (2001) *Taking education really seriously: Three years hard labour*. London: Routledge.

GAMBLE, A. (1994) *The free economy and strong state*. London: Macmillan.

GRANT, W. (2000) *Pressure groups and British politics*. Basingstoke: Palgrave.

GRANT, W. (2002) *Economic policy in Britain*. London: Palgrave.

LUND, B. (1996) *Housing problems and housing policy*. Harlow: Longman.

NUGENT, N. (ed). (2004) *European Union enlargement*. Basingstoke: Palgrave.

SAVAGE, S. and ATKINSON, R. (eds). (2001) *Public policy under Blair*. London: Palgrave.

SUMMERFIELD, C. and BABB, B. (eds). (2004) *Social trends 2004*. London: National Statistics.

TAYLOR, G. (ed). (1999) *The impact of New Labour*. London: Macmillan.

Regulation

INTRODUCTION

A key issue in public policy is how the interface between the state and the market should be managed. That is the role of state regulation which is carried out in a number of ways. At one level, regulation sets the rules within which market activity takes place. In this category comes competition and employment law, company law and regulations covering health, safety and the environment. At another level, regulation can be used to achieve policy objectives set by the elected government. The alternative to regulated markets, whether by the law or institutions such as government agencies, is 'free' markets. These are markets 'free' from social and political control, as in mid-nineteenth century England. Earlier, economic life had been constrained by the need to maintain social cohesion and was conducted in inter-related 'social markets'. These were markets that were embedded in society and were subject to many kinds of regulation and constraint. But the goal of leading politicians and some political theorists in mid-Victorian Britain was to demolish these social markets and replace them with 'deregulated' ones. By 1914, however, the 'free market' had ceased to exist in its most extreme form, because of its dysfunctional elements and its failure to meet human needs. Subsequently, government legislation, provoked by different aspects of the free market in action, regulated markets so that their impact on other social institutions and on human needs was tempered. The so-called 'free market' policies of UK governments in the 1980s and 1990s produced their own dysfunctions and since then 'New' Labour governments have legislated a series of regulatory enactments to alleviate those effects. This chapter outlines some key aspects of the 'regulatory' state in the early twenty-first century.

THE SOCIAL AND HISTORICAL CONTEXTS OF LEGAL REGULATION

The law or legal regulation is that body of rules, formally enacted or customary, which the state recognises as binding on its citizens. It has also been described by Kahn-Freund (1977, p3) as 'a technique for the regulation of social power', where power is the ability to direct and affect the behaviour of others, ultimately by sanctions. Sanctions that are positive reward people; negative ones threaten them. In any liberal society, naked power to determine rules and decisions and enforce them, by individuals, organisations or government, is insufficient to maintain social stability and social order. The power to act needs to be accepted as legitimate by those affected by such decisions, whether property owners, employers, workers, consumers or citizens. To be acceptable in democratic societies, the right of those with power to take decisions has to be recognised by those without positional or resource power, irrespective of any sanctions the powerful may possess. In an ordered society, ultimate power and the right to enforce it rest with those controlling the machinery and agencies of the state. These are the legislative, executive and judicial organs of government.

In liberal democratic states, the concept of the 'rule of law' is a fundamental one. First, it reflects the preference of citizens for 'law and order' rather than anarchy or civil strife. It implies that conflicts and disputes between parties should be settled by peaceful and constitutional means rather than by use of armed force, terrorism or physical coercion. If the state is identified with force and coercive might, the rule of law lacks any moral authority or legitimacy.

Second, the rule of law means that government itself must be conducted in accordance with the law and that the machinery of government must always operate through the law. Thus the law acts as a buttress of democratic principles, since only the law-making assembly, ie Parliament in the United Kingdom, can confer new governmental powers on the executive and administrative authorities.

Third, as law develops, it results in the rule of law reflecting changing social values, because the legal system exists in a wider social and economic context. Harris (1997) argues that understanding of the law cannot be acquired unless it is examined in close relationship to the social, economic and political contexts in which it is created, maintained and implemented. Law is part of the overall social structure and has links and dependencies with other social elements and forces. Within society, some institutions and social groups are more important than others, some have more power than others and some enjoy considerable prestige. These include:

- political institutions, such as Parliament, political parties and pressure groups
- economic institutions, including employing organisations, trade associations and unions
- cultural institutions such as literature, the arts, the press and television.

Law plays an important part in defining and regulating all kinds of social relationships, including relations between individuals, organisations, individuals and organisations, and citizens and the state. Laws are made, interpreted and applied but there are differing viewpoints about the nature of the law and the legal system in which the law operates. The social ambiguities inherent in creating and applying the law were summed up by Harris and Buckle (1967, p6):

> *Law may be regarded as a benign facilitating mechanism, making transactions possible between men [sic] and solving awkward problems as they arise; it may, alternatively, be seen as a mechanism of social control, regulating activities and interests in the name of either the community, a ruling class or the state. The state itself may be*

defined as either 'neutral arbiter' or 'interested party' in the solution of disputes and the balancing of interests. Again, law may be seen as an institution for the futherance and protection of the welfare of everyone, or it may be seen, crudely, as an instrument of repression wielded by the dominant groups in society.

Society and the law

Viewpoints about the relationship between law and society are dichotomous. On the one side, society and the legal system are seen as reflections of a prevailing social consensus. On the other, they are seen as reflecting fundamental social conflict between competing interest groups. The former perceives the law to be protecting social values to which all subscribe, while the latter holds that the law is less than neutral, protecting some values and interests at the expense of others. Developments in the law also reflect the historical, political and social contexts in which society evolves and changes. The emergence of a free labour market, for example, was a product of the industrial revolution. With the breakdown of the feudal agrarian system by the mid-eighteenth century, landless labourers moved to the expanding towns to become wage earners in the developing factory system. The growth of market capitalism and *laissez-faire* individualism led to the relationship between 'master' and 'servant', for example, being based on a legal contract, despite the vast disparity in bargaining power between them. The contract of service was viewed as a legally binding agreement between the two parties in the employment relationship, containing agreed rights and obligations for each of them. Any breach of these legal rules entitled the aggrieved party, normally the master, to seek a legal remedy by bringing a civil action against the other for breach of contract.

The doctrine of *laissez-faire* assumed that all members of society, including masters and servants, were free and equal parties before the law, able to regulate and arrange their affairs with one another without constraints being placed upon them by third parties or the law. It assumed that individuals were equal in terms of their bargaining position and, if people were left free to make their own decisions, that competitive trade and industry would flourish and the national economy thrive. In practice, of course, there were fundamental inequalities in terms of bargaining power, social position and wealth between most masters and servants. None the less, the employment contract, supposedly freely made between what later came to be known as employer and employee, was deemed legally to be made between consenting parties of equal standing.

Given the early predominance of these ideas about freedom and equality of contract, it took many years before the state began to intervene to provide basic legal protections for individual employees in their contractual relations with employers. It was the infinite variability of the terms of employment contracts, together with the fact that in many cases employees could neither negotiate their terms nor readily ascertain the terms dictated by the employer, that led over the years to growing state intervention in regulating the employment relationship. This was done through a series of statutes.

A number of factors had led slowly to the furthering of legislative intervention in employment matters, so that law now provides a wide range of protections for employees in terms of information about the terms of their contracts, their job rights, health and safety at work and union membership rights. The social and political factors leading to this development included:

- changed philosophies about the role of the state in society
- the reforming zeal of some politicians and social reformers
- absorption of working people into the democratic process
- growth of trade union power and influence.

It is not only in the field of employment and employment relations that the nineteenth-century emphasis on *laissez-faire* gave way to state and legal intervention, although there was a revival of *laissez-faire* ideas during the 1980s and early 1990s. Slowly, *laissez-faire*, with its emphasis on state abstention or 'voluntarism', gave way to the view that government through legislative and other measures should participate in economic affairs in an active and direct way. Prior to the Second World War, however, notions of free trade and freedom of competition dominated economic ideas, with the corollary that the economy was best left to regulate itself, unimpeded by any form of state intervention. This was accompanied by an assumption that the state should support that sort of economy by creating, through the law, an economic environment conducive to trade, industry and business interests, as demonstrated by various measures protecting the economic interests of the business community in preference to other interests. State support for the growth and consolidation of the industrial and commercial economy came from a number of sources. One was an imperialist foreign policy. Another was the judiciary, which constructed a legal framework within which business affairs could operate smoothly and predictably. The legal notion of 'contract' was, and remains, the essence of the legal relationship between buyers and sellers in product, capital and labour markets.

The basic legal rules governing contract stem almost wholly from cases determined by superior courts in the nineteenth century. The insistence of nineteenth-century judges on deciding cases, and creating legal contractual rules, using the juristic equivalent of *laissez-faire* economics – notions of freedom and equality of contract – eventually led to legislative intervention in the twentieth century, especially in the areas of employment and consumer protection. This was done to redress imbalances in power between employers and employees and businesses and consumers (Harvey and Parry 2000).

The nineteenth century also saw the development of legal rules relating to the form that business enterprises might take and of the legal protections that particular types of enterprise enjoyed. The most common form of business enterprise was, and still is, the limited company. In the case of the limited company, for example, its most striking legal feature is its 'corporate personality'. Once created, the company is regarded in law as if it were a person, a legal entity in its own right, separate from the people owning and running it, with legal rights and duties including owning and transferring property, entering into contracts and suing or being sued. By treating the company as a legal person, having ownership of corporate assets, the law not only allows the relatively free use of those assets in the running and expansion of the business but also provides significant legal protections for individual shareholders.

The legal systems of market economies, therefore, inevitably exhibit comprehensive sets of legal rules and rights concerning private property, because private property is of such fundamental importance to these societies. Yet the law does not treat property as a homogeneous category. Because it has taken different forms and values at different times, each type of property has particular legal rules attached to it. The legal rules dealing with land, for instance, can be traced back to feudalism, while those relating to manufactured goods, plant and machinery emerged during the development of early capitalism. Since capitalist market economies, such as those in Europe, depend upon the creation and acquisition of private personal wealth, legal systems concern themselves, to a large extent, with protection of that wealth, how it can be invested and consolidated and how it can be transferred. Yet, while the law purports to afford equality of treatment to everyone in society, regardless of social class, wealth or position, in practice it is used primarily for protecting and transferring property within the population.

The legal profession

The law is one of the most potent carriers of dominant definitions of acceptable and unacceptable social behaviour, as well as being the most significant institution for settling disputes, so it is important to understand the social background of lawyer practitioners. The law embodies dominant social norms and values and lawyers engage in maintaining these values in their daily work, through their function of applying the law. Like most professional groups, the legal profession remains predominantly middle-class in its origins and outlook. Research shows the predominance of professional and managerial backgrounds among lawyers, as indicated by fathers' occupations. Methods of recruitment into the legal profession and its unique position in the social structure tend to favour middle-class aspiring lawyers. Further, the high cost of legal education, especially post-graduate training, is prohibitive for many potential recruits. Once dominated by white males, the female-to-male ratio has changed dramatically since the 1970s in favour of females entering the profession and there are more ethnic minorities practising.

Senior judges have traditionally been appointed largely from the ranks of experienced and established barristers and it may be fairly said that members of the higher levels of the judiciary represent a distillation of those social-class currents within the legal system (Harris 1997). The uniform social and educational background of senior judges, largely from independent schools and Oxbridge backgrounds, raises questions about the general social and political outlook of the judiciary as a whole. In analysing cases with political elements coming before judges, Griffith (fifth edition, 1997, p34 and p320) wrote that:

> ... we find a remarkable consistency of approach in these cases concentrated in a fairly narrow part of the spectrum of political opinion. It spreads from that part of the centre which is shared by right-wing Labour, Liberal and 'progressive' Conservative opinion to that part of the right which is associated with traditional Toryism – but not beyond the reaches of the far right.

Griffith concluded that UK judges cannot be politically neutral 'because they are placed in positions where they are required to make political choices which are sometimes presented to them'. Lord Devlin (1978, p510), in replying to this analysis, declared that too much was made by Griffith of the 'politics of the judiciary'. Their politics, he argued, 'are hardly more significant than those of the army, the navy, and the air force; they are as predictable as those of any institution where maturity is in command'.

Some have argued, then, that at the apex of the legal system there is still a body of judges whose social class and educational background is likely to persuade them towards a conservative perhaps even reactionary outlook on the social world. On the other hand, there is the rest of society, comprising groups and individuals with very heterogeneous beliefs, values and attitudes. In Harris's (1997) view, it is no answer for the judiciary to argue that changes in society and the law are the business of Parliament, not of the judges. The problems which critics of the judiciary raise are not merely legal problems; they are at the heart of the political structure. Significant changes in the judiciary have been proposed by the New Labour government and these may go some way to bringing the judiciary into the twenty-first century.

Examine recent proposals to reform the judiciary and assess what impact if any they are likely to have on the composition of the judiciary and the interpretation of the law by judges.

CLASSIFICATION AND SOURCES OF LAW

Because of its history and origins, the English legal system differs from that of Scotland and continental Europe. English law is a 'common law' system, as are those in Ireland and the Anglo-Saxon states of the United States, Canada, Australia and New Zealand. European legal systems are based on civil law (or codified Roman law) as in France, Italy, Germany, Spain, the Netherlands and Portugal. The laws of Scotland, and South Africa, Quebec, Louisiana and Israel, embody elements of both (David and Brierley 1978). Given limitations of space, this section concentrates on law in England and Wales and does not cover Scottish law, which is governed by different legal principles and has different courts.

There are various ways of classifying English law and its rules are derived from a variety of legal sources. English law is divided into two main branches, the criminal and the civil law. Criminal law relates to the relationship between the state and the individual, while the civil law concerns relationships between individuals. The distinction between a crime and a civil wrong does not rest on the nature of the wrongful act itself but on the legal consequences that may follow it. Normally, criminal and civil proceedings are easily distinguishable, brought in different courts, with different procedures, different outcomes and different legal terminology. Crimes are divided into 'indictable' and 'summary offences', with indictable offences, the more serious crimes, tried by judge and jury in higher courts and summary offences tried, often before magistrates, in lower courts.

One branch of civil law, however, does concern government of the state and its relationship to individual citizens and this is constitutional and administrative law. Constitutional law is largely concerned with the organs of government, explaining where these bodies have come from and how they derive their constitutional power. It deals with: royal prerogative; functions of the executive, legislature and judiciary; the role of cabinet government and that of the prime minister; and the position of the courts and judiciary in the constitution. Administrative law is that branch of the law focusing on administrative agencies of the state, such as public corporations, delegated legislation and administrative tribunals. The essential difference between these branches of the law is that constitutional law studies the organs of the state, while administrative law studies them in operation.

Alternative classifications of law include:

- private law and public law
- substantive law and procedural law
- civil law and common law
- statute law and common law
- common law and equity.

Private law incorporates all the branches of law concerning cases where one party is making a claim against another. It takes in contract, tort and family law. Public law concerns cases where the state is involved and the public has a direct interest in the outcome. It includes criminal, constitutional and administrative law, and law affecting welfare services and local government. Substantive law focuses on the legal principles established by the courts in particular branches of the law, while procedural law is concerned with how law is used in those courts. Civil law and common law distinguish between those legal systems, as on the continent of Europe, based on codes of law – civil law systems – and those, such as in England and Anglo-Saxon countries, based on legal precedents and interpretation of statute law – common law systems.

The main sources of law are:

- legislation (or statute)
- common law
- equity
- custom
- books of authority
- European law.

Statute law

Until the nineteenth century Parliament was primarily a deliberative body and in practice parliamentary legislation, or statute law, was not a very important source of law. With the rapid changes in society following industrialisation and growth of modern government, statute is now the most important source in English legal theory. Sources of policy come from the party in power, departments of state and public opinion, represented by pressure groups and the mass media. Normally, the legislative process represents a continuous interaction between these forces. There is also the Law Commission, which acts as a major source of ideas for legal reform and plays an advisory role to Parliament on less controversial matters.

Parliament, or more exactly the monarch in Parliament, is defined as the supreme law-making body in the United Kingdom. Before becoming an act, a bill is initiated in Parliament and proceeds through various stages of the legislative procedure. Public bills deal with matters affecting the public generally, and private bills deal with matters of limited or sectional interest. Ministers or MPs introduce public bills; in the latter case they are called 'private members' bills'. Government bills originate from:

- government's election manifesto
- national emergencies
- government investigations
- recommendations of the Law Commission.

Private members' bills are normally the result of MPs being approached to support proposals put forward by pressure groups operating outside Parliament. In practice, the amount of time allocated to private members' bills is strictly limited and the majority of such bills fail to reach the statute book. For government bills, the parliamentary process falls into three phases: a period of consultation before a bill is introduced; a debate and examination or amendment of the bill in the Commons and Lords; and the granting of the royal assent before the bill becomes an act.

Common law

The 'common law' originally meant law that was not local (ie law that was 'common' to the whole of England). This may still be its meaning in particular contexts but is not the usual meaning. More usually the term signifies law that is not the result of legislation, that is, it is law created by the custom of the people and decisions of the judges. Within narrow limits, popular custom creates law, as do the decisions of the courts, which are called 'precedents'. The term 'common law' may also mean law that is not equity (ie law that was developed by the old courts of common law as distinct from the system technically called 'equity', developed by the old Court of Chancery). In this sense, common law may even include statutory modifications of the common law. The precise meaning of the phrase 'the common law' therefore depends upon the particular context in which it is used. A third meaning sometimes attributed to the term is law that is not foreign law. Used in this context, it contrasts English law, and that of other countries like the United States that have adopted it, with the continental legal tradition based on Roman law.

Judge-made common law, then, as developed through the doctrine of binding precedent, is one of the oldest and most fundamental features of the English legal system. The doctrine of precedent states that a decision made by a court in one case is binding on all equal or subordinate courts in later cases involving similar facts. Precedent is the basis of the common law and its essence is both its certainty and flexibility. On the one hand, judicial decisions can be determined in accordance with previous cases. On the other, the possibility always exists for judicial pronouncements to be modified if the decision proves unjust, inadequate or out of date. Moreover, one of the peculiarities of common law is its ambiguity. For every precedent cited by one counsel in support of a client's case, another proffers precedents supporting the case of his or her client. Judicial discretion does, then, make a difference. As Twining and Miers (1982, p291) argue:

> The exercise of discretion in choosing one particular formulation of the [rule of law] of a prior case involves basically the search for the most persuasive or cogent argument in its favour. While it is difficult to classify these reasons according to their acceptability or to the weight and priority that is attached to them, the status, acceptability, and permanence of decisions is in this country to a large degree controlled by judicial recognition of and adherence to a great number of constraints that operate on interpreters of precedent cases.

Judges, in other words, select creatively from the mass of precedents cited and, by virtue of their different interpretations of precedent, their decisions can oscillate between the certainty and flexibility of the common law.

Judges also interpret statute law, since the doctrine of precedent also applies to statutory interpretation. The courts define their role in interpreting statutory provisions as applying the statute to the facts before them and giving effect to the intentions of Parliament, as expressed in that statute. The courts have various techniques of interpretation. These are important given the complex nature of modern statutes, which are sometimes poorly drafted. The three common-law techniques used are the 'literal rule', 'golden rule' and 'mischief rule'. The literal rule requires that words in statute are given their ordinary meaning. The golden rule aims, in interpreting words literally, that the courts ensure that no absurdity or inconsistency results. The mischief rule is the principle whereby courts ask themselves what the 'mischief' is that the statute seeks to remedy. According to Harris (1997), there are two basic issues in statutory interpretation: what were the intentions of Parliament in passing a particular statute and do the facts in the case fall within the ambit of the provisions of the statute in question?

Equity, custom and books of authority

Equity came into being in the Middle Ages, when the courts of common law failed to give redress to individuals in certain cases. A rule of equity means that it has to be read in the light of the whole complex of rules developed by the Lord Chancellor but these rules do not necessarily apply if the rule in question is a rule of the common law. In other words, claiming that a particular right is an equitable right means that all subsidiary rules of equity apply to it. On the other hand, saying that a particular right is a common-law right is shorthand for saying that it is to be interpreted in a common-law atmosphere, leaving out of account such equitable rules as apply only to equitable rights. There is always the possibility that those relying on an equitable rule may find themselves outside its limits.

There are three generally accepted meanings of the term 'custom' in English law: 'general custom', 'mercantile custom' and 'local custom'. General custom is common law built up on the basis of existing customs of the various regions of what was Anglo-Saxon England. It is now accepted that general custom is no longer a creative source of law, since it has been absorbed into legislation or case law. Internationally accepted legal customs are known as mercantile customs, where they are accepted into the English legal system as part of commercial law. As these customs develop, the law takes notice of the changes and they become formalised as laws. Local custom is the term used where people claim by virtue of a local custom, such as a right of way or use of common land, that they have a legal claim that can be adjudicated by the courts. When the courts accept the claim, local custom is treated as local law.

Other sources of English law are the books of authority, largely books of antiquity. Certain ancient textbooks fall into this category and are treated by the judges and the legal profession as universally accepted in each branch of law to which they apply. Whether a book is accepted as authoritative depends on its professional reputation. There is no way of knowing this other than by a study of professional legal practice. It is these books of authority that are often the course of the prerogative which are the ancient rights of monarchy, which today form the basis of the executive powers exercised by the prime minister and Home Secretary.

> What are the major differences between criminal and civil law and what are the sources of both?

European law

Since the United Kingdom's admission to the European Economic Community, under the European Communities Act 1972, legal provisions contained in the relevant treaties have become part of UK law, thus challenging the legislative sovereignty of Parliament. There is provision for European legislation to be incorporated into UK law. In addition to the various treaties themselves, the most important legal devices are 'regulations' and 'directives'. EU regulations automatically become legally binding on all member states, while directives normally need to be specifically implemented. Member states have no powers to question European legislation, except through the European Court of Justice (ECJ), and since they are implemented in the United Kingdom by subordinate legislation, or administrative circulars, such laws are not debated in Parliament in the same way as public or private bills. There is, however, a special joint committee of the two Houses of Parliament that reviews European legislation and draws the attention of the Commons to matters of importance (Blackstone's Law 2003).

In addition to regulations and directives, non-binding EU instruments and the European Convention on Human Rights (ECHR) are relevant to UK legal regulation. Non-binding EU instruments are principally 'recommendations' and 'resolutions.' From 2000, the ECHR was incorporated into the UK law through the Human Rights Act 1998. For example, all legislation must be implemented in compliance with the Convention. This means that where there are two possible interpretations of a statutory provision, the one that is compatible must be adopted.

A major area where European law influences the United Kingdom is employment law. The direct sources of this are:

- Treaty of EU 1992
- Community legislation

- Social Dialogue
- European Court of Justice.

The EU Treaty (or Treaty of Maastricht)

Articles 2 and 3 of the Treaty list the purposes of the EU and include the following social objectives:

- promotion of a high level of employment and social protection
- equality between men and women
- protection and improvement of the environment
- raising standards of living and quality of life
- economic and social cohesion among member states.

Other relevant treaty articles include:

- combating discrimination based on sex, race, ethnic origin, religion or belief, disability, age, sexual orientation
- facilitating freedom of movement of workers
- developing a co-ordinated strategy for employment and a skilled, adaptable workforce responsive to economic change.

Issues where the EU can enact social provisions are:

- improvement of the working environment to protect workers' health and safety
- working conditions
- information and consultation of workers
- integration of people excluded from the labour market
- equality of men and women in the labour market and treatment at work.

Issues requiring unanimous agreement of the Council of Ministers are:

- social security and social protection of workers
- protection of workers where their employment contract is terminated
- representation and defence of the interests of workers and employers
- conditions of employment for third country nationals
- financial contributions for promoting employment and job creation.

Issues reserved for the competence of member states are:

- pay
- rights of association
- rights to strike
- rights to impose lock-outs.

Community legislation

Community law is mainly in the form of directives and covers issues such as:

- safeguarding employee rights in transfers of undertakings
- rights to consultation in collective redundancies
- protecting employees in the event of employer insolvency
- informing employees of conditions applicable to the contract of employment

- organising working time
- protecting young people at work
- European works councils
- protecting pregnant employees and those giving birth
- parental leave
- rights of part-time workers
- equal treatment and equal pay
- protecting workers on fixed-term contracts.

Social dialogue

Social dialogue at EU level is a method of involving employer and union representatives in decision-making on matters concerned with social and employment policy. The social partners are the Union of Industrial Employers' Confederations (UNICE), representing private employers' associations, the European Centre of Enterprises with Public Participation (CEEP), representing public employers, and the European Trade Union Confederation (ETUC) representing trade union organisations. The Commission has to promote consultation between the social partners representing management and labour at community level and must consult them before submitting proposals in the social policy field. This may involve the partners submitting joint recommendations or their own opinions (Cini 2003).

European Court of Justice

The ECJ is responsible for determining the application and interpretation of European law in areas such as whether a member state has fulfilled a treaty obligation or to give preliminary rulings on points of European law at the request of a national court. The ECJ must ensure that the law is not interpreted differently in each member state, since Community law is an independent legal order that takes precedence over that of member states. Apart from judgements interpreting the Treaty of Union, the ECJ impacts on employment law in the United Kingdom in the following ways:

- by actions taken by the Commission against member states failing to transpose community legislation into national law
- by national courts referring matters to it for interpretation of community law
- by using the principle of 'direct effect' where individuals can enforce their legal rights through starting proceedings in their national courts.

(i) What is the relationship between European and English law?
(ii) How is a conflict between European and national law resolved?

ELEMENTS OF THE LAW OF CONTRACT

A contract is, in essence, an exchange of promises. Sometimes the agreement refers to a promise to be fulfilled by one party in the future, which is called an 'executory' contract. More usually, in everyday contracts, exchange is instantaneous and the contract completed straight away, as in the case of purchases in shops: these are called 'executed' contracts. The law of contract, as developed by the judges, paralleled the development of social and economic *laissez-faire* in the nineteenth century, which held that the affairs of business, manufacturing, trade and employment were best left to the individuals concerned, with minimum state intervention or parliamentary legislation. Legal counterparts to this individualist philosophy were the twin assumptions of freedom and equality of contract. In a free market economy, competition is crucial and the attitude of judges and legislators was that it was up to the individuals concerned to strike the best bargains that they could negotiate. It was not up to the courts or Parliament to repair bad bargains.

Within the legal framework, it is contract that remains the legal cornerstone in business, consumer and employment transactions. Contract is the legal device facilitating exchange of goods or services between individuals and organisations in liberal democratic societies. It is a legally binding agreement between two parties, where each party undertakes specific obligations or enjoys specific rights conferred by that agreement. The expression 'breach of contract' (ie breach of a term of the contract) underlines the fact that one party can sue and obtain a remedy through the courts, if the other party fails to honour part of the bargain.

What makes a valid contract?

The essential elements in a valid contract are:

- offer and unconditional acceptance
- intention to create legal relations
- capacity of the parties
- consideration
- genuine agreement between the parties
- the contract must not be contrary to public policy
- the requirement of written formalities in some cases.

An offer must state all the terms of the offer, be communicated to the offeree and distinguished from an invitation to treat. It must not be vague and can be terminated before it is accepted by revocation, lapse of time, rejection or death. Acceptance must be unconditional or else it is regarded as a counter-offer. Acceptance, in turn, must be communicated to the offeror, though it can be implied from the party's conduct and it has to be made within a reasonable or stipulated time.

In determining a valid contract, there must be genuine agreement and consent between the parties and a number of factors affect this. Misrepresentation, for example, may be either fraudulent or innocent. Where fraudulent misrepresentation occurs, the aggrieved party may avoid the contract with or without seeking damages. Alternatively the aggrieved party can affirm the contract and seek damages. With innocent misrepresentation, the main remedy is to avoid the contract, though damages may be awarded even after performance has taken place. Similarly, fraud, if proved, allows the injured party to avoid the contract, with or without seeking damages. Mistake involves the subject matter of the contract, or the identity of the parties, and if the mistake is fundamental the contract is normally rendered void in law. Duress and undue influence also affect the genuineness of consent. Duress is actual or threatened violence against, or imprisonment of, the party concerned, and, at common law, any contract induced by duress is void. Undue influence is where a party is coerced and precluded from the exercise of free judgement. Contracts induced by undue influence are voidable at the court's discretion.

There are two presumptions regarding intention to create legal relations. In social or domestic agreements the courts hold that there is normally no intention to create legal relations. In business agreements, by contrast, the courts presume that there is such an intention. This presumption is rebutted, however, if there is express provision to that effect between the parties.

It is essential that the parties to a contract have proper capacity to make one. The contractual capacity of contracting parties is affected by a number of factors. For their own protection, for example, minors have limited contractual capacity. As a general rule, minors can enforce contracts against other people but cannot, with certain exceptions, have contracts enforced against them. The main exceptions are contracts for 'necessaries', contracts for minors' benefit and voidable contracts. Thus, if goods are deemed necessaries, minors are obliged to pay a reasonable price for them, not necessarily the contract price. Contracts for minors' benefit include educational, service or apprenticeship contracts, provided it can be shown that the fundamental purpose of such contracts is to the minor's ultimate benefit. By statute, certain contracts are void and cannot be enforced against a minor, including contracts for repaying money debts or money loans and contracts for goods supplied or to be supplied, other than necessaries.

Contracts with persons of unsound mind are generally valid but there are a number of exceptions. First, if the contracting party is aware of the other party's mental disability the contract is voidable at the discretion of the mentally unsound person. The onus of proof lies with any persons claiming insanity. They must prove that their disabilities prevented them from understanding the consequences of the transaction and that the other party knew this. Second, where the property of the mentally ill person has been placed under the courts' control, any contract involving disposal of the property does not bind the patient. Contracts are also voidable if individuals who were drunk at the time of making a contract can prove that they were incapacitated owing to intoxication and that the other party was aware of it. Although bankrupts are not devoid of contractual capacity, certain limitations are placed upon them. It is an offence for undischarged bankrupts, for example, to obtain credit beyond a limited amount without disclosing their position.

Another feature of contract law is that, at the time of its formation, the contract should be capable of being performed. Where it is reasonable to do so, future difficulties should be anticipated and provided for. A contract that is illegal at its formation is devoid of legal effect. Where a contract is legal when made, and subsequently becomes illegal, because of a change in the law, such a contract is normally discharged on the ground of frustration. Contracts may be illegal because statute or common law forbids them. Examples of contracts, which are contrary to common law, include contracts for immoral purposes, interfering with the course of justice, in restraint of trade, or defrauding the Inland Revenue.

The general rule in English law is that unless something of value is given in exchange for a promise or undertaking, the promise cannot be enforced against the promisor. Consideration or form, therefore, may be regarded as the element of the bargain in a contract and, at its simplest, involves a *quid pro quo* between the parties. There are a number of legal rules relating to consideration, though there are many exceptions arising from case-law decisions. The main ones are:

- Every simple contract has to be supported by a consideration, which must be legal.
- Consideration must move from the person making the promise to the person to whom the promise is made. This rule is connected with the legal doctrine of privity of contract, which means that only those who are parties to the contract acquire rights and obligations under it.
- Consideration must be something beyond the promisor's existing obligations to the promisee.
- Consideration must not be in the past. This means that a promise made in return for some past benefit or service is normally unenforceable at law. Where it can be shown that services were rendered at the express or implied request of the promisor, however, the courts take the view that this is sufficient consideration to support a subsequent promise to pay.
- Consideration must be real, though it need not be adequate, since it is up to the parties to make their own bargain.

Breach of contract, torts and breach of trust

Breach of contract, torts and breach of trust are civil wrongs. In civil cases, where proceedings result in judgement for the plaintiff, the courts may order the defendant to:

- perform a contract
- pay the plaintiff money
- do or not do something through an injunction
- transfer property to the plaintiff.

A breach of contract occurs where one party breaks the terms of a legally enforceable contract with the other party. The following remedies are available for breach of contract:

- actions for damages
- claims for *quantum meruit*
- applications for decrees of specific performance
- applications for injunctions.

An award of damages by the courts is intended to be compensatory, not punitive. If a legal right has been infringed, but no actual loss has resulted, the courts normally award nominal damages only. Further, injured parties are expected to take all reasonable steps to mitigate the extent of any damage and are unable to claim compensation for losses due to their own failure to act in a reasonable way after the breach occurred. A distinction is drawn between 'liquidated' and 'unliquidated' damages. The former are damages agreed upon by the parties at the time of entering into the contract; the latter are damages agreed upon after the contract has been entered upon. Only the fact that a breach has occurred needs to be proved; no proof of loss is required. To be enforceable by the courts, liquidated damages must be shown to be a genuine pre-estimate of loss and not a penalty inserted as a threat of punishment in the event of breach of contract. Where the courts conclude that the prearranged sum is in fact a penalty, it will not be awarded.

To determine whether a penalty is involved, the courts apply a number of legal rules, including where either the words used by the parties are not conclusive or a single sum is payable as damages for breaches or the sum is extravagant. The essence of a penalty is a payment to frighten defaulters into carrying out their side of the bargain, while the essence of liquidated damages is a genuine pre-estimate of the likely loss in case of default.

Quantum meruit is a claim based on reasonable remuneration and is distinct from a claim for compensation for loss based on action for damages. A claim for *quantum meruit* offers an alternative course of action to plaintiffs who might otherwise seek damages. The following are circumstances where a claim based on *quantum meruit* is appropriate:

- Work has been carried out under a contract that subsequently turns out to be void and damages cannot be awarded for the breach of a void contract.
- Substantial performance of the contract has been carried out.
- There was an express or implied contract to render services, with no agreement to remuneration.
- The original contract has been replaced by a new implied contract.

Awards for specific performance were formerly available only in courts of equity but are now available in any court. However, courts exercise discretion according to the following principles:

- Action must commence within a reasonable time, since delay defeats equity.
- The plaintiff's conduct is also taken into account by the courts, with those going to equity needing to have 'clean hands'.
- Specific performance is never granted: where damages are an adequate and appropriate remedy; where the contract is one for personal services; where the courts are not able to supervise the contract; where a promise is not supported by consideration and where undue hardship would be caused to the defendant; or where the contract is not binding on both parties.

Injunctions are another equitable remedy that the courts may award in cases where damages are neither an adequate nor an appropriate remedy. At their simplest, injunctions are court orders restraining an actual or contemplated breach of contract. There are several forms of injunction, such as 'interlocutory', 'prohibitory', 'perpetual' and 'mandatory'.

Torts include wrongs such as assault, battery, trespass, false imprisonment, defamation of character, negligence or nuisance. Thus a tort is a civil wrong independent of contract. It gives rise to an action for damages irrespective of any agreement not to do the act complained of.

A trust is an obligation enforced by the courts and occurs when a person, technically called a settlor, transfers property to another person, called a trustee, on trust for someone else, called a beneficiary. If a trust is breached, the courts can enforce it

---

What are the grounds for breach of contract and how is a breach of contract remedied?

ELEMENTS OF COMPETITION AND CONSUMER LAW

The theory of perfect competition demonstrates how, in conditions of perfect competition, consumer welfare is maximised. It also shows how this leads to allocative, productive, distributive efficiency. Competition, it is argued, allows goods and services to be supplied exactly in the forms and quantities desired by consumers at the lowest possible prices. However, as Doern and Wilks (1996, p1) have affirmed: 'Neither competition nor the market is inevitable or natural. Markets have to be created through processes of social exchange and public regulation.' There is therefore little agreement about what 'workable' competition means in terms of public policy.

The purpose of competition policies is to provide regulatory frameworks within which governments can maintain or encourage competition. Such policies are based on the assumptions that economic performance ultimately benefits from such an approach and that such policies promote both competition and consumer welfare. They are deemed necessary, as under conditions of monopolistic competition, oligopoly and monopoly, firms normally behave in ways that are detrimental to competition and the 'public interest'. Competition policies are drafted to prevent, deter or persuade firms from acting in ways harmful to consumers and the public interest. However, as Cini and McGowan (1998) have asserted, there can be a number of objectives associated with competition policies. These include:

- consumer welfare
- protecting consumers
- redistributing wealth
- protecting small and medium-sized enterprises

- regional, social and industrial considerations
- market integration.

Just as there are different competition policy objectives, there are different competition policies. Anti-competitive practices take a number of forms and a variety of responses are required. These are:

- *Cartels or restrictive practices policy*. Cartels or restrictive practices include price-fixing, market sharing, horizontal agreements and vertical agreements among firms. A restrictive practices policy aims to deal with such constraints on competition.
- *Monopoly policy*. Here dominant firms (whether pure monopolies or oligopolies) drive out competitors or charge higher prices by restricting supply. Monopoly policies aim to deal with such behaviour by firms.
- *Merger policy*. Mergers and joint ventures have anti-competitive implications because they can lead to situations where monopolies or oligopolies are formed. Merger policies allow the authorities to assess the potential impact of mergers on competition and to decide whether a merger should be allowed to proceed or not.

Business enterprises now have to deal with a spectrum of law covering fair trading and fair competition. This branch of the law has grown piecemeal, especially in the post-war period. Legislation against restrictions on trade arose from changing government attitudes to business arrangements after the Second World War. Prior to this, trading monopolies and restrictive practices were generally tolerated and even encouraged as means of protecting industry and employment. A different philosophy developed subsequently, supporting the view that the economy is better stimulated by competition than by protectionism. Hence, over the years, Parliament passed legislation aimed at prohibiting a wide range of restrictive or collusive practices and at controlling monopolies and mergers. Legislation to limit restrictive practices and monopolies was first passed in the 1940s and 1950s. Unlike in the United States, British public opinion was not preoccupied by notions of concentrated power and anti-trust arrangements associated with individualism, fairness and free enterprise and it was not until post-war Britain that the monopoly problem and the benefits of competition really appeared on the political and social agenda. This change of attitude among policy-makers was largely to pre-empt inflationary pressures and encourage productivity. Another revival of interest in competition reform was initiated by the Labour government post-1997 (Lowe and Woodruffe 2004).

The main legislation covering current competition policy is the Competition Act 1998 and Enterprise Act 2002. These two acts have sharpened competition law and two bodies have been created to enforce UK competition policy: the Office of Fair Trading (OFT) and the Competition Commission (CC). OFT's investigating and enforcement powers have been extended and the CC has replaced the former Monopolies and Mergers Commission. It conducts in-depth inquiries into mergers, markets and regulation of the major regulated industries.

The Office of Fair Trading

The Competition Act 1998 gives OFT, and industry regulators, powers to combat anti-competitive practices, as well as abuse of a dominant position in the marketplace by firms. Basically, the task of OFT is to make markets work for consumers and its functions are based on the assumption that markets work well when 'fair-dealing' businesses are in open and vigorous competition with each other for customers. This approach is based on the belief that when there is competition and consumers understand what they are buying, and they are not misled by deceptive or unfair practices, they have genuine 'power of choice.' In OFT's view, a market cannot work well for consumers unless it is also working well for businesses that serve the interests of their customers. In short, OFT seeks to understand markets and help them work better. OFT has enforcement responsibility under the following legislation:

- Competition Act 1998
- Enterprise Act 2002
- Consumer Credit Act 1974
- Unfair Terms in Consumer Contracts Regulations 1999
- Broadcasting Act 1990
- Courts and Legal Services Act 1990
- Financial Services Act 1986
- Financial Services and Markets Act 2002.

As an independent organisation, OFT plays a leading role in helping consumers understand their rights, protecting consumer interests and ensuring that business practices are fair and competitive under competition and consumer legislation. Its main work is conducted under a number of activities (Office of Fair Trading 2003).

- *The Consumer Regulation Enforcement Division.* This co-ordinates enforcement action throughout the United Kingdom, with other regulatory partners, and it takes action, where necessary, against unfair traders and encourages business and industry to adopt voluntary codes of practice. This Division enforces a wide range of consumer legislation including:
  - co-ordinating enforcement action with other regulatory partners
  - taking action against traders that trade unfairly
  - approving and promoting codes of practice
  - offering a range of information to help consumers understand their rights and make sound choices in the marketplace
  - liaising closely with regulatory bodies in other countries that also have powers of enforcement.
- *The Unfair Contract Terms Team.* This deals with standard terms in consumer contracts that are unfair. The team:
  - seeks to negotiate with business to stop use of unfair terms and where necessary to seek injunctions in the courts
  - issues guidance about the effect of regulations on different markets
  - provides advice and information about unfair terms that might arise in contracts
  - co-ordinates enforcement activities with other regulatory bodies.
- *Consumer Credit.* OFT regulates the consumer credit market, with the aim of ensuring that there is fair dealing by those businesses lending money to consumers, introducing consumers to lenders, offering debt advice or dealing with debt collection or credit worthiness information. Central to consumer credit is a licensing system, run by the consumer credit licensing team. This team:
  - assesses the fitness of applicants to hold a licence and monitors this
  - issues and updates licences
  - keeps a public record of applicants and those who are already licensed
  - issues guidelines to explain how the law is to be enforced.
- *The Competition Enforcement Division.* This plays a key role in enforcing competition law and stopping abuse of a dominant market position by firms. Its activities include stopping cartels and anti-competitive behaviour and investigating proposed and completed mergers. A cartel is a group of firms or businesses that agree to 'rig' a market by keeping prices high. Under the Competition Act 1998, any firm or business involved in a price cartel risks

being fined up to 10 per cent of its UK turnover for up to three years. The Enterprise Act 2002 has also introduced a criminal offence for individuals dishonestly engaging in cartel agreements. The functions of this Division include:

- working across all market sectors
- conducting on-site investigations when appropriate
- stopping and deterring cartels and other anti-competitive agreements
- stopping and deterring abuse of dominant market positions
- disqualifying directors who engage in serious breaches of competition law
- promoting a strong competitive culture across the economy
- referring to the Competition Commission mergers that lessen competition
- referring to the Competition Commission markets in which competition appears not to be working well
- informing business, through a widespread education programme, about new legislation and to comply with it
- liaising closely with relevant authorities around the world.

- *Analysing whether markets are working well for consumers.* OFT does this by:
  - advising on the effects of existing and proposed legislation on markets
  - ensuring that a competitive environment is maintained
  - publishing the results of its investigations and research
  - enforcing consumer legislation by court orders against businesses breaching the law.

- *Communicating with consumers, business, government and others with influence on markets.* This is done by:
  - showing how competitive markets that work well are important for consumers, fair-dealing businesses and overall economic performance
  - explaining OFT decisions openly and accessibly
  - promoting a culture of compliance by explaining to business what the law is and how OFT applies it
  - helping raise consumer awareness and confidence
  - co-ordinating activities with OFT's enforcement partners locally, nationally and internationally
  - providing advice to government on prospective legislation.

The Competition Commission

The Competition Commission is an independent public body established by the Competition Act 1998. It replaced the Monopolies and Mergers Commission on 1 April 1999. The Commission's prime function is to conduct in-depth inquiries into mergers, markets and regulation of the major regulated industries. Every inquiry is undertaken in response to a reference made to it by another authority, usually OFT. But in certain circumstances the Secretary of State, or regulators under sector-specific legislative provisions relating to the regulated industries, do this. The Commission has no power to conduct inquiries on its own initiative.

The Enterprise Act 2002 introduces a new regime for the assessment of mergers and markets in the United Kingdom. In most merger and market references, the Commission is responsible for making decisions on competition questions and for making and implementing decisions on appropriate remedies. Under earlier legislation, the Commission had to determine whether matters were against the public interest. The public interest test is replaced by tests focused specifically on competition issues. The new regime also differs from the previous regime where the Commission's power in relation to remedies was only to make recommendations to the Secretary of State.

The Secretary of State for Trade and Industry appoints members for an eight-year term following an open competition. They are appointed for their individual experience, ability and diversity of background, not as representatives of particular organisations, interests or political parties. There are usually about 50 members and except for the Chairman, they work part-time. There are specialist panels for utilities, telecommunications, water and newspapers. The utilities panel is the specialist panel for gas and electricity inquiries. The Chairman appoints a group of members (usually four or five) to undertake each inquiry. Members (other than newspaper panel members) may be appointed for any type of inquiry. Utility, telecommunications, water and newspaper inquiries have to have at least one member from the appropriate panel.

Aims, objectives and competence

The CC aims to become a 'world-class' competition authority. The Commission's activities are aimed at contributing an increase in the level of competition in the UK economy and to the UK's economic performance and productivity in the international economy, where competitive pressures are increasingly global. The Commission is also seeking to make markets work well for consumers based on the assumption that consumers will benefit from:

- lower prices
- a wider range of choice
- more innovation
- higher quality products and services.

The Commission has a number of objectives (www.competition-commission.org.uk). These include:

- making evidence-based decisions with remedies where required for effective competition
- providing advice to government on regulations
- contributing to the competition regime nationally and internationally
- operating cost effectively and providing value for money
- publishing decisions on inquiries within time limits
- establishing and maintaining robust, fair and thorough processes
- creating and maintaining effective governance and accountability
- consulting and maintaining good working relationships with its stakeholders
- ensuring that the Commission is responsive to the public
- communicating the world-class nature of the Commission.

Relationship between the Department of Trade and Industry (DTI) and the Commission

The White Paper on Competition in 2001 set out government's vision for the CC as a world-class competition authority and asserted its commitment to promoting competition in the economy to improve UK productivity performance and make markets work well for consumers, so as to achieve prosperity for all. DTI has a Public Sector Agreement (PSA) target with the Treasury, directed at:

- placing empowered consumers at the heart of an effective competition regime
- bringing UK levels of competition, consumer empowerment and protection up to the level of the best
- measuring the effectiveness of the regime by peer review and other evidence to ensure a fair deal for consumers and business
- working in collaboration with the relevant regulatory authorities.

DTI's responsibilities are to set overall policy and the legal framework for competition and consumer issues in the United Kingdom and negotiate in the EU and increasingly internationally. The Secretary of State is responsible specifically for appointing Members of the Commission, providing and monitoring its funding and assessing the Commission's contribution towards the overall DTI PSA target.

The CC has statutory powers and responsibilities covering competition issues, conducts in-depth inquiries into mergers and markets and makes decisions against the competition tests set out in the Enterprise Act 2002. In the event of adverse findings, it decides on appropriate remedies. The CC also investigates references on the regulated sectors of the economy. Given its expertise on competition issues, the CC contributes to government policy when requested. But in such interaction the CC does not refer to any specific current inquiries or contribute in any way that would bring its independence into question.

Key Performance Indicators

The CC provides a rolling corporate and business plan for each financial year, which is sent to DTI by March the previous year. This includes a range of qualitative and quantitative measures. DTI monitors progress towards these according to key performance indicators (KPIs), which the DTI monitors. These include progress in achieving high skills and expertise of staff and members, which is covered in the annual review. For the purposes of accountability DTI monitors a particular set of KPIs including:

- level of satisfaction of the Commission's stakeholders as measured annually by an independent third party
- assessment of the CC's performance against the objective of being a world-class competition authority carried out by independent consultants (every three years)
- value for money offered as measured by budget compliance and progress achieving annual efficiency improvements to be agreed with DTI.

> Refer to the latest reports of the OFT and the CC. Identify the last two cases and discuss the rationale for the decisions taken in each of them.

ELEMENTS OF EMPLOYMENT LAW

The relationship between employers and employees, covering terms and conditions of employment, execution of work and collective bargaining between them, is complex and of vital importance to both parties and society generally. It is important to the community that employer—employee relations are relatively harmonious and mutual, while social considerations demand that employers should not exploit employees by underpaying or exposing them to unnecessary dangers in carrying out their job tasks. The legal relationship between the two parties has evolved over the centuries by the application of common law rules on contract, tort and crime in various employment situations. Since the complex and special needs of employers and employees are not always adequately met by the application of broad common law principles, statutory provisions have been established to create a detailed framework of legal rules affecting them. These are aimed at regulating and controlling the conflicting demands of employers and employees in the labour market and the place of work. Given the wide scope of employment law (and what is covered extensively in other CIPD standards), this section is highly selective and outlines only the nature of the contract of employment and some basic employment rights for individuals (Sargent 2003).

The contract of employment

In law, employees are individuals working under a 'contract of service' for an employer, in return for wages or a salary. This contrasts with the self-employed, who work under 'contracts for services' for fees, commission or similar payments. Since the nineteenth century the relationship between employers and employees has been legally embodied in the contract of employment, which is an arrangement whereby an employee agrees to work for an employer, who agrees, in turn, to pay for the work done, thus resulting in a 'pay—work' bargain. Formation of the contract is according to the general law of contract. Apart from merchant seafarers and apprentices, who are covered by special provisions, the contract may be oral, or in writing, or both. Until required by statute, it was usual to find only a few terms of the contract specified, such as rates of pay and hours of work. Today, the employment contract derives from a variety of sources that have developed from the law, collective bargaining, managerial rules and custom and practice over the years.

The express terms of the contract are those that are spelled out, either in writing or orally, and can include the following:

- identity of the parties
- date of starting work
- terms of payment
- hours
- holiday entitlements
- holiday pay
- sickness pay
- grievance and disciplinary procedures
- pension arrangements and so on.

Some of these terms may be expressly incorporated in the contract of employment by reference to documents such as collective agreements, works rules or employee handbooks. Express terms take precedence over all other sources of the contract, apart from statutorily implied terms. Under current legislation, employers are required to provide their employees, including part-timers, with a written statement of the main terms and conditions of their contract within two months of commencing work. This contractual statement is not the contract of employment itself but is normally the best evidence of its express terms.

The implied terms of the contract are those inferred by the courts. Both employers and employees have certain common-law duties implied in the contract. In the case of the employer, there is the duty to provide agreed pay, take reasonable care of the employee's safety, maintain the trust and confidence of the employee, and not to expose the employee to grave danger of health or person. On the employee's part, there is the duty to give honest and faithful service, use reasonable skill and care when working, and obey all lawful and reasonable instructions given by the employer or its agents. The latter is sometimes known as the duty of co-operation and provides the basis of the employer's common-law powers of discipline.

A collective agreement, or particular terms of it, may be incorporated into individual contracts of employment, either by express words or by implication. It is quite common in individual contracts to find words stating that the employee's pay and hours of work are to be determined in accordance with the relevant collective agreement. Even where no express words are used, and the normal practice is to pay wages and provide conditions negotiated with union representatives, there is no difficulty in implying a term that pay and conditions are to be provided in accordance with the collective agreement. This normally applies to union members and to non-unionists working for the same employer.

Works rules, or those incorporated in an employee handbook, may also become terms of the contract of employment. Like collective agreements, these employment rules may be incorporated into the contract, either expressly or by implication. Where employees sign a document saying that such rules form part of their contract, they become express terms and bind the signatories. Works rules and those found in employee handbooks may also become part of the contract by being displayed prominently in the workplace or where they are proved to be local custom in the establishment. Works rules offer an advantage to employers because the employer determines them unilaterally.

A custom or practice may be implied as a term of the contract of employment if it is 'reasonable, certain and notorious'. To be reasonable, judges must approve it. To be certain, it must be precisely defined. To be notorious, it must be well known. Not every custom and practice, therefore, can be considered as part of the contract of employment. However, 'with workers increasingly getting written statements of terms which cover most of their workplace rights and duties this incorporation is becoming less relevant' (Painter *et al* 1998, p50).

Dismissal

Dismissal involves terminating an employee's contract, with or without notice and requires that there is a fair reason for the dismissal (substantive fairness), the disciplinary process leading to dismissal conforms with standards of fairness and natural justice (procedural fairness) and the decision is fair in the circumstances. Dismissal is 'unfair' when it is contrary to statutory criteria and relevant case law and 'wrongful' where it is not in accordance with the contract of employment. Wrongful dismissal usually arises where an employer fails to give 'due notice' of terminating the contract. The Employment Rights Act 1996 contains a statement of the right of employees not to be unfairly dismissed by their employer, where they have been employed for a year's continuous service. Employees are also entitled to a written statement giving particulars of the reasons for dismissal (Willey 2003).

There are now a number of important instances where dismissal is automatically unfair including:

- family reasons
- health and safety
- working time
- pension scheme trustees
- employee representatives
- assertion of a statutory right (such as union activities and time off for trade union duties)
- the national minimum wage
- working family credits
- participation in protected industrial action
- part-time work
- redundancy
- transfer of undertakings
- fixed-term work
- flexible work
- sex
- race
- disability.

Employers have to show that there is a fair reason for dismissal. Dismissal is fair when it is on the grounds of the employee's:

- capability and qualifications
- conduct
- redundancy
- contraventioning of a statutory duty or restriction
- 'some other substantial reason'.

Dismissal can be reasonable in the circumstances on the grounds of:

- previous warnings
- different treatment for different employees
- reasonable belief in misconduct cases
- evidence from informants
- criminal convictions unconnected with work
- capability and ill health.

Procedural fairness is determined by statutory dismissal, disciplinary and grievance procedures, the Advisory Conciliation and Arbitration Service (ACAS) code of practice and the right for employees to be accompanied.

- *Statutory dismissal, disciplinary and grievance procedures.* The Employment Act 2002 introduced for the first time a statutory dismissal, disciplinary and grievance procedure, which has the effect of incorporating these procedures into the contract of employment. There must be a statement setting out in writing the employee's alleged conduct, a meeting must take place before any action is taken and there must be a right of appeal. Each step must be taken without undue delay, the timings of the meetings should be reasonable and meetings must be conducted in a way enabling both parties to explain their cases.
- *ACAS code of practice.* Management is responsible for maintaining discipline and setting performance standards within their organisation. *Inter alia*, disciplinary procedures should not be seen as means of imposing sanctions but as encouraging improved performance. When deciding a disciplinary penalty, an employer must have regard to acting reasonably.
- *The right to be accompanied.* The Employment Relations Act 1999 introduced the right for workers to be accompanied by a 'companion' if requested reasonably and in writing. The companion can be a union official or another worker of the employer. The companion can address the hearing and may confer with the worker during the hearing but cannot answer questions on behalf of the worker.

Where employees consider that the employer has acted unfairly, they may make a claim to an employment tribunal. The normal remedies for employees where the tribunal finds the complaint well founded, and decides that the dismissal is unfair, are:

- compensation based on a 'basic award' linked to the number of years' continuous service and a 'compensatory' award related to the actual loss incurred by the employee
- reinstatement to the same job on the same terms and conditions
- re-engagement to a comparable position to that from which the employee has been dismissed.

Discrimination

Discrimination is a phenomenon occurring widely in communities, organisations and societies. It encompasses patterns of economic, social and political behaviour that justifies stereotyping, victimising and discriminating against particular groups of people. Discrimination against such groups, based on sex, race, national origin, religion, disability, sexual orientation and age, is rooted in presumptions that individuals within these groups possess certain 'less desirable' characteristics distinguishing them from the dominant groups around them. Many political, economic and social pressures have changed attitudes and behaviours towards discriminatory actions during the last 30 years. A major player in this respect is the European Union, where the EU treaty states in article 13 (Cini 2003):

> Without prejudice to the other provisions of this Treaty and within the limits of the powers conferred by it upon the Community, the Council, acting unanimously on a proposal from the Commission and after consulting the European Parliament, may take appropriate action to combat discrimination based on sex, racial or ethnic origin, religion or belief, disability, age or sexual orientation.

Sex and race

The principal statutes dealing with sex and race discrimination are the Sex Discrimination Act 1975 and Race Relations Act 1976 (RRA 1976). Article 141 of the EU treaty and the Equal Treatment Directives on equal treatment in employment and occupation and equal treatment between persons of racial or ethnic origin have also influenced the UK courts when interpreting its anti-discrimination legislation.

Discrimination in employment may be direct or indirect. Direct discrimination on the grounds of sex is where a person discriminates against a woman because of her sex, by treating her less favourably than that person treats or would treat a man. Discrimination is reversed where men are treated less favourably on the grounds of their sex. These provisions are mirrored in the RRA 1976, which provides that a person is regarded as discriminating against another if, on racial grounds, they treat that person less favourably than they would treat another person.

Indirect discrimination in employment on the grounds of sex is where a person applies a provision, criterion or practice to a woman which they would equally apply to a man but is such that it would be to the detriment of a considerably larger proportion of women than of men and it is not justifiable irrespective of the sex of the person to which it is applied. In terms of race, a person discriminates indirectly against another person, if that person applies to that other person a requirement or condition to persons not of the same racial group and:

- The proportion of persons of the same racial group who can comply with it is considerably smaller than the proportions of persons not of that racial group who can comply with it.
- The person cannot show it to be justifiable irrespective of the colour, race, nationality or ethnic origins of the person to whom it is applied.
- It is detrimental to the other person because they cannot comply with it.

The Equal Pay Act 1970 inserts an equality clause into all contracts of employment, when a person is employed on like work, work rated as equivalent or work of equal value to that of a person of the opposite sex in the same employment. Employers need to show that any differences in pay are the result of a genuine material difference, not related to the sex of either employee.

However, discrimination on the grounds of sex or race is lawful in certain circumstances. This includes when there is a statutory requirement with the purpose of protecting women in relation to pregnancy or maternity provisions and when sex or race is a 'genuine occupational qualification'. In the case of sex, for example, this can occur where the job needs to be held by a particular sex to preserve decency or privacy, because it is likely to involve physical contact where members of the opposite sex might reasonable object such as where people are undressed or using sanitary facilities. Another example is where a job holder provides personal welfare services that can most effectively be provided by persons of a particular racial group. Being a member of a racial group can also be a genuine occupational advantage for a post on the grounds of 'authenticity' – such as in acting or entertainment – and as the most effective way of promoting the welfare of a particular racial group, where knowledge of an ethnic group is required.

Persons alleging discrimination in employment on the grounds of sex or race may take a complaint to an employment tribunal. Where a tribunal finds the complaint well founded, it may:

- make an order declaring the rights of the claimant and respondent in relation to the act complained of
- make an order requiring the respondent to pay compensation to the claimant
- make a recommendation that the respondent takes action, within a specified period, to obviate the adverse effect on the complainant of any act of discrimination.

Disability and age

The Disability Discrimination Act 1995 outlaws discrimination against disabled people. The Act makes if unlawful for employers to discriminate against employees or job applicants for reasons related to disability. A disability within the meaning of the act is a physical or mental impairment which has a substantial and long-term adverse effect on the ability of an individual to carry out normal day-to-day activities. This means that an employer has a duty to take steps and make adjustments in order not to place a disabled person at a substantial disadvantage to abled persons. In approaching the question whether a person has a disability, the tribunal has reference to the impairment condition, the adverse effect condition, the substantial condition and the long-term condition. Where a tribunal finds the complaint well founded, it may make a declaration on the rights of the complainant and respondent, order the respondent to pay compensation to the applicant or recommend action to be taken by the respondent.

The UK government is committed to make age discrimination unlawful by 2006, so as to comply with the EU Equal Treatment in Employment Directive. The government's voluntary code of practice on age diversity (Department of Education and Employment 1999) looks at all stages of the employment cycle and makes recommendations for good practice by employers.

Health and safety

Managing health and safety at work means dealing with a range of factors including the ways in which work is organised and carried out, the scheduling of work activities, staffing levels, the technology used, the nature of the products or services and ergonomic considerations. Health and safety regulation in Britain has a long history, going back to the early years of the nineteenth century. However, health and safety legislation was generally piecemeal and was concerned with specific industries or occupational groups. It was not until after the Robens report in 1972 that a new statutory framework was enacted, with bipartisan support in the House of Commons, resulting in the Health and Safety at Work Act (HASAWA) 1974. This extended statutory protection to some seven million additional working people.

HASAWA 1974 sets out the general duties of employers towards their employees and members of the public, as well as those that employees have towards themselves. Every employer with five or more employees must prepare and revise a written statement of their general policy on health and safety at work and the organisation and arrangements for carrying out that policy. There is a duty on employers to provide information and consult with employees and their representatives, who are either appointed by trade unions or directly elected. Safety committees need to be established that represent employees and have responsibility for consultations with employers, investigating potential hazards and dangerous occurrences, investigating complaints by employees on health and safety issues and making representations to employers on general matters affecting health and safety at work. Employers must also distribute leaflets or display posters providing general information about the requirements of health and safety law. Certain injuries, incidents or accidents must be reported if they occur out of or in connection with work activities.

The Management of Health and Safety (MHSW) Regulations 1992 were the main method of enacting the European Community Framework Directive on Health and Safety. This places primary responsibility for ensuring health and safety on employers. These regulations have been amended a number of times and now cover pregnant women, young workers and fire precautions. The MHSW Regulations impose a duty on all employers and the self-employed to conduct a risk assessment. The purpose of this assessment is to identify the measures needing to be taken to ensure compliance with the relevant statutory provisions contained in HASAW 1974 and approved codes of practice providing practical advice of how to comply with the law and examples of good practice.

HASAWA 1974 established two bodies, the Health and Safety Commission (HSC) and the Health and Safety Executive (HSE), to enforce the act:

- *Functions of HSC*
  - assisting and encouraging persons concerned with matters relevant to HASAWA 1974 to further these purposes
  - arranging and carrying out research and providing information and training to encourage others to perform these functions
  - providing an information and advisory service to those needing it.
- *Functions of HSE*
  - managing health and safety inspectors who can enter premises, investigate occurrences, take action on substances or equipment and obtain information
  - issuing improvement notices, issuing prohibition notices and bringing criminal proceedings in the courts.

Work–life balance

Considerable tensions exist between the demands of employment and an employee's dependency responsibilities. This has given rise to the debate about 'work–life balance'. Basically, this is a concept seeking to facilitate a balance for individual workers between the requirements of their employers, individual expectations about work, and individual expectations and responsibilities in their non-work lives. It has been argued that demographic changes, a more diverse workforce, business imperatives and government policy have been driving this (Taylor 2002). Some of the main legal provisions are outlined below (Lewis and Sargent 2004).

Statutory maternity, paternity and adoption pay
A pregnant woman is entitled to 26 weeks statutory maternity pay, providing she has been in continuous employment for at least 26 weeks ending with the week immediately preceding the fourteenth week before the expected week of childbirth. Statutory paternity pay was introduced

in 2003, for a period of two consecutive weeks, within a period of 56 days beginning with the date of the child's birth. Statutory adoption pay is payable for a period not exceeding 26 weeks commencing on the day that ordinary adoption leave starts.

Maternity leave entitlements

A pregnant employee has the right not to be unreasonably refused time off during working hours to attend a medical appointment. She is also entitled to:

- ordinary maternity leave of up to 26 weeks, irrespective of length of service
- additional maternity leave of 26 weeks, starting when ordinary maternity leave ends; this is provided that the employee has been continuously employed for 26 weeks on the fifteenth week before the expected week of childbirth and that the employee notifies the employer of her intention to return to work.

Parental, paternity, adoption and dependency leave

Following the European Parental Leave Directive 1996 (enacted through the Maternity and Parental Leave Regulations 1999), 13 weeks unpaid leave is provided for men and women when they have a child or have adopted one to enable them to take care of the child. For parents of a disabled child, the period is 18 weeks.

Employees with 26 weeks continuous employment at the fifteenth week before the expected week of childbirth are entitled to two weeks paid paternity leave in respect of birth or adopted children but the leave must be taken within 56 weeks of the child's birth date. Employees with 26 weeks continuous service are entitled to 26 weeks of ordinary adoption leave, paid at a flat rate, and a further 26 weeks of additional adoption leave, giving a total leave period of one year that mirrors the provision of maternity leave.

Every employee, irrespective of length of service, is entitled to reasonable time off for dependants. This includes:

- providing assistance when a dependant falls ill, gives birth or is injured
- making arrangements for the provision of care for a dependant who is ill
- resulting from the death of a dependant
- dealing with an incident involving a child of an employee, where this occurs unexpectedly.

Requesting flexible working

Under the Employment Act 2002, employers have the legal duty to consider application for flexible working from employees who are parents of children under 6 years or of disabled children under 18 years of age. Employees with 26 weeks continuous employment can apply to the employer for a change to their terms and conditions of employment relating to:

- hours of work
- the times required to work
- where they are required to work
- other aspects of terms and conditions specified by the secretary of state.

Changes can cover annualised hours, compressed hours, flexitime, homeworking, job sharing, self rostering, shift working, staggered hours and term time working. If agreed, such changes are permanent and the employee does not have the right to revert to the former working patterns. Employers can only refuse applications for flexible working on the grounds, for example, of additional costs, inability to reorganise work among existing staff and the detrimental impacts on quality or performance.

(i) What are the sources of an employment contract and how does an employee know what the content is?

(ii) Consider the view that the EU has done more for advancing employee rights than any UK government.

THE IMPACT OF REGULATION ON ORGANISATIONS AND SECTORS

Regulation of the contemporary state by government is carried out in a number of overlapping ways. At one level, regulation sets the rules within which market activity takes place. In this category of regulation, there is competition, consumer and employment law, and rules governing health and safety, which have been outlined above. At another level, regulation can be used to achieve policy objectives set by government in terms of general economic and social policy. In public utility regulation, there are ongoing debates about how much each of these levels of regulation is appropriate for each sector. There is also disagreement about how far regulators are simply a surrogate for competitive markets in industries having unavoidable elements of monopoly or whether they have a wider social role.

Industries and sectors

Table 8.1 outlines the scope of some current regulatory demands placed on particular industries and sectors within the UK economy, derived from Competition Commission investigations. Given the broad range of legislation identified in Table 8.1, these sources of regulatory interventions indicate that regulation is about both economic efficiency and 'social values' in public policy. Thus regulation of potential monopolies and mergers is concerned largely with arguments of economic efficiency, whilst utility regulation is linked closely with increased use of the private sector to provide and deliver 'public services'. Arguments about the depth and spread of the regulatory state reflect different views of how market economies work, what externalities exist within them and what the state has to do about these externalities. They also reflect different views on the efficacy of public policy and different values about the weight to be given to concepts such as 'equality', 'social cohesion' and 'sustainable development'. This is why politics cannot be taken out of regulation. Utility regulation, for example, depends on the policy framework within which regulation takes place. This can only be given and changed by government. Regulation also depends on the various interactions of government, regulators, regulated and other stakeholders in the regulatory regime. 'The promise of a neutral, value-free approach [to regulation] given by the once powerful ideas of New Public Management theory is simply an illusion' (Corry 2003, p5).

On the basis of his experience as a Treasury economist, special advisor to government and policy researcher, Corry (2003) has concluded that in regulating public utilities:

- The role of regulation and regulators was not unchanging; it was continually evolving according to circumstances.
- Since the late 1990s, the role of regulators has been appropriate to the situations facing them and they have made regulation work better.
- Competition remained a means not an end in the regulatory environment.

Table 8.1 Sources of Competition Commission investigations

Type of inquiry	Legislation	Referral made by:
Market	Enterprise Act 2002	OFT, Secretary of State or certain Utility Regulators
Merger	Enterprise Act 2002 EC Merger Regulation	OFT, Secretary of State
Newspaper merger	Fair Trading Act 1973	Secretary of State
Water merger	Water Industry Act 1991	Secretary of State
Broadcasting	Broadcasting Act 1990	Independent Television Commission or holder of regional Channel 3 licence
Telecommunications	Telecommunications Act 1984	Director General of Telecommunications
Gas	Gas Act 1986

Gas (N Ireland) Order 1996 | The Gas and Electricity Markets Authority
The Northern Ireland Authority for Energy Regulation |
| Water | Water Industry Act 1991 | Director General of Water Services |
| Electricity | Electricity Act 1989

Electricity (N Ireland) Order 1992 | The Gas and Electricity Markets Authority
The Northern Ireland Authority for Energy Regulation |
Airports	Airports Act 1986 Airports (N Ireland) Order 1994	Civil Aviation Authority Civil Aviation Authority
Railways	Railways Act 1993	Rail Regulator/Strategic Rail Authority
Postal Services	Postal Services Act 2000	Postal Services Commission
Air Traffic Services	Transport Act 2000	Civil Aviation Authority
Financial Services	Financial Services and Markets Act 2000	OFT

Source: derived from the Competition Commission (www.competition-commission.org.uk)

- Where balances needed to be achieved between different policy objectives, the public limited company (PLC) model should first be looked at for attaining them.
- There was a need for more transparency and openness in regulation to make it accessible, not only to experts but also to the public.
- Government cannot abdicate policy-making to sectoral regulators.
- Where a major government subsidy is involved, a regulated PLC model was unlikely to work in the longer term.
- Alternative solutions (such as public ownership or not-for-profit organisations) have to show how they can overcome some of the above problems, as well as keeping incentives for efficiency.

The general function of industry and sector-wide regulators is to ensure that providers deliver 'world-class' services to their customers. Their overall aim is to regulate industries/sectors in ways that give incentives to suppliers that encourage them to achieve quality and value-for-money for their customers. Sometimes regulators work with government, other bodies and agencies to monitor the ways in which the providers operate. They also make comparisons between providers and seek to raise the standards of those needing to improve. As a bottom line, regulators want customers to get good quality and efficient services at a fair price. The ways in which they do this in their sectors/industries are by:

- setting limits on what companies can charge
- ensuring companies are able to carry out their responsibilities under relevant legislation
- protecting the standard of service customers receive
- encouraging companies to be more efficient
- helping to encourage competition where appropriate.

Regulating the public sector

Starting under the Conservatives, with the creation of the Audit Commission in 1983, regulation in the public sector has increased dramatically under New Labour, as its attention was turned from controlling inputs to public services to concentrating on outputs. As government has assumed a steering role, it needs to increase its control over the 'rowers', or bodies such as agencies, trusts, schools, universities, that deliver public services. In addition to the Audit Commission, which is no longer concerned with financial regularity but delivery of services, there are Her Majesty's Inspectorate of Constabulary, the Social Security Inspectorate, the Best Value Audit, various bodies in the NHS and also a new body to regulate the plans for providing bursaries and financial support for low income students in universities when 'top-up' fees are introduced. In every case, government investigates the performance of these bodies, sets targets for them to achieve and penalises them if they fail to achieve them. It is not regulation by the law, although the law authorises the creating of these bodies, but 'administrative regulation' by bodies theoretically independent but, in practice, doing government's bidding. Like the courts, these bodies are making judgements about performance. This sort of regulation is aimed at ensuring that government policies are achieved and at controlling standards, for example, in old peoples homes, hospitals, schools, universities and so on. Such public sector regulation also claims to increase accountability and transparency (Jackson and Price 1994).

The Audit Commission is an independent public body responsible for ensuring that public money is spent economically, efficiently and effectively in local government, housing, health, criminal justice, and fire and rescue services. The Commission's work relates most closely to that of the Office of the Deputy Prime Minister, Department of Health and National Assembly for Wales and seeks to ensure that public sector organisations deliver value for money. Its mission is to be a driving force in improving public services. It promotes good practice and helps those responsible for public services to achieve better outcomes for citizens, with a focus on those people who need public services most. The values underpinning the work of the Commission are:

- promoting the delivery of high-quality public services
- achieving excellence and value for money in its work
- maintaining independence and commitment to a robust evidence base
- supporting local democracy and public accountability
- acting with openness and honesty, both externally and internally
- valuing diversity, treating people fairly and being a good employer.

The Commission appoints independent auditors to local government, health and criminal justice organisations and regulates the work they do. Most auditors come from its Operations Directorate, with the rest coming from private firms. The Commission also inspects public services and report backs to the public on the results. Through inspections of local services, it assesses their quality and cost effectiveness, and helps local authorities to continually improve. It does this by:

- publishing information on how council services, including housing, are performing against measures in a number of specific areas set down by government
- assessing the overall performance of every council in England through the Comprehensive Performance Assessment initiative
- conducting national value-for-money studies looking at local services from the user's perspective, comparing performance and identifying and promoting good practice
- undertaking research covering a range of services including health, housing, social care, police, fire and education
- operating a 'studies programme' designed to make a major contribution to achieving the Commission's aim of improving public services and helping to improve people's lives (Audit Commission 2004).

Describe and comment on the main ways in which your organisation/sector/industry is regulated.

IMPLICATIONS FOR ORGANISATIONS AND P&D PROFESSIONALS

Given the wide range of consumer, competition, employment and other regulatory legal provisions with which organisations now have to comply, it is necessary for top management in each case to accept responsibility for ensuring that the enterprises they lead comply with the minimum standards required. This requires direction from the top of organisations.

Because of the expense of litigation, organisations are normally reluctant to call on lawyers and the courts to resolve any contractual disputes involving them. They also recognise the need to maintain good working relations with other organisations with which they deal, so they try to avoid undermining these relations by using the courts to resolve business disputes. For these reasons, business contracts almost invariably contain agreed methods for resolving specified problems when they arise. Where this fails, arbitration can be used. Arbitrators act impartially and provide a relatively informal method of enabling private sector and public service organisations determine any contractual difficulties involving them. However, the conduct and outcome of any arbitration proceedings are subject to the overriding control of the law.

Legal control of arbitration proceedings is necessary because, first, however detailed the contractual specifications are, there may be gaps in the provisions which neither party has anticipated. Second, there is a general principle, under contract law, that it is against public policy for any contractual term to exclude jurisdiction of the ordinary courts. Third, legislation on arbitration contains provisions upholding the courts' involvement in arbitration as a means of last resort. However, any legal appeal against an arbitration award requires the consent of the parties or leave of the court.

The regulatory area of most concern to a majority of organisations today – and certainly P&D professionals – is employment law. With the extension of employment legislation since the 1970s, employees now have a wide range of employment protection rights which, if infringed, permit applicants to take their claims to an employment tribunal for determination. One implication is that managements need to know their obligations under legislation and ensure that subordinate managers do not flout employee legal rights. This requires organisations developing effective HR policies and procedures, embodying at least the minimum standards provided by the law. These, in turn, need to be monitored and evaluated regularly by management to make sure that they are being implemented fairly and effectively. These policies and procedures need to be adapted and modified in the light of experience. HR departments have a vital role in creating, implementing and evaluating such policies.

One of the most significant legal provisions aimed at promoting greater job security for individual employees is the right not to be unfairly dismissed. If employers are to minimise the risk of being taken to an employment tribunal for claims of unfair dismissal, they need properly designed and administered disciplinary and dismissal procedures. Subordinate managers need training in using and applying them. In this way, consistency and equity for employees and legal protection for employers can be achieved in the disciplinary process.

It is also necessary for employers and managers to exercise greater care in recruiting, selecting and appraising employees than was the case in the past. When there was no employment protection legislation, employers and managers could take risks in recruitment and selection on the ground that they could readily dismiss unsuitable employees. Now managers need to be more professional when engaging people so that they have some confidence that new employees are suitable for the job for which they have been selected. Properly monitored induction and probationary periods are part of this process. As a result, employee recruitment and selection now take longer and are more costly in real terms than they were in the past. Another implication is that more managerial attention is being devoted to undertaking HR planning, promoting 'good' human resources management (HRM) practices and facilitating human resources development than before. This is especially the case in organisations where the effective managing of people is seen as a necessary condition of employee efficiency and corporate success.

Clearly the regulatory legal framework within which for-profit and not-for-profit organisations operate is complex and specialised. Organisations need not only appropriate legal advice but also to ensure that subordinate managers are aware of their legal duties and responsibilities. This means, in practice, that managers require informing and training in various aspects of the law. These include basic principles, as well as specialist areas such as consumer, competition and employment law. Larger organisations are likely to have their own legal specialists, while smaller enterprises are more likely to need legal advice on an ad hoc basis. One way of obtaining this is by membership of appropriate employers' or trade associations. Managerial updating of legal matters can be done through regular scanning of trade journals, professional journals and law reports and by attending relevant seminars and workshops. Investing in such training and development by employers is a necessary strategy for dealing with the provisions of an ever expanding regulatory state.

CONCLUSION

This chapter discusses the role of regulation in the contemporary state. Regulation provides the interface between the state and the market. In the regulatory state, the law plays a crucial role in mitigating the worst external effects of unregulated, free markets. Law defines and regulates all kinds of social relationships, between individuals, organisations, individuals and organisations, and citizens and the state. English law is a common law system developed through the doctrine of binding precedent. Precedent states that a decision made by a court in one case is binding on other courts in later cases involving similar facts.

The main sources of English law are legislation (or statute), common law (or judge-made law), equity, custom, books of authority and, increasingly, European law. The EU Treaties are the juridical base from which the EU institutions derive their authority to make legislation. The most important European legal devices are 'regulations' and 'directives'. Regulations become legally binding on all member states; directives normally need to be specifically implemented.

Contract is the legal cornerstone in business, consumer and employment transactions. It is the legal device facilitating exchange of goods or services between individuals and organisations and is a legally binding agreement between two parties, where each party undertakes specific obligations or enjoys specific rights conferred by that agreement.

Competition policy provides regulatory frameworks within which governments maintain or encourage competition. The objectives of competition policy include: consumer welfare, protecting consumers, redistributing wealth, protecting small and medium-sized enterprises, regional, social and industrial considerations, and market integration. In Britain, OFT and the Competition Commission (CC) have major roles in promoting competition. OFT's powers have been extended and the CC has replaced the Monopolies and Merger Commission. The CC conducts in-depth inquiries into mergers, markets and regulation of the major regulated industries.

In employment, statutory provisions have been established to create a detailed framework of legal rules, aimed at regulating and controlling the conflicting demands of employers and employees in the labour market and place of work. These include the contract of employment, dismissal, discrimination, health and safety and work—life balance. Finally, special regulatory requirements cover markets, mergers, public utilities, transport, postal services and financial services, with the Audit Commission having a special role in the public sector.

USEFUL READING

AUDIT COMMISSION. (2004) *Improving public services: Inside the Audit Commission*. London: Audit Commission.

BLACKSTONE'S LAW. (2003) *Blackstone's EC legislation 2003–04*. Oxford: Oxford University Press.

CINI, M. (ed). (2003) *European Union politics*. Oxford: Oxford University Press.

CINI, M. and McGOWAN, L. (1998) *Competition policy in the European Union*. Basingstoke: Macmillan.

CORRY, D. (2003) *The regulatory state*. London: Institute of Public Policy Research.

HARVEY, B. and PARRY, D. (2000) *The law of consumer protection and fair trading*. London: Butterworth.

JACKSON, P.M. and PRICE, C. (eds). (1994) *Privatisation and regulation*. London: Longman.

LEWIS, D. and SARGENT, M. (2004) *Essentials of employment law*. London, CIPD.

LOWE, R. and WOODRUFFE, G. (2004) *Consumer law and practice*. London: Sweet and Maxwell.

OFFICE OF FAIR TRADING. (2003) *A guide to the OFT*. London: OFT.

SARGENT, M. (2003) *Employment law*. London: Longman.

WILLEY, B. (2003) *Employment law in context*. London: FT/Prentice-Hall.

Developing Strategy

CHAPTER 9

CHAPTER OBJECTIVES

By the end of this chapter, readers should be able to:

- contribute to the process of strategy making and strategic review
- lead strategy-making in response to environmental developments which primarily affect P&D
- advise on effective strategic leadership in response to environmental developments.

In addition, readers should be able to understand, explain and critically evaluate:

- diverse approaches to strategy-making; the concepts of strategic search, choice and implementation
- the major constraints on an organisation's activities created by its business environment
- the role played by the P&D function in developing organisational strategies.

INTRODUCTION

This chapter introduces readers to some basic ideas about strategy, strategy-making, the strategic process and strategic management. Strategy has a long history and there are many conflicting perspectives of the strategic process, so the approach adopted here is a selective but demanding one. With organisations operating in increasingly complex, unstable external environments, those leading them – in the private, public and voluntary sectors – are using systems and techniques of strategic management in response to uncertainty, change and market competition. One major view of strategy, the deterministic view, is rationalist and is concerned with assessing where an organisation is at the moment, how it got there, analysing the directions in which it might go in order to survive and prosper, determining how it can get there and subsequently evaluating whether it has achieved its objectives. Another major view is that strategy can be 'shaped', without any predetermined objectives, and that it 'emerges' over time in response to changing organisational needs. In this case, the final objective of strategy is unclear and its elements are developed as strategy unfolds. It is the tensions between these two approaches to strategy that are explored in this chapter, as well as some of the tools and techniques of environmental analysis, major stages in strategy-making, constraints on strategy, ways in which organisations help shape the corporate environment and debates about strategic leadership.

DEBATES ABOUT STRATEGY

Strategy is a disputed concept, with different meanings for different people at different times. As de Wit and Meyer (2004, p3) have put it: 'there are strongly differing opinions on most of the key issues within the field and the disagreements run so deep that even a common definition of the term strategy is illusive'. Originally 'strategy' – from the ancient Greek *strategia*, 'generalship' –

was associated with the planning and winning of wars. Nowadays strategy, such as business strategy, marketing strategy or P&D strategy, is mainly linked with the management function in organisations and with those people and groups responsible for planning organisational success in the marketplace. But the term strategy is also used in a personal sense. Someone might have 'a strategy for developing their career'; another might claim to have a 'strategy for the good life'; and someone else a 'strategy for self-development and personal growth'. More generally, however, strategy is used in the collective sense. Thus people might say that 'the team's strategy for beating its opponents is to base our position on past experience' or 'the company's strategy for recruiting the best staff is to provide career opportunities internally'. In this chapter, strategy is used primarily in this collective sense and, in particular, its relation to the processes and contexts of organisational planning in uncertain, turbulent environments.

Conceptualised in these terms, strategy is a vital part of the management process. It arises as organisations face increasingly uncertain conditions. As a result, those leading and taking strategic decisions within organisations seek more structured ways of meeting these challenges in a world dominated by shortages of skills and resources and by market uncertainties or political competition. The development of relevant 'strategic frameworks' by top business and organisational leaders is one response to these demanding contextual challenges. However, developing strategic responses is not limited to top people in organisations; it takes place at all organisational levels – corporate, business unit and operational. Indeed, the phrase 'strategic choice' implies that there is no single way in which strategic direction, implementation and evaluation may be determined and that strategy operates at a multiplicity of organisational levels. This means that the vocabulary of strategy is a linguistic minefield of competing models, paradigms and values, rooted strongly in Anglo-American private sector literature, whereas public sector strategic management literature is more limited (Elcock 1996, Joyce 1999). For some observers, the search for an effective strategy is more realistically seen as a pseudo-rational process in which individual, organisational and group attitudes and beliefs play just as important a part in the process as do chosen techniques, logical thinking and sound judgement.

Quinn (1980), for example, has distinguished the words 'strategy', 'objectives', 'goals', 'policy' and 'programmes'. For him, a strategy is the pattern or plan that integrates an organisation's major goals, policies and actions into a coherent whole, while objectives or goals state what is to be achieved, when the results are to be achieved, but not how to achieve them. All organisations have multiple goals within a complex hierarchy of goals, so Quinn defines an enterprise's major goals as those affecting its overall direction and viability. These are its 'strategic goals'. Policies are rules or guidelines expressing the limits within which action takes place, with the major ones being called 'strategic policies'. Programmes, in turn, specify the step-by-step sequence of actions required to achieve major objectives, with strategic decisions being those determining the overall direction of an enterprise and its viability. Quinn also accepts that strategies exist at different levels in large organisations. In distinguishing between 'strategies' and 'tactics', Quinn argues that the primary difference lies in the scale of action or the perspective of the leader. What appears to be a 'strategy' to a departmental head may seem to be a 'tactic' to the chief executive; tactics are of relatively short-term duration in their impact on the organisation.

Drawing on analyses of military and diplomatic strategies, Quinn goes on to argue that effective formal strategies contain four main elements:

■ They incorporate the most important goals to be achieved, policy guidelines for action and programmes to accomplish defined goals.

- Effective strategies develop around a few key concepts and thrusts, giving them cohesion, balance and focus.
- Strategies deal with not only the unpredictable but also the unknowable, with organisations needing to build 'strong postures' so that they can achieve their goals despite the external forces acting on them.
- Organisations have a number of hierarchic and mutually related supporting strategies.

Effective strategies also appear to encompass certain critical success factors such as:

- clear, decisive objectives
- maintaining the initiative
- concentration
- flexibility
- co-ordinated and committed leadership
- surprise
- security.

Mintzberg (1987a) sees the need for eclecticism in defining strategy. He provides five interpretations of strategy, arguing that a good deal of confusion stems from contradictory and ill-defined uses of the term. Mintzberg examines various definitions of strategy to avoid this confusion and to enrich people's ability to understand and manage the processes by which strategies are formed. He believes, however, that these different definitions of strategy interrelate and each one 'adds important elements to our understanding of strategy, indeed encourages us to address what is really intended'. These definitions are:

- *Strategy as plan*. This is defined as some kind of consciously intended course of action or set of guidelines to deal with a situation.
- *Strategy as ploy*. This is where a specific manoeuvre is developed which is intended to outwit opponents or competitors to bring their strategies into the open.
- *Strategy as a pattern*. This involves patterns of actions where intended strategies are realised through resulting behaviours that emerge as substantive 'strategy' only in retrospect. Thus, as one business executive has said, 'Gradually the successful approaches merge into a pattern of action that becomes our strategy. We certainly don't have an overall strategy on this' (Mintzberg *et al* 1998, p15).
- *Strategy as position*. This is a means of locating an organisation in its environment. By this definition, strategy becomes a mediating force between organisations and their environment. This definition of strategy is compatible with those obtained through a preselected plan or position, aspired to through a plan or ploy, or reached through a pattern of behaviour.
- *Strategy as perspective*. Here strategic content consists of not only a chosen position but also an ingrained way of seeing the world. This definition suggests that strategy is a 'concept' and an abstraction, existing only in the minds of interested parties. It is a shared perspective, in the 'collective mind', which unites individuals by common thinking and behaviour.

Another attempt to provide an understanding of the nature of strategy is suggested by Hax (1990). While agreeing that a simple definition of strategy is not easy, he argues that some elements have universal validity and can be applied to any organisation. His starting point is the assumption that strategy embraces all the critical activities of a firm or organisation and that, as a concept, it can be considered separately from the process of strategy formation. He identifies six critical dimensions to be included in any unified definition of strategy:

- strategy as a coherent, unifying and integrative pattern of decisions
- strategy as a means of establishing an organisation's purpose in terms of its long-term objectives
- strategy as a definition of a firm's competitive domain
- strategy as a response to external opportunities and threats and to internal strengths and weaknesses as means of achieving competitive advantage
- strategy as a logical system for differentiating managerial tasks at corporate, business and functional levels
- strategy as a definition of the economic and non-economic contribution the firm intends to make to its stakeholders.

Since the concept of strategy embraces the overall purpose of an organisation, Hax (1990) believes that it is necessary to examine the many facets making up the whole strategic dimension. By combining these, a comprehensive definition is obtained. In this way, strategy becomes the fundamental framework through which organisations assert their continuity, whilst at the same time enabling them to adapt to their changing environments to gain competitive advantage. For Hax, the ultimate objective of strategy is to address the needs of organisational stakeholders: 'to provide a base for establishing the host of transactions and social contracts that link a firm to its stakeholders'.

The concept of strategy, then, is a problematic one. To provide a precise definition is misleading, since there is widespread disagreement among practitioners, academics and researchers about the boundaries, methods and philosophical underpinnings of the strategic process. Determining and applying strategic processes is a contingent, complex activity, in part rational, in part humanistic and in part value driven. As de Wit and Meyer (2004, p4) conclude: 'the variety of partially conflicting views means that strategy cannot be reduced to a number of matrices or flow diagrams that one must learn to fill in'. There is, in short, no simple definition of what strategy is. A number of perspectives, conceptual tools and approaches may be identified, but no definitive answer is possible.

Examine the view that 'strategy is about beating your enemies'.

THE RATIONAL APPROACH TO STRATEGY

There are a number of approaches to conceptualising, analysing and describing the strategy process. Each one provides specific ways in which the process and tools of strategic management can be explained and explored. A simple typology suggests a spectrum of models ranging from 'rational planning' approaches, on the one side, to 'natural selection' ones, on the other, with 'logical incrementalism', 'the emergent approach', 'chaos theory' and 'institutional' approaches in between these extremes. The basic dichotomy is between the 'planning' and 'incrementalist' perspectives. In the planning perspective, emphasis is on deliberate strategy, where strategy is intentionally designed. Strategy is formally structured, implementation is focused on programming and strategic change is implemented from the top down. In the incrementalist perspective, emphasis is on 'emergent' strategy, where strategy is unstructured, fragmented, and shaped gradually. Implementation is focused on learning or organisational development, with strategic change requiring cultural and cognitive shifts.

The rational or planning approach to strategy provides 'textbook' models of the strategy process. It emphasises the rational, scientific nature of the strategic process which if properly applied can improve the effectiveness and growth of organisations in conditions of change. The underlying principle is that strategies are the outcome of objective analyses and planning. It is rooted in the assumption that analytical, logical methods of managing strategy can be prescribed, individuals can be trained to use these methods and pay-offs can be demonstrated by using them effectively. This approach is predicated on the belief that rational decision-making points to the future direction of the organisation, through formal planning systems.

The rational approach is a prescriptive one, where strategies have objectives defined in advance, although they may be adjusted if circumstances change. The rational strategic process includes:

- analysing the environment
- analysing resources and identifying vision, mission and objectives
- developing strategic options
- choosing among these options
- implementing and evaluating the chosen strategy.

The advantages of this prescriptive approach include: the opportunity it provides of giving an overview of the organisation; the possibility of making comparisons with defined objectives; and the ability to monitor what has been agreed, so that evaluation of progress can be made. There are many versions of the rational, planning model of strategy; three are presented here: the 'hopper method', 'recipe view' and 'linear sequential view' approaches.

The hopper method

Andrews (1987, p28) illustrates the hopper method. This approach 'feeds' or 'funnels' (like a hopper) a number of variables into the strategy process, such as organisational, informational and managerial variables, and integrates them to create organisational responses capable of facilitating corporate purpose. For Andrews, corporate strategy is:

> ... the pattern of decisions in a company that determines and reveals its objectives, purposes or goals, produces the principal policies and plans for achieving those goals, and defines the range of business the company is to pursue, the kind of economic and human organisation it is or intends to be and the nature of the economic and non-economic contribution it intends to make to its shareholders, employees, customers and communities.

In this method of determining strategy, interdependence of purposes, policies and action is seen to be crucial to any individual strategy, so as to achieve competitive advantage for the organisation. The essential elements of strategy for Andrews are 'formulation' and 'implementation'. Formulation is about deciding what to do and implementation is about achieving results. Formulation involves identifying 'opportunity and risk', 'determining the company's material, technical, financial, and managerial resources', taking account of 'the personal values and aspirations of senior management', and acknowledging the company's 'non-economic responsibility to society'. Implementation, in turn, necessitates adopting appropriate 'organisational structures and relationships', designing necessary 'organisational processes and behaviour' and drawing on the strategic and personal skills of 'top leadership'.

This method of formulating and implementing suitable strategies for organisations begins by identifying 'opportunities and risks' in the environment and links these with the organisation's 'distinctive competence' and 'corporate resources'. The matching of opportunities and resources results in the schematic development of a viable economic strategy. In undertaking this to determine choice of products and markets, top managers are expected to take account of economic, technical, physical (eg locational), political, social and global factors, and match them with the company's competence and resources. The former might include the organisation's financial, managerial and organisational competence, as well as its reputation in the marketplace. 'In each company, the way in which distinctive competence, organizational resources and organizational values are combined is or should be unique.'

The recipe view

The recipe view of strategy provides structured procedures for determining strategy and is illustrated by a major British text by Johnson and Scholes (2002, p11 and p17). They define corporate strategy as being 'concerned with the overall purpose and scope of the organisation to meet the expectations of owners or major stakeholders and add value to the different parts of the organisation'. In arguing that strategic management is different from other aspects of management, because of its ambiguity, complexity, organisational impact, fundamental nature and long-term implications, Johnson and Scholes provide a three-dimensional model of strategic management. They analyse it in terms of 'strategic analysis,' 'strategic choice' and 'strategic implementation'.

Strategic analysis is concerned with the strategic position of the organisation 'in terms of its external environment, internal resources and competences, and the expectations and influence of stakeholders'. In language similar to that of Andrews (1987, pp20–22), they define strategic choice as 'understanding the underlying bases guiding future strategy, generating strategic options for evaluation and selecting from among them'. Strategic implementation translates strategy into organisational action 'through organisational structure and design, resource planning and the management of strategic change'.

Johnson and Scholes identify at least three different levels of organisational strategy: corporate, business unit and operational. The first is concerned with the organisation's overall purpose and scope; the second with how to compete successfully in the market; and the third with how resources, processes and people can effectively deliver corporate and business level strategies. They also explore the vocabulary of strategy, defining key terms such as: 'mission', 'vision', 'goal', 'objective', 'core competencies', 'strategies', 'strategic architecture' and 'control'. In arguing that different organisations are likely to emphasise different aspects of the strategic management process, Johnson and Scholes conclude that strategic priorities need to be understood in terms of the particular contexts of organisations.

The linear sequential view

The linear sequential implementation approach is a logical, rationalist approach to conceptualising corporate strategy, using a systems model of 'inputs', 'processes' and 'outputs'. It is epitomised in many basic US texts, such as those of Higgins and Vincze (1993) and David (1997), and British ones such as Bowman (2000). Higgins and Vincze (1993, p5), for example, define strategic management as the process of managing the organisation's mission and the relationship of the organisation to its internal and external environments. They provide a five-stage model of strategic management and details for determining objectives and formulating strategy:

- formulation of vision statement, mission statement and goals
- determination of strategic objectives
- formulation of strategies
- implementation of strategies
- evaluation and control of strategies.

The first three stages make up 'strategic policies', with the last two providing 'policies that aid implementation' and 'control policies'. In the determination of organisational objectives and strategy formulation, Higgins and Vincze argue that business leaders take account of organisational mission, internal and external environmental analyses and an assessment of the organisation's 'strengths, weaknesses, opportunities and threats'. This leads on to a set of 'strategic alternatives', 'evaluation of alternatives', decision-making and a 'hierarchy of strategies'.

David (1997, p4ff) defines strategic management 'as the art and science of formulating, implementing and evaluating cross-functional decisions' enabling an organisation to achieve its objectives. He sets out three stages in the strategic management process: strategy formulation, strategy implementation and strategy evaluation.

- *Strategy formulation*. This includes developing a business mission, identifying an organisation's external opportunities and threats, determining internal strengths and weaknesses, establishing long-term objectives, generating alternative strategies and choosing particular strategies to pursue. Strategy formulation also decides 'what new businesses to enter, what businesses to abandon, how to allocate resources, whether to expand operations or diversify, whether to enter international markets, whether to merge or form a joint venture and how to avoid a hostile takeover'.
- *Strategy implementation*. This requires organisations to establish annual objectives, devise policies, motivate employees and allocate scarce resources so that formulated strategies can be executed.
- *Strategy evaluation*. This is the primary means of determining whether or not particular strategies are working and involves reviewing external and internal factors that provide bases for current strategies, measuring performance and taking corrective actions.

In David's model, strategy implementation demands developing a 'strategy-supportive culture', creating an effective structure, directing marketing efforts, preparing budgets, utilising information systems and linking employee compensation to performance. This is often the most difficult stage in strategic management and hinges upon the abilities of managers to motivate employees and carry them with them to achieve organisational purpose. He sees interpersonal skills as being especially critical for successful strategic implementation. For David, 'the challenge of implementation is to stimulate managers and employees throughout an organization to work with pride and enthusiasm towards achieving stated objectives'.

For David, strategy formulation, strategy implementation and strategy evaluation take place at three hierarchical levels in large organisations. He classifies these as corporate, divisional or strategic business unit, and functional levels. In his view, by fostering communication and interaction among managers and employees across hierarchical levels, strategic management helps firms and organisations work as a team. This model of the strategic process is based on the belief that organisations 'should continually monitor internal and external events and trends so that timely changes can be made as needed', so as to adapt to change (David, p7). In his view (David, p22), 'it is a known and accepted fact that people and organisations that plan ahead are much more likely to become what they want to become than those who do not plan at all'.

Lynch (1997) regards corporate strategy as important because it deals with the fundamental issues affecting the future of an organisation. It does this by integrating an organisation's functional areas and activities to ensure its survival and growth. In his view, strategy develops out of considering the resources of an organisation in relation to its environment, with the prime purpose of adding value to it and then distributing the added value among its stakeholders. He identifies five key elements of strategy, which are principally related to the need to get competitive advantage in the marketplace. These are sustainability, distinctiveness, competitive advantage, exploitation of linkages between the organisation and its environment, and vision. He identifies three 'core areas' of corporate strategy: 'strategic analysis', 'strategy development' and 'strategy implementation'.

- Strategic analysis is concerned with the organisation's environment, its resources and its vision, mission and objectives.
- Strategic development focuses on the strategic options available to the organisation, rational selection of the ways forward, finding the strategic route ahead and considering strategy, structure and style.
- Strategy implementation enables selected options to be put into operation, although there may be practical difficulties in motivating staff and from external pressures such as legislation, regulation and market forces.

Lynch identifies the major environmental factors impacting on corporate strategy as:

- increased global competition
- consolidation and development of trading blocks
- cheap telecommunications and computer technology
- collapse of the command economies of eastern Europe
- emergence of Asian economies
- better-educated workforces.

As a result, corporate strategy becomes international in scope and has moved out of being the preserve of North American and European countries. Markets have become more international, thus making it necessary to balance global interests with variations in local demand. In describing the essential elements of what he calls a 'prescriptive corporate strategy', he identifies these as:

- developing and defining the organisation's objectives
- analysing the external environment
- reconsidering the organisation's objectives
- developing strategy options
- selecting the option against the likelihood of achieving the objectives, and
- implementing the chosen option.

For Lynch, the advantages of the prescriptive approach are that it provides:

- an overview of the organisation
- the possibility of comparing objectives
- a summary of the demands on an organisation's resources
- a picture of the choices that the organisation may need to make, and
- the possibility of monitoring agreed plans.

Drawing on Mintzberg (1994), Lynch also highlights six difficulties with the prescriptive strategic process:

- The future may not be predicted accurately enough to make rational choices.
- It may not be possible to determine the long-term good of an organisation.
- The strategies proposed may not be capable of being managed in the ways expected.
- Top management may not be able to persuade others to follow their decisions.

- Strategy decisions may need to be altered because circumstances change.
- Implementation is not necessarily a separate and distinctive phase and comes only after a strategy has been agreed.

Identify and discuss the similarities and differences amongst rationalist models of strategy.

EMERGENT AND OTHER APPROACHES TO STRATEGY

In contrast to rational approaches to strategy, there are also non-rationalistic approaches, based around the 'emergent approach'. The emergent approach to strategy is where final objectives are unclear and the elements of which are developed as strategy proceeds. It arises from the observation that human beings do not always react rationally and logically to situations and that strategy emerges over time in adaptation to human needs. Logical incrementalism, which derives out the emergent approach, is where strategic management is seen, not as a formal planning process, but as a series of subprocesses by which strategies develop on the basis of the experiences of managers and their sensitivity to changes in their environments. It is the process of developing strategy by small, incremental and reasonable steps rather than by macroscopic 'grand plans'. Incrementalists do not question the value of planning and control as means of managing organisational processes but claim that strategy formation is not one of them, since planning is less suitable for non-routine activities such as innovation and change.

The emergent approach

According to de Wit and Meyer (2004, p151):

> the distinction between deliberate and emergent strategy goes to the heart of the debate on the topic of strategy formation. While theorists disagree on many points, the crucial issue is whether strategy formation should be deliberate or more emergent.

The key principle of emergent strategy is that it does not have a single, definitive objective and that strategy develops over time. The test for emergent strategy is to examine how strategy has developed in practice over a defined period. The emergent approach identifies corporate vision, mission and objectives, analyses the environment and its resources and out of these processes strategy is developed, implemented and evaluated in response to the issues facing it.

According to Lynch (1997), the advantages of the emergent approach are that it:

- accords with organisational practice
- takes account of people issues, such as motivation, that make the rational approach unrealistic in some cases
- allows strategy to develop as more is learnt about the strategic situation
- redefines implementation so that it becomes an integral part of the strategy development process
- provides opportunity for the culture and politics of an organisation to be included in the strategic process
- provides flexibility to respond to changes, especially in fast-moving markets.

Concerns about the emergent approach include:

- In multifunctional or multidivisional organisations, resources need to be allocated between the demands of competing units and this requires some central strategic overview.
- In some industries where long-term issues are involved, decisions have to be taken and adhered to by direction from the centre.
- Management control is simpler where the basis of the actions to be taken has been planned in advance.

Emergent strategies develop, then, when strategies emerge from situations and issues rather than being planned and prescribed in advance. Such strategies came to the fore in the light of market turbulence in the 1970s, when some researchers argued that the basis of rational, prescriptive strategy was false. Three types of emergent strategic theory are distinguished: 'survival-based theories', 'uncertainty-based theories' and 'human resources-based theories'.

Survival-based theories are rooted in the belief that strategy is decided primarily in the marketplace, hence the optimal strategy for organisational survival is to be efficient. As Williamson (1991, p75) writes: 'economy is the best strategy'. If organisational survival is paramount, survival-based theorists argue, the most appropriate strategy is to pursue a number of strategic initiatives at any one time and let the market decide the best one (Whittington 2001).

Uncertainty-based theories use mathematical probability to show that development of corporate strategy is complex and uncertain, thus making accurate predictions of the future impossible. Because the environment is turbulent and uncertain, only limited strategies are possible. Miller and Friesen (1984) found, for example, that sudden shifts in strategy and in the organisational structures of companies occurred before they had reached a steady state. It is possible to provide mathematical models of such systems and show that they oscillate between stable and turbulent states. Stacey (1993) suggests that the environments of many businesses, such as computer firms, are inherently unstable, so business strategy has to emerge rather than aiming at the false certainties of the prescriptive approach.

Human resources-based strategies stress the importance of people in strategy development. They highlight the motivation of people, politics and cultures of organisations, and desires of individuals in developing strategy. The ways in which people act and interact in strategic development is vital and a process of trial and error can be used to devise acceptable strategies. These theories particularly emphasise the difficulties arising as new strategies are introduced, which confront people with the need to change. Recently, there has been discussion on the learning aspects of strategic development. In his conceptualisation of the learning organisation, Senge (1990) suggests, for example, that there are five learning disciplines, crafted to enable individuals and organisations to learn, where learning is creative activity aimed at developing new strategies and opportunities. These are:

- personal mastery that creates an organisational environment encouraging groups to develop goals and purposes
- mental models that reflect upon the images that managers and workers have of the world, and how these influence actions and decisions
- shared vision that builds commitment to achieve group aims by agreeing what these aims are
- team learning that uses group skills to develop individual abilities and competencies
- systems thinking that enables groups to understand the major forces influencing them.

Logical incrementalism

One of the best-known pioneers of emergent strategy is Quinn (1978) who is widely credited with being influential in developing the logical incrementalist perspective. In his view, 'when well-managed major organizations make significant changes in strategy, the approaches they use frequently bear little resemblance to the rational-analytical systems so widely touted'. The processes that are used to arrive at total strategy are typically fragmented, evolutionary and intuitive. He criticises both the formal systems planning approach, which underemphasises power-behavioural factors, and the power-behavioural approach because studies of these have been conducted in settings far removed from the realities of strategy formation. His research into 10 major companies in the 1970s provided the following important findings:

- Neither the formal systems planning nor power-behavioural models adequately characterise the ways in which successful strategic processes operate.
- Effective strategies tend to emerge from a series of 'strategic subsystems', each of which attacks a specific strategic issue in a disciplined way but is blended incrementally and opportunistically into a cohesive pattern that becomes the company's strategy.
- The logic behind each subsystem is so powerful that it may serve as a normative approach for formulating these key elements of strategy in large companies.
- Because of cognitive and process limits, almost all these subsystems – and the formal planning activity itself – are managed and linked together by an approach best described as 'logical incrementalism'.
- Incrementalism is not muddling through: it is purposeful, effective, proactive management for improving and integrating both the analytical and behavioural aspects of strategy formulation.

According to Quinn, strategic decisions do not lend themselves to aggregation in a single massive decision. Successful managers link together and bring order to a series of strategic processes and decisions. They proceed incrementally to handle urgent issues. In his view, logic dictates that managers proceed flexibly and experimentally from broad concepts towards specific commitments. Managers make the latter concrete as late as possible in order to narrow the bands of uncertainty and to benefit from the best available information. This is the process of logical incrementalism. It is logical in the sense that it is reasonable and well considered. It is incremental in the sense that it is structured on a piecemeal basis. Properly managed, logical incrementalism allows executives to bind together the contributions of rational systematic analyses, political and power theories and organisational behaviour concepts, thus allowing them to attain cohesion and focus.

Mintzberg's (1987b) 'crafting strategy' complements Quinn's analysis. For Mintzberg, the crafting image of strategy captures the actual process by which effective strategies are made, rather than using the rational planning approach. Using metaphor, Mintzberg argues that 'managers are craftsmen and strategy is their clay. Like the potter, they sit between the past of corporate capabilities and a future of market opportunities.' To manage strategy is to craft it, which involves dedication, experience, involvement with the material, the personal touch, mastery of detail, a sense of harmony and integration by practitioners. Ultimately, for Mintzberg, the crafting of strategy, like managing a craft, requires a natural synthesis of the future, present and past. This process incorporates:

- managing stability, not change
- programming a strategy which has already been created, not actually creating it
- detecting subtle discontinuities that might undermine a business in the future
- knowing the business, on the basis of personal knowledge and understanding
- managing emerging patterns of strategy and helping them take shape, which requires creating a climate within which a variety of strategies can grow
- reconciling both change and continuity.

Other approaches to strategy

Other ways of looking at strategy include 'complexity and chaos theory', the 'institutional' and 'natural selection' approaches. Those adopting the 'complexity and chaos' perspective argue that organisations exist in complex and unstable worlds that are difficult to understand, let alone manage. However, it is possible for people to experience particular contexts so that they become sensitive to the complexities and uncertainties around them. When there are deviations from these established patterns, they sense them intuitively. Strategic management is to do with building upon the capacity to be intuitive and to take action based on that capacity.

Institutionalists, such as Scott (1995), argue that managers can choose what strategies to develop because these arise from similarities in institutional settings. These enable managers to see how their organisations operate within a particular environmental context. Managers can understand these institutionalised assumptions, such as how a university 'works' or how a retail firm operates and the ways in which things are 'done' within them. Ways of seeing things and behaving become institutionalised, so that organisational strategies tend to develop within institutionally similar cultural parameters.

An approach far removed from the idea that managers can control their organisations is that of 'natural selection' theorists, such as Hannan and Freeman (1989). Drawing on the views of population ecologists, they argue that the success of organisations depends on how 'doing things' coincides with the needs of the environment. Where they coincide, organisations prosper; where they do not, organisations wither away. Some organisational cultures are suited to their external environments; others are less so and the extent to which managers are able to influence this is overstated.

> (i) Consider the view that logical incrementalism is the only approach to strategy appropriate for public sector organisations.
> (ii) Your manager has come across the term 'logical incrementalism' when reading a book on strategy. He has asked you to define the term and explain its relevance for your organisation. What will you say?

TOOLS AND TECHNIQUES OF ENVIRONMENTAL ANALYSIS

A major task that organisational strategists need to undertake in determining an organisation's strategic direction is assessing the external environmental forces acting upon it. These forces vary in importance depending on the type of organisation but most organisations are affected by their political, economic and legal contexts. Increasingly, technological developments and social changes are impacting too, as well as issues of environmentalism and changing public attitudes. All have to be appraised, if an organisation is to respond effectively to these forces insofar as they influence corporate, business and operational strategies. An analysis of these help senior managers not only to understand the complexities and interrelationships to be taken into account in predicting future trends affecting their organisations but also to be aware of the key factors affecting the success or otherwise of the organisations they manage. The relationship between organisations and their environment is a two-way one. Organisations have to respond to changes in the environment and the environment reacts, in turn, to organisational changes. Ultimately, if an organisation does not respond effectively to the environmental forces acting on it will fail regardless of how well its internal affairs are managed.

The scope of environmental analysis

The main areas necessitating some strategic environmental analyses by senior management are the political environment, economic forces, social factors, technology and legal factors. Some indicative examples are considered below.

The political environment

This is important because government decisions, and increasingly EU decisions, affect the ways in which organisations are managed. Organisations have continually to respond to public and EU policy changes. Government and EU regulations cover a range of issues including, for example, product competition, consumer interests and workers' rights. These demand relevant actions from organisational leaders so that they can develop appropriate strategic responses. Recent political changes such as the rise in number of interest groups in the community, and of activism amongst interest groups (such as consumer, animal welfare and ecological groups), need to be observed and acted upon by business leaders of for-profit and not-for-profit organisations. Such demands necessitate developing appropriate strategies facilitating product development, market opportunities and business innovation.

Economic forces

These are of vital concern to organisations. The overall economic climate determines business opportunities, because an expanding economy stimulates demand for goods, services, investment and labour, whilst a declining economy (or one going into recession) chokes off demand for production, consumption and resources. Top people leading organisations have to be able to distinguish between short-term and long-term economic trends, since long-term trends relate to more fundamental changes in the economy at large, which need to be addressed proactively. In addition to the general economic situation, each organisation has to examine specific trends in the industry or sector in which it operates, including competitor behaviour. The sort of areas requiring industry/sector appraisal include:

- availability of materials, finance capital and labour
- research and development
- pricing policy
- marketing and advertising
- cost structure of the sector.

Social factors

These include demographic trends and population projections. They require robust assessment, since they influence demand for goods and services and provide indicators of future labour supply. The size, distribution, age structure, ethnic mix, income levels and geographic distribution of the population are important indicators in undertaking environmental analyses. Such analyses need to give specific consideration to the impact of demographic change on the industry or sector in which the organisation operates or is competing. To survive, organisations have to be certain that their products or services are wanted and, to this end, consumer behaviour has to be examined and analysed. Consumer behaviour affects sales, or results in negative purchase decisions, and has to be assessed effectively, if an organisation is to react rationally and appropriately to such forces.

Technology

Technological change is one of the most visible and pervasive forms of change and it brings in its wake new products, processes and materials, so awareness of technological developments is essential for most organisations. Technology directly impacts on transportation, energy use, communications, entertainment, health care and so on. Organisations having knowledge of technological breakthroughs, for example, are likely to have distinct advantages in the market-place over those that do not. If organisations affected by technological change only become aware of it through subsequent publicity, then it may be too late to respond to it. A further feature of technological change is the reduction in time between scientific discovery and commercial application. Top management need to be aware of relevant technological develop-ments and to assess their impacts on their own organisations. Some innovations create new industries but destroy old ones. Technological innovation also affects not only operational systems but also functions such as finance, administrative and P&D.

Legal factors

Various legal factors can affect an organisation's reactions to its external environment (for details see Chapter 7) and they can constrain an organisation's actions or facilitate them. Areas affected by legal regulation include:

- type of products or services produced
- how products or services are developed
- labelling of products
- pricing of products
- amounts spent on advertising and promotion
- how employees are hired
- salaries and other payments
- workplace design and health and safety
- accounting practices.

The process of environmental analysis

Environmental analysis can be divided into four analytical stages: scanning the environment, monitoring specific environmental trends or patterns, forecasting the future direction of environ-mental changes, and assessing current and future environmental change for their organisational implications. There are two approaches to environmental analysis. One is a 'macro' (outside-in) approach; the other is a 'micro' (inside-out) approach. Using the macro-approach, organisations engage in scanning, monitoring, forecasting and assessing to identify and examine plausible alter-native future environments that might confront them. The driving force is to ensure organisations understand the dynamics of change within each environment, before deriving organisational spe-cific implications. The micro-approach takes the organisation as the starting point – its products, markets, technologies and so on. This approach asks the question, given these contexts, what elements of the external environment should the organisation scan, monitor, forecast and assess? (Fahey and Narayanam 1986).

Scanning

Scanning involves general surveillance of all environmental segments (political, economic, social, technological and legal) and their interactions. This is done either to identify early signals of pos-sible environmental change or to detect changes already underway. Environmental scanning is aimed at alerting organisations of potentially significant external developments before they are fully formed. The fundamental challenge is to make sense of vague, ambiguous and unconnect-ed data, using judgement, observation and consulting experts inside and outside the organisation for their specialist views. Analysts have to make connections among diverse data, so that signals of future events are created. The outputs of scanning are, therefore, signals of potential change and detection of change underway and the organisational outcomes are greater awareness of the general environment.

Monitoring

Monitoring involves tracking the evolution of environmental trends, sequence of events or streams of activities. It involves following signals or indicators identified during environmental scanning. The purpose of monitoring is to assemble sufficient data to discern whether certain predicted trends or patterns are emerging. Data sources are focused reading, selective use of individual expertise and focus groups. The outputs of monitoring are specification of trends and identification of scanning needs. The organisational outcomes are, first, consideration and detailing of specific developments and, second, time for developing flexibility.

Forecasting

Scanning and monitoring provide pictures of what has already taken place in the external environment and what is currently happening there. Strategic decision-making, however, requires a future orientation and the need to develop plausible projections of the future. The data sources are outputs of monitoring, with data being collected via forecasting techniques (see below). The outputs are alternative forecasts of the future and identification of scanning and monitoring needs. The organisational outcomes are understanding future environmental changes.

Assessment

Scanning, monitoring and forecasting are not ends in themselves. Assessment involves identifying and evaluating how and why current and projected environmental changes are affecting or are likely to affect the strategic management of the organisation. The outputs are specific organisational implications and the organisational outcomes are specific actions. Assessment thus answers questions such as what are the key issues presented by the environment and what are the strategic implications of these for the organisation?

Techniques of environmental analysis

There is a range of environmental analysis techniques. Some are data-gathering methods, others are forecasting techniques. Data-gathering methods specify data sources and methods of data collection. Sources of data are either primary or secondary and may be collected on *ad hoc*, periodic, real-time or continuous bases. Primary sources are organisational data or specialist agencies may be hired to provide them. The sources are individuals, sampled populations or expert panels. Secondary sources are gathered by various agencies for general purposes and are typically available to all organisations. The nature of the data may be quantitative, qualitative or inferential. Inferential data are arrived at as a result of drawing conclusions from various data sources. For example, social values may not be directly manifest or self-explanatory but they have 'meanings' for those internalising them that imply certain substantive behaviours.

Forecasting techniques are procedures for transforming data so as to provide answers to questions posed by environmental analysts in manners consistent with the data available. Forecasting techniques serve three main purposes: they verify 'hunches' or intuitive judgements; they answer 'what if?' questions; and they facilitate the forecasting of trends, events and patterns.

Forecasting techniques are deterministic, adaptive or inventive. Deterministic techniques assume that the future can be known from the past, provided that the analyst has a model of the underlying causes at hand. Adaptive techniques do not assume that the future is knowable and are oriented to creating descriptions of how the future is unfolding and reveal the process of change that is taking place. Inventive techniques are directed towards 'open futures'. They emphasise how an organisation can 'redesign' its future and its environment. The analyst is guided by the intentions of the organisation and the analysis is oriented towards creating 'pathways' to the intended future. Three widely used techniques for environmental analysis are Dephi forecasting, cross-impact matrices and scenarios.

Delphi forecasting

The Delphi technique brings a number of experts together to analyse specific aspects of the current and future environment. It is intended as a technique to enable them to contribute to each other's understanding of the issues and to refine their opinions as a result of their interactions with one another. The Delphi technique involves the following steps.

- Each expert is asked to make an initial prediction.
- Predictions are tabulated and clarified by a neutral investigator.
- The output of the above is fed back to the experts who are asked to make a second round of predictions based on the information provided to them. The process of making predictions and receiving feedback may go on for several rounds.

Cross-impact matrices

Cross-impact matrices provide a systematic approach to identifying and tracing through chains of effects among several forecasts or elements in the environment that are believed to interact with one another. The matrix provides a means of identifying secondary and tertiary consequences. When one environmental phenomenon being forecast affects the likelihood or timing of another, cross-impact matrices allow assessment of the consequences to be made in an explicit manner. The raw material of a cross-impact matrix is a set of events that are forecast to happen within a specified time period (the horizontal axis). The analyst specifies the time period within which the event is likely to occur and its probability of occurrence (the vertical axis).

Scenarios

Scenarios represent hypothetical descriptions of sequences of future events and trends. They are plausible, alternative futures. They allow analysts to explore the possible consequences of a series of complex, interrelated possibilities about the future. A scenario typically includes some trends, patterns, events, assumptions pertaining to these, conditions in the current environment and the dynamics leading from the present state of the environment to some future state. They allow the analyst to lay out possible blueprints for the future and assess the risks and implications of environmental change. The following steps are involved:

- Identify the strategic decision context.
- Identify key industry, competitive and organisational forces.
- Identify key macro-environmental forces.
- Analyse the key forces.
- Develop scenario logics or explanations for how the elements in the scenario fit together.
- Elaborate the scenarios.
- Determine the implications for strategic decisions.

(i) Why is environmental analysis of such importance to organisations today?

(ii) How can the results of an environmental assist the strategic management process?

(iii) Outline how you would carry out an environmental analysis of your organisation (or part of it).

FORMULATING STRATEGY

In the private sector, it is generally recognised that the profit-maximising model of the firm has serious shortcomings when trying to explain strategic decision-making in practice. Firms have to make some level of profit to survive but they do not maximise profits and, in some cases, managerial goals may be an important element in determining the strategic goals of organisations (Mintzberg 1989). In the public (and voluntary) sectors, or 'not-for-profit' bodies, organisations have different, more complex goals from those of private sector ones.

There are many ways of describing and analysing the major stages in strategy-making. Johnson and Scholes (2002), for example, provide a model of strategic management incorporating three main elements: 'strategic position', 'strategic choices' and 'strategy into action'. For Lynch (1997), the three core areas of strategy are 'strategic analysis', 'strategy development' and 'strategy implementation'. Basically, however, making strategy can be analysed in terms of formulation (ie searching and choosing strategy) and implementation. In this section, the formulation of strategy is considered and the following section examines strategy implementation.

Vision, mission statements and strategic objectives

Strategy formulation begins with an organisation's 'vision', 'mission' and 'strategic objectives'.

Vision

Like all terms and concepts used in describing and analysing strategy, 'vision' has a number of meanings. Vision is the strategic intent or desired future state of an organisation, as defined by its leading strategists, normally the chief executive. Johnson and Scholes (2002) state there are a number of ways in which strategic vision may be determined. It might be formulated deliberately, as part of the planning process. It might be associated with the founder of a business. It might be derived from external forces, such as privatisation, market testing or compulsory competitive tendering in the public services. It might even be related to intuition. The crucial point is that vision encapsulates a view of a realistic, credible and successful future for the organisation. For Bartlett and Ghoshal (1989), building a shared corporate vision gives context and meaning to every manager's roles and responsibilities and it helps individuals understand the company's stated goals and objectives. In their view, vision must be crafted and articulated with clarity, continuity and consistency because:

- clarity of expression makes corporate objectives understandable and meaningful
- continuity of purpose underscores those objectives' enduring importance
- consistency of application across business units ensures uniformity throughout the organisation.

Vision is not the same as an organisation's mission and objectives. Vision is awareness of where the organisation is now and how it and its competitors will be competing in the future, whereas mission and objectives are concerned with current issues facing the organisation. Vision underpins the purpose and strategy of an organisation. Hamel and Prahalad (1994) have put forward five criteria for judging the relevance and appropriateness of an organisation's vision:

- foresight
- breadth
- uniqueness
- consensus
- actionability.

Mission

The mission of an organisation is a general expression of its overall purpose and the broad directions it seeks to follow. The mission derives out of its leaders' vision and takes account of

229

the values and expectations of its leaders and major stakeholders. Some claim that corporate mission is an organisation's reason for existence. Others view corporate mission as encompassing the basic points of departure that direct an organisation in a particular direction. Corporate mission can be articulated in a 'mission statement', although there is disagreement over exactly what a mission statement is and what it should include. Some have questioned the lengthy nature and content of mission statements, whilst others have indicated that organisations should concentrate on short, concise statements of 'strategic intent' (Hamel and Prahalad 1989). The sorts of items included in mission statements, although the list is neither exclusive nor exhaustive, are:

- direction of the organisation
- organisational purpose
- values of the organisation
- points of departure for the strategy process
- nature of the business on which the company intends to focus
- competitive ambitions of the organisation.

Whatever is in the mission statement, it has a number of functions. First, it points the organisation along a stated pathway, by defining the boundaries within which strategic choices and actions take place. Second, it conveys to stakeholders that the organisation is pursuing valued activities affecting their interests. Third, by specifying the fundamental principles driving organisational actions, the mission statement can inspire individuals to work together co-operatively. In formulating mission statements, those responsible take account of factors such as:

- nature of the business of the organisation
- importance of customer interests
- basic values and beliefs of what the organisation stands for
- the need to address the business's market niche and competitive advantage
- reasons for adopting its choice of approach.

Strategic objectives

These state more precisely than mission statements what is to be achieved and when the results are to be achieved but are distinguished from functional and business unit objectives. The purpose of strategic objectives is to focus the tasks of management on specific outcomes and to provide means of assessing whether the outcomes have been attained. In the past, writers like Ansoff (1965) were keen to stress the importance of setting quantifiable objectives but nowadays it is generally recognised that some strategic objectives cannot be easily quantified.

In developing corporate objectives, those responsible normally recognise that overall strategic objectives need subsequently to be translated into objectives for different functions and, in larger organisations, for different business units. Further, in larger organisations, strategic objectives need to be adjusted to take account of the circumstances and business conditions of different parts of the organisation. Strategic objectives commonly relate to overall financial, marketing and other targets. Financial targets relate to issues such as profitability, costs relative to key competitors, financial stability, earnings on capital invested, revenue growth, dividends, cash flow and share price. Marketing targets include market share, products or service diversity, growth opportunities, ability to compete in international markets and quality issues. Other strategic objectives cover customer relations, customer service, product/service leadership, research and development, investment in human resources, training and development, and operational costs.

Levels of strategy, strategic options and preferred strategy

Strategy is the key link between what the organisation wants to achieve (its objectives) and the policies guiding its activities. However, organisations can have more than one strategy, since strategies can exist at:

- *Corporate level.* Corporate strategy is concerned with the type of business the firm is in and addresses issues such as the balance of the organisation's portfolio, markets, contribution to profits, growth and possible diversification.
- *Business level.* Business strategy is concerned with how operating units within the organisation can compete in particular markets, divisional plans and the strategies of strategic business units that are 'parts of the whole'.
- *Operational level.* Operational strategy is concerned with how various functions (such as finance, marketing, operations, P&D and research and development) contribute to corporate and business strategy.

Approaches to strategy formulation involve identifying strategic options and selecting a preferred strategy (or strategies). The generation of strategic options is not a random process but may be stimulated by shortfalls in current performance or business effectiveness. Hrebiniak and Joyce (1984) have suggested that five factors affect identification of strategic options:

- organisational learning
- distinctive competencies
- past performance and type of search activity
- power differentials in organisations
- absorption of uncertainty.

Organisations approach the task of strategy formulation differently, depending on the type of markets they operate in, their culture, management style, external environment and so on. 'Top-down', 'bottom-up', 'interactive' or 'semi-autonomous' approaches are used:

- *The top-down approach.* Strategy formulation is driven by corporate management and strategy is unified, coherent and provides corporate direction and performance targets.
- *The bottom-up approach.* Strategy formulation takes place at business unit level and is passed upwards for approval and integration with the strategies of other business units; as a result corporate strategy may lack unity, coherence and consistency.
- *The interactive approach.* Strategy formulation is managed jointly by corporate and business unit managers, with the process being participative, negotiated and reflecting links between corporate centre and business units.
- *The semi-autonomous approach.* Strategy formulation is determined by relatively independent strategy formulation activities at corporate and business unit levels; at corporate level, formulation is virtually continuous; at business unit level, formulation is suited to each business unit's circumstances and objectives.

At corporate level, selecting a preferred strategy utilises techniques such as 'portfolio analysis' and 'horizontal strategy'. At business level, strategy selection draws upon techniques such as SWOT analyses which examine the internal strengths and weaknesses and external threats and opportunities facing organisations. Such approaches have been described as normative, however, and addressed implicitly at organisational leaders as formulators of strategy (Leavy and Wilson 1994).

The Boston Consultancy Group (BCG) growth share matrix

One of the most publicised business portfolio techniques is the BCG growth share matrix. The matrix plots a firm's relative market share position in an industry (or market) on the horizontal axis against business growth rates of industry (or market) on the vertical axis.

- *Stars*. These are businesses with strong market share in a high growth industry and represent the best profit and growth opportunities.
- *Cash cows*. These are businesses with high market share in a low growth industry. They represent a valuable resource, because the cash they generate can develop new 'stars' and provide funds for corporate spending.
- *Dogs*. These are businesses with low market share in a low growth industry because of their poor competitive position and are not usually very profitable.
- *Question marks*. These are businesses with low market share in a high growth industry. Their high growth rate makes them an attractive market position but their weak market share means their cash generation is low.

The weaknesses of the BCG model include its relative simplicity, business growth rate is not a sufficient description to describe industry attractiveness and business growth rate and relative market share are not the only factors determining the standing of a business in its portfolio.

The nine-cell General Electric (GE) matrix

The GE matrix relates a firm's competitive position on the horizontal axis (whether 'strong', 'average' and 'weak') to the industry's attractiveness on the vertical axis (whether 'low', medium' and 'high'). Measurement of a firm's competitive position includes indicators such as market share, competitive ability, knowledge of customers, knowledge of markets, technological capability, calibre of management and so on. Industry attractiveness, in turn, is a function of a number of factors including market growth rate, market size, profitability, market structure, competitive rivalry, seasonality, economies of scale, technological requirements, capital requirements, and social, legal and environmental issues. Unlike the BCG model, the GE matrix takes into account a wider range of strategic variables and it allows for intermediate rankings between 'high' and 'low' and between 'strong' and 'weak'.

The product/market evolution matrix

Hofer and Schendel (1978) have provided a 15-cell matrix model, in which a firm's competitive position, on the horizontal axis (whether 'strong', 'average' and 'weak'), is related to the stage of product/market evolution on the vertical axis in terms of 'development', 'growth', 'shake-out', 'maturity/saturation' and 'decline.' Future positions can be plotted and used to identify major strategic issues.

Horizontal strategy

Porter (1998a, pp318–319) has described horizontal strategy as 'a co-ordinated set of goals and policies across distinct but interrelated units', which he regarded as 'the essence of corporate strategy.' In his view, without horizontal strategy, 'there is no convincing rationale for the existence of a diversified firm because it is little more than a mutual fund.' The main analytical steps in this approach are:

- identifying all interrelationships deriving from opportunities to share activities among related businesses
- tracing such interrelationships outside the boundaries of the firm
- identifying possible interrelationships involving the transfer of managers' knowledge between businesses

- identifying competitor interrelationships
- assessing the importance of interrelationships to competitive advantage
- developing a co-ordinated strategy to achieve and enhance the most important interrelationships
- creating horizontal organisational mechanisms to ensure implementation.

SWOT analyses

Here emphasis is on strategy-related strengths, weaknesses, opportunities and threats, as illustrated in Tables 9.1 and 9.2. These are only illustrative examples but SWOT analyses provide a useful way of screening strategic options, where an option maximising a 'strength' or an 'opportunity' is preferable to one that is not. The first case is an organisation in the market sector; the second is an NHS hospital trust.

Table 9.1 Example of a SWOT analysis for an organisation in the market sector

INTERNAL	
Strengths	*Weaknesses*
Market position	Management skills
Economies of scale	Lack of key skills/competencies
Cost advantages	Weak image in the market
Financial resources	Lack of strategic direction
Staff skills and competencies	Competitive disadvantage
EXTERNAL	
Opportunities	*Threats*
Potential new markets and products	Possible new competitors
Reputation	Potential substitute products
Vertical integration	Low market growth
Demographic changes	Government policies
Competitor complacency	Power of customers

Table 9.2 Example of a SWOT analysis for an NHS hospital trust

INTERNAL	
Strengths	*Weaknesses*
Expertise of professional staff	Management skills
Range of medical provision	Lack of key skills/competencies
Up-todate technology	Low 'star rating'
Financial resources	Lack of strategic direction
Good facilities and estate	Lack of resources
EXTERNAL	
Opportunities	*Threats*
Additional government funding possibilities	Possible new competitors
Potential new services	Demographic changes
Developing new partnerships locally	Loss of key staff
Private financial initiatives	Changing government policies
Generating new revenue sources	Power of patients

(i) Undertake a business portfolio analysis of your organisation using the Boston Consultancy Group growth share matrix.

(ii) Do a similar exercise using the nine-cell General Electric matrix.

(iii) What do these indicate about selecting a business strategy for your organisation?

IMPLEMENTING STRATEGY

Strategy implementation is crucial to effective strategic management. Most of the time and efforts of senior managers are directed towards strategy implementation and it is planning and control systems that are the main means through which the strategic objectives and policies of an organisation are translated into specific, measurable, attainable goals and plans. However, the importance of people in the implementing process is not to be underrated, since issues such as motivating employees, communicating with them and facilitating the managing of change all need to be addressed if strategies are to be turned into practical results and actions.

Large organisations may decide to use a pilot study or demonstration project as an initial implementation strategy. This becomes an opportunity for organisational learning. Projects are a synthesis of strategy formulation and implementation. Bryson and Farnum (1995) have identified pilots as being particularly appropriate to technically difficult situations, where it is important to test the relationships between solutions and effects. Pilots are also useful where there is scepticism or opposition to change. Pilots can be used to demonstrate the effects of the change and win over those who are wavering.

Planning, budgeting and communicating

The budget is the common method used for strategic implementation and incorporates the communication of attainable goals and targets, whilst engaging the participation and support of all levels of management in the process. Budgeting is central to the planning and control process, because it converts all elements of an organisation's plans into financial numbers. The overall budget includes a number of elements, such as sales, production/operations and administration, each of which in turn is broken down into smaller segments, although there are some inherent problems in budgets:

- They are dependent upon predictions about future performance and a range of assumptions, which are subject to error, so budgets are not exact tools.
- They can facilitate modification of plans and strategies in the light of the latest information.
- They are often misused, particularly during evaluation of the actual outcomes with the planned ones.
- They involve use of resources, as with any management information system.
- They result in the production of elaborate reports that are not always easy to understand.

The function of budgeting in converting strategy into action plans has three main elements:

- *Planning*. This is not simply an estimate based on past performance. The budget is designed to articulate in greater detail the agreed strategic direction of the organisation. This includes preparing a projected income statement and balance sheet to ensure that the aggregate detailed action plans meet predetermined criteria such as return on investment and profit levels.

- *Co-ordination.* This requires dovetailing individual elements of the budget to ensure internal consistency. Co-ordination of budgets determines the iterative nature of the budgetary process.
- *Control.* This requires an effective communication system, including both formal and informal methods. Formal measures include written policy statements, procedural manuals, job descriptions and meetings. Informal measures include informal gatherings and interpersonal communications. Control is important because management control is the process guiding organisations to their objectives. Fundamental to the exercise of control is reporting appropriate information at the appropriate level.

In order to implement strategy, organisations also need to have commitment to the achievement of the goals that have been stated by those responsible for the organisation. This requires employee motivation. Motivation can be best achieved by positive means such as higher pay, promotion and intrinsic reward. Once the budget is recognised to be an element helping motivate people, attention needs to be paid to individual needs, group needs and enterprise values. When these elements are incorporated in the overall planning and control process, the resulting budget is likely to fulfil its function as an aid to employee motivation.

Alexander (1985) has identified five main features for successful strategy implementation and these are based on the assumption that successful implementation requires preventing problems occurring. This is followed by quick action to resolve any problems that occur. Successful implementation involves doing things that help to promote success rather than just preventing problems. These five features are:

- *Communicating.* Clear communication on strategic decisions to all employees is required. Communication is two-way, permitting questions about formulated strategy, issues to be considered and potential problems to be raised.
- *Starting with a good idea.* This must be fundamentally sound, since nothing can rescue a poorly-formulated strategic decision.
- *Gaining employee commitment and involvement.* This suggests that managers and employees should be involved right from the start in the formulation process. Where people are involved in the implementation process, commitment typically follows.
- *Providing sufficient resources.* These include money, time, technical expertise and people.
- *Developing an implementation plan.* Likely problems and their contingent responses need to be addressed and the plan needs to strike a balance between too much detail and too little.

Managing change

Implementing strategic decisions inevitably involves changes within organisations. Gaining commitment of key people in the organisation to any 'new vision' and the development of new skills is critical to this purpose. Change can be accepted or rejected by staff and behavioural and attitudinal responses to change depend on two main factors. The first is individual perceptions of the change and its effects. The second is individual perceptions of responses and their effects. Attitudinal responses to change, such as hostility, do not necessarily translate into resistance, since there are other considerations that might determine the response. Behavioural and attitudinal responses to change depend on individual perceptions of change, the range of responses available and their likely effects.

From the individual's viewpoint, there are two main types of change resulting from strategic decisions: social changes and technical changes. Social changes affect the employee's social relationships with others in the organisation and changes in status, workgroup or supervisor. Technical changes are connected with the job itself such as changes in pay, hours worked, conditions of service, promotion and type of work. Social changes to groups, status and supervision are often perceived as more disruptive than are technical changes to the work performed.

Personal factors, group factors and organisational factors influence perceptions of change and possible responses to it. Personal factors include general attitudes, personality, self confidence and tolerance of ambiguity. Group factors include group norms and group cohesiveness. The more cohesive the group, the higher the level of conformity within it. Organisational factors include the record of change within an organisation, its structure and management style. Those responsible for change management have little control over most of these factors.

INTERNAL CONSTRAINTS ON STRATEGY

Determining an organisation's current position and the way forward to the future also involves consideration of its internal resources. Unless these resources are adequate to the task, they act as internal constraints on developing an effective organisational strategy. An internal analysis of these resources and appraising their utilisation involves:

- developing a profile of the organisation's principal skills and resources
- comparing this resource profile with the product and market requirements, so as to identify strengths and weaknesses
- comparing the strengths and weaknesses with major competitors to identify where significant competitive advantage exists.

Such an internal appraisal requires reviewing the main functional areas of the organisation: human resources, finance, marketing, operations, and research and development in terms of their added value to the business. The aim of assessing these functional areas is to determine their effects on the organisation's strategy and address any internal constraints on it.

Human resources

The importance of analysing the human resources of an organisation should not be understated, although it is a problematic area in which to form balanced judgements. Some of the key issues to be considered include:

- the relationship between individuals and the organisation
- the impact of informal groups and whether they are supportive of the formal organisation
- management sensitivity to human resources issues
- morale in the organisation and the 'health' of the organisational climate
- the qualifications and expertise of staff, given the present and projected activities of the organisation
- the organisation's policy in terms of recruitment, selection, placement, rewards, employee relations and training
- the organisation's relationship with trade unions (if they are recognised)
- the organisation's position in relation to its competitors regarding pay, promotion, fringe benefits and so on
- the extent to which HR is considered strategically within the organisation and its role in formulating and implementing strategic decisions.

Finance

A financial analysis is important to strategy because it evaluates the financial resources of the organisation and how well they are being utilised. Financial indicators also provide important pointers concerning the way that the organisation is managed and the systems used in the management process. This information is crucial in assessing the appropriateness of past, present and future strategies. Some of the main issues to be considered include:

- the financial results and financial status of the organisation
- links between financial budgets and overall strategic and operating plans
- consistency between divisional budgets and overall budgets
- the process of budget preparation and whether management across the organisation participate in this process
- utilisation of forecast profit and loss statements, balance sheets and cash flow projections
- the information provided for management control
- the attitude of managers to planning and control reports
- whether such documents are utilised as motivational elements in the organisation
- utilisation by management of control reports for evaluating performance and formulation of strategy, in particular whether the reports compare actual results with budgets or standards and whether corrective action is taken.

Marketing

The marketing function encompasses market research, sales forecasting and promotions activity and represents a vital communication link between the organisation (whether 'for-profit' or 'not-for-profit') and the outside world. Marketing does this by considering changes in the economic, technological, social and other external contexts and bringing such knowledge into the organisation, as well as making information about the organisation available to customers and potential customers. Two important internal relationships are between marketing and operations and between marketing and research and development. The way in which marketing relates to and communicates with these two functions is vital, since this provides the information required by marketing staff for the strategic decisions they take. The main issues to be considered include:

- the use made of market research and the extent to which it influences product or service development
- the relative position of each 'product group' in terms of sales and contribution to profits or organisational objectives
- the market share of each product group and its stage in the product life cycle
- the distribution channels used and the extent to which new distribution development indicates need for change
- the relationship between sales price and sales volumes
- the pricing policy pursued by the organisation
- the organisation's competitive features such as quality, price, service and delivery, as well as the extent to which such features are appropriate to the industry or sector
- the extent to which the marketing function is aware of competitor moves, technological change and environmental aspects relevant to the organisation.

Operations

The operations function within organisations, whether in manufacturing, service or public organisations, has responsibility for more physical, financial and human resources than any other function.

But the links between operations and research and development are fundamental to the successful development of products in terms of cost, quality and effectiveness. The main issues to be considered in the operations function include:

- production planning and control and their interface with marketing and production
- information received from sales and marketing, accounting and quality control, with particular reference to its usefulness in managing the operations function
- production costs and their movement in relation to sales prices and identification of the causes of cost changes
- use of performance standards and the exercise of cost control
- control over key cost elements such as labour, materials and packaging
- stock levels in relation to output and sales and the relationship between levels of raw material stocks, work in progress and finished goods
- plant and equipment, their adequacy, age, state of repair and level of investment in relation to industry/sector norms
- the extent of computerisation of production facilities and the organisation's policy on replacement
- communications between all aspects of the operations function and other areas of the organisation
- the organisation of the function including purchasing and materials management
- the reputation of the organisation as a producer, coupled with the requirements of the industry and environmental conditions.

Research and development

Research and development (R&D) is aimed at improving products, introducing new ones or enhancing the production process. For non-manufacturing organisations, R&D is unlikely to be of great importance. But for manufacturing, R&D is crucial to survival and future success. The effectiveness of the R&D function is dependent upon the past record of R&D in product and process innovation and upon future expectations for R&D-driven innovations. The main issues to be considered include:

- industry/sector expenditure on R&D and the organisation's commitment to it
- the nature of the organisation's products and whether they require continual development
- whether the market requires such development
- the nature of the production process and whether it requires enhancement
- the return to the organisation for a product breakthrough
- the resources that the organisation can devote to R&D, analysed between projects and products
- the record of the organisation in terms of new or improved products and the present state of likely innovations for future exploitation
- the way in which R&D is organised, in particular its links with marketing and operations
- links between the R&D organisation and others such as universities and hospitals
- whether the organisation has R&D joint ventures with other bodies.

Identify and discuss the main internal constraints on strategy at:

(i) corporate level
(ii) business level
(iii) operational level in your organisation.

EXTERNAL CONSTRAINTS ON STRATEGY AND SHAPING THE EXTERNAL ENVIRONMENT

As stated in Chapter 2, Porter (1998a) has identified the immediate environments in which business organisations operate. His study provides a framework for examining the industry or sector relevant to particular firms. It is these 'competitive forces' that are potential constraints on the success of each firm, or organisation operating in a competitive market, and of its strategic responses to environmental change. But they also provide potential opportunities for developing appropriate strategic responses to environmental change. Such forces affect all firms in a sector and each firm tries to respond to these forces by 'shaping' the external environment.

Porter's five basic competitive forces – threat of new entrants, rivalry among existing firms, threat of substitutes, the bargaining power of buyers and the bargaining power of suppliers – determine the state of competition and its underlying structure. Firms have to identify the key structural features of their sector, so that the strength of the five competitive forces, and hence industry profitability, can be determined. The essence of such an analysis is to identify the sources of each force so as to enable the firm to develop a strategy that builds on the 'opportunities' provided and avoids the 'threats'. An important feature of Porter's model is recognition that competition in an industry goes beyond immediately competing firms. All five forces determine the intensity of competition and profitability; identifying the strongest force (or forces) is critical in effective strategy formulation.

The five forces influencing competition in an industry have been explored in Chapter 2 and are not repeated here. However, after a firm has identified how these forces affect it, it can consider its own position in relation to the underlying causes of each competitive force. Porter (1998a) argues that an effective strategy has to be designed to establish a defendable position *vis-à-vis* the five competitive forces. There are three possible approaches:

- positioning the organisation so that it has the best defence against these competitive forces (ie matching the organisation's strengths and weaknesses to the given industrial structure)
- influencing the balance of forces by altering their causes in order to improve the organisation's relative position. This requires structural analysis to identify key factors and where action influencing the balance yields the best 'pay-off'
- forecasting changes in the factors underlying the five forces and responding to them, thus exploiting change by selecting an appropriate strategy before the organisation's competitors recognise the change.

Having analysed the nature of the environment and an industry's structural features, business leaders can then identify the environmental issues most likely to have an impact on their organisation. This provides focus in strategy formulation. Two issues need to be addressed by top management in looking at possible opportunities and threats in the external environment.

First, consideration needs to be given to the extent to which the strategy of an organisation matches or fails to match its external environment: an organisation's environment may have changed but not its strategy. Alternatively, the structure of an organisation may not be suited to the conditions prevailing in the environment and different structures may be needed. Management has to assess those changes in the environment, in relation to the nature of the organisation and its business, in order to determine whether the change is permanent or just short-term, a well as the speed and extent of the change. For example, change in the wider environment may significantly affect the structure of an industry. On the other hand, the balance in competitive forces may have altered because barriers to entry may have been reduced by technological innovation. Examining the external environment and its constraints on an organisation is an important part of any systematic approach to strategy-making.

Second, consideration needs to be given to the strengths of the organisation relative to the environmental changes it faces. These strengths depend on a variety of factors such as an organisation's record of product/service innovations that can involve changes in working practices, new organisational structures, entry into new markets and so on. This could indicate that the organisation is well placed to deal with and respond to change effectively. Its key strength may be not product/service development but its flexibility in response to change (Porter 1998b).

In managing change in organisations in response to internal and external constraints on strategy, business leaders have five main strategies from which to choose:

- *Participative strategies*. These are particularly effective where management needs the active co-operation of staff but participation can be regarded sceptically, if it is used manipulatively.
- *Power strategies*. These are appropriate where change must be introduced rapidly and where commitment of those affected is not necessary for successful implementation.
- *Manipulation strategies*. This involves conscious restructuring of events so that others behave in the way that the manipulator wants. The manipulator can either restructure the situation or alter the subjects' perception of the existing situation.
- *Negotiation strategies*. This is useful where there are likely losers resulting from change and where losers can disrupt implementation of change.
- *Contingency strategies*. This approach suggests that all relevant factors in the situation should be considered before selecting the appropriate change strategy.

DEBATES ABOUT EFFECTIVE STRATEGIC LEADERSHIP

Just as 'strategy' is an elusive concept, so too is 'leadership'. The essence of strategy has been described as the direction and scope of an organisation over the long term 'which achieves advantage for the organisation through its configuration of resources within a changing environment and to fulfill stakeholder expectations'. The essence of leadership has been described as the process of influencing an organisation or group within an organisation 'in its efforts towards achieving an aim or a goal' (Johnson and Scholes 2002, p10 and p549). In practice, however, a full understanding of these two concepts and their interrelationships is problematic, since there is lack of theoretical integration between the strategy and leadership fields. As indicated earlier in this chapter, the concept of 'strategy' has multiple meanings and interpretations. So too has the concept of 'leadership'. As Bennis and Nanus (1985, p4) have commented: in the field of leadership research 'never have so many labored so long to say so little'.

For some, strategy is a plan for the future or a pattern from the past (Bennis and Nanus 1985). For others, it is an intellectual product or a craft process (Mintzberg 1987b). For some, leadership is an attribute, style or capacity for visionary thinking. And for others, it is a science or performing art (Zaleznik 1992). The central issue is are leaders of organisations in control of its destiny? Or is the environment of an organisation or its contexts the controlling and determining factor? Where does the 'locus of influence' over leadership and strategy lie? The debate and research in these areas are polarised into competing views along the 'human agency-determinist' spectrum.

Human agency views of leadership and strategy

The assumption that underlies much understanding of effective leadership starts with rational theories of the firm, workgroups or individuals. These theories try to get a 'best fit' between the functional demarcations of organisations and the performance of managers. The same process is assumed where groups and individuals are concerned. Thus effective leaders are seen to be those who match their leadership styles to the needs of the organisation, group or individuals (Lickert 1967). The overriding theoretical framework linking such studies and approaches is one that ascribes primacy to the role of human agency in these situations (Gouldner 1980). It assumes that the leader makes an important contribution to the strategy of an organisation and that such actions are linked directly to its economic performance. Leadership is identified as the key factor in securing the assumed link between management and organisational performance.

Human agency theory also runs through much of the literature on strategic management. Studies here support the view that patterns of organisational action should be based on the assumption (ie they are normative) that forming this pattern is a matter of a leader's will, intellect and administrative skills. Generic strategy models are all addressed at organisational leaders as formulators of strategy, with linear-rational models of decision-making supporting such theories (Cyert and March 1992). Within this frame of reference, the role of leaders is to reduce unwanted constraints on an otherwise 'optimal' managerial process. Development of the human agency perspective, however, extends beyond the field of strategic management. Total quality management also takes a proactive, human agency view of leadership as achievable and desirable. Deming (1986) has argued, for example, that effective leadership acts as a substitute for structure, hierarchy and organisational controls. Strategic objectives can best be met by leaders who know how they can be met, whilst emphasising quality and empowering others to perform to their highest ability. Ultimately, strategy and the performance of the organisation are seen to be in the hands of effective leaders.

Determinist views of leadership and strategy

Determinist views of leadership and strategy, in contrast, focus on identifying the determinants of organisation structures within which leaders are constrained in taking strategic actions. In her pioneering studies, Woodward (1965,1970) saw structure as setting parameters around managerial processes, while Perrow (1972) drawing upon substantial empirical evidence supported the thesis that structure was determined largely by the type and complexity of technology being used. Burns and Stalker (1961) demonstrated the importance of links between organisation structure and the nature of the task environment. The 'open systems' model followed shortly afterwards, providing a unifying, integrated conceptual framework of the deterministic view of organisations (Katz and Kahn 1966).

Building on earlier works, socio-technical systems theory viewed organisations as social and technical systems located within, and in constant interaction with, through permeable boundaries, a 'supra-system' or environment. Within these perspectives, the role of the leader was to work within such constraints and take charge of what little autonomous discretion remained.

Contingency views of leadership and strategy

There are, however, a number of contributions that have challenged the determinist paradigm. For example, Child (1972) has argued that when the facts of organisational life are faced, and the contingencies spelled out, organisations do have choices. Child reviewed the case for 'contingent' determinants such as organisation size, technology and environment, concluding that 'strategic choice' was a critical variable in the theory of organisations. Further, Astley (1985, p239) rejected the total determinism of the population ecology perspective, arguing for a 'community ecology' perspective. This was one in which 'chance, fortuity, opportunism and choice are the dominant factors determining the direction in which the evolution of populations of organisations progresses.'

The debate is ongoing. The field of industrial economics, for example, has traditionally seen the 'invisible hand' of the market as the prime regulator of organisation and strategy in the market economy. Chandler (1977), however, has shown that over time retained earnings within organisations have outstripped new capital as the primary source of funding for the expansion of US businesses. He concluded that the 'visible hand' of managerial capitalists has long since replaced the 'invisible hand' of capital markets as the basic mechanism for strategic resource allocation in western economies. Galbraith (1952, 1984), in turn, has argued that the tendency towards the concentration of economic power in business corporations has invoked a countervailing tendency in the organisational environment. This suggests that the 'locus of influence' over leadership and strategy is contextually dynamic and historically shifting over cycles of time.

Models of strategic leadership

Johnson and Scholes (2002, p549) have argued that strategic leadership is commonly directly linked with the managing of change, where leadership is 'the process of influencing an organisation (or a group within an organisation) in its efforts towards achieving an aim or goal'. Leaders are often categorised as either 'charismatic' or 'instrumental or transactional.' Charismatic leaders are characterised as building 'visions' of their organisations and energising people to achieve it. Instrumental or transactional leaders focus on designing systems and controlling the organisation's activities.

The leadership literature suggests that successful leaders have exceptional personal characteristics including: visionary capacity, good team players, effective team builders, capacity for self-analysis and self-learning, mental agility, ability to cope with complexity, self-confidence and creating commitment (de Vries 1994). Peters and Waterman (1982) have argued that effective strategic leaders need to be both charismatic and instrumental. This requires:

- ability to undertake detailed analysis in strategy creation and be visionary about the future
- ability to demonstrate insights about the future in achieving credibility for a strategy
- ability to maintain credibility and carry people with change when challenging the status quo
- ability to summarise complex issues of strategy in communicating strategic intent
- ability to make things happen and maintain organisational performance in consolidating strategy.

Farcas and Wetlaufer (1996), however, have provided evidence of different strategic leadership approaches in managing strategy and change, in different circumstances. This depends upon the 'focus of attention' in managing strategy, resulting in different indicative behaviours, roles of other managers and implications for managing change.

- Where the focus of attention is on strategic analysis and strategy formulation (the *strategy* approach), indicative behaviour is scanning markets and technological change, while managing of change is delegated. The role of other managers is to concentrate on day-to-day operations.
- Where the focus of attention is on developing people (the *human assets* approach), indicative behaviour is getting the right people and creating a coherent culture, while the implications for managing change are recruiting and developing people capable of managing strategy locally. The role of other managers is involvement in strategy development.

- Where the focus of attention is on disseminating expertise as a source of competitive advantage (the *expertise* approach), indicative behaviour is cultivating and improving areas of expertise, while the implications for managing change are doing so in line with the expertise available. The role of other managers is being immersed in and managing the area of expertise.

- Where the focus of attention is on setting procedures and measures of control (the *control box* approach), indicative behaviour is monitoring performance against controls to ensure uniform predictable performance, while the implications for managing change are to carefully monitor and control change. The role of other managers is to ensure uniform performance against control measures.

- Where the focus of attention is on continual change (the *change* approach), indicative behaviour is communicating and motivating through speeches, meetings and so on, while the implications for managing change are to make change central to the approach. The role of other managers is to act as change agents and be open to change themselves.

Linking strategy and leadership

For Leavy and Wilson (1994), the leader is only one important element in strategy formation. The others are 'context' and 'history'. Their empirical study of 13 leaders in four Irish organisations – a state agency, public limited company, state-owned enterprise and producer co-operative – examined how leadership, context and history interacted in the formation of organisational strategy, which changed over time. They classified these leaders as 'builders', 'revitalisers', 'turnarounders' and 'inheritors'. They also identified and analysed the five most salient contextual factors influencing strategy formation in the four case study organisations: technology, industry structure, international trading environment, national public policy, and social and cultural transformation. But the 'key theme' to emerge from this study was 'that of the historical perspective'. Long time-frames of analysis lent 'a perspective to the potency and powerlessness of individual action.' They also re-emphasised the role of strategic choice: leaders might be 'tenants of time and context but are rarely reduced to purely passive agents.'

Leavy and Wilson (1994, p187) concluded that leaders often could and did make the histories of their organisations, although not always in circumstances of their own choosing. Their findings revealed a variety of ways in which the 'leader–organisation–context' interaction fitted together but did not reveal any single best way to manage for long-term success. What their case studies demonstrated was:

- The strategies and development of their sample organisations never appeared 'at any stage' to be wholly pre-determined by managerial action or external events.
- Any patterns and predictability that did emerge in both the strategies of organisations and the actions of leaders were 'significant only with regard to historical context'.
- Variations in context emerged as the dominant unit of analysis rather than individual or organisational strategies.
- Their data questioned the pre-occupation with 'transformational leadership' as the sole route of organisational success or revival.

From your observations and reading, which model of strategic leadership is the most effective one to achieve the business goals of your organisation (or one known to you)? Justify your response.

IMPLICATIONS FOR ORGANISATIONS AND P&D PROFESSIONALS

Building appropriate organisational designs and structures is an important response to strategic implementation, if organisations are to deliver their missions and objectives effectively. Factors that are taken into account in developing appropriate organisational designs include: the age of the organisation, its size, degree of centralisation and decentralisation, the technical content of the work, the different tasks in different parts of the organisation, leadership style and its dominant culture. Four main types of organisational structure can be distinguished:

- *Functional structures*. These are based on an organisation's managerial functions (eg operations, finance, marketing, personnel, and so on).
- *Multidivisional structures*. These are based at corporate headquarters with separate divisional units linked with products or geography, each with their own functional substructures (the 'M-form' structure).
- *Holding company structures*. These are based on a central holding company, with a number of subsidiaries, whose role is to act as the central shareholder and to allocate funds to the most attractive profit opportunities (the 'H-form' structure).
- *Matrix organisational structures*. These are based on dual responsibilities such as for products (horizontally) and geographical areas (vertically).

Where innovation is important, other structures have been noted. In Kanter's (1984) study of the structures and processes most conducive to innovation, she demonstrates the importance of matrix structures, problem-solving 'parallel' organisations looking for innovative solutions to problems and participative styles of management.

The sorts of criteria taken into account in developing appropriate organisational structures include: simplicity, least-cost solutions, motivating staff, and adopting a pertinent culture, as well as environmental factors, such as market changes, market complexity and competition, and impact on structure. Generally, change and complexity indicate the necessity for flexible, decentralised structures; standardisation and mass production require more centralised structures. In modern technical systems, which rely on specialised controls and expert knowledge, decentralisation is recommended, since there is little point in having such knowledge without decision-making power to use it. Since staffing issues such as recruitment, rewards, appraisal and training are all affected by strategic implementation, formal procedures have to be built into those systems in order to develop revised HRM policies and procedures.

It was assumed that business strategies merely defined the nature of competition in the marketplace, leaving the personnel management contribution to be secured pragmatically. Thomason (1991) has rebutted this view by arguing that historically the acquisition and utilisation of human resources in organisations have been approached in a number of different ways at different times. He has identified four historical approaches, delineating particular periods where 'typical' organisations tended to adopt a distinct approach to labour acquisition and utilisation in broadly comparable conditions. He was not arguing that market conditions solely determined the approach adopted but that they imposed limits on available options, as well as predisposing enterprises to adopt one approach in preference to others.

For Thomason, all organisations need strategies to decide how to survive in their business environments. Private firms are likely to express business strategies in terms of how they can compete in the marketplace. Public services do this in terms of how they can secure their revenues in the face of competing calls on the public purse. 'In any organisation, the answers to this question can be given only by taking some account of both the opportunities and threats offered by its product/service markets and the strengths and weaknesses of its own combination of resources, and not just the one' (Thomason 1991, p3). Decisions relating to opportunities and threats in product or service markets suggest that they have tendencies to one of four main types of business strategy:

- *Low-cost leadership*. This aims to supply mass production goods or services more cheaply than competitors.
- *Differentiation*. This emphasises a superior product or service commanding a premium price.
- *Focus*. This relies upon either differentiation or low-cost leadership to supply a niche market.
- *Asset parsimony*. This depends on high entry costs as protection against competitors, or flexible use of limited assets to generate high output performance.

The second set of decisions takes account of whether the markets for the organisation's resources are capable of meeting these demands and determines whether the preferred competitive strategy will be facilitated or frustrated by availability of the resources needed. As Porter (1998b) has argued, competitive advantage depends not only on conditions in product or service markets but also on the availability of factors of production.

Thomason identified three historical shifts in business strategy. The first was associated with the onset of the industrial revolution; the second with industrial rationalisation in the late nineteenth century; and the third with 'new wave rationalisations' from the 1960s. In the first period, typical business strategy was one of differentiation; in the second period, cost leadership; and in the third period 'focus', where competitive advantage was secured by paying attention to customer needs and emphasising quality, reliability, delivery and teamwork. Currently, enterprises can be found following any one of these strategies, although the strategy of asset parsimony is losing ground as a source of competitive advantage, because cheapness of modern technologies allows freer entry by competitor firms into many markets.

The approaches to labour acquisition adopted by typical enterprises have varied, depending on what the business strategy required of its workforce or on labour force capacity in the labour market. The differentiation strategy was dependent upon the availability of a core workforce of skilled labour, which in industrialising Britain was satisfied by its apprenticeship system and flow of workers from countryside to towns and cities. The low-cost strategy in the period of mass production needed a workforce capable of doing short-cycle tasks for relatively low wages. Recruiting workers from the external labour market and subjecting them to close supervision and linking their pay to output secured this.

When enterprises had to develop new customer relationships, in the face of global competition, the strategic remedy lay in developing internal labour markets, because most skills were job-specific and non-transferable between firms and industries. Firms needed to train and develop their employees to assure the future supply of labour and retain them until they had recouped their investment from the flexible performance of employees. In terms of labour utilisation, work during the first period was organised by putting it in workshops and factories. In the second period it was fragmented. In the third period, work is characterised by being flexible, versatile and multiskilled, with workers being expected to achieve quality, reliability and delivery in their job tasks.

This indicates that labour acquisition and utilisation vary with business strategy and the capacity of the external labour market to supply the necessary labour that firms want. In the first historical period, labour acquisition of the core workforce was paramount. In the second period, acquisition was important but the emphasis switched to labour utilisation. And in the latest, third period, two distinct developments associated with creation of internal labour markets are discernible. In one, the criteria to be satisfied in labour acquisition are related to trainability, with provision of learning opportunities becoming a salient feature of labour utilisation. In the other, the criteria are extended to embrace broader personality traits, related to capacity for handling change and personal learning from opportunities created by 'learning organisations'.

Thomason concluded that different human resources strategies were necessary for different circumstances and serve different business strategies:

- *Pre-personnel management*. This still exists in parts of the small firm sector and depends on the ability of firms to recruit skilled labour in external labour markets in response to business needs. A selection strategy is used as the main mechanism of labour control.
- *Traditional personnel management*. With mass production, firms depend on their ability to draw on the external labour market to supply the workers they need. A supervision strategy of labour control is adopted, where company rules are policed in order to secure targeted levels of performance.
- *A development strategy for staff flexibility.* In modern niche-markets, and where the business relies on price leadership, labour supply is obtained by developing internal labour markets, using appropriate training and development strategies.
- *A partnership strategy for worker commitment.* In cases where business strategy relies on differentiation, labour supply is obtained by using a partnership strategy aimed at worker commitment. This requires problem-solving and creative skills within the workforce.

CONCLUSION

This chapter examines some basic concepts of strategy and the strategy process. With organisations operating in increasingly unstable external environments, those leading them use strategic management techniques in response to uncertainty and market competition. The deterministic view of strategy is rationalist and prescriptive and it assesses where an organisation is, how it has got there, and how to achieve its objectives. The rational planning approach adopts a 'scientific' methodology, underpinned by processes that are the outcome of objective analyses, rooted in logical methods of managing strategy.

Another view of strategy is that it can be 'shaped', without predetermined objectives, and that it 'emerges' over time in response to changing organisational needs. The emergent approach is where final objectives are unclear and its elements are developed as strategy proceeds. Logical incrementalism derives out of the emergent approach. Here strategic management is seen not as a formal planning process but as a series of subprocesses by which strategies develop. These draw upon the experiences of managers and their sensitivity to changes in their environments.

A major task for organisational strategists in determining strategic direction is assessing the external environmental forces acting upon their organisations. These include political issues, the economy, social factors, technology and the law. Environmental analysis scans the environment, monitors specific environmental trends, forecasts the future direction of environmental changes, and assesses current and future environmental change and their organisational implications.

The major stages in strategy are strategy formulation and strategy implementation. Internal constraints on strategy are human resources, finance, marketing, operations, and research and development. Porter provides a framework for examining the industry or sector relevant to particular firms. It is these 'competitive forces' that are external constraints on the success of each firm and its strategic responses to environmental change. These forces also provide opportunities for developing appropriate responses to environmental change. A central issue is whether organisational leaders are in control of their destinies or whether the environment is the determining factor. Finally, in considering the role of leadership in the strategy process, the evidence suggests that there is no single best way of managing long-term organisational success. Strategic effectiveness is contingent upon a range of personal and organisational factors.

USEFUL READING

BOWMAN, C. (2000) *Strategic management*. Basingstoke: Macmillan.

JOHNSON, G. and SCHOLES, K. (2002) *Exploring corporate strategy*. Hemel Hempsted: Prentice Hall Europe.

JOYCE, P. (1999) *Strategic management for the public services.* Buckingham: Open University Press.

LEAVY, D. and WILSON, D. (1994) *Strategy and leadership*. London: Routledge.

LYNCH, T. (1997) *Corporate strategy*. London: Pitman.

MINTZBERG, H. (1994) *The rise and fall of strategic planning.* London: Prentice-Hall.

MINTZBERG, H., QUINN, J. and GHOSHAL, S. (1998) *The strategy process*. London: Prentice-Hall.

PORTER, M. (1998a) *Competitive strategy*. New York: Free Press.

PORTER, M. (1998b) *The competitive advantage of nations*. Basingstoke: Macmillan.

QUINN, J. B. (1980) *Strategies for change*. Homewood, Ill.: Irwin.

SENGE, P. (1990) The leader's new work: building learning organisations. *Sloan Management Review.* Fall. pp7–22.

WHITTINGTON, R. (2001) *What is strategy and does it matter?* London: Thomson Learning.

WIT, B. and MEYER, R. (2004) *Strategy: process, content, context – an international perspective.* London: Thomson Learning.

Business Ethics and Social Responsibility

INTRODUCTION

Various attempts have been made to classify complex, formal organisations and to whom they are accountable. A classical approach was provided by Blau and Scott (1963, p42ff) whose classification was based on the criterion of who the 'prime beneficiary' of the organisation was. They identified four basic categories of 'stakeholders' with relationships in organisations: owners or managers, workers or rank-and-file participants, 'clients' and 'the public-at-large'. On this basis, four types of organisation were identified: businesses, mutual benefit concerns, service organisations and 'commonweal organisations', such as co-operatives or trade unions. The prime beneficiaries in each case were identified as the owners, members, client groups and 'public-at-large' respectively. This simple typology was by no means a definitive one but it illustrates the complexity of analysing exactly who the stakeholders of an organisation are and whose interest an organisation primarily or otherwise serves. It also implies that most organisations have multiple 'stakeholders' (ie all parties with an interest in an organisation), different types of organisation have different types of stakeholders and some stakeholders are more influential and powerful than others. Most importantly, stakeholder interests sometimes conflict with one another in the same organisation, which can give rise to ethical problems within it. For example, if a business's prime legal accountability is to its 'shareholders', then paying 'extra' wages to its workforce may adversely affect its shareholders' interests, because 'more' money going to its workers results in 'less' money going to its shareholders, and vice versa. Similarly, if one objective of a public service organisation, such as a local authority, is keeping its council tax down, then this could result in poorer services being provided to its residents. This raises a number of questions about the corporate social responsibilities of organisations. For example, who are an organisation's stakeholders? To whom is an organisation accountable, legally and morally? How can differing stakeholder interests be reconciled? What are some of the ethical problems arising out of such dilemmas? Does an ideal solution to these issues present itself? This chapter examines some of the issues arising out of these ethical dilemmas in the business community and it discusses the social responsibilities and ethical stances of for-profit and not-for-profit organisations in the contemporary world.

DEBATES ABOUT CORPORATE ETHICS

What is ethics? What is morality? There are many definitions of these two concepts and they are often used interchangeably but a neat distinction has been made by Lawton (1998, p16) who states: 'Ethics is a set of principles often defined as a code that acts as a guide to conduct. This set of principles provides a framework for acting.' Morals, in contrast, are concerned with actions and how a person lives up to the demands of what is perceived to be right action. Thus an individual may be aware of ethical principles but still act immorally.

The ethical code that has guided the conduct of people within the western world is based largely upon Christian and humanistic principles. Other societies have different ethical codes reflecting different religions and secular traditions. But they all relate to human behaviour, to 'right' and 'wrong' actions and to the values attached to them. Underpinning all codes of ethics are values but these may change over time. Values are beliefs that are deemed to be socially and personally desirable and are recognised as being important. Cultural relativism is significant in understanding ethical standards in different cultures but it is also possible that individual values may conflict with organisational values. Just as there is no universal model of personal ethics, there is no universal model of business ethics.

Ethical theory distinguishes between theories based on deontological principles and those based on teleological principles. These two theories, although not often stated in discussions about business ethics and social responsibility, underpin the arguments that are explored below.

- *Deontology*. This branch of ethics inquires into the nature of moral duty and the rightness of actions. Deontology is absolutist and is based on the assumption that there are fundamental rights and wrongs, such as it is wrong to kill, steal or lie, irrespective of the consequences. It derives its ethical principles from either 'God's Law' or 'right' reason and takes the principles of duty or obligation, (ie those laying down what individuals morally ought to do), as self-evident or self-substantiating.
- *Teleology*. This branch of ethics (sometimes called consequentialism) argues that actions must be judged by their consequences. Rightness is not an intrinsic property but is dependent on the 'goodness' or 'badness' of the consequences. Thus killing may be justified if it saves lives. Stealing may be justified if it is to feed starving children. The use of human embryos is justified if it creates life or saves lives through medical research. The invasion of Iraq was justified because it freed people from oppression and removed a dictator. Consequentialism is based on pragmatism and moral pluralism. It recognises contradictions and the inability to order values, so focuses on the effects of actions and tends to be utilitarian. One problem of consequentialism is that it is not always easy to evaluate the consequences of actions and, even where this is possible, they may be in conflict with each other.

Also there is a major distinction in debates about corporate or business ethics between those supporting the stockholder theory of organisations and those supporting stakeholder theory. Stockholder theory states that companies exist to serve the interests of their owners or shareholders alone and that the sole or at least overriding duty of executives is to serve that interest.

This contrasts with stakeholder theory which says that business organisations exist for the benefits of all those with a stake in them. In terms of organisational stakeholders, Post, Lawrence and Weber (2002) have identified a variety of primary stakeholders, including shareholders, employees and their unions, suppliers, creditors, customers, competitors and wholesalers. They have also identified a number of secondary stakeholders including the local community, local government, national government, social pressure groups, the media, business support groups and the general public. These perspectives are also examined throughout this chapter.

Business organisations and the marketplace

Creating, exchanging and distributing wealth in market economies like that of the United Kingdom is full of moral ambiguities. In the private sector, for example, businesses exist primarily to make profits. To earn profits, businesses produce goods or services and engage in the buying and selling of goods, services and other factor inputs. If profit making is the first claim on business activities, therefore, supporters of stockholder theory (ie that businesses exist primarily for those owning 'stock' or 'shares' within them) argue that there is no need for businesses to act ethically towards their stakeholders, other than shareholders, because the prime responsibility of business is to make money. Others argue, in contrast, that all producers should consider the effects of their actions on stakeholders and take their interests into consideration. Producing goods like tobacco and alcohol for profit, for example, is explicitly unethical because of the danger to the health of consumers and others. Some also argue that it is unethical for top business executives to receive excessive reward packages (the 'fat cats' syndrome), while groups of their company's employees are on low wages, non-permanent contracts and are doing what many would perceive as demanding, stressful low-quality work. Those arguing for social responsibility and ethical responses in business organisations, therefore, say business is not exempt from ethical concerns but must recognise, respond to and manage them (Mellahi and Wood 2003).

Extreme supporters of the market, on the other hand, say that businesses and people in business should not be concerned with ethical issues. This is because the market itself is 'amoral' and exists merely to satisfy the economic wants that people demand and businesses are prepared to supply, within the framework of the law. They consider that any form of social responsibility or any ethical considerations are inappropriate in business and market transactions, because it is the law that is the final arbiter of morality, not the business sector itself. Ethical language is simply not the language of business. Thus Friedman (1970), a major apologist of the free market, has argued that there is only one responsibility of business; it is to use its resources as efficiently as possible and undertake its business activities to increase profits, so long as it stays within the rules of the game. For him, this means free competition, without deception or fraud. In his view, when business people talk of social responsibility in terms of environmental protection or employment protection, they are guilty of 'pure and unadulterated socialism' and are 'unwilling puppets of the intellectual forces that have been undermining the basis of the free market society' (Chryssides and Kaler 1993, p249).

Most people would not nowadays accept the free market 'amoral' model of organisations and managerial decision-making articulated by commentators like Friedman. Indeed it is increasingly accepted that issues of moral responsibility do impinge on the private and public corporate sectors and on the ways in which their decisions affect organisational stakeholders, each with their own particular interests. These moral responsibilities have to be examined in terms of how corporate decisions impact not only on shareholders (or taxpayers) but also on primary stakeholders, secondary stakeholders and the environment – just as individuals in their everyday lives have to consider how their actions affect others. Such matters involve, in short, issues of moral responsibility, which take two basic forms: 'duties' and 'causal responsibility'. Duties are owed explicitly to other people, groups, organisations or communities and mean 'having responsibilities' to or for others. They require the party concerned to behave morally, because of legal, social or personal constraints on them, so that they fulfil those moral duties in an appropriate way. Causal responsibility means 'being responsible' and bearing responsibility for actions that did or did not happen.

Defend and challenge the proposition that business organisations are amoral.

Analysing business ethics

De George (1999) says that business ethics, defined as the interaction of ethics and the business community, can be analysed at four levels. The first is at macro-level or the level of the economic system and possible modifications of it. The second is concerned with the study of the business system but also includes moral evaluation of the public sector, trade unions, voluntary bodies, small businesses, consumerism and so on. The third focuses on the moral evaluation of individuals and their actions in economic and business transactions. Last, because business is becoming more internationalised, a fourth level of analysis is global or international, including the actions of multinational corporations, use of natural resources and other activities affecting humankind generally.

The study of business ethics, in turn, typically involves five kinds of activities:

- applying general ethical principles to particular cases or practices in business
- investigating whether terms used to describe moral individuals, and the actions that they take, can also be applied to businesses and other organisations
- analysing the moral presuppositions of business
- going beyond the field of ethics into other areas, such as philosophy, economics or organisation theory to resolve problems in business ethics
- describing morally praiseworthy and exemplary actions of either individuals or organisations.

According to De George (1999, p25ff), 'business ethics can help people approach moral problems in business more systematically and with better tools than they might otherwise have'. Business ethics can help people see issues which they might typically ignore and impel them to make changes that they might not otherwise make. 'But business ethics will not, in and of itself, make anyone moral.'

Business ethics in the private sector

An interesting development in the private sector is creation of codes of written ethical policies for organisations. Schlegelmilch and Houston (1999, p39) have defined these codes of conduct as statements 'setting down corporate principles, ethics, rules of conduct, codes of practice or company policy concerning responsibility to employees, shareholders, the environment or any other aspect of society external to the company'.

An example of a formal ethics policy is provided by a US company, Johnson Controls, whose stated corporate ethical 'creed' is that:

> We believe in the free enterprise system. We shall consistently treat our customers, employees, shareholders, suppliers and the community with honesty, dignity, fairness and respect. We will conduct our business with the highest ethical standards.

> (Johnson Controls 1999, p3ff)

The company goes on to say that it is an organisation where honesty and integrity are essential to the ways in which it does business and how it interacts with people. It believes that customer satisfaction is the source of employee, shareholder, supplier and community benefits and it will 'exceed customer expectations through continuous improvement in quality, service, productivity and time compression'. The company also states that it is committed to the fair and effective selection, development, motivation and recognition of employees and that it will provide them with training and support 'to achieve excellence in customer satisfaction'. In addition to seeking improvements and innovations in its business, the company claims that its products, services and workplaces 'reflect our belief that what is good for the environment and the safety and health of all people is good for Johnson Controls'. Thirteen detailed issues are covered by the code in this company:

- reporting risks
- promoting the health and safety of its employees and reporting deficiencies
- providing equal opportunity and diversity in all its employment and purchasing practices
- protecting the environment, including waste management, recycling and energy conservation
- protecting the company's information that is critical to its competitive position and reputation
- avoiding conflicts of interest and building trust in the company
- using corporate funds properly and honestly
- upholding the integrity of the company's record-keeping and accounting systems
- not making any political or governmental contributions
- upholding the rule of law
- complying with the laws relating to the protection and disclosure of classified information
- not acting with competitors to fix prices or violate anti-trust laws
- complying with laws restricting the company to where it can do business and with whom
- expecting all employees to carry out their work in accordance with the company's business standards of conduct and reporting any violations of the ethics policy to the company.

Business ethics in the public sector

The ethical beliefs and values associated with what is considered to be justifiable behaviour in public organisations are somewhat different from those of the private sector – although there are overlaps. Indeed it is argued by some that the very essence of public organisations is their need to act socially and responsibly to all their stakeholders at all times. Thus one of the arguments favouring nationalisation was that the 'commanding heights' of the economy, such as public utilities, needed not only to be controlled by and accountable to government but also socially responsible to their plural set of stakeholders. How this was to be done was not always spelt out in practice. Yet there was an assumption underpinning the actions of public officials in nationalised industries, as in other parts of the public sector, that they would be fully accountable, be beyond financial reproach and would treat their users, suppliers and employees fairly and reasonably and in accordance with 'good' practice. One example of this was the idea of public employers being 'good practice', 'model' employers, acting as an example for private employers to follow (Beaumont 1992, Farnham 2000). It was also a legislative requirement for boards of nationalised industries to recognise appropriate unions and negotiate and consult with their representatives on terms, conditions, health and safety and related issues. In the 1970s, there were even experiments in worker directors appointed to the boards of some nationalised industries, such as in iron and steel (Brannen *et al* 1976).

These features of public service organisations are associated with what has been called the 'public service ethos', which is traditionally characterised as comprising honesty, integrity, impartiality, recruitment and promotion on merit, probity and accountability and is associated with a notion of 'acting in the public interest'. In the United Kingdom, it has its roots in the Northcote–Trevelyan report (1854) on the civil service and can be found in the workings of public services elsewhere.

Pratchett and Wingfield (1994), in their research on the public service ethos in local government, described the generic ethos as comprising accountability, bureaucratic behaviour, a sense of community, motivation and loyalty. An assumption is that there is something distinctive about the public service ethos, since there are differences between the ways in which public and private organisations are managed. Factors inducing the public sector ethos are claimed to be the statutory framework within which public services operate, the public sector's concern with equitable outcomes and the processes and structures that they adopt to achieve a complexity of goals.

Others factors are that recipients of public services are citizens or clients, as opposed to being market-driven customers, and public services are uniform services, provided nationally. Yet Pratchett and Wingfield (1994, p14) have questioned whether there is a generic public service ethos, even in local government. For them, it is a concept 'only given meaning by its organisational and functional situation and may be subject to very different interpretations over both time and location'. They have argued that today different local authorities adopt a differing ethos, varying between a community-based approach and a commercial one.

Another way of examining ethical issues in public organisations is by identifying the 'principles of public life', which are guidelines for action based on ethical values. These were identified by the Nolan committee (1995) in its report on standards in public life. The committee's objectives were to examine concerns about standards of conduct of public office holders in the United Kingdom, so as to ensure the highest standards of propriety in public life. Nolan identified seven principles of public life. These were:

- *Selflessness*. Public office holders should take decisions solely in terms of public interest.
- *Integrity*. Public office holders should not put themselves under financial obligations to outside individuals or organisations.
- *Objectivity*. In carrying out public business or making appointments, public office holders should make choices based on merit alone.
- *Accountability*. Public office holders are accountable for their decisions and actions to the public and must submit themselves to scrutiny for this.
- *Openness*. Public office holders should be as open as possible about the decisions and actions they take, giving reasons for their decisions.
- *Honesty*. Public office holders have a duty to declare any private interests relating to their public duties and take steps to resolve any conflicts arising from this.
- *Leadership*. Public office holders should promote and support these principles by leadership and example.

In an interesting observation about why people join public service, a former senior civil servant, in his evidence to the Nolan committee, recorded his view. It is 'because they want to serve ... They have some consciousness of what it means in serving the public ... I think that the continuation of the desire to serve, that almost ethical view of the thing, will continue' (Nolan 1995, para 194).

> To what extent is there an argument for having different ethical codes for private businesses and public organisations? Justify your response.

International comparisons

In international and comparative contexts, it is observable that a number of OECD countries are responding to general concerns about public confidence in ethical standards in public organisations, by integrating ethics into new ways of managing public sector organisations (Hondeghem 1998). Three key values have been identified in guiding the behaviour of contemporary public servants. First, there is 'responsibility', with public servants being expected to behave in responsible ways involving personal judgement and being aware of the consequences of their behaviour on others. A second important set of values is transparency, openness and service to the public, with all public servants being expected to do what they can to inform and serve the public. Third, there is the value of integrity, which means that the general interest, not personal interests, must determine the behaviour of public servants.

Maguire (1998) identifies four main tendencies in recent ethical initiatives in OECD countries:

- *Countries like the United Kingdom, United States, Finland, the Netherlands and Norway.* Here the primary focus is checking for gaps in existing ethical infrastructures and reinforcing them rather than completely overhauling them.
- *Countries like Australia, Canada and New Zealand.* Here a great deal of attention is being given to refocusing ethical management in relation to overall public management reforms and redefining the nature of accountability.
- *Countries like Spain, Portugal and Mexico.* Here ethical frameworks are being included in the modernisation programmes of public administration.
- *Countries such as the transition economies of east Europe.* Here ethical infrastructures are being created from the 'bottom up' as part of their development of new democratic systems.

Maguire (1998, p33) concludes that regardless of where a country may wish to situate itself regarding managerial reforms, ongoing attention to ethics will remain essential to retain public confidence. Governments 'will be judged by their citizens not only on how efficient and effective they are, but on how well they safeguard the public trust invested in them'.

You have been asked by a colleague to identify and discuss the ethical dilemmas faced by organisations expanding their operations into developing countries. What will you say and why?

APPROACHES TO CORPORATE ETHICS

There are a number of approaches to business and corporate ethics. These include the following:

- *The 'business is business' approach.* This is what Chryssides and Kaler (1996) have called the basic view of business ethics which assumes that a firm's aims are purely commercial and that it is the responsibility of its stakeholders to determine whether the firm is acting ethically or not and how the firm's actions affect their interests. It is not the firm's and its leaders' duty to do this.
- *Coincidence theory approach.* This view of business ethics is that 'good ethics coincides with good business.' It argues that if companies behave ethically in relation to their stakeholders, then virtue is its own reward. Firms selling high-quality goods, rather than defective ones, for example, are likely to retain their customers. Similarly, ethical employment policies are more likely to benefit both staff and the company than are unethical ones.
- *'Act consistently with the law' approach.* This view of business ethics is that legislation provides a floor of ethical standards below which firms should not fall. By this approach,

firms must at least fulfil their legal obligations regarding their customers, suppliers, bankers, government, the community, the environment and their employees. Further, since regulatory legislation applies to all companies, it is reasonable to suppose that one's competitors, in accepting the same constraints on their corporate behaviour as one's own firm, face the same *pro rata* costs as those covered by legal requirements.

■ *The 'conventionalism' approach*. This view of business ethics is that business people should act in accordance with conventional standards of morality (ie the prevailing standards accepted by the public) or with those standards typically associated with good business practice.

■ *The 'no difference theory' approach*. This view of business ethics argues that business people should maintain the same standards in business life, as they do in their private lives. Just as we do not expect neighbours to dispose of their garden rubbish in our gardens, then neither should we expect firms to pollute the environment.

There is, then, no universal model of corporate ethics. Business ethics, or ethical corporate practices, are both subjective and contingent upon those pursuing or evaluating them. Corporate ethics raise questions about how firms should deal with those business issues that have implications for their stakeholders but they do not produce universalistic answers to these questions. Chryssides and Kaler (1996, p3) claim that business ethics has two aspects. 'One involves the specific situations in which ethical controversy arises; the other concerns the principles of behaviour by which it is appropriate to abide.'

Some examples where ethical controversy arises include the following (though this list is neither inclusive nor exhaustive):

■ ethics of employment, including pay, unions, workers' rights, equal opportunities and non-discrimination

■ ethics of accounting, finance, corporate restructuring and investing

■ ethics of marketing, truth and advertising

■ ethics of information technology

■ ethics of intellectual property, corporate disclosure and insider trading

■ ethics of safety, risk and environmental protection

■ ethics of whistle-blowing

■ ethics of international business.

Central to the study of corporate ethics is the assumption that 'moral rules' apply to business behaviour, just as they do to individual behaviour and that certain actions are wrong or immoral and others are right or moral. Thus it is generally agreed that employers expect their employees not to steal from them, parties to a contract expect each other to honour it and suppliers expect the businesses dealing with them to pay them promptly. The problem is that there is no universal benchmark of morality. Different people resolve moral dilemmas in business using different approaches and alternative frames of reference (Sternberg 1994).

Moral responsibility in business is largely concerned with considerations of duty. First, there are the duties that people in business owe to each other, such as managers to workers, workers to managers and managers to shareholders. Second, there are duties that each of these groups owes to the organisation as a whole. Third, there are the duties, which, as organisations, businesses owe to their customers, suppliers, creditors and so on. Fourth, there are the duties of businesses to the environment. Fifth, there are duties that business organisations owe to society as a whole. The last is to some extent the most fundamental issue in corporate ethics, as it is asking the question: what is the 'social responsibility' of business? To explain the duties of business organisations in society is to prescribe their function in society. This specifically social role sets the moral standards against which business may be judged and it identifies the ultimate ends towards which businesses ought to be directed and steered. In the US context, for example, De George (1999, p7ff) argues that the American business system incorporates the values of 'freedom', 'profit, money, and goods', 'fairness and of equal opportunity', 'pragmatism' and 'efficiency'. In his view, the American business value system is, consequently, a mixture of both good and bad. He asks:

> Should freedom be emphasized more than security, or competition more than equality? ... Is the value system changing? Are some of the values ... obsolete? Many people ask these questions, as our society struggles with the realities of limited resources ... Which values are morally justifiable? And is the system of free enterprise itself morally justifiable? If so, under what conditions?

There are at least six perspectives on morality, which can be applied to the corporate sector. These can affect decisions and choices made within organisations:

- *Moral subjectivism*. This suggests that there is no objective answer to moral dilemmas and that it is up to individuals to choose between what is right and what is wrong. Thus existentialists, for example, would argue that the important thing in ethics is not what you decide but that you decide.
- *Cultural relativism*. This is where what is right and wrong is relative to the circles in which you move. By this view, moral 'truth' varies according to time, place and circumstances and it acknowledges that environments shape people's moral values and beliefs.
- *Moral absolutism*. This approach, based on religious morality, suggests that there are absolute answers to moral questions and what is right and what is wrong are not capable of personal interpretation. Fundamental moral principles do not vary but stand for all time and in all places.
- *Reason as the arbiter of truth*. This approach, based on Kantian principles, says that human reason is the arbiter of truth. The essence of morality by this view is that it is the process of rational deduction that determines the basis of right and wrong, implying that morality is not the same as self-interest, and reason demands that one's duty is to be done for duty's sake.
- *Utilitarianism*. This argues that in making moral decisions it is necessary to balance one person's welfare against someone else's to reach a decision based on the course of action achieving the greatest good. Utilitarianism finds the seat of morality in humankind, not in religion or a God. Moral acts result in human happiness, while immoral ones harm people by causing them pain.
- *Universal human rights and natural law*. This approach to solving moral dilemmas claims that rights rather than duties are the basis of moral choice and moral decisions. In recognising rights, natural law sets limits to the degree to which the law may intrude upon people. Not all laws are just laws, however, and when the state or businesses deprive people of any of their fundamental natural rights this is contrary to natural law (Singer 1995).

ETHICS AND PROFESSIONALISM

Ethical statements in private and public organisations are concerned with establishing agreed normative principles as guidelines to right or 'moral' actions by those managing enterprises and those employed by them. Thus organisations have formal and informal rules, aiming to ensure consistency, continuity, control and accountability within their boundaries. These rules can embrace ethical principles or even incorporate explicit ethical policies and individual managers and employees are expected to adhere to them as a contribution to good ethical practice.

In the post-industrial, knowledge-based, service economy, however, increasing numbers of professional workers are employed in both private and public organisations. These include diverse professional groups such as architects, accountants, computer and IT specialists, doctors, engineers, nurses, scientists, social workers, teachers, technologists and P&D professionals. As professional workers, these groups often belong to professional associations with their own professional codes of practice and good conduct. Professionals, therefore, often look to their own profession for a professional ethos, rather than to the organisations employing them. Belonging to an appropriate professional association normally involves being bound by its professional code of conduct, which regulates the activities of the group's members and sets out its ethical position and professional standards of behaviour to the public. There are a number of descriptive and prescriptive models of professionalism.

Trait models of professionalism

These models list the attributes claimed to represent the common core of professional occupations. Millerson (1964) has listed 23 elements incorporated within definitions of professions. These include skills based on professional knowledge, provision of training and education, testing the competence of members, altruistic service to clients and adherence to professional codes of conduct. A weakness of trait approaches is that they tend to incorporate the professionals' own definition of what it means to be a professional.

Functionalist models of professionalism

These make no attempt to present exhaustive lists of traits. Instead, the components of professionalism are limited to those said to have functional relevance for society and the professional–client relationship. Thus Barber (1963) has claimed that professional behaviour may be defined in terms of four essential attributes. These are a high degree of generalised and systematic knowledge, primary orientation to community rather than personal self-interest, a high degree of control of behaviour through internalised codes of ethics, operated by the professionals themselves, and a system of rewards that are mainly symbols of work achievement. Like the trait model, the functional one excludes from consideration the power dimension of professionalism (ie potential conflicts between professionals and their clients), which suggests that there are variations in the institutionalised ways in which occupational activities are controlled.

The occupational control model of professionalism

Johnson (1972, p45) has responded to this omission by arguing that professionalism can be defined as 'a peculiar form of occupational control rather than an expression of the inherent nature of particular occupations'. For him, a profession is not an occupation 'but a means of controlling an occupation'. He provides a three-fold typology of institutionalised forms of professional control. The first is where the professionals define the needs of their clients and the manner in which these needs are to be catered for. This is 'collegiate control', based on either occupational authority or a guild system, as in the medical profession. A second form of control is 'patronage', where clients define their own needs and the manner in which they are to be met. This may be 'oligarchic' patronage (as in the patron–artist relationship) or 'corporate' patronage (such as how some large organisations recruit and promote professional staff). The third form of professional control is 'mediation', which is where a third party (either business or the state) mediates the relationship between the professionals and their clients (such as between government and professional nurses or schoolteachers).

The jurisdictional model of professionalism

Abbott (1988, p20) has developed a 'jurisdictional' model for understanding professionalism. He has proposed an approach for analysing the development of professions in terms of the link between a particular profession and the nature of work undertaken by that profession. He has used the term 'jurisdiction' to denote the link between a profession and the tasks constituting the work it does:

> *The central phenomenon of professional life is thus the link between a profession and its work, a link I shall call jurisdiction. To analyse professional development is to analyse how this link is created in work, how it is anchored by formal and informal structure, and how the interplay of jurisdictional links between professions determine the history of individual professions themselves.*

Abbott has argued for a scheme that examines how professions develop jurisdictional control by filling in 'jurisdictional gaps' and that there is no reason for expecting that the process of professionalisation follows any particular pattern of development. This analysis has led Holmes (1998, p10) to conclude that the functionalist approach of the CIPD to developing the skills and competencies of the personnel profession is flawed. In his analysis, this was particularly a problem with the former 'Core Management' and 'Core Personnel and Development' fields in CIPD's former Professional Qualification Scheme. Using Abbott's framework would in his view enable the profession to reframe its 'jurisdictional claims'. He argued that the dominant managerialist orientation of the scheme, which reduced the personnel profession to managerial definitions of the personnel or human resources function, had placed 'the profession in a vulnerable position likely to lead to its withering or decline'. He believed that the personnel and development profession should lay claim to a broader jurisdiction than solely the management and development of employees within organisations.

Professional codes of conduct

By definition all professions have codes of conduct. These concentrate on the individual behaviour of professional workers and serve to regulate the behaviour of professionals with their clients and other stakeholders. Clients, for example, may want some guarantees that they are being treated with due professional care and attention, with sanctions being invoked where this is lacking. Lawton (1998, p88) has suggested that professional ethical codes serve a number of purposes:

- promote ethical behaviour and deterrence of unethical behaviour
- provide a set of standards or written benchmarks against which to judge behaviour
- act as guidance when faced with difficult decisions
- establish rights and responsibilities
- provide a statement of principles indicating what the profession stands for
- create a contract between professionals and their clients
- act as a statement of professional development
- legitimise professional norms and justification for sanctions, when those norms are ignored, or unethical conduct occurs
- enhance the status of the profession
- provide a statement of professional conduct, identifying client expectations.

A code of professional conduct, then, can function as a public statement of ethical principles and inform others of what to expect. Kernaghan (1975) reported that such codes lie on a continuum. At one end is the short, '10 commandments' approach that provides general statements of broad ethical principles, with few if any administrative arrangements. At the other extreme is the 'Justinian Code' approach. This provides a comprehensive coverage of principles and administrative arrangements in some detail.

(i) Does membership of CIPD mean that HR practitioners are a profession?

(ii) Is professionalism a guarantee of ethical behaviour?

(iii) How would you respond to a colleague who expresses the opinion that professionalism is best defined in terms of orientation towards the community rather than professional self-interest?

STAKEHOLDER THEORY

The main significance of stakeholder theory of the firm is that it contrasts with the conventional 'input–output model' of business organisations. Donaldson and Preston (1995, pp68–69) have argued that in the 'input–output model' of the firm, three sets of 'contributors' – investors, employees and suppliers – supply inputs to firms, which the 'black box' of the firm transforms into 'outputs' for the benefit of a fourth party, its customers. Each contributor receives appropriate compensation for its inputs but 'as a result of competition throughout the system, the bulk of the benefits will go to customers'. These writers went on to point out that stakeholder theories argue that all persons or groups with legitimate interests participating within enterprises have economic and moral claims upon it. These include investors, employees, suppliers plus customers, communities, political groups, trade associations and governments. Each of these interests 'do so to obtain benefits and there is no *prima facie* priority of one set of interests and benefits over another'. Donaldson and Preston also stressed that 'at the outset' stakeholder theory represents 'a controversial or challenging approach to conventional views' that vary 'greatly among market capitalist economies'. As *The Economist* (1993, p52) has stated, in America, 'shareholders have a comparatively big say in the running of the enterprises that they own; workers ... have much less influence'. In many European countries, however, shareholders have less say and workers more. And in Japan, managers have been left to run their companies as they see fit – namely for the benefit of employees and allied companies, as much as for shareholders.

Identifying organisational stakeholders

Lynch (1997, p810) has defined stakeholders as 'the individuals and groups who have an interest in the organisation, and, therefore, may wish to influence aspects of its mission, objectives and strategies'. He listed the typical stakeholders in large businesses as employees, managers, shareholders, banking institutions, customers, suppliers and government. This concept of stakeholding extends beyond just those working in the organisation. Thus in a limited company, for example, stakeholders with legitimate interests in the ways in which the company conducts its business affairs would include shareholders who have invested in it, employees and managers working in it, banks lending it money, governments concerned about employment, investment and trade, and its customers and suppliers. Interests may be informal, such as in the case of a football supporters' club and its influence in and on a privately owned football club. In the case of a PLC football club with quoted shares, it may be formal, with supporters owning shares in that company. Unless an organisation's stakeholders remain satisfied with it, or at a minimum 'satisficed' (ie not fully satisfied but not dissatisfied either), then employees and managers are likely to leave, shareholders sell their shareholdings, banks stop providing credit, customers go elsewhere and suppliers look for other outlets for their products or services.

Cannon (1994) has provided another model of stakeholders. He has distinguished between owners, employees, customers, creditors, suppliers, community and government. Each of these, he has argued, has 'primary' and 'secondary' expectations about a business. Owners want a financial return on their invested capital and added value for their investments. Employees want good pay, followed by good working conditions, work satisfaction and proper training opportunities. For customers, the primary expectation is effective supply of required goods and services and, secondly, that these are of sufficiently high quality in relation to price. Creditors want creditworthiness and payment on time; suppliers want payment for items received and long-term relationships with the purchasing organisation; and the community wants jobs, a safe environment, and the firms located in their community to make a contribution to it. Government, in turn, wants employment for people, compliance with its regulations, laws and taxation rules, and improved competitiveness of firms. Clearly, satisfying these divergent needs is a major issue facing most organisations, each with their multiple stakeholders.

Lawton (1998) has used a different classification of organisational stakeholders in the 'new' public sector. He identifies six sets of key stakeholders: customers, citizens, clients, colleagues, ministers and contractors. Customers are characterised as having 'purchasing power', citizens 'rights and duties' and clients 'lack of power and information'. Ministers, in turn, are characterised by having 'authority', colleagues 'equal status' and contractors 'specifications'. Thus dealing with customers, citizens and clients involves different sets of relationships. Customers are concerned with purchasing power, protected by a legal framework providing consumer protection and rights. The language of citizenship, on the other hand, is that of general rights and solidarity. Clients, in contrast, are interested in ensuring that they receive their entitlements and that their interests are protected. Colleagues in public service organisations normally have expectations about being managed 'collegially', which means being involved in the decision-making processes affecting them, being treated equitably by their managers and being promoted on the basis of merit. Ministers and contractors are external stakeholders and they too have interests in the ways in which public organisations are managed. Ministers are concerned with all aspects of public organisations, because they are accountable to Parliament for any matters that have aroused public interest. Contractors are concerned with how contracts are specified and monitored, and want payments made on time. Managing such diverse stakeholders in public organisations, therefore, means that different interests need to be balanced, while common ones need to be identified and conflicting ones reconciled.

What role stakeholders actually play in organisations depends partly on their legal status and partly on their power in or over the organisation. The prime legal responsibility of the boards of PLCs in the United Kingdom, for example, is to their shareholders but they also have certain statutory obligations to their employees, customers and suppliers, as well as having to pay their taxes to government and protect the environment. An organisation's system of governance plays a key function here but there are different models of corporate governance internationally and, in the United Kingdom, between private and public organisations, with the latter, for example, being more likely to have some element of employee involvement imposed on them.

In Germany, public companies have two-tier boards, a supervisory board and a management board. The supervisory board has shareholder, employee and third-party representatives sitting on it and the management board is responsible to it. Thus the legal accountability of German companies is both to their shareholders and employees. The strengths of this European model of corporate governance are that it promotes long-term business growth, has strong governance procedures and sustains a highly stable system of capital formation and accumulation. The major weakness is its vulnerability to global economic pressures. The Anglo-Saxon model of corporate governance, in contrast, while providing a dynamic market orientation and fluid capital resources, promotes short-term business policies, mainly concerned with corporate profits rather than long-term investment and growth in the company. The strength of the Asian model of corporate governance, in turn, is its promotion of long-term industrial strategies and overseas investment. Its weaknesses include: financial speculation; activism among institutional investors; and, sometimes, corrupt internal procedures.

Typologies of stakeholders

Mitchell *et al* (1997, p854) have argued that stakeholder theory has become a popular heuristic device for describing the management environment for many years but lacked theoretical status. They proceeded to produce a comprehensive typology of stakeholders based on the normative assumption that these variables define the field of stakeholders: 'those entities to whom management should pay attention'. In their view, classes of stakeholders can be identified as those possessing one or more of the following attributes:

- the stakeholder's *power* to influence the firm
- the *legitimacy* of the stakeholder's relationship with the firm
- the *urgency* of the stakeholder's claim on the firm.

Power

This first attribute is defined as the probability that one actor within a social relationship is in a position to carry out his/her will despite resistance (Weber 1964). It is, in short, the ability of individuals or groups to persuade or coerce others to follow certain courses of action. Sources of power within organisations include formal hierarchical power, informal power (such as charismatic leadership), controlling strategic resources, possession of strategic knowledge and IT and negotiating skills. Internal indicators of power are visible signs that internal stakeholders have been able to get their own way. First is the status of the individual or group, such as position in the hierarchy or reputation within and outside the organisation. The second is the individual's or group's claim on organisational resources, as measured by size of budget, number of employees in the group and so on. The third is representation in powerful positions, which might be assessed in terms of the corporate governance arrangements for the organisation, or who is represented on its important committees. The fourth indicator is 'symbols of power', such as size, location and fittings of offices, amount of support services that the group has, and so on. Johnson and Scholes (2002, p222) have concluded: 'No single indicator of power is likely to uncover the structure of power within a company. However, by looking at all four indicators, it may be possible to identify which people or groups appear to have power by a number of these measures.'

Sources of power for external stakeholders are both similar and different from those for individuals and groups within organisations. The sources of power of external stakeholders are control of strategic resources (such as materials, labour and money), involvement in the organisation (such as distribution outlets and agents) and possession of specialist knowledge (such as that possessed by subcontractors). Another is through internal links and informal influence in the organisation and organised pressure groups.

Indicators of power for external stakeholders are, first, the status of the external party. The status of suppliers, for example, is normally indicated by the way that they are discussed among employees and whether the company responds quickly to the suppliers' demands. A second indicator is 'resource dependence' or the extent to which the organisation depends on the resources of particular external stakeholders to conduct its affairs successfully. These include the relative sizes of shareholdings, loans by banks and proportion of the business linked with particular customers or suppliers. The third key indicator here is the ease with which shareholders, financiers or customers can switch their resources out of the organisation at short notice. A fourth indicator is negotiating arrangements, including whether external parties are treated at arm's length or are actively involved in negotiations with the company in doing business with it. Thus customers or suppliers invited to negotiate over the price of a contract are in more powerful positions than those treated on a fixed-price or a 'take-it-or-leave-it basis'. Last, symbols provide clues about the power of external stakeholders including how the organisation treats its customers, suppliers or bankers, as well as the level of person dealing with its stakeholders.

Few individuals have sufficient personal power to influence the direction, policies and their own personal interests within an organisation. Even chief executives need to carry influential groups of senior managers and their staff with them. Influence arises because particular individuals share similar expectations with others in the same stakeholder group. Here external stakeholders can be important, such as bankers, customers, suppliers, shareholders and trade unions. These may seek to influence what is happening in the company through their links with internal stakeholders such as managers and others working in the organisation. Thus individuals are more likely to identify themselves with the aims of specific stakeholder groups, such as the corporate board, institutional investors or the trade unions having members within the organisation. There have been several examples in the public sector recently, where internal employee pressure groups, organised and coordinated by the trade unions, have produced 'votes of no confidence' in an organisation's chief executive. As a result, the person in question has resigned and been replaced by a new incumbent.

The significance of Mitchell *et al's* (1997, p865) conception of power in stakeholder analysis is that 'a party to a relationship has power, to the extent it has or can gain access to coercive, utilitarian, or normative means, to impose its will in the relationship.'

Legitimacy

Power and legitimacy are distinct attributes and they can combine to create authority (Weber 1964), as well as existing independently. An entity may have legitimate standing in society, or it may have a legitimate claim on the firm, but unless it has either power to enforce its will in the relationship or a perception that its claim is urgent, it will not achieve salience for the firm's managers. For this reason, a theory of stakeholder salience requires, first, that separate attention be paid to legitimacy as an attribute of stakeholder–management relations. Suchman (1995, p574) has defined the second attribute of legitimacy as 'a generalized perception or assumption that the actions of an entity are desirable, proper, or appropriate within some socially constructed system of norms, values, beliefs, and definitions.' Mitchell *et al* (1997, pp866–867) accepted this definition, implying that legitimacy is a desirable social good 'that is something larger and more shared than a mere self-perception' and may be defined and negotiated differently at various levels of social organisation. The most common of these 'are the individual, organizational, and societal.'

Urgency

Mitchell *et al's* (1997, pp867–868) third attribute of classes of stakeholder – the urgency of the stakeholder's claim on the firm – was posited as moving their model from a static one to a dynamic one. They defined 'urgency' as 'the degree to which stakeholder claims call for immediate attention', arguing that urgency was based on two factors. One was 'time sensitivity' or the degree to which managerial delay in attending to a claim or relationship is unacceptable to the stakeholder. The second was 'criticality' or the importance of the claim or relationship to the stakeholder. In their view, their theory 'captures the resulting multidimensional attribute as urgency, juxtaposes it with the attribute of power and legitimacy, and proposes dynamism in the systematic identification of stakeholders.'

Classifying stakeholder classes

Combining these attributes of power, legitimacy and urgency results in three generic groups of stakeholders ('latent', 'expectant' and 'definitive') and a sevenfold typology of stakeholder classes. This recognises that entities with no power, legitimacy or urgency in relation to the firm are not stakeholders and they have no salience with the firm's managers.

- *Latent stakeholders*. These are low-salience classes and are identified by their possession or attributed possession of only one of the three possible attributes. They incorporate three typologies of stakeholders, defined as:
  - 'dormant stakeholders' (with power only)
  - 'discretionary stakeholders' (with legitimacy only)
  - 'demanding stakeholders' (with urgency only).
- *Expectant stakeholders*. These are moderate-salient classes and are identified by their possession or attributed possession of two of the three attributes. They incorporate three typologies of stakeholders, defined as:
  - 'dominant stakeholders' (with both power and legitimacy)
  - 'dangerous stakeholders' (with both power and urgency)
  - 'dependent stakeholders' (with both legitimacy and urgency).
- *Definitive stakeholders*. These are highly salient classes and are identified by their possession of all three attributes. This typology of stakeholder is defined as:
  - 'definitive stakeholders' (with power, legitimacy and urgency).

In summary, Mitchell *et al* (1997, p882) have argued that many scholars of stakeholder theory have only searched for bases of legitimacy in stakeholder–management relationships. Their aim was to expand managerial understanding beyond legitimacy to incorporate stakeholder power and urgency of a claim in their analysis. They have argued that these attributes of actual or potential stakeholders in a firm's environment 'make a critical difference in managers' ability to meet legitimate claims and protect legitimate interests.' For them, stakeholder theory must account for power and legitimacy and urgency. Managers need to know about entities in their organisation's environment that have power and intend to impose their will upon the firm. In their view: *'Power and urgency must be attended to if managers are to serve the legal and moral interests of legitimate stakeholders.'*

Carry out a stakeholder analysis of your organisation, explaining how each group you identify influences or constrains the process by which organisational strategy is made and operationalised.

ACCOUNTABILITY IN ORGANISATIONS

In satisfying the demands of the market place or of their political masters, organisations are ultimately accountable through their governing bodies, government ministers or local public officials, for the actions that they take. Organisations and those leading them have a duty to use responsibly the resources they employ, taking into account their obligations to a variety of organisational stakeholders, whoever these may be. A mixture of market, legal, social and moral imperatives enforces the multiple accountabilities of contemporary organisations today.

The private sector

The distinctive feature of private-sector businesses is that they are market-driven and market-led organisations. This means that the ways in which private businesses are managed reflect the market environment in which they operate. They buy their factor inputs in the market (ie land, labour, capital and other resources), sell their products or services in the market and, if they are to survive, prosper and grow, they are ultimately judged as organisations in the market by their ability to generate profits.

> *Unless, over time, private organisations are able to satisfy customer demand in the market, provide a surplus of revenues over costs and ensure capital investment programmes for the future, they cease to trade as viable organisations.*
>
> (Farnham and Horton 1996, p28)

In satisfying the demands of the marketplace, business organisations are ultimately responsible through their governing bodies for the actions they take.

Private businesses are held accountable in a number of ways but, legally, are accountable to their shareholders who may attend meetings and vote on issues affecting company policy. Shareholders, which are increasingly other companies, also have rights to appoint and remove directors, receive annual reports, examine their accounts and share in corporate profits. To those supporting the stockholder perspective of businesses, this is the norm and incontestable. For them, companies exist solely or primarily to serve the interests of their shareholder owners. There are certainly interests other than shareholders, whose fortunes are tied up with the company but this is beside the point. These other interests do not own the company. The essential point from the stockholder perspective is that the company is simply a piece of property, no different, in principle, from other property such as land, houses and other artefacts that people own. From the stakeholder perspective, in contrast, corporate status transforms a business into something closer to 'public' property, ie something for which just and fair property ownership rights must be recognised. From both stockholder and stakeholder perspectives, this is nothing to do with being private or public in the legal sense of whether shares are on public sale or not. What is crucial is being incorporated. For stockholder theory, which places organisations more in a moral context, this does not lift a business out of the merely private property category. For stakeholder theory, which places organisations more in a moral context, it does.

In practice, however, private organisations are also legally accountable, amongst others, to their employees, suppliers and consumers in terms of the minimum standards expected of them by the state. Employees, for example, have a series of common law and statutory employment rights, preventing them from being exploited by 'bad' or exploitative employers. Some employees, the low-paid, have a statutory right to a legally enforceable minimum wage. All employees, except those derogated by the law, have statutory rights to maximum working hours per week and paid holiday entitlements. The legal obligations of private businesses to their suppliers are embodied in the law of contract, which provides a legal framework around which business organisations build their mutual commercial activities together. Corporate legal accountability to consumers is largely through consumer protection laws, while the Office of Fair Trading publishes information, proposes new laws and takes action on behalf of consumers who think that their rights have been infringed by offending businesses.

Legal accountability of private businesses to the community incorporates a variety of measures. These relate to controls over land use, building development, pollution control and noise abatement. The law relating to land use, for example, seeks to achieve a balance between the interests of people within their communities and those of business organisations. Pollution control is aimed at minimising the potentially hazardous impacts of effluents and noxious substances released into the air, land or waterways. Legislation also exists to prevent damage to individuals and households by excessive noise levels from factory machinery, motor vehicles and aircraft.

The social and moral accountabilities of private businesses have become more important in recent years, as businesses have increasingly accepted that they have extra-legal responsibilities, in response partly to pressure group lobbying and partly to changes in public opinion. These have to be taken into account when managements take decisions about issues of production, pricing, resource utilisation and distribution of profit. Businesses are also becoming increasingly customer aware and environmentally conscious. Failing to satisfy these obligations can result in fines, loss of customer loyalty and damage to their corporate reputation. Ultimately, however, the accountability of business organisations is to the market. If they do not satisfy the marketplace, they eventually go bankrupt and out of business.

Public organisations

Public organisations in contrast, since they are political bodies created by the state, are ultimately accountable to the 'public' whom they serve. The public is particularly interested in public organisations because:

- Public bodies are often monopoly providers, leaving the public no choice but to take what they provide.
- Public bodies exercise power to ensure compliance with public laws and can fine people or ultimately deprive them of their liberty if they break the law.
- They provide merit goods or public goods (ie goods that everyone contributes to or benefits from), which directly affect the quality of people's lives.
- They levy compulsory taxation to fund government activities.
- They regulate many areas of social life, including licensing alcohol, providing street lighting and highways, checking building designs and monitoring building plans.

As citizens, taxpayers and consumers, therefore, the public is obviously interested in the use of public power, the efficiency with which public money is spent, and the quality of public services provided.

It is this exercise of public power that necessitates public organisations being held accountable in a democratic society. Public officials are expected to act as stewards of the public interest and the public purse, as well as being responsible for ensuring that public organisations provide the goods and services to those entitled to them. The forms that public accountability takes vary according to type of public agency, level of government and its particular functions. As Lawton and Rose (1991, p17) state, it is difficult to generalise about accountability in the public sector. 'The mechanics of accountability in local authorities are different from those in central government, which in turn vary from those in the NHS.' In practice, it is arguable that there are four main types of public-sector accountability: legal, political, consumer and 'professional'. All public bodies operate within a strict legal framework. Unlike private businesses, which can do anything that the law does not specifically forbid or prevent them from doing, public ones can do only what the law permits and prescribes for them. This legal rule known as *ultra vires* means that public officials require legal authority for all the actions they perform. Failure to exercise their legal responsibilities, or actions which exceed their legal authority, means that public officials can be mandated or restrained by the courts. Unlike in most other European countries, there is no system of public law courts in the United Kingdom, it is ordinary courts that hold public organisations to account, both for their actions and the procedures they use. Public officials are required to demonstrate that they have complied with substantive law, procedural law and the rules of natural justice.

Political accountability manifests itself in a number of ways. All public officials are accountable directly or indirectly to a political person or body. Civil servants are accountable to a minister, local government officers to elected councillors and the boards of public corporations to appropriate ministers. This model assumes that powers are vested in ministers who are responsible for what public servants do and who are accountable, in turn, to Parliament for their actions. Similarly, power is vested in elected local authority councils that are responsible to the public for the actions of their officials. The reality of ministerial responsibility has long been disputed, however, and civil servants are now more directly accountable to Parliament, through its specialist committees, than they were in the past (Drewry 1989). Local officials also deal with the public. In both cases, ultimate accountability to the public, as the electorate, is through periodic elections and the ballot box. Between elections, the press and pressure groups keep public organisations alert and inform the public what is going on inside them.

Accountability to users and clients of public organisations is through institutions established for dealing with complaints and grievances. Various tribunals deal with appeals against administrative decisions. The Parliamentary, Health Service or Local Government Commissioners each deals with complaints about maladministration and, in addition, each public body has its internal complaint procedure. Since the 1980s, the rights of public consumers have come to the fore and all public organisations have had to look at ways in which they are responsive and accountable to the public. The *Citizen's Charter* (Prime Minister's Office 1991) and *Service First* (Cabinet Office 1997) set down standards that users of services can expect. Most public organisations now have their own charters or charter standards (Horton and Farnham 1999).

Professional accountability is particularly pertinent to the public sector, since it employs many professional workers, such as doctors, nurses, teachers, social workers, engineers and so on. Public service professionals seek, where they can, not only to control entry into their occupations but also to determine how they work and how to police their fellow professionals. They claim professional autonomy, clinical freedom or academic freedom, as the case may be. This is because professionals see themselves as being primarily accountable to their professional colleagues and their internal codes of ethics. The Law Society deals with complaints against lawyers and the British Medical Association hears complaints against doctors. However, counter to this, public-service professional workers are increasingly being held accountable to public managers, who may or may not be drawn from among the ranks of the professionals they supervise.

(i) Compare and contrast the ways in which private and public organisations are held accountable.
(ii) What do you think are the most significant differences between them and which methods are the most effective ones?

CORPORATE SOCIAL RESPONSIBILITY AND ETHICAL RESPONSES

Theory and practice in the field of corporate social responsibility (CSR) build upon stakeholder theory. The European Commission has defined CSR as situations where 'companies integrate social and environmental concerns in their business operations and in their interaction with their stakeholders on a voluntary basis' (European Commission 2001, p7). It is generally accepted in market economies that the main function of business enterprises is to create added value through producing goods and services demanded by people and other organisations in society. This generates profit for their owners and shareholders and provides benefits for society through consumption, investment and job creation. New social and market pressures, however, are leading to changes in the values and horizons of business activities.

There is a growing perception within the business community that sustainable business success and shareholder value cannot be achieved solely through maximising short-term profits. This must be done instead through market-oriented yet responsible corporate behaviour. Companies are therefore becoming aware that they can contribute to sustainable development by managing their operations in ways enhancing economic growth and increasing competitiveness, whilst at the same time promoting social responsibility (such as consumer interests) and ensuring environmental protection. With increasing numbers of firms embracing CSR, there is growing consensus on its main features.

- CSR is behaviour by businesses over and above their legal requirements, which is voluntarily adopted because businesses deem it to be in their long-term interests to do so.
- CSR is linked to the concept of sustainable development, with businesses needing to integrate the economic, social and environmental impacts of their operations.
- CSR is not an optional 'add-on' to core business activities but is about the ways in which businesses are managed.

Socially responsible initiatives by businesses have a long tradition in the United Kingdom (as with Quaker firms and organisations such as Cadburys in Victorian Britain) and elsewhere. But the distinguishing feature of CSR today, compared with past initiatives, is in attempts to manage it strategically and to develop instruments for doing this. CSR adopts a business approach putting stakeholder expectations and the principle of continuous improvement and innovation at the heart of business strategies. What constitutes CSR depends on the specific situations of particular organisations and the contexts within which they operate. Whatever forms it takes, however, CSR has found increasing recognition among businesses, policy-makers and other stakeholders as an important element of new and emerging forms of corporate governance (European Commission 2002).

CSR helps organisations respond to some of the following changes:

- Globalisation has created new opportunities for enterprises but also increased organisational complexity. The increasing extension of business activities internationally has led to these new responsibilities on a global scale.
- Considerations of image and reputation play an increasingly important role in the competitive business environment. This is because consumers and pressure groups ask for more information about the conditions in which products and services are generated and their impact on sustainability. These parties tend to reward socially and environmentally responsible firms.
- Because of this, financial stakeholders seek disclosure of information about conditions going beyond traditional financial reporting. This allows them to identify the success and risk factors inherent in a company and its responsiveness to public opinion.
- As knowledge and innovation become more important in response to competitiveness, businesses have more motivation to retain highly skilled and competent personnel.
- Because of the need to respond to international environmental pressure groups, plus the pressure from international organisations to reduce hydrocarbon emissions and reduce pollution, organisations have had to develop, implement and evaluate ecological and environmental measures to address these issues.

How does your organisation (or one known to you) EITHER demonstrate OR not demonstrate CSR? Provide examples.

An action framework for CSR

CSR has international dimensions. For example, the European Commission has promoted a European framework for CSR, building on the Lisbon Summit of 2000. For the Commission, CSR is seen as making a contribution to achieving the strategic goal of the EU of becoming by 2010 'the most competitive and dynamic knowledge-based economy in the world, capable of sustainable economic growth with more and better jobs and greater social cohesion' (European Commission 2002, p4). A subsequent green paper argued that CSR was about managing change at company level in a socially responsible manner. This required companies seeking trade-offs between the needs of their various stakeholders that were acceptable to all parties. In this way, if companies manage change in a socially responsible way, there is a positive impact on the macro-economy.

Following a period of consultation, the Commission reported that all its respondents – including businesses, employers' organisations, trade unions, civil society organisations and European institutions – had welcomed the green paper and supported action in this field. Unsurprisingly, however, and demonstrating the practical difficulties in achieving CSR, there were significant differences among the positions expressed:

- *Enterprises*. These stressed the importance of the voluntary nature of CSR and the need not to adopt a 'one-size-fits-all' solution.
- *Trade unions and civil society organisations*. These emphasised that voluntary initiatives were not sufficient in themselves to protect workers and citizens rights. They wanted a regulatory framework, establishing minimum standards and ensuring a level playing field.
- *Investors*. These stressed the need to improve disclosure and transparency of corporate practices.
- *Consumers' organisations*. These underlined the importance of trustworthy and complete information about the ethical, social and environmental conditions in which goods and services are produced and traded.

As a result of these consultations, the Commission proposed building its strategy to promote CSR on principles recognising the voluntary nature of CSR, the need for credibility and transparency of CSR practices, and a balanced approach to CSR – including economic, social and environmental issues, as well as consumer interests. The Commission also recognised that attention had to be paid to the needs of small and medium size enterprises, as well as support for existing international agreements and instruments. The Commission proposed focusing its strategy around the following areas:

- increasing knowledge about the positive impact of CSR on business and societies
- developing exchanges of experience and good practice on CSR amongst enterprises
- promoting development of CSR management skills
- fostering CSR among SMEs
- facilitating convergence and transparency of CSR practices and tools including:
  - codes of conduct
  - management standards
  - accounting, auditing and reporting provisions
  - labels
  - socially responsible investment
- launching a multi-stakeholder forum on CSR at EU level
- integrating CSR into Community policies covering:
  - Employment and Social Affairs Policy
  - Enterprise Policy

- Environment Policy
- Consumer Policy
- Public Procurement Policy
- External Relations Policy.

The internal dimensions of CSR

Within firms, socially responsible business practices largely involve employees in terms of investing in human capital, health and safety, and managing change, whilst environmentally responsible practices relate mainly to managing the natural resources used in the production process (European Commission 2003b).

Human resources management

A major challenge for enterprises is attracting and retaining skilled workers. Relevant measures include lifelong learning, employee empowerment, better information provision, better work–life balance, greater workforce diversity, equal pay and career prospects for women, profit sharing, share ownership, employability and job security. Further, responsible recruitment practices can facilitate selection of people from ethnic minorities, older workers, the long-term unemployed and disadvantaged people.

Health and safety at work

This has traditionally been advanced by legislation and enforced by the law. However, companies, government and not-for-profit bodies are looking at additional voluntary and preventative ways of promoting health and safety. As the focus on occupational health, safety performance and quality of products and services is increasing, there is rising demand for measuring, documenting and communicating these in marketing material.

Adapting to change

Restructuring in a socially responsible manner means balancing and taking into consideration the interests and concerns of all those affected by organisational change and business policy decisions. In practice, the process of change is often as important as its substance to the success of restructuring. In particular, facilitating the participation and involvement of those affected by change through using open information and communication channels is crucial to this process.

Managing environmental impacts and natural resources

Cutting consumption of resources, reducing polluting emissions and minimising waste can abate the environmental impact of business organisations. They can also reduce energy and waste disposal bills and lower input and depollution costs. Companies have found that using less natural resources and paying attention to environmental issues can lead to increased profitability and competitiveness.

The external dimensions of CSR

CSR extends into the community and is concerned with business partners and suppliers, customers, public authorities, local communities and the environment. In a world of multinational investment and global supply chains, CSR extends beyond national borders. Rapid globalisation has encouraged an examination of the role and development of global governance and the use of voluntary CSR practices contributing to this (European Commission 2003b).

Business partners, suppliers and consumers

Working closely with their business partners means companies can reduce complexity and costs, as well as increasing quality of product or service. Selection of suppliers is not always exclusively through competitive bidding. Relationships with alliance and joint venture partners are equally important. Building such relationships can result in fair prices, good terms and realisable expectations, along with quality and reliable delivery.

Large companies are also business partners of smaller ones, as customers, suppliers, subcontractors or competitors. Companies need to be aware that their social performance can be affected by the practices of their partners and suppliers throughout the whole supply chain. The effect of CSR activities is not limited to the company itself but touches upon their economic partners, especially in the case of large companies that have outsourced part of their operations or services.

As part of CSR, companies are expected to provide products and services that consumers want in an efficient, ethical and environmentally friendly way. Companies building lasting relationships with customers focus on their whole organisation by understanding customer requirements and providing them with superior quality and safe products that are reliable. They also give good service. These companies are also likely to be more profitable than companies not doing this.

Local communities

CSR is also about integrating companies into their local settings, nationally and, in the case of MNCs, internationally. Companies contribute to local communities by providing jobs, pay and benefits, and tax revenues. On the other hand, they also depend on the health, stability and prosperity of the communities in which they operate. They recruit the majority of employees from local labour markets and often have clients and customers in the surrounding area. The reputation of a company at its location(s), its image as an employer and as a player in the local community also influences its competitiveness.

Companies interact with their local physical environment. They rely on a clean environment for producing or offering services, such as clean water, clean air or non-congested roads. There is also a relationship between the local physical environment and the ability of a business to attract its workforce there. However, businesses can also be responsible for noise, light, water, air and soil pollution or for environmental problems arising out of transport congestion and waste disposal.

Many companies become involved in community causes, notably by providing vocational training, assisting environmental charities, recruiting socially excluded persons, providing childcare facilities for employees, creating partnerships with communities, sponsoring local sports and cultural events, and donating to charitable activities. Developing positive relations with local communities adds to the accumulation of social capital locally and is particularly relevant to non-local companies. MNCs increasingly use these relations to support the integration of affiliates into the markets in which they are present. Familiarity of companies with local actors, local environment and local traditions is an asset from which they can benefit and capitalise.

Human rights

CSR has a strong human rights dimension. Human rights are a complex issue presenting political, legal and moral dilemmas. Under increasing pressure from non-governmental organisations and consumer groups, companies and sectors are adopting codes of conduct covering working conditions, human rights and environmental aspects, in particular those of subcontractors and suppliers. They do so for various reasons, notably to improve their corporate images and reduce the risk of negative consumer reaction. However, codes of conduct and other voluntary initiatives can only complement these, by promoting higher standards for those subscribing to them. It is also being recognised that the impact of a company's activities on the human rights of workers and local communities extends beyond issues of labour rights. This is the case, for example, where companies work with state security forces having records of human rights abuses. There is also need for ongoing verification where implementation and compliance with codes is concerned.

Global environmental concerns

MNCs can pursue social responsibility internationally and at local, national and regional levels. They can encourage better environmental performance throughout the supply chain and make larger use of international management and product related tools. Investment and the activities of the companies in third-world countries have a direct impact on social and economic development within them. The debate on the role of business in achieving sustainable development is gaining importance on the global stage.

(i) How likely is it that the framework for corporate social responsibility will be implemented throughout the corporate sector?
(ii) In what ways can the EU ensure its adoption?

ORGANISATIONAL ETHICS

Ethical organisations have always existed but most businesses have traditionally been driven by economic goals not ethical ones. In the nineteenth century, for example, Quaker companies operated on distinctive ethical principles and firms such as Cadburys incorporated welfare policies into their business philosophies, which benefited their workforces. This was in contrast to most other firms at that time that were driven solely by the profit motive. Today examples of successful businesses noted for the ethical principles they promote include the Co-Operative Bank, Scott Bader and Traidcraft.

Some people argue that business organisations cannot have 'ethics' or be 'ethical', as they are not agents and are not driven by moral imperatives. However, organisations have sufficient structural complexity to be agents, so that they can be called to account for their actions and the consequences of those actions. If a body can take decisions and implement them, then it must be responsible for those decisions (Kaptein and Wempe 2002). Indeed, as corporate legal entities, business organisations are accountable in law for some of their actions. Therefore part of corporate responsibility is legal – such as in the areas of employment law, health and safety and consumer protection – but part of this responsibility is moral or ethical. Being profitable is a virtue of business organisations but it is not their only virtue. As Kitson and Campbell (1996, p98) have argued: 'We can expect organisations to be socially responsible because that is part of the contract out of which they were created.' It is a 'condition of the permission that society granted that they exist in the first place.'

One measure of the notional 'ethical organisation' is the practice in the United States of corporate ethics programmes. These incorporate four elements: ethics audits; advice and guidance for publicly stated expectations about employee behaviour; the need for organisational structures to support ethical behaviour; and for ethical behaviour to be supported by the reward systems of organisations (Post et al 2002). Another measure indicating 'ethical' organisations is using corporate governance structures that reinforce the connections between ethical behaviour and governmental processes in firms. In 1992, for example, the Cadbury report (1992) presented a voluntary code of best practice, aimed at boards of listed companies based in the United Kingdom. Broadly, it argued for adequate disclosure of financial information and for checks and balances within the governance structures of companies. Following such a code means that it 'is more likely than not to lead to a corporate governance regime with greater openness of information, less likelihood of domination by one or a few people and fewer excesses in the remuneration packages of senior executives' (Kitson and Campbell 1996, p115).

Ethical issues in accounting

The strongest pressures for ethical accounting practices come from self-regulation by members of the accounting profession. The prevailing standards are to be found in the ethical rules regulating the behaviour of members of the accounting bodies. Members of these bodies are expected to behave with integrity in all business relationships, strive for objectivity in making professional judgements and carry out their work with courtesy and consideration towards all with whom they come into contact. Additionally, members should not perform work that they are not competent to do and should carry out their professional work with due skill, care and diligence. There are codes of professional ethics governing professional practice in accounting and professional bodies can discipline members for misconduct, incompetence and inefficiency. Punishments include suspension from membership, fines, reprimands and withdrawals of practising certificates.

Ethical issues in buying

Purchasing managers occupy a boundary-spanning role and have to face situations where they must judge what is right (or ethical) and what is wrong (or unethical) in undertaking transactions between their employing organisation and its suppliers. Many issues of ethical concern in business practices arise within purchasing departments. These include deception, bribery, price rigging, unsafe products and public safety. One area of concern is the offering of gifts or favours by sellers, who try to influence buying decisions. A second area is where buyers exaggerate the difficulties their company is experiencing in order to pressurise suppliers. A third concern is discrimination, by showing favouritism towards certain suppliers. There is also the issue of information disclosure, where some suppliers seek information on their competitors with the implied promise that it will benefit the purchaser. Most surveys demonstrate that such practices by purchasing personnel are viewed as unethical by them but these practices still persist. The nature of the purchasing function is such that it is a problematic area in which to maintain ethical standards, since the dividing line between ethical and unethical behaviour is so finely drawn.

Ethical issues in human resources management

There is relatively little mention of ethics in the literature of human resources management (HRM) in the United Kingdom, although it is growing. A different picture emerges in the United States, where ethics and ethical behaviour feature prominently in both HR practice and academic research studies. Yet almost every HR decision and issue poses ethical questions, since they deal with people issues covering recruitment and selection, managing performance, equal opportunities, learning and development, employee relations, rewards and termination of employment. Marchington and Wilkinson (2005) have argued that ethical and socially responsible HR practices may become even more elusive as organisations devolve HR activities to line managers who are required to meet corporate targets that stress production and service targets as their first priority. However, ethical recruitment and selection, for example, demand properly drafted job descriptions and personnel specifications, candidates only being invited to interview where they meet the essential requirements and unsuccessful candidates having their applications returned to them with the selectors' reasons for their decision. Applicants could also be given the results of any assessments made of them. Perhaps the underlying argument for ethical HR practices is that companies adopting them benefit by gaining employee commitment, the trust and loyalty of their workforce and improved organisational performance.

Ethical issues in marketing

The marketing function is open to deceptive advertising, price fixing, withholding product test data and falsifying market research. The areas where ethical dilemmas emerge in marketing include marketing strategy, marketing mix, decisions about products, price, distribution and promotion. It would seem that ethics in marketing cannot be divorced from issues concerning business ethics as a whole. As with any less than scrupulous business practice, compromising ethical standards in marketing is a tactic of short-term value. The need to repeat business may guard against unethical behaviour but the best protection appears to lie in the company's overall ethical stance, reflected in its policies on internal standards and in its commitment to its external stakeholders. The most persuasive idea to convince top management that adopting an ethical corporate policy is beneficial to their company is that it has a positive effect on corporate success and the firm's bottom line.

Ethical issues in strategy

Strategy is the sphere where business ethics plays the most decisive role in organisations. Strategic decisions have a major integrative function, so ethics at this level also inform the ethics of other management functions. Ethical issues of strategic management need to be examined in relation to the current debate about stakeholder interests. How stakeholder interests within organisations are balanced depends partly on the legal structure of business organisations, so to some extent strategic ethical issues must be worked out within what is provided for legally. Substantively, however, the ethical issues arising out of business strategy decisions relate to areas such as setting the organisation's vision, aims and objectives, leadership, senior managers' remuneration, implementing strategic change, changes in organisational ownership and global strategic operations. All these areas have ethical dimensions. Stakeholder theory, for example, stems from the principle that business organisations have responsibilities to a wider range of people and institutions than just to shareholders, directors and creditors. It therefore challenges traditional belief in management's right to manage and it raises broader questions about responsibility and accountability within organisations.

Strategic change often breaches the psychological contract. Although reorganisations may benefit shareholders, lifetime employees may lose their jobs. The ethical issue here lies in persuading people that the changes are legitimate so that a sense of continued loyalty to the company can be regenerated. Similarly, in MNCs, being a global player is an increasingly important strategy for long-term survival, so difficult ethical issues surrounding 'cultural relativism' (ie business leaders accepting the ethical norms of the countries that the company is in) are likely to increase, as is regulation of MNCs.

Strategic management addresses fundamental issues about the ends and means of business organisations. These have been strongly influenced since the creation of joint-stock limited companies in the nineteenth century, since the Companies Acts recognise only shareholders, directors and creditors. This remains the case today. British company law preceded the world of MNCs, the Welfare State, trade unions, privatised monopolies and the social expectations of having certain democratic rights. Company law does not recognise frontline staff, technicians, managers and the wider stakeholders of organisations. Yet it is getting out of line with social reality and people's expectations as workers, consumers and citizens.

Your manager asks you to draft an ethical code of practice for the P&D function in your organisation. What will you include and why?

IMPLICATIONS FOR ORGANISATIONS AND P&D PROFESSIONALS

Issues of business ethics, stakeholding, accountability and social responsibility are becoming increasingly important in both private and public organisations. Those leading organisations are recognising, responding to and managing the multiple interests making demands on organisational resources and policies. Because of mass communications, greater public awareness and the activities of external pressure groups, business leaders and public managers are finding it more difficult to ignore these conflicting power-centres and pressures acting on them. Also with the shift towards free markets in recent years and the internationalisation of business activity, more people are questioning the market's ability to deliver real progress and quality of life, rather than just economic growth. It is also becoming increasingly difficult for the business sector to define its role solely in the narrow sense of the 'business is business' approach. As a result, some business leaders are redefining their leadership roles in organisations. This means placing responsibility on top management – not just on the state, the market or technology – for dealing with the multiplicity of morally ambiguous problems associated with the emerging strategic business context of the twenty-first century. These include:

- issues of justice and equity in organisations
- maintaining environmental sustainability
- creating jobs
- narrowing social cleavages in organisations
- managing technological change and developing corporate ethical policies, as well as making profits.

The demands of these forces on organisational leaderships are immense. The sort of leadership required to drive this needs to see organisations as learning systems, where an ethical perspective provides a valuable insight for determining both rational and moral choices in times of exponential change. These responses support the ideas of Fisher and Lovell (2003, p299) who do not share the pessimistic view that 'debates about business ethics are hopeless ... because of the fundamental contradictions within market-based, capitalist relationships'. They argue that 'a more proactive citizenry is required to shape business relationships so that citizens and societies exercise greater influence over business behaviour'.

As concerns about the broad impacts of business on society have increased, there has been expansion in the development of CSR-related instruments used to measure, evaluate, improve and communicate corporate performance in relation to social, environmental and ethical criteria. CSR-related instruments include auditable instruments, broad guidelines, codes of conduct, charters, investment screening and benchmarks. They draw upon simple statements of principles that an individual company might subscribe to, industry-led initiatives in which groups of companies collectively implement agreed codes of practice, and instruments voluntarily adopted by companies and regulated by accredited bodies.

CSR-related instruments attempt to close the gap between enforceable, mandatory laws and the universal principles and values embodied in agreements such as the Universal Declaration of Human Rights. They include instruments setting out: aspirational principles for corporate behaviour, underlying engagement in partnerships, benchmarking best practice, the basis for communicating levels of performance directly to consumers and other stakeholders, and the terms of trade for investing. Such instruments fulfil a vital need in providing robust process guidance and indicators of historic and future environmental, social and financial performance. They have the potential to enhance performance of whole companies, significantly advancing realisation of CSR across sectors, industries and whole economic regions.

CSR-related instruments by which organisations can be measured are vitally important for comparing and contrasting levels of performance. Initially, the function of instruments is to establish minimum levels of performance. They also help organisations manage the quality process or systems designed to manage impacts and processes. Over time, use of instruments encourages, facilitates and mandates best practice (European Commission 2003b).

In terms of P&D professionals, Winstanley *et al* (1996, p5ff) have argued that recently 'the relationship between ethics and human resource management is emerging as a subject of serious academic enquiry'. They have identified three main issues in the area: ethical concerns, ethical frameworks and putting ethics into practice. They have raised concerns about the lowering of employment standards, for example, where several types of undesirable change have been identified. These are, first, insecurity and risk in terms of jobs and employment opportunities. Second, new forms of work organisation and management control are giving rise to surveillance and control of employees at work. Third, deregulation of management decision-making in firms is leaving little scope for power-based employee participation in the workplace and this element in contemporary HRM 'is at best unsympathetic to the exercise of democratic rights by employees or to stakeholder models of corporate governance'. Fourth, the rhetoric of HRM, with its themes of commitment and identification, fits poorly with the trend towards less secure employment and evidence of diminished employer commitment to employees, with 'a relentlessly instrumental orientation to the employment relationship on the part of employers'.

Winstanley *et al* (1996, p9ff) have also argued that the prevailing common sense ethical framework justifying contemporary HRM policies based on its utilitarianism to organisations is a weak principle for ethical action. They have identified a number of alternative ethical frameworks lending themselves to analysing HRM. These are:

- *Basic human, civil and employment rights*. This framework seeks greater job security, openness and transparency, and avoiding scapegoating at work.
- *Social and organisational justice*. This framework aims at providing procedural principles for evaluating current employment practices.
- *Universalism*. This framework emphasises the Kantian principle of treating individuals as ends in themselves and not just means to ends.
- *Community of purpose*. This framework seeks adoption of a stakeholder and more communitarian view of the firm rather than just a stockholder one.

Another level of engagement with ethics is for P&D professionals to utilise appropriate ethical frameworks helping to explain and analyse the nature of changes taking place in the employment relationship and to use the frameworks 'more prescriptively'. In seeking ways of putting ethical principles into practice in the P&D area, Winstanley *et al* (1996, p11) have proposed the use of employment charters, legal regulation, innovation in good practice and challenging 'the inevitability thesis' on the demise of job security. They are unconvinced that the 'ethical stewardship' role of P&D professionals in raising awareness of ethical issues is a viable one. 'There is the risk that assuming ownership of the "ethical" issues and conscience in the organization might yet again serve to decrease their status'. Drawing on Connock and Johns (1995), they have concluded that ethical leadership must come from the top of organisations. It must 'not be part of the ghetto of human resource management'. In their view, growth in interest in stakeholding, ethical consumerism and international labour standards are some of the significant developments putting ethics and HRM on the political agenda.

CONCLUSION

This chapter has focused on business ethics, stockholder theory, stakeholder theory and corporate social responsibility (CSR). Business ethics is the application of general ethical ideas to business behaviour. There are a number of approaches to business ethics but there is no universal model of corporate ethics. Business ethics (sometimes described as ethical corporate practices) are both subjective and contingent upon those pursuing or evaluating them. However, business ethics raise questions about how firms should deal with corporate issues that have implications for interested parties other than shareholders. But business ethics do not produce universalistic answers to these questions.

The major debate in business ethics is between supporters of stockholder theory of organisations and those supporting stakeholder theory. Stockholder theory holds that companies exist to serve the interests of shareholders alone and that the overriding duty of management is to serve these interests. Those supporting stakeholder theory, in contrast, argue that business organisations exist for the benefits of all those with a stake in them. These include primary stakeholders (such as shareholders, employees and their unions, suppliers, creditors, customers, competitors and wholesalers) and secondary stakeholders (such as the local community, local government, national government, social pressure groups, the media, business support groups and the general public).

Since stakeholder theory claims that all persons or groups with legitimate interests who participate within an enterprise have economic and moral claims upon it, it analyses how those individuals, groups, institutions and communities are affected by organisational strategies, policies and actions. Classes of stakeholders are identified as those possessing one or more of three attributes: the stakeholder's power to influence the firm, the legitimacy of the stakeholder's relationship with the firm and the urgency of the stakeholder's claim on the firm. In addition to legitimacy, therefore, power and urgency must be taken into account, if managers are to serve the legal and moral interests of legitimate stakeholders.

Theory and practice in CSR build upon stakeholder theory. CSR is where companies integrate social and environmental concerns in their business operations and in their interactions with their stakeholders voluntarily. CSR adopts a business approach putting stakeholder expectations and the principle of continuous improvement and innovation at the heart of business strategies. Finally, ethical businesses need to demonstrate ethical responses in mainstream managerial activities such as ethical accounting, buying, HRM, marketing and strategy.

USEFUL READING

CANNON, T. (1994) *Corporate responsibility*. London: Pitman.

CHRYSSIDES, G. and KALER, J. (1993) *An introduction to business ethics*. London: Chapman and Hall.

DE GEORGE, R. (1999) *Business ethics*. New Jersey: Prentice Hall.

EUROPEAN COMMISSION. (2001) *Promoting a European framework of corporate social responsibility.* Luxembourg: Office for Official Publications of the European Commission.

EUROPEAN COMMISSION. (2002) *Corporate social responsibility: A business contribution to sustainable development.* Luxembourg: Office for Official Publications of the European Communities.

EUROPEAN COMMISSION. (2003b) *Mapping instruments for corporate social responsibility.* Luxembourg: Office for Official Publications of the European Communities.

FISHER, C. and LOVELL, A. (2003) *Business ethics and values.* London: Prentice Hall.

HONDEGHEM, A. (ed.). (1998) *Ethics and accountability in a context of governance and new public management.* Amsterdam: IOS Press.

KITSON, A. and CAMPBELL, R. (1996) *The ethical organisation: Ethical theory and corporate behaviour.* Basingstoke: Macmillan.

LAWTON, A. (1998) *Ethical management for the public services.* Buckingham: Open University Press.

LAWTON, A. and ROSE, A. (1991) *Organisation and management in the public sector.* London: Pitman.

MELLAHI, K. and WOOD, G. (2003) *The ethical business: Challenges and controversies.* Basingstoke: Palgrave.

MITCHELL, R., AGLE, B. and WOOD, D. (1997) Towards a theory of stakeholder identification and salience: defining the principle of who and what really counts. *Academy of Management Review.* Vol. 22, No. 4, 853–886.

NOLAN COMMITTEE. (1995) *Standards in public life: Vol 1.* London: HMSO.

POST, J., LAWRENCE, A. and WEBER, J. (2002) *Business and society: Corporate strategy, public policy, ethics.* Boston, MA.: Irwin/McGraw-Hill.

PRATCHETT, L. and WINGFIELD, M. (1994) *The public service ethos in local government.* London: Commission on Local Democracy.

WINSTANLEY, D., WOODHALL, J. and HEERY, E. (1996) Business ethics and human resource management. *Personnel Review.* Vol. 25, No. 6.

Bibliography

ABBOTT, A. (1998) *The system of the professions*. Chicago: University of Chicago Press.

ABERCROMBIE, N. and WARDE, A. (eds). (2000) *Contemporary British society*. Cambridge: Polity.

ALDCROFT, D. H. (1993) *The European economy 1914–1990*. London: Routledge.

ALEXANDER, L. (1985) Successfully implementing strategic decisions. *Long Range Planning*. Vol. 18, No. 3, 91–97.

ALLSOP, J. (1995) *Health policy and the NHS*. Harlow: Longman.

ALWIN, D. and SCOTT, J. (1996) Attitude change: its measurement and interpretation using longitudinal surveys. In: B. Taylor and K. Thomson (eds). *Understanding change in social attitudes*. Aldershot: Dartmouth.

ANDREWS, K. (1987) *The concept of corporate strategy*. Homewood, Illinois: Irwin.

ANGELES, J. (2002) *Fundamentals of robotic mechanical systems*. New York: Springer.

ANNESLEY, C. and GAMBLE, A. (2004) Economic and welfare policy. In: C. Ludlam and M. Smith (eds), *Governing as New Labour: Politics and policy under Blair*. Basingstoke: Palgrave.

ANSOFF, I. (1965) *Corporate strategy*. Harmondsworth: Penguin.

AOKI, M. (1988) *Information, incentives and bargaining in the Japanese economy*. Cambridge: Cambridge University Press.

ARBER, S. and GINN, J. (2004) Ageing and gender. In: *Social Trends No. 34*. London: National Statistics.

ASTLEY, W. (1985) The two ecologies: population and community perspectives on organisation theory. *Administrative Science Quarterly*. Vol. 30, pp245–273.

AUDIT COMMISSION. (2004) *Improving public services: Inside the Audit Commission*. London: Audit Commission.

AUERBACH, P. (1998) *Competition: The economics of industrial change*. Oxford: Blackwell.

AUGAR, P. (2000) *The death of gentlemanly capitalism: The rise and fall of London's investment banks*. Harmondsworth: Penguin.

BACON, R. and ELTIS, W. (1976) *Britain's economic problem*. London: Macmillan.

BALL, A. and MILLARD, F. (1986) *Pressure group politics in industrial society*. Basingstoke: Macmillan.

BARBER, B. (1963) Some problems in the society of professions. *Daedalus*. Fall issue.

BARTLETT, C. and GHOSHAL, S. (1989) *Managing across borders*. Boston, Mass.: Harvard Business School Press.

BARUCH, Y. and NICHOLSON, N. (1997) Home, sweet work. *Journal of General Management*. Vol. 23, No. 2, pp15–30.

BASU, K. (2000) *Prelude to political economy: A study of the social and political foundations of economics*. Oxford: Oxford University Press.

BATRAM, D. (2000) Internet recruitment and selection: kissing frogs to princes. *International Journal of Selection and Assessment*. Vol. 8, No. 4, pp261–274.

BEATSON, M. (1995) *Labour market flexibility*. London: Employment Department.

BEAUMONT, P. (1992) *Public sector industrial relations*. London: Routledge.

BEGUM, N. (2004) Employment by occupation and industry. *Labour Market Trends*. Vol.112, No.6, June, 227–233.

BELL, D. (1973) *The coming of post-industrial society*. New York: Basic Books.

BELLAMY, C. and TAYLOR, J. (1998) *Governing in the information age*. Buckingham: Open University Press.

BENNIS, W. and NANUS, B. (1985) *Leaders: The strategies for taking charge*. New York: Harper and Row.

BERESFORD, P. (2005)*The Sunday Times rich list 2005: Britain's richest 1,000*. London: The Sunday Times.

BERGER, B. and CARLSEN, A. (1993) Liberty, order and the family. In: J. Davies (ed). *The family: Is it just another lifestyle?* London: Institute of Economic Affairs.

BERLAGE, T. (1997) Information technology in medicine. *European Research Consortium for Informatics and Mathematics News*. No.29, April.

BEVERIDGE, F., NOTT, S. and STEPHEN, K. (2000) Mainstreaming and the engendering of policy making: a means to an end? *Journal of European Public Policy*. Vol.3, No. 3, pp385–405.

BEVERIDGE, W. (1942) *Social insurance and allied services*. London: HMSO.

BIENEFELD, M. (1996) Is a strong national economy a utopian goal at the end of the twentieth-century? In: R. Boyer and D. Drache (eds), *States against markets*. London: Routledge.

BLACKABY, F. (ed). (1979) *De-industrialisation*. London: Heinemann.

BLACKSTONE'S LAW. (2003) *Blackstone's EC legislation 2003–04*. Oxford: Oxford University Press.

BLAIR, T. (1998) *The third way*. London: Fabian Society.

BLAKEMORE, K. (1998) *Social policy: An introduction to social policy*. Milton Keynes: Open University Press.

BLAKEMORE, K. and DRAKE, R. (1996) *Understanding equal opportunity policies*. London: Prentice-Hall/Harvester Wheatsheaf.

BLAU, P. and SCOTT, W. (1963) *Formal organisations*. London: Routledge.

BOOTH, A. (1995) *British economic developments since 1945*. Manchester: Manchester University Press.

BOSANQUET, N. (1983) *After the New Right*. London: Heinemann.

BOSANQUET, N. (1986) Interim report: public spending and the welfare state. In: R. Jowell, S. Witherspoon and L. Brook (eds), *British social attitudes: The 1986 report*. Aldershot: Gower.

BOURDIEU, P. (1986) *Distinction: A social critique of judgements of taste*. London: Sage.

BOWMAN, C. (2000) *The essence of strategic management*. London: Prentice Hall.

BOXALL, P. and PURCELL, J. (2003) *Strategy and human resource management*. Basingstoke: Palgrave.

BOYER, R. and DRACHE, D. (eds). (1996) *States against markets*. London: Routledge.

BRADLEY, H. (1996) *Fractured identities: Changing patterns of inequality*. Oxford: Blackwells.

BRANNEN, P. *et al.* (1976) *The worker directors: A sociology of participation*. London: Hutchinson.

BRITTAN, S. (1964) *The treasury under the Tories 1951–64*. Harmondsworth: Penguin.

BRITTON, A. (1991) *Macro-economic policy in Britain 1974–1987*. Cambridge: Cambridge University Press.

BROMLEY, C. (2003) Has Britain become immune to inequality? In: A. Park, J. Curtice, K. Thomson, L. Jarvis and C. Bromley (eds), *British social attitudes: The 20th report*. London: Sage.

BRYSON, J. and FARNUM, K. (1995) *Creating your strategic plan*. San Francisco: Jossey-Bass Publications.

BUDD, A. (1978) *The politics of economic planning*. Manchester: Fontana.

BUDGE, I., CREWE, I., MCKAY, D. and NEWTON, K. (2004) *The new British politics*. London: Pearson Education.

BURNS, T. and STALKER, G. (1961) *The management of innovation*. London: Tavistock.

BUTLER, D. and KAVANAGH, D. (2001) *The British general election of 2001*. London: Macmillan.

CABINET OFFICE. (1997) *Service first: The new charter programme.* London: Stationery Office.

CABINET OFFICE. (1999) *Modernising government.* London: Stationery Office.

CAIRNCROSS, A. (1992) *The British economy since 1945*. Oxford: Blackwell.

CALLENDER, C. (1996) Women in employment. In: C. Hallet, *Women and social policy*. Hemel Hempsted: Harvester Wheatsheaf.

CANNON, T. (1994) *Corporate responsibility*. London: Pitman.

CARNOY, M. (1993) *The new global economy in the information age*. University Park, Pennsylvania: Penn State University Press.

CASTELLS, M. (1996) *The rise of the network society*. Oxford: Blackwell.

CERNY, P. (1995) Globalisation and the changing logic of collective action. *International Organisation*, No 49, pp595–625.

CERTIFICATION OFFICER. (2004) *Annual report of the Certification Officer 2003–2004*. London: Certification Office for Trade Unions and Employers' Association.

CHANDLER, A. (1977) *The visible hand: The managerial revolution in American business*. Cambridge, Mass.: Harvard University Press.

CHESNAIS, F. (1994) *La mondialisation du capital*. Paris: Syros.

CHIEF MEDICAL OFFICER. (2003) *On the state of public health: Annual report of the Chief Medical Officer of the Department of Health*. London: The Stationery Office.

CHILD, J. (1972) Organisational structure, environment and performance: the role of strategic choice. *Sociology.* Vol. 6, pp1–22.

CHRYSSIDES, G. and KALER, J. (1993) *An introduction to business ethics.* London: Chapman and Hall.

CHRYSSIDES, G. and KALER J. (1996) *Essentials of business ethics.* London: McGraw-Hill.

CINI, M. (ed). (2003) *European Union politics.* Oxford: Oxford University Press.

CINI, M. and McGOWAN, L. (1998) *Competition policy in the European Union.* Basingstoke, Macmillan.

CLARK, T. and LIPSET, S. (eds). (1996) Are social classes dying? In: D. Lee and B. Turner, *Conflicts about class.* London: Longman.

COHEN, M. (1996) Democracy and the future of nations. In: R. Boyer and D. Drache (eds), *States against markets.* London: Routledge.

CONNOCK, S. and JOHNS, T. (1995) *Ethical leadership.* London: IPD.

CORIAT, B. (1994) Neither pre- nor post-Fordism: an original and new way of managing the labour process. In: K. Tetsuro and R. Steven (eds), *Is Japanese management post-Fordism?* Tokyo: Mado-sha.

CORRY, D. (2003) *The regulatory state.* London: Institute of Public Policy Research.

COUNCIL OF MINISTERS. (2001) *Employment and social policies: A framework of investing in quality.* Brussels: Council of Ministers.

COWLES, M. and DINAN, D. (eds). (2004) *Developments in the European Union.* Basingstoke: Palgrave.

CRAIG, J. (2005) *Introduction to robotics: Mechanics and control.* Upper Saddle River, New Jersey: Pearson Education.

CROMPTON, R. *et al.* (2000) *Renewing class analysis.* Oxford: Blackwell Publishers.

CROMPTON, R., BROCKMANN, M. and WIGGINS, R. (2003) A woman's place ... Employment and family life for men and women. In: A. Park, J. Curtice, K. Thomson, L. Jarvis and C. Bromley (eds), *British social attitudes: The 20th report.* London: Sage.

CURTICE, J. and SEYD, B. (2003) 'Is there a crisis in political participation?' In: A. Park, J. Curtice, K. Thomson, L. Jarvis and C. Bromley (eds), *British social attitudes: The 20th report.* London: Sage.

CURWEN, P. (ed). (1997) *Understanding the UK economy.* London: Macmillan.

CUTLER T., WILLIAMS, K. and WILLIAMS, J. (1986) *Keynes, Beveridge and beyond.* London: Routledge and Kegan Paul.

CYERT, R. and MARCH, J. (1992) *A behavioral theory of the firm.* Englewood Cliffs, New Jersey: Prentice Hall.

DAHRENDORF, R. (1982) *On Britain.* London: BBC.

DAVENPORT, T. and PEARLSON, K. (1998) Two cheers for the virtual office. *Sloan Management Review.* Vol. 39, No. 4, pp51–65.

DAVID, F. (1997) *Strategic management.* London: Prentice Hall International.

DAVID, R. and BRIERLEY, J. (1978) *Major legal systems in the world today*. London: Stevens.

DAWSON, P. (2003) *Understanding organisational change: The contemporary experience of people at work*. London: Sage.

DE GEORGE, R. (1999) *Business ethics*. New Jersey: Prentice Hall.

DE VRIES, M. (1994) The leadership mystique. *Academy of Management Executive*. Vol. 8, No. 3, pp73–89.

DE WIT, B. and MEYER, R. (2004) *Strategy: process, content, context – an international perspective*. London: Thomson Learning.

DEAKIN, N. (1994) *The politics of welfare*. Hemel Hempsted: Harvester Wheatsheaf.

DEMING, W. (1986) *Out of crisis*. Cambridge, Mass.: MIT Center for Advanced Engineering Study.

DENNIS, N. and ERDOS, G. (1993) *Families without fatherhood*. London: Institute of Economic Affairs.

DEPARTMENT FOR EDUCATION AND SKILLS. (2003) *Education and training skills for the United Kingdom*. London: The Stationery Office.

DEPARTMENT OF EDUCATION AND EMPLOYMENT. (1999) *Code of practice on age diversity in employment*. London: DFEE.

DEVLIN, LORD. (1978) Judges, government and politics. *Modern Law Review*. No. 41.

DINAN, D. (2004) *Europe recast: A history of the European Union*. Basingstoke: Palgrave.

DOERN, G. and WILKS, S. (1996) *Comparative competition policy: Nation institutions in a global market*. Oxford: Oxford University Press.

DONALDSON, T. and PRESTON, L. (1995) The stakeholder theory of the firm: concepts, evidence and implications. *Academy of Management Review*. Vol. 20, pp65–91.

DOOGAN, K. (2001) Insecurity and long-term employment. Work, *Employment and Society*. Vol. 15, No. 3.

DREWRY, G. (1989) *The new select committees*. Oxford: Clarendon.

DRUCKER, P. (1993) *Post-capitalist society*. Oxford: Butterworth-Heinemann.

DURDEN, P. (2001) Housing policy. In: S. Savage and R. Atkinson (eds), *Public policy under Blair*. London: Palgrave.

ECCLES, T. (1994) *Succeeding with change: Implementing action-driven strategies*. London: McGraw-Hill.

THE ECONOMIST. (1992) *Special edition on corporate governance*. 11 September, pp52–62.

ELCOCK, H. (1996) Strategic management. In: D. Farnham and S. Horton, *Managing the new public services*. Basingstoke: Macmillan.

EUROPEAN COMMISSION. (2001) *Promoting a European framework of corporate social responsibility*. Luxembourg: Office for Official Publications of the European Communities.

EUROPEAN COMMISSION. (2002) *Corporate social responsibility: A business contribution to sustainable development*. Luxembourg: Office for Official Publications of the European Communities.

EUROPEAN COMMISSION. (2003a) *Energy: Science and society – issues, options and technologies*. Luxembourg: Office for Official Publications of the European Communities.

EUROPEAN COMMISSION. (2003b) *Mapping instruments for corporate social responsibility.* Luxembourg: Office for Official Publications of the European Communities.

EUROPEAN COMMISSION. (2004a) *Key facts and figures about the European Union.* Luxembourg: Office of Official Publications of the European Communities.

EUROPEAN COMMISSION. (2004b) *Report of the high-level group on the future of social policy in an enlarged European Union.* Luxembourg: Office for the Official Publications of the European Communities.

EUROSTAT. (2003) *Migration statistics.* Luxembourg: Office of Official Publications of the European Communities.

EUROSTAT. (2004) *European social statistics.* Luxembourg: Office of Official Publications of the European Communities.

EUSEPI, G. and SCHNEIDER, F. (2004) *Changing institutions in the European Union: A public choice perspective.* Cheltenham: Elgar.

EVANS, P. (1995) *Embedded autonomy: States and industrial transformation.* Princeton, New Jersey: Princeton University Press.

FAHEY, L. and NARAYANAM, V. (1986) *Macroenvironmental analysis for strategic management.* St Paul, MN.: West Publishing.

FARCAS, C. and WETLAUFER, S. (1996) The ways chief executive officers lead. *Harvard Business Review.* May–June, pp110–112.

FARNHAM, D. (2000) *Employee relations in context.* London: IPD.

FARNHAM, D., BARLOW, J., HORTON, S. AND HONDEGHEM, A. (eds). (1996) *New public managers in Europe: Public servants in transition.* Basingstoke: Macmillan.

FARNHAM, D., HONDEGHEM, A. and HORTON, S. (2005) *Staff participation and public management reform: Some international comparisons.* Basingstoke: Palgrave.

FARNHAM, D. and HORTON, S. (eds). (1996) *Managing the new public services.* London: Macmillan.

FARNHAM, D. and HORTON, S. (eds). (2000) *Human resources flexibilities in the public services: International perspectives.* London: Macmillan.

FERGUSON, P. and FERGUSON, G. (1994) *Industrial economics: Issues and perspectives.* Maidenhead: Macmillan.

FIELDING, M. (ed). (2001) *Taking education really seriously: Three years hard Labour.* London: Routledge.

FINN, D. (2001) Welfare to work: New Labour and the unemployed. In: S. Savage and R. Atkinson (eds), *Public policy under Blair.* London: Palgrave.

FISHER, C. and LOVELL, A. (2003) *Business ethics and values.* London: Prentice Hall.

FLYNN, N. (2002) *Public sector management.* Harlow: FT/Prentice Hall.

FORESTER, T. (1987) *High-tech society.* Oxford: Blackwell.

FRIEDMAN, M. (1970) *The counter revolution in monetary theory.* London: Institute of Economic Affairs.

FUKUYAMA, F. (1992) *The end of history and the last man.* London: Hamish Hamilton.

GALBRAITH, J. (1952) *American capitalism*. Boston: Houghton Miffin.

GALBRAITH, J. (1967) *The new industrial state*. Harmondsworth: Penguin.

GALBRAITH, J. (1984) *Anatomy of power*. London: Hamish Hamilton.

GALBRAITH, J. (1993) *The culture of contentment*. Harmondsworth: Penguin.

GALLIE, D. *et al* (1998) *Restructuring the employment relationship*. Oxford: Clarendon Press.

GAMBLE, A. (1994) *The free economy and strong state*. London: Macmillan.

GEORGE, S. (1998) *An awkward partner: Britain in the European Community*. Oxford: Oxford University Press.

GIDDENS, A. (1981) *The class structure of advanced societies*. London: Hutchinson.

GIDDENS, A. (1985) *Contemporary critique of historical materialism: Vol 2 the nation state and violence*. London: Polity Press.

GIDDENS, A. (1990) *The consequences of modernity*. Cambridge: Polity Press.

GIDDENS, A. (1998) *The third way: The renewal of social democracy*. Cambridge: Polity Press.

GIDDENS, A. (2001) *Sociology*. Cambridge: Polity Press.

GITTINS, D. (1993) *The family in question*. London: Macmillan.

GOODE, J., CALLENDER, C. and LISTER, R. (1998) *Purse or wallet? Gender inequalities and income distribution within families on benefits*. London: Policy Studies Institute.

GOODMAN, A. and SHEPHARD, A. (2002) *Inequality and living standards in Great Britain: Some facts*. London: Institute for Fiscal Studies.

GOULDNER, A. (1980) *The two Marxisms*. London: Macmillan.

GRANT, W. (2000) *Pressure groups and British politics*. Basingstoke: Palgrave.

GRANT, W. (2002) *Economic policy in Britain*. London: Palgrave.

GRAY, J. (1998) *False dawn: The delusions of global capitalism*. London: Routledge.

GRIFFITH, J. (1997) *The politics of the judiciary*. London: Fontana.

GRIFFITHS, A., and WALL, S. (eds). (2004) *Applied economics*. Harlow: FT/Prentice Hall.

GRINT, K. and WOOLGAR, S. (1997) *The machine at work: Technology, work and organisation*. Cambridge: Polity Press.

GRÜBLER, A. (1998) *Technology and global change*. Cambridge: Cambridge University Press.

HALL, P. and PRESTON, P. (1988) *The carrier wave: New information technology and the geography of innovation*. London: Unwin Hyman.

HALSEY, A. (2000) A hundred years of social change. In: *Social Trends No. 30*, London: Office for National Statistics.

HAMEL, G. and PRAHALAD, C. (1989) Strategic intent. *Harvard Business Review*. May–June, pp63–76.

HAMEL, G. and PRAHALAD, C. (1994) *Competing for the future*. Boston, Mass.: Harvard Business School Press.

HAMPDEN-TURNER, C. and TROMPENAARS, F. (1995) *The seven cultures of capitalism*. New York: Piatkus.

HAMPSHIRE and ISLE OF WIGHT COMMUNITY. (2005) *NHS health records*. Hampshire and Isle of Wight Community.

HANNAN, M.J. and FREEMAN, J. (1989) *Organisational ecology*. Boston, Mass.: Harvard University Press.

HARDT, M. and NEGRI, A. (2000) *Empire*. Cambridge, Mass,: Harvard University Press.

HARKER, L. (1996) "The family friendly employer in Europe" in S. Lewis and J. Lewis (eds) *The work and family: Rethinking employment*. London: Sage.

HARRIS, P. (1997) *An introduction to law*. London: Butterworth.

HARRIS, P. and BUCKLE, J. (1976) Philosophies of the law and the law teacher. *The Law Teacher*.

HARRISON, B. (1994) *Lean and mean: The changing landscape of corporate power in the age of flexibility*. New York: Basic Books.

HARVEY, B. and PARRY, D. (2000) *The law of consumer protection and fair trading*. London: Butterworth.

HAX, A. (1990) Redefining the strategy concept. *Planning Review*. May/June.

HEATHER, K. (2004) *Economics: Theory in action*. Harlow: FT/Prentice Hall.

HELD, D., GOLDBLATT, D. and PARRATON, J. (1997) *Global transformations*. Cambridge: Polity Press.

HERTZ, N. (2001) *The silent takeover: Global capitalism and the death of democracy*. London: Heinemann.

HESTER, R. and HARRISON, R. (eds). (2004) *Transportation and the environment*. Cambridge: Royal Society of Chemistry.

HIGGINS, J. and VINCZE, J. (1993) *Strategic management: Text and cases*. Fort Worth: The Dryden Press.

HIRSCH, F. (1976) *Social limits to growth*. London: Routledge and Kegan Paul.

HIRST, P. and THOMPSON, G. (1996) *Globalisation in question*. Cambridge: Polity Press.

HM TREASURY. (2004) *Central government expenditure*. London: Stationery Office.

HOBBES, T. (1947) *Leviathian*. Oxford: Blackwell.

HOBSBAWN, E. (1964) The machine breakers. In: E. Hobsbawn, *Labouring Men*. Weidenfeld and Nicolson.

HOBSBAWN, E. and RUDÉ, G. (1969) *Captain Swing*. London: Lawrence and Wishart.

HOCHSCHILD, A. (1997) *The time bind*. New York: Metropolitan Books.

HOFER, C. and SCHENDEL, D. (1978) *Strategy formulation: Analytical concepts*. St Paul MN: West Publishing.

HOLMES, L. (1998) W(h)ither the personnel profession. Unpublished paper, IPD Professional Standards Conference: University of Warwick.

HOME OFFICE. (1998) *Consultative paper on families*. London: HMSO.

HOME OFFICE. (2003) *Asylum statistics: United Kingdom*. London: Home Office.

HONDEGHEM, A. (ed). (1998) *Ethics and accountability in a context of governance and new public management*. Amsterdam: IOS Press.

HORTON, S. (2000) The employee relations environment. In: D. Farnham, *Employee relations in context*. London: Institute of Personnel and Development.

HORTON, S. (2005) Trajectories, institutions and stakeholders in public management reform. In: D. Farnham, A. Hondegehem and S. Horton, *Staff participation in public management reform: Some international comparisons*. London: Palgrave.

HORTON, S. and FARNHAM, D. (eds). (1999) *Public management in Britain*. London: Macmillan.

HORTON, S, HONDEGEHEM, A. and FARNHAM, D. (2002) *Competency management in the public sector*. Amsterdam: IOS Press.

HREBINIAK, L. and JOYCE, W. (1984) *Implementing strategy*. New York: Macmillan.

HUTTON, W. (1995) *The state we're in*. London: Cape.

HUTTON, W. (2001) *The world we're in*. London: Little Brown.

JACKSON, P.M. and PRICE, C. (eds). (1994) *Privatisation and regulation*. London: Longman.

JACKSON, P. and VAN DER WIELEN, J. (eds). (1998) *Teleworking: International perspectives, from telecommuting to the virtual organisation*. London: Routledge.

JEWELL, B. (1993) *The UK economy and Europe*. London: Pitman.

JOHNSON CONTROLS. (1997) *Ethics policy: The cornerstone of customer satisfaction*. Milwaukee, Wisconsin: Johnson Controls.

JOHNSON, G. and SCHOLES, K. (2002) *Exploring corporate strategy*. Hemel Hempsted: Prentice Hall Europe.

JOHNSON, T. (1972) *Professions and power*. London: Macmillan.

JOYCE, P. (1999) *Strategic management for the public services*. Buckingham: Open University Press.

KAHN-FREUND, O. (1977) *Labour and the law*. Stevens: London.

KANTER, R. M. (1984) *The change master*s. London: Allen and Unwin.

KAPTEIN, M. and WEMPE, J. (2002) *The balanced company: A theory of corporate integrity*. Oxford: Oxford University Press.

KATZ, D. and KAHN, R. (1966) *The social psychology of organisations*. New York: Wiley.

KAY, J. (2003) *The truth about markets: Their genius, their limits, their folies*. London: Allen Lane.

KENDALL, I. and HOLLOWAY, D. (2001) Education policy. In: S. Savage and R. Atkinson (eds), *Public policy under Blair*. London: Palgrave.

KERNAGHAN, K. (1975) *Ethical conduct*. Toronto: Institute of Public Administration.

KEYNES, J. M. (1936) *The general theory of employment, interest and money*. London: Macmillan.

KICKERT, W. (ed.). (1997) *Public management and administrative reform in Western Europe*. Cheltenham: Edward Elgar.

KITSON, A. and CAMPBELL, R. (1996) *The ethical organisation: Ethical theory and corporate behaviour*. Basingstoke: Macmillan.

KONTRAKOU, V. (ed.). (2004) *Contemporary issues and debates in EU Policy*. Manchester: Manchester University Press.

LABOUR FORCE SURVEY. (2004) *Labour market summary*. London: The Stationery Office.

LANDES, D. (1998) *The wealth and poverty of nations*. London: Little Brown.

LAWTON, A. (1998) *Ethical management for the public services*. Buckingham: Open University Press.

LAWTON, A. and ROSE, A. (1991) *Organisation and management in the public sector*. London: Pitman.

LEAVY, D. and WILSON, D. (1994) *Strategy and leadership*. London: Routledge.

LENAGHAN, J. (1998) *Rethinking IT and health*. Institute for Public Policy Research: London.

LEWIS, D. and SARGENT, M. (2004) *Essentials of employment law*. London: CIPD.

LICKERT, R. (1967) *The human organisation*. New York: McGraw-Hill.

LOCKE, J. (1947) *An essay concerning the true original, extent and end of civil government*. Oxford: Oxford University Press.

LOCKWOOD, D. (1958) *The blackcoated worker*. London: Allen and Unwin.

LOWE, R. and WOODRUFFE, G. (2004) *Consumer law and practice*. London: Sweet and Maxwell.

LUKES, S. (2005) *Power: A radical view*. Basingstoke: Palgrave.

LUND, B. (1996) *Housing problems and housing policy*. Harlow: Longman.

LYNCH, T. (1997) *Corporate strategy*. London: Pitman.

LYON, J. and GORNER, P. (1995) *Altered fates: Gene therapy and the retooling of human life*. New York: Norton.

MACPHERSON, C. (1962) *The political theory of possessive individualism*. Oxford: Clarendon Press.

MAGUIRE, M. (1998) Ethics in the public service. In: A. Hondeghem (ed), *Ethics and accountability in a context of governance and new public management*. Amsterdam: IOS Press.

MANN, M. (1997) Has globalisation ended the rise and rise of the nation state? *Review of International Political Economy*. No 4, pp472–496.

MARCHINGTON, M. and WILKINSON, A. (2005) *Human resource management at work: People management and development*. London: CIPD.

MARRIS, R. (1964) *The economic theory of managerial capitalism*. London: Macmillan.

McLAREN, L. and JOHNSON, M. (2004) Understanding the rising tide of anti-immigrant sentiment. In: A. Park, J. Curtice, K. Thomson, C. Bromley and M. Phillips (eds), *British social attitudes: The 21st report*. London: Sage.

McORMOND, T. (2004) Changes in working trends over the past decade. *Labour Market Trends*. January, Vol. 112, No. 8, pp25–35.

MELLAHI, K. and WOOD, G. (2003) *The ethical business: Challenges and controversies.* Basingstoke: Palgrave.

MILL, J. S. (1972) *Utilitarianism, liberty and representative government.* London: Dent.

MILLER, D. and FRIESEN, P. (1984) *Organisations: A quantum view.* New York: Harper.

MILLERSON, G. (1964) *The qualifying associations.* London: Routledge and Kegan Paul.

MINISTRY OF HEALTH. (1997) *The new NHS: Modern, dependable.* London: Ministry of Health.

MINTZBERG, H. (1987a) The strategy concept I: The five P's for strategy. *California Management Review.* Fall.

MINTZBERG, H. (1987b) Crafting strategy. *Harvard Business Review.* Vol. 65, No. 4, pp65–75.

MINTZBERG, H. (1989) Strategy formation: schools of thought. In: J. Fredrickson (ed), *Perspectives on strategic management.* California: Ballinger.

MINTZBERG, H. (1994) *The rise and fall of strategic planning.* London: Prentice-Hall.

MINTZBERG, H., QUINN, J. and GHOSHAL, S. (1998) *The strategy process.* London: Prentice-Hall.

MITCHELL, R., AGLE, B. and WOOD, D. (1997) Towards a theory of stakeholder identification and salience: defining the principle of who and what really counts. *Academy of Management Review.* Vol. 22, No. 4, pp853–886.

MONBIOT, G. (2001) *The captive state: The corporate takeover of Britain.* London: Pan Books.

MWENDA, I. and KUMARI, K. (2005) *Drug offenders in England and Wales.* London: Home Office.

NEGROPONTE, N. (1995) *Being digital.* New York: Alfred A. Knopf.

NELSON, R. (1994) An agenda formal growth theory. Unpublished paper, Columbia University, Department of Economics.

NOLAN COMMITTEE. (1995) *Standards in public life: Vol 1.* London, HMSO.

NONAKA, I. (1995) *The knowledge-creating company: How Japanese companies create the dynamics of innovation.* Oxford: Oxford University Press.

NONAKA, I. and TAKEUCHI, H. (1995) *The knowledge creating company.* Oxford: Oxford University Press.

NORRIS, P. (1997) *Electoral change since 1945.* Oxford: Blackwell.

NORTH, N. (2001) Health policy. In: S. Savage and R. Atkinson (eds), *Public policy under Blair.* London: Palgrave.

NUGENT, N. (ed). (2004) *European Union enlargement.* Basingstoke: Palgrave.

OECD. (2004) *Economic outlook.* Paris: OECD.

OECD. (2005) *This is the OECD.* Paris: OECD.

OFFICE OF FAIR TRADING. (2001) *The role of market definition in monopoly and dominance inquiries.* London: HMSO.

OFFICE OF FAIR TRADING. (2003) *A guide to the OFT.* London: OFT.

OFFICE FOR NATIONAL STATISTICS. (2001) *Census 2001*. London: The Stationery Office.

OFFICE FOR NATIONAL STATISTICS. (2003a) *Annual abstract of Statistics*. London: The Stationery Office.

OFFICE FOR NATIONAL STATISTICS. (2003b) *Regional trends*. London: The Stationery Office.

OFFICE FOR NATIONAL STATISTICS. (2003c) *Birth statistics*. London: The Stationery Office. 2003c.

OFFICE FOR NATIONAL STATISTICS. (2004a) *Population trends*. London: The Stationery Office.

OFFICE FOR NATIONAL STATISTICS. (2004b) *The state of the labour market*. London: The Stationery Office.

OFFICE FOR NATIONAL STATISTICS. (2004c) *Labour force survey*. London: The Stationery Office.

OFFICE FOR NATIONAL STATISTICS. (2004d) *Labour market trends*. London: The Stationery Office.

OHMAE, K. (1995) *The end of the nation-state*. London: Harper Collins.

ORMEROD, P. (1998) *Butterfly economics: A new general theory of social and economic behaviour*. London: Faber and Faber.

OULTON, N. (1995) Supply side reform and UK economic growth: what happened to the miracle? *National Institute Economic Review*. No. 154.

OWEN, G. (1999) *From Empire to Europe: The decline and revival of British industry since the second world war*. London: HarperCollins.

PAINTER, C. and ISAAC-HENRY, K. (1999) Local government. In: S. Horton and D. Farnham, *Public management in Britain*. London: Macmillan.

PAINTER, C., PUTTICK, K. and HOLMES, A. (1998) *Employment rights*. London: Pluto Books.

PARK, A. and SURRIDGE, P. (2003) Charting change in British values. In: A. Park, J. Curtice, K. Thomson, I. Jarvis and C. Bromley (eds), *British social attitudes: The 20th report*. London: Sage.

PEET, R. (2003) *Unholy trinity: The IMF, World Bank, and WTO*. London: Zed.

PENSIONS COMMISSION. (2004) *Pensions: challenges and choices – the first report of the pensions commission*. London: The Stationery Office.

PERROW, C. (1970) *Complex organisations*. Glenview, IL: Scott Foresman.

PETERS, G. AND SAVOIE, D. (eds). (1998) *Taking stock: Assessing public management reforms*. Montreal and Kingston: Canadian Centre for Management Development and McGill-Queen's University Press.

PETERS, T. and WATERMAN, R. (1982) *In search of excellence*. New York: Harper Row.

PETRELLA, R. (1996) Globalisation and internationalisation. In: R. Boyer and D. Drache (eds), *States against states*. London: Routledge.

PFEFFER, J. (1998) *The human equation: Building profits by putting people first*. Boston: Harvard Business School Press.

PHELAN, J., LINK, B., STUEVE, A. and MOORE, R. (1995) Education, social liberalism and economic conservatism. *American Sociological Review*. Vol. 60, No. 1, pp126–140.

PIORE, M. and SABEL, C. (1984) *The second industrial divide: Possibilities for prosperity.* New York: Basic Books.

POLANYI, K. (1944) *The great transformation.* Boston: Beacon Press.

POLLARD, S. (1969) *The development of the British economy 1914–1967.* London: Allen and Unwin.

POLLITT, C. (1993) *Managerialism and the public services.* Oxford: Blackwell.

POLLITT, C. (1998) Evaluation and the new public management: An international perspective. *Evaluation Journal of Australasia.* Vol. 9, No. 1, pp7–15.

POLLITT, C. and BOUCKAERT G. (2004) *Public management reform: A comparative analysis.* Oxford: Oxford University Press.

PORTER, M. (1985) *Competitive advantage.* New York: Free Press.

PORTER, M. (1998a) *Competitive strategy: techniques for analysing industries and competition.* New York: Free Press.

PORTER, M. (1998b) *The competitive advantages of nations.* Basingstoke: Macmillan.

POST, J., LAWRENCE, A. and WEBER, J. (2002) *Business and society: Corporate strategy, public policy, ethics.* Boston, Mass.: Irwin/McGraw-Hill.

POULANTZAS, N. (1975) *Classes in contemporary capitalism.* London: New Left Books.

POWELL, M. (ed). (1999) *New Labour, new welfare state? The third way in British social policy.* Bristol: The Policy Press.

PRATCHETT, L. and WINGFIELD, M. (1994) *The public service ethos in local government.* London: Commission on Local Democracy.

PREECE, D. (1995) *Organisations and technological change: Strategy, objectives and involvement.* Routledge: London.

PRIME MINISTER'S OFFICE. (1991) *The citizen's charter.* London: Stationery Office.

QUINN, J. B. (1978) Strategic change: logical incrementalism. *Sloan Management Review.* Fall.

QUINN, J. B. (1980) *Strategies for change.* Homewood, Ill.: Irwin.

RANDALL, A. (1991) *Before the Luddites: Custom, community and machinery in the English woollen industry, 1776–1809.* Cambridge: Cambridge University Press.

RATLEDGE, C. and KRISTIANSEN, B. (2001) *Basic biotechnology.* Cambridge: Cambridge University Press.

REICH, R. (1991) *The work of nations.* New York: Alfred A. Knopf.

ROBERTSON, R. (1992) *Globalisation: Social theory and global culture.* London: Sage.

RUIGROK, W. and VAN TAULDER, R. (1995) *The logic of international restructuring.* London: Routledge.

SAMPSON, A. (2004) *Who runs this place? The anatomy of Britain in the 21st century.* London: Murray.

SANDERS, D. (1999) The impact of left/right ideology. In: G. Evans and P. Norris (eds), *Critical elections.* London: Sage.

SARGENT, M. (2003) *Employment law*. London: Longman.

SAVAGE, M. *et al.* (1992) *Property, bureaucracy and culture: Middle class formation in contemporary Britain*. London: Routledge.

SAVAGE, S. and ATKINSON, R. (eds). (2001) *Public policy under Blair*. London: Palgrave.

SCHILLER, D. (2000) *Digital capitalism: Networking the global market system*. Cambridge, Mass.: MIT Press.

SCHLEGEMILCH, B. and HOUSTON, J. (1999) Codes of corporate ethics. *Management Decision*. Vol. 28, No. 7.

SCOTT, R. (1995) *Institutions and organisations*. London: Sage.

SEFTON, T. (2003) What we want from the welfare state. In: A. Park, J. Curtice, K. Thomson, L. Jarvis and C. Bromley (eds), *British social attitudes: The 20th report*. London: Sage.

SELDON, A. (1990) *Capitalism*. Oxford: Blackwell.

SENGE, P. (1990) The leader's new work: building learning organisations. *Sloan Management Review*, Fall. pp7–22.

SILVA, E. and SMART, C. (1999) *The new family*. London: Sage.

SINGER, P. (1995) *A companion to ethics*. Oxford: Blackwell.

SMART, B. (1993) *Postmodernity*. London: Routledge.

SMART, C. and SHIPMAN, B. (2004) Visions in monochrome: families, marriage and the individualisation thesis. *British Journal of Sociology*. Vol. 55, No. 4, pp291–309.

SOROS, G. (1995) *Soros on Soros*. New York: Wiley.

SOROS, G. (2000) *Reforming global capitalism*. New York: Little Brown.

STACEY, R. (1993) *Strategic management and organisational dynamics*. London: Pitman.

STALLING, W. (2004) *Data and computer communications*. Upper Saddle River, New Jersey: Pearson Education.

STERNBERG, E. (1994) *Corporate governance: Accountability in the marketplace*. London: Institute of Economic Affairs.

STIGLITZ, J. (2002) *Globalisation and its discontents*. London: Penguin.

SUCHMAN, M. (1995) Managing legitimacy: strategic and institutional approaches. *Academy of Management Review*. Vol. 20, pp571–610.

SUMMERFIELD, C. and BABB, B. (eds). (2004) *Social trends 2004*. London: National Statistics.

SWART, J., KINNIE, N. and PURCELL, J. (2003) *People and performance in knowledge-intensive firms*. London: CIPD.

TAYLOR, G. (ed). (1999) *The impact of New Labour*. London: Macmillan.

TAYLOR, R. (2002) *The future of work–life balance*. Swindon: Economic and Science Research Council.

THOMAS, L. and WORMALD, E. (1989) Political participation. In: I. Reid and E. Stratta, *Sex differences in Britain*. Aldershot: Gower.

THOMAS, R. (2001) UK economic policy: the Conservative legacy and New Labour's third way. In: S. Savage and R. Atkinson (eds), *Public policy under Blair*. London: Palgrave.

THOMASON, G. (1991) The management of personnel. *Personnel Review*. Vol. 20, No. 2.

THUROW, L. (1999) *Building wealth: The new rules for individuals, companies, and nations in a knowledge-based economy*. New York: Harper Business.

TIMMINS, N. (2001) *The five giants: A biography of the Welfare State*. London: HarperCollins.

TOFFLER, A. (1970) *Future shock*. New York: Random House.

TOFFLER, A. (1981) *The third wave*. New York: Bantam Books.

TOMKINS, C. (1987) *Achieving economy, efficiency and effectiveness in the public sector*. London: Routledge.

TWINING, W. and MIERS, D. (1982) *How to do things with rules*. London: Wiedenfeld and Nicolson.

UNITED NATIONS. (2004) *United Nations demographic yearbook*. New York: United Nations.

UNITED NATIONS. (2005) *Millennium ecosystem assessment synthesis report*. New York: United Nations.

VELJANOVSKI, C. (ed). (1991) *Regulators and the market*. London: Institute of Economic Affairs.

WARLEIGH, A. (2004) *European Union: The basics*. London: Routledge.

WEBER, M. (1930) *The protestant ethic and the spirit of capitalism*. London: Allen and Unwin (Translated by Talcott Parsons).

WEBER, M. (1964) *The theory of social and economic organisation*. London: Free Press, Collier Macmillan.

WEBER, M. (1968) Status groups and classes. In: G. Roth and C. Wittlich (eds), *Economy and society*. New York: Bedminster Press.

WEBER, M. (1971) Class, status and party. In: K. Thompson and J. Tunstall (eds), *Sociological perspectives*. Harmondsworth: Penguin.

WHITMARSH, A. (1995) *Social focus on women*. London: HMSO.

WHITTINGTON, R. (2001) *What is strategy and does it matter?* London: Thomson Learning.

WILKINSON, B., MORRIS, J. and NICH, O. (1992) Japanising the world: the case of Toyota. In: J. Marceau (ed), *Reworking the world: Organisations, technologies and cultures in comparative perspective*. Berlin: de Gruyter.

WILLEY, B. (2003) *Employment law in context*. London: FT/Prentice-Hall.

WILLIAMSON, O. (1991) Strategising, economising and economic organisation. *Strategic Management Journal*. Vol. 12, pp75–94.

WINSTANLEY, D., WOODHALL, J. and HEERY, E. (1996) Business ethics and human resource management. *Personnel Review*. Vol. 25, No. 6.

WISE, E. (2000) *Applied robotics*. Indianapolis: Sams Technical Publishing.

WOMEN'S UNIT. (1997) *The minister for women*. London: The Stationery Office.

WOOD, S. (ed). (1989) *The transformation of work*. London: Allen and Unwin.

WOODWARD, J. (1965) *Industrial organisation: Theory and practice*. Oxford: Oxford University Press.

WOODWARD, J. (ed). (1970) *Industrial organisation: Behaviour and control*. Oxford: Oxford University Press.

YOUNG, M. (1958) *The rise of the meritocracy 1879–2033*. Harmondsworth: Penguin. 1958.

ZALENICK, A. (1992) Managers and leaders: are they different? *Harvard Business Review*. Vol. 70, pp126–135.

Index